Critical Perspectives on Agrarian Transition

This book evaluates the relevance of classical debates on agrarian transition and extends the horizon of contemporary debates in the Indian context, linking national trends with regional experiences. It identifies new dynamics in agrarian political economy and presents a comprehensive account of diverse aspects of capitalist transition both at theoretical and empirical levels. The chapters discuss several neglected domains in agricultural economics, such as discursive dimensions of agrarian relations and limitations of stereotypical binaries between capital and non-capital, rural and urban sectors, agriculture and industry and accumulation and subsistence.

With contributions from major scholars in the field, this volume will be useful to scholars and researchers of agriculture, economics, political economy, sociology, rural development and development studies.

B. B. Mohanty is Professor, Department of Sociology, Pondicherry University, Puducherry, India. His research interests are agrarian transition, farmer suicides and local governance. His recent work includes the edited volume *Agrarian Change and Mobilisation* (2012).

'Readers of this splendid collection will encounter a set of thematically and regionally diverse, uniformly erudite and politically provocative studies that link India's past to its troubled present and that situate national realities in broader international debates about the agrarian question.'

Marc Edelman, *Professor of Anthropology, Hunter College and the Graduate Center, City University of New York, USA*

'[This book's] thought-provoking contributions span from a close interrogation of classic theories of the relationship between agrarian and industrial development, to new analyses of agrarian transition, class and the peasantry in India from a range of critical approaches.'

Jens Lerche, *Editor, Journal of Agrarian Change*

'Focused primarily on India and its regionally diverse trajectories of change, this volume tries to open up . . . questions [of rural and agrarian distress] afresh by invoking some of the classical debates and the dynamics of contemporary realities. Instead of offering simple or generalizable solutions it raises questions that need further engagement, empirically, theoretically and politically.'

Surinder S. Jodhka, *Professor of Sociology, Jawaharlal Nehru University, New Delhi, India*

Critical Perspectives on Agrarian Transition

India in the global debate

Edited by B.B. Mohanty

LONDON AND NEW YORK

First published 2016
by Routledge
2 Park Square, Milton Park, Abingdon, Oxon OX14 4RN

and by Routledge
711 Third Avenue, New York, NY 10017

First issued in paperback 2017

Routledge is an imprint of the Taylor & Francis Group, an informa business

© 2016 B.B. Mohanty

The right of B.B. Mohanty to be identified as the author of the editorial material, and of the authors for their individual chapters, has been asserted in accordance with sections 77 and 78 of the Copyright, Designs and Patents Act 1988.

All rights reserved. No part of this book may be reprinted or reproduced or utilised in any form or by any electronic, mechanical, or other means, now known or hereafter invented, including photocopying and recording, or in any information storage or retrieval system, without permission in writing from the publishers.

Trademark notice: Product or corporate names may be trademarks or registered trademarks, and are used only for identification and explanation without intent to infringe.

British Library Cataloguing-in-Publication Data
A catalogue record for this book is available from the British Library

Library of Congress Cataloging-in-Publication Data
A catalog record has been requested for this book.

ISBN 13: 978-1-138-48831-1 (pbk)
ISBN 13: 978-1-138-99838-4 (hbk)

Typeset in Goudy
by Apex CoVantage, LLC

Dedicated to the memory of
Professor Baburao Shravan Baviskar

Contents

List of figures	ix
List of tables	x
Notes on Contributors	xii
Foreword	xiv
TERENCE J. BYRES	
Preface and Acknowledgements	xxv
List of Abbreviations	xxvii

Introduction: Agrarian transition: from
classic to current debates   1
B. B. MOHANTY

PART I
Agrarian transition: theoretical discourse   41

1 Back to the future? Marx, modes of production and
the agrarian question   43
A. HAROON AKRAM-LODHI AND CRISTÓBAL KAY

2 Revisiting agrarian transition: reflections on long
histories and current realities   67
HENRY BERNSTEIN

3 Contours of the agrarian question: towards
political question of 'the peasantry' in
contemporary India   92
D. NARASIMHA REDDY

viii Contents

PART II
Global capitalism, neoliberalism and changing agriculture

113

4 Capitalist trajectories of global interdependence and welfare outcomes: the lessons of history for the present
UTSA PATNAIK

115

5 Declining credibility of the neoliberal state and agrarian crisis in India: some observations
D. N. DHANAGARE

138

6 Neoliberal reforms, agrarian capitalism and the peasantry
B. B. MOHANTY AND PAPESH K. LENKA

164

PART III
Agrarian transition: regional responses

197

7 Loosening ties of patriarchy in agrarian transition in Tamil Nadu
JUDITH HEYER

199

8 Agro-ecological double movements? Zero Budget Natural Farming and alternative agricultures after the neoliberal crisis in Kerala
DANIEL MÜNSTER

222

9 Stressed commerce and accumulation process: a farm-level study of agrarian transition in West Bengal
SANTANU RAKSHIT

245

10 Punjab's small peasantry: thriving or deteriorating?
SUKHPAL SINGH AND SHRUTI BHOGAL

276

Index

293

Figures

4.1	Food grains availability per capita during economic reforms period, India 2011–12	129
6.1	Rural workforce in agriculture	184
6.2	Rural main workers	185
6.3	Rural population	186
7.1	Education levels of males and females aged 15–25 years	206
9.1	Closed circuit with government support	248
9.2	Trends of gross output, gross value added in advanced and backward regions in 2003–4	257
9.3	Trend of farm-labour surplus or deficit per holding, acre and worker	257
9.4a	Synoptic view of the process described for agriculture only (Capital and Non-capital)	263
9.4b	Synoptic view of the process described for agriculture only (Non-capital)	263
9.5	Open circuit under neoliberalism	264

Tables

4A.1	Annual per capita output of wheat, England and Wales, in bushels and in kilograms	132
4A.2	Share of primary products in world trade 1876–80 to 1913	132
4A.3	Land productivity in China, India and the United States, 2007	133
4A.4	Trends in rural and urban poverty measured directly and by the official method	133
4A.5	Cereal supply and utilisation 2011 selected countries/regions	134
5.1	Sector-wise availability of jobs	144
5.2	Share of agricultural sector in GDP to industry and service sectors	145
5.3	Agencies where farmers from Uttar Pradesh prefer to sell their farm produce	146
5.4	Summary statistics on bonded labour cases documented, 2011	156
5.5	Investment in rural infrastructure: projections for the 11th Five-Year Plan	158
6.1	Changes in cropping pattern	170
6.2	Use of agricultural machinery	173
6.3	Per hectare share of hired labour and market purchased inputs	174
6.4	Total value of output agriculture	176
6.5	Size class-wise distribution of land cultivated by households	178
6.6	Agricultural labour households without cultivated land	181
6.7	Rural cultivators and agricultural labourers	182

6.8	Rural households that did not cultivate any land	184
6.9	Level of capitalist development and response of peasantry	187
7.1	Caste composition of village households in 1981–2	201
7.2	Landholding size distributions, Gounder households	203
7.3	Class breakdown, Gounder households	204
9.1	Quantitative criterion for village selection	254
9.2	Indicative criterion for village selection	255
9.3	Final villages selected in Memari, Bardhaman	255
9.4	Average operational holding according to economic class in acres	256
9.5	Surplus retention ratio 2003–4	260
9.6a	Details of cost, production and surplus – producers/traders in 2013–14	261
9.6b	Details of surplus distribution and retention between traders and producers	262
9A.1	Development indices of the districts of West Bengal	268
9A.2	Village-wise distribution of population and sample	270
10.1	Sampling design of the study	278
10.2	Distribution of number of operational holdings in Punjab and India	279
10.3a	Changing structure of rural workforce in Punjab	280
10.3b	Percentage point change in the structure of rural workforce in Punjab	281
10.4	Surplus from agriculture and non-farm income on various farm categories in different zones of Punjab	282
10.5	Magnitude of debt in Punjab	284
10.6	Degree of indebtedness in relation to income, Punjab	284
10.7	Farmers' suicides in Punjab, 2000–2011	285
10.8	Number of families who had left farming in Punjab	287
10.9	Reasons for leaving farming in Punjab	287
10.10	New occupations of farmers who left farming	289
10.11	Level of satisfaction from present profession of sample families, Punjab	290

Notes on Contributors

A. Haroon Akram-Lodhi is Professor in the Department of International Development Studies and teaches agrarian political economy at Trent University, Peterborough, Canada.

Henry Bernstein is Professor Emeritus of Development Studies at the School of Oriental and African Studies, University of London, and Adjunct Professor at the College of Humanities and Development, China Agricultural University, Beijing.

Shruti Bhogal is Research Fellow in the Department of Economics and Sociology, Punjab Agricultural University, Ludhiana, Punjab.

D. N. Dhanagare has taught at Agra University-Institute of Social Sciences (1961–68) and IIT Kanpur (1968–77). He also held such positions as Member-Secretary, ICSSR (1991–93) on deputation, and also as Vice-Chancellor, Shivaji University, Kolhapur (1995–2000). He was also invited as National Fellow by the Indian Institute of Advanced Study, Shimla (2012–14).

Judith Heyer is Emeritus Fellow of Somerville College, Oxford. She has held a post in Oxford University's Economics Department from 1975 to 2005 before which she was affiliated to Nairobi University.

Cristóbal Kay is Emeritus Professor in Development Studies and Rural Development at the International Institute of Social Studies (ISS), Professorial Research Associate of the Department of Development Studies at the School of Oriental and African Studies (SOAS) at the University of London and Visiting Professor at the Facultad Latinoamericana de Ciencias Sociales (FLACSO) in Quito, Ecuador.

Papesh K. Lenka is a Research Fellow in Sociology at Pondicherry University, Puducherry, India.

Notes on Contributors xiii

B. B. Mohanty is Professor, Department of Sociology, Pondicherry University, Puducherry, India.

Daniel Münster is a social and cultural anthropologist working on South Asian agrarian environments, the anthropology of food and agriculture, political ecology, and economy and social theory. He is leader of the Junior Research Group 'Agrarian Alternatives' at Heidelberg University's Cluster of Excellence 'Asia and Europe in a Global Context'.

Utsa Patnaik is Professor Emeritus of Economics at the Centre for Economic Studies and Planning, Jawaharlal Nehru University, New Delhi.

Santanu Rakshit is Associate Professor of Economics, Department of Rural Studies, Visva Bharati University, Santiniketan, West Bengal.

D. Narasimha Reddy was formerly Professor of Economics at the University of Hyderabad, and late Sankaran Chair Professor, National Institute of Rural Development, Hyderabad. Presently, he is ICSSR National Fellow, CSD, Hyderabad, and Hon. Visiting Professor, Institute for Human Development, New Delhi.

Sukhpal Singh is Professor at the Department of Economics and Sociology at Punjab Agricultural University, Ludhiana, Punjab.

Foreword

It seems useful to suggest a broad historical and comparative context for this book – broad in the widest possible sense. This helps place agrarian transition in due perspective.

Agrarian transition and three agrarian transitions

The term 'agrarian transition' is, perhaps, misleading. Such transition is termed 'agrarian' inasmuch as it encompassed change – profound change – in the countryside. That change related to agriculture (an *agricultural revolution*), from its very beginnings, with the advent of a more productive means of acquiring food, with the possibility of an agricultural surplus, a *potential* surplus. Agrarian transition was not, however, confined to agriculture, although agriculture was intrinsic to it. It involved the *appropriation* of a portion of the agricultural surplus, especially of food, but in diverse forms, financial as well as physical, and on favourable terms, whether by the state or dominant classes. This enabled accumulation outside of agriculture: accumulation that was not possible without that surplus. Such accumulation, in *different historical contexts*, might be as part of the creation, or extension, of an *urban* civilisation, a so-called *urban revolution*; or, more narrowly, of manufacturing industry, *industrialisation*. Agrarian transition, however, remains a useful, shorthand term, so long as we bear in mind its wider meaning.

There have been three distinct, powerfully transformative *agrarian transitions* in human history, although one of them was aborted *in statu nascendi*. Each was wide in its geographical scope. The *prehistoric agrarian transition* extended over millennia; and the second, the *capitalist agrarian transition*, advanced over centuries. The second, characterised by distinctly different 'paths', is still incomplete over large parts of the world. A third, a *socialist agrarian transition*, was planned, and although dramatic and far-reaching in its relatively very short life, was ultimately incomplete and was concentrated in decades.

The prehistoric agrarian transition

It was Gordon Childe (1892–1957), the outstanding prehistorian of the twentieth century, who first identified the prehistoric agrarian transition, although he did not use that term. He did so with immense erudition, lightly worn, and analytical skill and within a Marxist framework. It had its origins in the Near East and created the basis for other transitions, far in the future. His relevant works on this remain essential reading.

It has been said of Childe that, 'like Hegel and Marx, he was a great historian of capitalism, of the genesis of capitalism' (Gathercole 1994: 28). Childe himself wrote in a letter in 1941, when he was composing his best-known 'popular' book *What Happened in History* (Childe 1942), that he was taking his treatment up to 'the dawn of capitalism' (Trigger 1994: 117). In his hands, it was an exhilarating and enlightening intellectual journey, in which capitalism's, as well as feudalism's, prehistory was explored with rare insight by a formidably informed scholar. That prehistory encompassed, critically, an agrarian transition.

Childe postulated two 'revolutions' in prehistory.[1] The first was the creation of sedentary agriculture and stock raising, what he first terms his 'economic revolution', and latterly the *Neolithic revolution*: as he said, 'the greatest revolution in human history after the mastery of fire' (Childe 1934: 23). It brought under man's control a richer and more reliable source of food than was possible under hunting and gathering (Childe 1934). A single family might now extract a multiple of the amount of food needed for domestic consumption. So it was that a significant *potential surplus* might be envisaged (p. 89), a *social surplus* (p. 115). That potential social surplus was realised and became the basis of the second 'revolution': Childe's *urban revolution*, encompassing industry and commerce. The ruling class/state forced the peasantry to produce that surplus and appropriated it. These revolutions took place in the Near East: first in Mesopotamia; then in Egypt; and thereafter in India, in the Indus valley, where the cities of Mohenjodaro, Harappa and Chanhudaro were the urban revolution's monuments (pp. 172–73 and 238). Here was a fundamental contribution to our understanding of prehistory. So it was that the 'archaeologist's picture'

xvi Foreword

of the regions in question 'no longer focused attention on communities of simple farmers, but on States embracing various professions and classes' (Childe 1936/1981: 119). Class societies and states had come into being.

It was far later that these revolutions 'spread' to Europe. Childe considered the spread of his two revolutions to Europe in his last book *The Prehistory of European Society* (1958). The *Neolithic revolution*, with its *potential surplus*, spread to Mediterranean and Temperate Europe: first to the Balkan Peninsula and round the Carpathians to the coasts and islands of the central and western Mediterranean to the löss lands of Central Europe, to the Iberian Peninsula and Atlantic Europe.[2] This was followed, eventually, by the *urban revolution*, or, at least, what Childe describes as 'ripples generated by the Urban Revolution' (p. 124), fuelled by the social surplus appropriated from sedentary agriculture. This was first in the Aegean coasts and islands (p. 99 et seq.); and then along the Atlantic and North Sea coasts of Europe, where megalithic tombs were to be found in abundance – in Portugal, Southern and Western France, Ireland, the western side of Britain and the North of Scotland.[3]

The word 'spread' is controversial. For Childe it was appropriate as he was a diffusionist, and argued that his revolutions did so spread from the Near East. That was to be strongly contested by other prehistorians/archaeologists, who stressed *internal development* rather than external influence. Childe's last book has a particular interest in that it was written just as the results of radiocarbon dating were becoming seriously available and casting considerable doubt on the chronologies that Childe had developed. Childe does cite some of the dates so yielded (see 1958a/2009: 12, 44) but expressed scepticism about the robustness of the results. In fact, Childe's dating generally has been shown to have been wildly out, along with that of archaeologists/prehistorians generally.

In the foregoing I have deliberately left out Childe's chronology. That would now have to be changed. In a sense, this does not matter. At least, it does not matter *analytically*. I would suggest that his 'interpretative concepts and methods of explanation', to use his own phrase, from one of his last essays 'Retrospect' (Childe 1958b/2004: 191) remain powerful and convincing, in the face of 'the massive accumulation of new [archaeological] information since the 1950s' (Shennan in Childe 1958a/2009: 4), and not least that of radiocarbon dating. Pre-eminently, they include his two revolutions. His great contribution was to identify the nature of the first agrarian transition in human history.

After the prehistoric agrarian transition

In what was so bequeathed, different modes of production were rooted and developed, with their particular class structures, forms of appropriation and contradictions. Prominent among them, throughout Europe, as well as in Asia, was *feudalism*. There was *no feudal agrarian transition*, on a par with the prehistoric agrarian transition, although, of course, there was a transition to feudalism, as feudal structures and forms were established. Feudalism had its own law of motion. But its logic was bounded by the outcome of the prehistoric transition. Feudal agriculture faced limits on its productivity and the surpluses it might generate: with its means of production constrained by its class structure. Ultimately, far in the future, it faced a crisis.

The second great agrarian transition would take place not in the Near East, but, first, in Europe and involved a transition from feudalism. It is that agrarian transition that is the concern of this book. It was also twofold. It involved the capitalist transformation of the countryside, via several different 'paths', and capitalist industrialisation that was fuelled by agricultural surpluses in various forms and in different ways.

Capitalist agrarian transition

The second agrarian transition was a *capitalist* transition that grew out of feudalism's eventual crisis. It was, obviously, completed successfully in the now-advanced capitalist countries but is yet to be negotiated universally.

That transition proceeded from feudalism, the dominant mode of production in medieval Europe, to capitalism, its usurper, although feudalism was not necessarily its base. It was Marx who analysed it first, in *Capital*, focusing on the English path. He did so within a powerful theoretical framework, complemented by illuminating empirical investigation. His classic statement of the *process of transition* is in his chapters in volumes 1 and 3 of *Capital*, on 'the so-called primitive accumulation'.[4] I would suggest that the appropriate analytical procedure is one informed by theory and pursued by careful empirical treatment.

The 'English model' has been influential among analysts of capitalist transition, largely because it was the one explored by Marx in great detail in *Capital*. But it was also because England has generally been seen as the first instance of a *full capitalist transition*, a capitalist transition in both agriculture and industry: as having won 'the race for capitalism' (Wood 1999: 129). That has been disputed by some. It is challenged by de Vries and Van der Woude (1997), who argue for *Dutch primacy* in 'raising up the first modern economy' (de Vries and van der Woude 1997: 716, with the argument made in full in chapter 13). They are not Marxists and do not use the notion of capitalist transition, but the thrust of their argument is clear.[5] Then, Robert Brenner, concentrating on agriculture, has clearly argued that the Dutch were first.[6] Ellen Meiksins Wood, however, has described Holland as 'a "failed transition" in the development of industrial capitalism' (Wood 1999: 129) and has issued a blistering attack on Brenner in this respect (Wood 2002). That it is crucial to explore the Dutch path is obvious. I would question this primacy attributed to the Dutch and argue that their *full* transition was not secured until the nineteenth century.

Capitalist transition started in sixteenth-century England and was complete there by 1750; was probably second in Scotland, between, say, 1690 and the early nineteenth century; and proceeded in other parts of Europe, in North America (where feudalism was not established) and in Japan (where feudalism did exist), and elsewhere, and is still in the process of unfolding. I discuss some of the different paths of successful transition in an early paper (Byres 1986, 1991): in England, Prussia, France, the northern United States, Japan, South Korea and Taiwan. This I brought up to date in 2003 (Byres 2003) and added the Netherlands to my treatment.

What is significant is the substantive diversity that emerges. Amidst that diversity one can distinguish 'capitalism from above', in which the landlord class was the major agent of change in the countryside, with Prussia as the classic example; and 'capitalism from below', where the major impulse came from the rich peasantry, and of which the northern United States has been seen as the exemplar; with England identified as a crucial instance of 'landlord-mediated capitalism from below'. I provided a full treatment of the US transition in my Capitalism *from Above and Capitalism from Below* (Byres 1996), where the American North and Prussia are examined. I also discussed the American South, where the transition from *slavery* to capitalism, via an important interlude of sharecropping, was critical. I consider the Scottish case in my forthcoming book *Capitalism and Enlightenment. An Essay on the Political Economy of Agrarian Transformation and Its Analysis in Eighteenth Century Lowland Scotland.* I also discuss the Dutch case there.

The key variables in, and the driving forces behind, capitalist agrarian transition have been the character of the landlord class, where there was a landlord class; the nature of the peasantry and the degree and course of social differentiation; relationships between the peasantry and

Foreword   xix

landlords; the changing nature of modes of surplus appropriation; labour supply and whether labour was scarce or abundant; class struggle, pre-eminently over surplus appropriation; the crucial role of the state; and the development of the productive forces and the form taken as transition proceeded. The nature of capitalist industrialisation cannot be understood without reference to agriculture and agrarian change and the way in which capitalism penetrates agriculture, whether with the establishment of capitalist relations of production or not: in both Japan and the American North there was a notable absence of wage labour in agriculture, usually seen as a crucial component of capitalist agriculture, while in both a critical contribution to capitalist industrialisation was made.

A critical issue is whether this varied experience of successful transition has analytical relevance with respect to contemporary poor countries. I argue that it does (in the various writings already referred to). There are those who suggest that it does not and that its relevance has been ruled out by the relentless progress of globalisation, most notably Henry Bernstein (see his chapter below and his various writings referenced there).

Capitalist agrarian transition has given rise to a rich literature, including the celebrated transition from feudalism to capitalism debate, the Brenner debate and much else encompassing extensive discussion of contemporary poor countries. That has included the Indian mode of production debate and a great deal more on India. These are all referenced among the chapters that follow.

Socialist agrarian transition and its aftermath

The third transition was an attempted *socialist agrarian transition*. Its classical sites were the Soviet Union and China, starting, respectively, in the 1920s and 1950s. Each entailed the *collectivisation of agriculture* and *socialist industrialisation*. Each involved, inter alia, the attempted generating of surpluses in agriculture, and the appropriation of agricultural surpluses to enable accumulation outside of agriculture. Appropriation of a surplus from agriculture was pursued via taxation of agriculture and shifting the internal/inter-sectoral terms of trade against agriculture and to industry's advantage.

There is a vast specialist literature on each, and several classic texts were published in the Soviet Union in the 1920s, which was a period of impassioned, high-quality debate. Especially important with respect to socialist agrarian transition is the writing of Eugene Preobrazhensky

xx Foreword

(1886–1937), and in particular his classic *The New Economics* (Preobrazhensky 1965, first published in Russian 1926), which is an exploration of what Preobrazhensky terms 'the law of primitive socialist accumulation' (for a definition, see pp. 84–85), in which he explores the critical matter of how the fledgling socialist state can finance industrialisation and lays emphasis on the appropriation of a surplus from agriculture, via price policy and taxation.

Preobrazhensky did not, in his writing, contemplate the collectivisation of agriculture. That was enforced in the Soviet Union between 1928 and 1940, following a crisis in 1927–28. Soviet agriculture was decollectivised in the early 1990s. It had lasted effectively for six decades. In China its lifespan was far less: agriculture, after a period of land reform, was collectivised suddenly in 1955–56, and decollectivised between 1978 and 1984, relatively slowly and at a different pace in different regions (Bramall 2000: 326–31), a period of three decades. In each case, with decollectivisation came the effective end of socialist agrarian transition.

In both instances there was some success in acquiring an agricultural surplus and using it to sustain industrialisation, though at considerable human cost in the Soviet Union. Preobrazhensky was executed in 1937, as were many other intellectuals in those fateful years. In the Chinese case, it has been argued, with plausible supporting evidence, that during the era of attempted socialist agrarian transition, 'the necessary infrastructure for modern economic growth was created' (Bramall 2000: 130). There was a considerable rise in the literacy rate, the rate of population growth was reduced and the stock of human capital was raised, while 'there was a massive investment in physical infrastructure: irrigation works, plant and machinery, factories and transport networks' (Bramall 2000: 130). Moreover, it was a success that would have future ramifications. Socialist agrarian transition left a considerable legacy. The same might be said mutatis mutandis of the Soviet Union.

With decollectivisation in China came so-called market socialism, which, according to Bramall, lasted from 1978 to 1996 (Bramall 2009). But the writing was on the wall. Socialist agrarian transition, to all intents and purposes, was over. By 1996, the pursuit of capitalism was openly embraced by the state (the Chinese Communist Party). A thoroughgoing capitalist agrarian transition was on the agenda. Thus, 'the rhetoric of socialism may have been retained, but the true aim of the CCP [from 1996] has been to effect a rapid transition to a full-blown capitalist economy' (Bramall 2009: 469). Bramall identifies the post-1996 era as that of 'the transition to capitalism'. There had been a traverse from a socialist

Foreword xxi

to a capitalist agrarian transition. Pursuit of capitalist agrarian transition has been wholeheartedly embraced before a full socialist agrarian transition had been secured. The same has been true of Russia.

China, in this new era, has enjoyed 'explosive' economic growth, in both agriculture and industry (Bramall 2000: 132). Many, in the West, have attributed this to 'decollectivisation, privatisation, and the creation of formal (and individual) property rights' (Bramall 2000: 132). There is a more convincing explanation. It has been argued that 'the galvanising effect of the shift in the terms of trade in 1979' in favour of agriculture was crucial, in 'creating a surplus in the rural sector which could be invested in both agriculture, and more importantly modern industry . . . [and so] set in train a process of cumulative causation' (Bramall 2000: 132). The shift in the terms of trade *against* agriculture, which had helped fuel industrialisation in the era of socialist agrarian transition, was now *reversed* during that of capitalist agrarian transition and contributed potently to both agricultural and industrial development. That, however, would not have been possible without the *prior creation of infrastructure*, in both agriculture and industry, as part of socialist agrarian transition.

Russia, however, has enjoyed no such success, although something of a legacy from the past has been posited. That is so in that 'former state and collective farms of Russia' are far from being 'nothing more than stagnant and unchanging "rural Gulags" waiting for the inevitable onward march of private family farming to consign them to oblivion' (Kitching 1998: 23). On the contrary, it is likely that a small minority of them 'will form the nucleus of the agrarian capitalism of Russia's future' (Kitching 1998: 22). That was written at the end of the 1990s. Whether it has proved so remains to be seen.

In a recent special issue of the *Journal of Agrarian Change* on 'Agrarian Change in Contemporary China' (Oya *et al.* 2015), the editors pose the question: 'Why is China important for the literature on agrarian change and agrarian transitions?' (p. 311). One of the reasons, they suggest,

> is because of the particular history of China and the possibility of devising new analytical categories of agrarian transition, with socialist transitions preceding and shaping more conventional capitalist transition. In comparative terms, the study of agrarian questions in China opens up a wealth of possibilities in the study of agrarian transitions worldwide, and therefore should be of interest to those working on other regions and countries of the developing word.
>
> (Oya *et al.* 2015)

xxii Foreword

Their argument is compelling. Readers of this book might read the collection with profit.

Themes in this book

There is no need to rehearse the arguments pursued and debated in this book. The editor provides an excellent summary of each chapter in his Introduction. Suffice it to say that in a wide array of chapters one finds a range of conflicting views, expressed with varying degrees of intensity in: consideration of classical debates on the agrarian question and their possible relevance for India; the theoretical and the empirical; examination of the historical roots of India's economic backwardness with analysis of colonialism and surplus appropriation/remittance; assessment of the impact of globalisation and whether it impedes agrarian transition; the neoliberal state; agrarian crisis and farmers' suicides; macro treatment at one level and village studies at another; the nature and the fate of different classes; exploration of regional diversity. For anyone concerned with agrarian transition in India, there is much to choose from.

Terence J. Byres
Emeritus Professor of Political Economy,
University of London
2 August 2015

Notes

1 Childe had first pointed to, and explained, these 'revolutions', in his *New Light on the Most Ancient East: The Oriental Prelude to European Prehistory* (1934). He stressed their nature and importance, with great clarity and cogency in the first of his 'popular' books *Man Makes Himself* (1936/1981: chapters 5, 6 and 7), and again, with equal clarity and force in his second 'popular' book *What Happened in History* (1942: see 18–19 for a concise statement; and chapters 5 and 6).
2 See Childe (1958a/2009, 43–44 and in detail 44–55 and 56–67).
3 See Childe (1958a: 125 and see 125–33 on the megalithic tombs).
4 See Marx (1961: 713–74, 1962: 63–93).
5 For their 'orthodox' conceptual apparatus, see de Vries and Van der Woude (1997: 693–99).
6 See Brenner (2001: 169, 212–13, 217, 231, 233).

References

Bramall, Chris. 2000. *Sources of Chinese Economic Growth 1978–1996*. Oxford: Oxford University Press.
Bramall, Chris. 2009. *Chinese Economic Development*. Abingdon: Routledge.

Brenner, Robert, 2001. 'The Low Countries in the Transition to Capitalism'. *Journal of Agrarian Change*, April, 1 (2): 169–242.

Byres, Terence J. 1986. 'The Agrarian Question, Forms of Capitalist Agrarian Transition and the State: An Essay with Reference to Asia'. *Social Scientist*, November–December, nos. 162–63, 14 (11–12): 3–67.

Byres, Terence J. 1991. 'The Agrarian Question and Differing Forms of Capitalist Agrarian Transition: An Essay with Reference to Asia'. In Jan Breman and Sudipto Mundle (eds). *Rural Transformation in Asia*. Delhi: Oxford University Press, pp. 3–76. Previously published in 1986.

Byres, Terence J. 1996. *Capitalism from Above and Capitalism from Below: An Essay in Comparative Political Economy*. Basingstoke and London: Macmillan.

Byres, Terence J. 2003. 'Structural Change, the Agrarian Question, and the Possible Impact of Globalization'. In Jayati Ghosh and C. P. Chandrasekhar (eds). *Work and Well-Being in the Age of Finance*. Delhi: Tulika Press, pp. 171–211.

Byres, Terence J. forthcoming. *Capitalism and Enlightenment. An Essay on the Political Economy of Agrarian Transformation and Its Analysis in Eighteenth Century Lowland Scotland*.

Childe, Vere Gordon. 1934. *New Light on the Most Ancient East: The Oriental Prelude to European Prehistory*. London: Kegan Paul, Trench, Trubner and Co., Ltd, pp. xiv + 208. Revised 2nd edition 1935; 4th edition rewritten 1952.

Childe, Vere Gordon. 1936. *Man Makes Himself*. London: Watts and Co., pp. xii + 275. 2nd impression 1937; 3rd impression 1939. Slightly revised edition in The Thinkers' Library. 1941. New impression 1948; 3rd edition 1956; 4th edition 1965. First illustrated edition by Moonraker Press and Pitman, 1981, with an Introduction by Sally Green.

Childe, Vere Gordon. 1942. *What Happened in History*. Harmondsworth and New York: Pelican Books, Penguin Books, p. 256. New impression 1943, 1946. Reset 1948. New impression 1950. New impression 1952. 2nd edition 1954; 3rd edition Book Club Associates 1973. Revised edition 1976.

Childe, Vere Gordon. 1958a. *The Prehistory of European Society*. Harmondsworth: Penguin Books. Reprinted 1962 by Cassells, London; and with a new Introduction by Stephen Shennan in 2009 by Spokesman, Nottingham.

Childe, Vere Gordon. 1958b. 'Retrospect'. *Antiquity*. XXXIII: 69–74. Reprinted in Thomas C. Patterson Jr. and Charles E. Orser. *Foundations of Social Archaeology: Selected Writings of V. Gordon Childe*, Oxford and New York: Berg (2004: 191–97).

Gathercole, Peter. 1994. 'Contribution to Discussion of Bruce G. Trigger, "Childe's Relevance to the 1990s"'. In David R. Harris (ed.). *The Archaeology of V. Gordon Childe*. London: UCL Press, pp. 28–29.

Kitching, Gavin, 1998. 'The Development of Agrarian Capitalism in Russia 1991–97: Some Observations from Fieldwork'. *Journal of Peasant Studies*, April, 25 (3): 1–30.

Marx, Karl. 1961. *Capital. Volume 1*. Moscow: Foreign Languages Publishing Press.

Marx, Karl. 1962. *Capital. Volume 3*. Moscow: Foreign Languages Publishing Press.

xxiv Foreword

Oya, Carlos, Jingzhong Ye and Qian Forrest Zhang (eds). 2015. Special issue on *Agrarian Change in Contemporary China*. *Journal of Agrarian Change*, July, 15 (3): 297–477.

Preobrazhensky, E. 1965. *The New Economics*. Oxford: Clarendon Press. First published in Russian in 1926.

Trigger, Bruce. 1994. 'Childe's Relevance to the 1990s'. In David R. Harris (ed.). *The Archaeology of V. Gordon Childe. Contemporary Perspectives*. London: UCL Press, pp. 9–27. And in the same volume comments on Childe, p. 117.

Vries, Jan de and Van der Woude. 1997. *First Modern Economy. Success, Failure, and Perseverance of the Dutch Economy 1500 to 1815*. Cambridge: Cambridge University Press.

Wood, Ellen Meiksins. 1999. *The Origins of Capitalism*. New York: Monthly Review Press.

Wood, Ellen Meiksins. 2002. 'The Question of Market Dependence'. *Journal of Agrarian Change*, 2 January (1): 50–87.

Preface and Acknowledgements

Over the past few decades, the agriculture and rural economy in countries like India has witnessed widespread restructuring in terms of productivity and output, intensification of production technology, rural livelihood, patterns of migration and the like in the context of neoliberal globalisation. However, this transformation indicates diverse trends with large regional variations and differential response from various categories of agrarian/rural population. To what extent the classical and contemporary political economy perspectives in agrarian change comprehend this complex change is the central concern of this book. It critically evaluates the relevance of classical debate and extends the horizon of contemporary debates in the Indian context linking the national trends with specifications of regional experiences.

The book is an outcome of an international seminar on Agrarian Transition in India held in January 2014. This seminar was organised by Pondicherry University in collaboration with French Institute of Pondicherry. I greatly acknowledge the financial support of the Indian Council of Social Science Research, New Delhi, National Bank for Agriculture and Rural Development, Mumbai, and Indian Bank, Puducherry. I am grateful to the vice-chancellor of Pondicherry University and the Director of French Institute of Pondicherry, for providing the necessary support for organising the seminar.

Scholars across the disciplines like Joan P. Mencher, Henry Bernstein, Utsa Patnaik, A Haroon Akram-Lodhi, D. Narasimha Reddy, Hira Singh, Marc Edelman, D. N. Dhanagare, Barbara Harriss-White, Jens Lerche, R. Vijay, Gaurang Ranjan Sahaya, Santanu Rakshit, Elumalai Kannan, Joseph Tharamangalam, Daniel Münster, Jonathan Pattenden, G. Venkatasubramanian, Joel Caballion, Mamata Swain, Joe Headly, Frehiwot Tesfaye and Tudor Silva presented papers and enriched the discussions in the seminar.

xxvi   Preface and Acknowledgements

Of the 25 papers presented in the seminar, only eight papers were selected for this book based on thematic coverage. As gender aspect of agrarian transition was not covered by the presentations in the seminar, to fill the gap, I requested Judith Heyer (who chaired one of the sessions and actively participated in the seminar) to contribute a chapter to the book. The last chapter on Punjab peasantry which was published earlier in *Economic and Political Weekly* (*EPW*) was also not presented in the seminar. It was included in the book as an anonymous reviewer suggested to include a chapter from traditional green revolution states. I am thankful to its authors, Sukhpal Singh and Shruti Bhogal, as well as the *EPW* for giving permission to reproduce the paper.

I am indeed grateful to Terence J. Byres for kindly writing a foreword to this book despite his preoccupation with other pressing commitments.

Most important, I have been benefitted from my regular consultations with D. N. Dhanagare, who was a great source of motivation and inspiration for me right from the inception of the seminar. He also went through the earlier draft of the introduction and made valuable comments and suggestions.

Thanks are due to Sujata Patel who intially motivated me to bring out a volume on agrarian transition.

I thank the anonymous reviewer who has read carefully the previous version of this book and suggested important changes.

At Routledge, it has been a pleasure to work with Shoma Choudhury, Antara Ray Chaudhury, Daniel Bourner and Rimina Mohapatra who have been immensely supportive throughout the publication process. I thank them all. I express deep sense of appreciation to Anita Selina for copy editing of the manuscript. I am equally thankful to Deepti Agarwal and her entire team at Apex CoVantage, LLC for organising the typesetting of the manuscript.

I would like to thank my colleagues G. Ramathirtham, K. Gulam Dasthagir, Sudha Sitharaman, C. Aruna, P. K. Parida, M. Mancy, Imtirenla Longkumer and Ramesh Nayak as well as all the research scholars, especially Hemalatha, Satish, Debadatta, Safeeque, Chita and Papesh for extending necessary help and cooperation.

My special thanks to Thanuja Mummidi and Ponnarasu Subramanian who have helped in many ways to complete this book.

Without the firm support and constant encouragement of my wife, Pritinanda, and son, Samarpit (Gudul), this book would never have been completed.

I express my deepest sense of gratitude to my parents whose unlimited love and blessings have always guided me in my all academic endeavours.

Needless to say, any errors and omissions are solely my own.

B. B. Mohanty

Abbreviations

AQ	Agrarian Question
CEC	Centre for Education and Communication
COA	Certified Organic Agriculture
CPI(M)	Communist Party of India (Marxist)
CSR	Child Sex Ratio
EGS	Employment Guarantee Scheme
EPRP	Export-Led Poverty Reduction Programme
EPW	*Economic and Political Weekly*
EU	European Union
FAO	Food and Agricultural Organisations
FDI	Foreign Direct Investment
FDS	Farm Disposable Surplus
FIR	First Information Report
FLS	Farm Labour Surplus
FTA	Foreign Trade Agreement
GATT	General Agreement on Tariffs and Trade
GCF	Gross Capital Formation
GDP	Gross Domestic Product
GoAP	Government of Andhra Pradesh
GoH	Government of Haryana
GoI	Government of India
GoM	Government of Maharashtra
GoP	Government of Punjab
GVA	Gross Value Added
HYVs	High-Yielding Varieties
IFAD	International Fund for Agricultural Development
IMF	International Monetary Fund
IRS	Increasing Returns to Scale
IT	Information Technology

xxviii Abbreviations

JOAC	*Journal of Agrarian Change*
KNMK	Kongu Nadu Munnetra Kazhagam
LDCs	Least Developed Countries
MGNREGA	Mahatma Gandhi National Rural Employment Guarantee Act
MLA	Member of Legislative Assembly
MNC	Multinational Corporation
MoRD	Ministry of Rural Development
MPCE	Monthly Per Capita Expenditure
MSP	Minimum Support Price
NABARD	National Bank for Agriculture and Rural Development
NGO	Non-Governmental Organisation
NRIs	Non-Resident Indians
NSSO	National Sample Survey Organisation
OBC	Other Backward Classes
PDS	Public Distribution System
RBI	Reserve Bank of India
SBI	State Bank of India
SEZs	Special Economic Zones
UN	United Nations
UPA	United Progressive Alliance
VAO	Village Administrative Officer
VM	Village Munsiff
WTO	World Trade Organisation
ZBNF	Zero Budget Natural Farming

Introduction
Agrarian transition: from classic to current debates

B. B. Mohanty

I. Introduction

One of the central questions that generated scholarly research and debate in social sciences throughout the major part of the twentieth century relates to the 'incomplete' transition in the Third-World countries from the pre-capitalist to capitalist mode of production. This question assumed even greater significance and has renewed interest among researchers in the past few decades in the context of profound transformation in the agrarian economy and society of the Global South under neoliberal reforms. According to the orthodox Marxist version, capitalist penetration in the Third World would produce the same trajectory of development as was observed in the Western homelands of capital. However, this view evoked a critical response since the 1960s; it was then argued that the possibility of the Third World experiencing a full-scale transition to capitalism in the line of the First World was ruled out, as the classic transition trajectories, exemplified by some European countries, represented only a minority of experiences of agrarian transition, which were not under colonial or imperial yoke. The variety of past and more recent studies of agrarian relations also raised complex theoretical issues that need interpretations within larger historical debates.

The World Development Report on Agriculture (2008: 26), however, indicated that the agrarian transition of Europe in the nineteenth century would be repeated throughout the Global South as populations move from country to city, agriculture to industry and subsistence production to wage labour.[1] On the contrary, a recent report released by the Food and Agriculture Organisation (2014) highlighted that family farms were by far the most prevalent form of agriculture in the world, and its estimate suggested that they occupied around 70 to 80 per cent

2 B. B. Mohanty

of farmland and produced more than 80 per cent of the world's food in value terms. It also noted that the vast majority of these small farms were from the Global South.

In view of the contradictory theoretical as well as empirical interpretations, the classical discussion and subsequent debates on agrarian transition, therefore, need to be further developed, not just to document the changes that took place in developing countries like India but also to critically analyse their specificities and generalities that they deserved but did not yet receive any attention. In India the recent pace of neoliberal globalisation has apparently transformed the forces and relations of production on a global scale, which has implications for agrarian transition. Changes in productivity and output, intensification of production technology, rural livelihood, patterns of migration and the like have to be understood and explained in relation to the rapid pace of global capitalist development, and their uneven impact across regions. While there has been much written on agrarian transformation and dynamics of capitalist transition across the world, there has been much less analysis of the nature of transition in countries like India and its linkage with the classical and contemporary transition debate. This volume, therefore, addresses itself to the following five major questions:

(1) What are the significant changes emerging in India's agrarian economy and society under the impact of neoliberal reforms and global capitalism? (2) Are these changes indicating the transition from rural/semi-feudal economy to urban-industrial capitalist economy? (3) Is this transition conforming to, or deviating from, the classical model of transition from feudalism to capitalism? (4) How have different regions and states in India, being at different stages of development, experienced and responded to this agrarian transition? (5) How are various agrarian classes and interest groups responding to this transition?

In the recent literature on agrarian change, the preceding questions have rarely been addressed or tangentially touched upon. In their book, though Akram-Lodhi and Kay (2009) offer a rare attempt to analyse the impact of agrarian transformation on peasantry in the context of capitalist globalisation within the larger historical and contemporary political economy perspective, they made little effort to examine the emerging process of capitalist transition and ongoing transition discourse in India and its relevance to the larger debate at the global level. Similarly, Kelly's book (2013) throws light on agrarian transition but confines itself only to the process of migration that derives from and

Agrarian transition: from classic to current debates　3

drives agrarian transition in Southeast Asian countries (e.g. Malaysia, Thailand and Philippines) which may not fit neatly into the Indian situation due to different sociopolitical and economic conditions as well as historical features. In their book, Patnaik and Moyo (2011) show how the neoliberal global capitalist accumulation is consuming the small producers of the periphery, the peasantry in Africa and India. The arguments in the book, however, lack fine-grained empirical analysis and are based on a high level of abstraction with political overtone. Chakrabarti and Cullenberg's book (2003) which presents a critical study of the theories of transition in India, including debates on modes of production and subaltern studies, is not based on any empirical exercise and overlooks the current debates on agrarian transition. Even the more recent book by Harriss-White and Heyer (2015), which focuses on various aspects of contemporary capitalism in India, paid little attention to Indian transition debate and bypassed the key conceptual and theoretical issues relevant to the understanding of current discourse on capitalist transition. The books on agrarian crisis in India (Reddy and Mishra 2009; Deshpande and Arora 2010) did not touch upon agrarian transition. In this context, this book provides a set of new perspectives on central questions concerning agrarian transition in India and their implications for the global debate. It has identified certain new dynamics of agrarian political economy and provides a comprehensive account of diverse aspects of capitalist transition at both theoretical and empirical levels.

An attempt is made in the following section to present a synthesis of several important debates on agrarian transition, starting from the classical to contemporary period, and to provide an analytical framework for interpreting the Indian situation, with a view to situating it in the context of the global debate on mode of production and agrarian transition in the Third World.

2. Agrarian transition: the classics

Although the study of agrarian structure goes back to the classical debate on political economy of the eighteenth century, a systematic analysis in agrarian change began only in the nineteenth century, with Marx's writings explaining the origins of capitalism. However, Marx being interested mainly in the development of industrial capitalism said little about agriculture and peasantry. His analysis of the development of capitalism in agriculture, developed towards the end of his life (in *Capital I* – the chapter on 'The So Called Primitive Accumulation'), explained how

4 B. B. Mohanty

capitalist methods of farming destroyed the English peasantry which he cited as the classic form of transition. Marx said,

> The capitalist system presupposes the complete separation of the labourers from all property in the means by which they can realise their labour . . . so-called primitive accumulation . . . is nothing else than the historical process of divorcing the producer from the means of production. . . . The starting-point of the development that gave rise to the wage labourer as well as to the capitalist, was the servitude of the labourer. . . . The expropriation of the agricultural producer, of the peasant, from the soil, is the basis of the whole process.
>
> (Marx 1965: 714–16)

In the context of France, Marx argued, 'A similar movement is seen during the last ten years in France; in proportion as capitalist production there takes possession of agriculture, it drives the surplus agricultural population into the towns' (1965: 693n).[2] However, though the analysis, made in *Capital I*, was applicable to all countries of Europe (Duggett 1975: 169), Marx pointed out elsewhere that the entry of capital into agriculture as an independent and leading power did not take place everywhere all at once, but rather gradually and in particular branches of production (Marx 1981: 937).

It needs to be emphasised here that Marx's analysis of historical development of capitalism was in fact tied to many significant considerations of structures and processes and that he cautioned against any straightforward and naïve application of his propositions in *Capital* to historical experiences outside Western Europe (Sen 1984). Marx and Engels remarked,

> Viewed apart from real history, these abstractions have in themselves no value whatsoever. They can only serve to facilitate the arrangement of historical material, to indicate the sequence of its separate strata. But they by no means afford a recipe or scheme, as does philosophy for neatly trimming the epochs of history.
>
> (Marx and Engels 1945: 15)

Engels reiterated the sentiments of Marx though he was not concerned with the issue of capitalist penetration of farming as did Marx. In his first major work *The Condition of the Working Class in England*, Engels explained that as the machine had given birth to an industrial proletariat, so it had also produced agricultural proletariat and the

Agrarian transition: from classic to current debates 5

tenant farmer too faced the same ruin that hounded the petty bourgeoisie in the cities (Hammen 1972: 683). In 'The Peasant Question in France and Germany' while writing on historical forms of land ownership, peasant movements and their specific characteristics, Engels indicated the extinction of small agricultural producers under the impact of capitalism in the long run (Engels 1950: 382). Engels continued to view peasants as almost always in a transition towards proletarianisation. Put precisely, from a theoretical point of view, both Marx and Engels felt that peasant and agricultural workers were subjected to the same nightmare of exploitation by capitalism as were the industrial proletariat.

The conventional Marxist analysis thus believed that introduction of capitalist relations of production in agriculture led to the emergence of agrarian capitalist and wage labour classes. However, Marx recognised the varied ways through which capitalist production was strengthened in agricultural economy. In his writings Marx had indicated that the development of capitalism in agriculture led to both peasant dispossession by displacement, or enclosure, and peasant dispossession by differentiation (Akram-Lodhi 2007; Araghi 2009; Akram-Lodhi and Kay 2010a). While Marx (1894/1981) described the English path to capitalism, Engels (1894/1950) explored the capitalist transition in Europe, indicating that only Great Britain and Prussia were able to solve their agrarian questions. However, Marx was unfamiliar with, what Lenin and Kautsky later recognised as, the specific laws of capitalist penetration into agriculture (Hazelkorn 1981: 300).

Two important and insightful writings that appeared in 1899, Lenin's *Development of Capitalism in Russia* and Kautsky's *Die Agrarfrage*, further extended and enriched Marx's idea on development of capitalism in agriculture. Lenin's work (which is regarded as an application of the theory of Marx's *Capital* to Russian conditions) demonstrated the process of capitalist development through his 'theory of market' based on *Zemstvo* statistics on peasant differentiation against the arguments of the *Narodniks* of the time that claim that capitalism could not develop in Russia. Like Marx, Lenin saw a contradiction between capitalist industry and capitalist agriculture and laid emphasis on the differentiation of the peasantry in helping the growth and enlargement of the home market. In addition to Marx's English path of transition which is known as 'enclosure' model of agrarian transition, Lenin identified two opposite patterns of capitalist transition – the Prussian or Junker path (the state-promoted capitalism from above) and the American path (capitalism from below) – resulting from the internal differentiation of

6 B. B. Mohanty

the peasantry. Moreover, Lenin was aware of diversity in the pattern of agrarian transition when he argued,

> Of course, infinitely diverse combinations of elements of this or that type of capitalist evolution are possible, and only hopeless pedants could set about solving the peculiar and complex problems arising merely by quoting this or that opinion of Marx about a different historical epoch.
>
> (Lenin 1964: 33)

Lenin, however, preferred to concentrate on the Prussian and the American paths while analysing Russian situation as he realised these two to be likely alternatives (Byres 1986: 13). While Lenin analysed the process of development of capitalism in agriculture and compared different paths of agrarian transitions, Kautsky explained the differential pace of capitalist development in agriculture and in industry and held the view that agricultural economy followed its own laws of development. Kautsky was more concerned with the extent of development of capitalism in the countryside, its forms and underlying barriers (Byres 1986: 11). To Kautsky, in order to understand the capitalist transition in agriculture, it is essential to address the question (which was precisely his agrarian question): 'whether, and how, capitalist seizing hold of agriculture, revolutionising it, making old forms of production and property untenable and creating the necessity for new ones' (1988: 12).

Drawing on the agrarian transition in West Europe, Kautsky argued that the prime cause underlying the transformation of conditions of production in agriculture was the urban industrial capitalism. Kautsky concluded that it was industry that acted as the motor of transition from feudalism to capitalist development in agriculture by converting peasant to a commodity producer. He stated,

> Industry forms the motor force not only of its own development, but also of the development of agriculture. It was urban industry, that smashed unity of industry and agriculture in the countryside, that converted the peasant into a pure agriculturalist, a commodity producer tied to an unknown market, that established the possibility of his proletarianisation. The agriculture of the feudal epoch ended in an impasse, from which it could not escape through its own dynamism. It was urban industry that generated the revolutionary forces that were bound to, and could, break down the feudal regime and open a new path of development for itself and agriculture.
>
> (Banaji 1980: 89)

Lenin–Chayanov (Russian) debate

Lenin's extensive research into the nature and dynamics of the peasant culture and production process, paths of rural transition and the character of class politics in Russia was contested by Chayanov (1966, 1991) using the same basic statistical data as Lenin had used; it is termed as the Lenin–Chayanov debate. The crux of this debate was the pattern of differentiation that small producers underwent as capitalist forms of agriculture appeared. To Lenin, class differentiation within peasantry was central to the understanding of the development of capitalism, and he constructed a model of three peasant classes – rich, middle and poor peasants – with the eventual polarisation of middle peasants into rich and poor peasants. Chayanov (1966) developed a model of the peasant economy that focused on the particular characteristics of 'middle peasants'. His central thesis was that the rationale of peasant economies differed from that of capitalist farming. Arguing that the economic rationality of peasants was rooted in the basic subsistence needs of peasant farming rather than in profit, Chayanov, therefore, claimed that peasant households increased their labour output and intensity when faced with difficult circumstances. In contrast to the theory of class differentiation, he advanced the theory of 'demographic differentiation'. Challenging Lenin, who argued that capitalist penetration of agriculture entailed eventual 'depeasantisation', Chayanov argued that the economic reproduction of each individual peasant family farm was governed by its demographic cycle. According to Chayanov (1966: 4–6), the key to the economic behaviour of family labour farms lay in the farmers' subjective evaluation of the amount of drudgery required in farm production weighed against the consumption demands of the household unit, which he called the 'labour–consumer balance' (ratio of producers – working adults to consumers – working adults and dependants). To him, under given conditions, peasant families worked longer and intensively, leading to 'self-exploitation of family labour'. Chayanov, therefore, concluded that the competitive power of peasant family–farms versus large-scale capitalist farms was far greater than had been foreseen by Marx, Kautsky and Lenin, because in crisis conditions capitalist farms would go bankrupt and peasant families could work more hours, sell at lower prices, obtain no net surplus and yet manage to carry on with their farming and survive (Thorner 1966: xviii).

In fact, Lenin–Chayanov debate[3] was the most fascinating debate covering a number of key issues on political economy of agrarian change like class differentiation, capitalist and socialist transition and

8 B. B. Mohanty

related issues. Thus, the twentieth-century debates on agrarian transition were built on these classical positions. A wealth of literature flourished from this debate that analysed historical as also contemporary developments in peripheral political economies and also in advanced capitalist formations.

3. After the classics

After the Second World War, with the availability of new and meaningful evidences on agrarian history, industrial and commercial evolution and demographic changes, volume of research grew and new directions in historical research emerged ultimately generating fresh insights and discourse on Marxist analysis. Of these, the Dobb–Sweezy debate in 1950s on the Marxist explanation of the transition from feudalism to capitalism in the light of the European experience was both crucial and significant contribution to the discourse.

Dobb–Sweezy debate

The reincarnation of the classical debate occurred when the transition question occupied the centre stage in the exciting debate between Maurice Dobb and Paul Sweezy; it began in the journal *Science and Society* in 1950 revolving around feudalism as a mode of production and its contradictions leading to the transition to capitalism. This debate had implications for the understanding of the agrarian question and transition (Akram-Lodhi and Kay 2010a: 196). It originated from Maurice Dobb, a British Marxist economic historian who published *Studies in the Development of Capitalism* (1946) explaining the dynamics of transition from feudalism to capitalism in Europe.

According to Dobb, feudalism could be defined by understanding in terms of the structure of relationship between 'the direct producer and his overlord' in which 'the producer was in possession of his means of production as an individual producing unit' (1976: 58). More important, however, Dobb conceived of the crisis of feudalism, and its ultimate decline, as developing within the boundaries of the feudal mode of production. He noted,

> The inefficiency of feudalism as a system of production, coupled with the growing needs of the ruling class for revenue, that was primarily responsible for its decline.
>
> (Dobb 1946: 42)

Agrarian transition: from classic to current debates 9

Dobb argued that formation of two distinct classes – a class of 'free' workers who sell their labour power and a class of individuals who accumulate wealth – was not enough to ensure the capitalist transition. The transformation of wealth into the means of production was also necessary, which in turn required new behaviour, lifestyles of the accumulating class and its propensity to invest accumulated wealth in discovering new means of production to ensure ever-enlarging production. Feudalism, Dobb argued, collapsed as a result of the intensification of its own internal contradictions. In other words, Dobb found that the roots of the transition lay in the struggle and conflicting interests between lords and peasants *internal* to the feudal economy that removed obstacles to the market. Paul Sweezy, an American Marxist economist, however, challenged Dobb's explanation. To Sweezy, the collapse of feudalism could only be explained as arising from causes external to the system. He argued that, not the articulation of internal contradictions, but 'the growth of trade was the decisive factor in bringing about the decline of western European feudalism' (1976: 41). Put precisely, while Dobb emphasised on 'relations of production', Sweezy laid stress on the 'growth of trade' as prime mover in the transition from feudalism to capitalism. Though subsequently many others joined the debate, it was Robert Brenner's revisionist analysis of multiple paths of agrarian transition that enlarged further the scope of Dobb–Sweezy debate, and overall Marxist discourse on transition.

Brenner debate

In his groundbreaking article 'Agrarian Class Structure and Economic Development in Pre-Industrial Europe' Brenner (1976) addressed himself to Marx's theory and elaborated the process by which feudal property relations gave rise to new capitalist property relations. His analysis of multiple paths of agrarian transition in Europe underscored the limitations of demographic, market and technological forces which sparked one of the liveliest debates on transition from feudalism to capitalism, known as *Brenner debate*; it took place in the pages of the English historical journal *Past and Present* between 1976 and 1982.

Though Brenner was clearly influenced by Dobb, like Sweezy he differed from certain aspects of Dobb's argument. Like Dobb, Brenner concluded that there was no capitalism, even in embryonic form that existed, to challenge feudalism. However, he did not agree with Dobb's implicit assumption that within the interstices of feudalism lay the basis of capitalism (Akram-Lodhi and Kay 2010a: 196). Like Sweezy, Brenner argued that the tenacity of feudalism should not be underestimated, but unlike Sweezy, he agreed with Dobb that the dynamic of change had to be found not in some external intervention, but within the constitutive relations of feudalism (Wood 2009: 51–52). In other words, Brenner, unlike Chayanov, did not overestimate the tenacity of peasant-family-farm producer against the capitalist onslaught.

Brenner made a frontal attack on two main competing models (demographic or Malthusian model and commercialisation or market model) frequently used for understanding the decline of feudalism and the rise of a capitalist agriculture in late-medieval and early modern Europe; instead, Brenner demonstrated that class-relations model provided a better explanation of cross-national differences than either the demographic or the commercialisation model. To quote Brenner (1976: 31),

> It is the structure of class relations, of class power, which will determine the manner and degree to which particular demographic and commercial changes will affect long-term trends in the distribution of income and economic growth – and not vice versa.

Brenner thus believed that demography cannot be the decisive variable; rather, it was the population trends mediated through class relations and class conflict that matter in explaining socioeconomic development. Similarly, for Brenner, the commercialisation explanations were inappropriate for the analysis of feudal crisis, since serfdom was quintessentially a power relationship, not just a form of free contractual exchange. To Brenner, in the development of agrarian capitalism the determining variable was the relative strengths of the two main feudal classes – the lords and the peasants. Within feudalism, according to Brenner, the limits on peasant production imposed by a coercive-extractive relationship between landlord and peasant led to inefficiencies and struggles that ultimately destroyed the system. Its outcomes varied significantly from region to region as variations are a function of historically specific conditions. Comparing the trajectories of the English and the French feudalism, Brenner argued that it was the relative weakness of the English peasantry which allowed the lords to establish absolute property in land and gradually led to capitalist relations based on wage labour. However, the strength of the French peasantry left them with access to their means of livelihood, leading to a very different resolution of the crisis of late-medieval feudalism, namely the centralisation of lordly power in the absolute monarchy. Put succinctly, what held the French back was a pattern of class relations in which lords were unable,

Agrarian transition: from classic to current debates   11

unlike their English counterparts, to undermine independent peasant proprietorship. Brenner made it clear that neither Eastern Europe nor France provided a feasible alternative route to capitalism. In his analysis it was not the class relations per se but class conflict that held the key to capitalist transition. Brenner (1976: 47) wrote,

> The breakthrough from 'traditional economy' to relatively self-sustaining economic development was predicated upon the emergence of a specific set of class relations in the countryside, that is capitalist class relations. This outcome depended, in turn, upon the previous success of a two-sided process of class development and class conflict: on the one hand the destruction of serfdom; on the other hand, the short-circuiting of the emerging predominance of small peasant property.

In a nutshell, Brenner viewed class structure, class relations and class struggle as the key dynamic variables in the analysis of agrarian transition to capitalism (Akram-Lodhi and Kay 2010a).

Brenner's analysis of transition however, raised many problems.[4] It was typically Eurocentric and comparisons were made within Europe rather than between Europe and other parts of the non-European world. The possible explanatory significance of other countries beyond Europe was notably absent both from Brenner's own account and from Brenner's debate in general. The real 'classic' formulation was that of Marx, whom all contributors to the debate look to for justification, and views of the subsequent Marxist revisionists like Lenin were overlooked; this was taken seriously later by Byres and his followers. Byres (1996) differed from Brenner's view of the roots of capitalist origins. He made the differentiation of the peasant class as the key to his notion of capitalist development, as against Brenner who minimised social differentiation within the peasantry, and stressed its homogeneity as a class. Byres argued that the process of peasant differentiation affected the balance of class forces both between lords and peasants and within the peasantry itself which ultimately shaped the process of agrarian transition (Akram-Lodhi and Kay 2010a: 197).

4. Agrarian transition: Byres and Bernstein

By the end of the twentieth century, new meanings had been added to the classical account of agrarian transition that was developed in the nineteenth century by Marx, Kautsky and Lenin, which were

12 B. B. Mohanty

explained clearly by Byres (1986) and subsequently elaborated systematically by Bernstein (1994). The agrarian transition began to be understood as a non-linear process. Taking the classical texts of Marx, Lenin and Kautsky as his point of departure, Byres (1986, 1996) suggested great diversity in historical circumstances under which agrarian transition could occur and illustrated six different comparative paths of successful agrarian transition (four paths of capitalist agrarian transition representing European/North American diversity: *the English path* leading to decline of feudalism accompanied by the emergence of capitalist farming, class struggle and class formation; *the Prussian path* whereby an impoverished peasantry was subordinated by and became the workforce of a landlord class that engaged directly in capitalist farming; *the American path* and *the French path* in which serfdom disappeared as a result of successful class struggle waged from below by peasantry against the landlord class; and two paths of transition representing Asian diversity: *the Japanese* and the *Taiwanese/South Korean paths*).[5] Like Brenner (1986), Byres (2009) identified class struggle as a critical variable in understanding a specific path of agrarian transition.

To Byres, how capitalism became dominant in a society without full development of capitalist social relations of production in agriculture represented the 'historical puzzles', which was not looked into seriously due to stereotypical and narrow understanding of successful agrarian transitions (1996: 3–4). According to Bernstein, this marks Byres's reformulation of the agrarian question as agrarian transition (Bernstein 1996: 24–25). For Byres (1986: 4), 'agrarian transition' refers to 'those changes in the countryside of a poor country necessary to the overall development of capitalism and to its ultimate dominance in a particular national social formation'.[6] To him, in order for agriculture to no longer pose any obstacles to capitalist transformation, the agrarian question[7] must be 'resolved' through some forms of successful 'agrarian transition' (Akram-Lodhi and Kay 2009: 21).

In his assessment of the work of Byres, Bernstein (1996) summarised three important 'problematics' of Byres's agrarian question, namely 'accumulation', 'production' and 'politics'.[8] While the 'problematic of accumulation' was referred to the understanding of the extent to which agriculture could act as a basis for accumulation, the 'problematic of production' was related to the extent to which capitalism developed in the countryside, the forms it took and the barriers which might impede it (Byres 1991: 10). The 'problematic of politics' was associated with the impact of political forces and forms on the evolution of rural change explicit in both the accumulation and production problematics

Agrarian transition: from classic to current debates 13

(Akram-Lodhi 1998: 138). It was argued that since Byres linked agrarian transition with overall development of capitalism and its ultimate dominance, 'agrarian transition may occur without necessarily changing the individual spheres of accumulation, production and politics' (*ibid* 146).

Bernstein debate

Bernstein's recent series of writings on agrarian question and its relevance in the context of globalisation generated intense debate in the political economy of agrarian change. To Bernstein, the classical agrarian question of the problematic of transition was the agrarian question of capital, specifically of industrial capital (Bernstein 1996: 52, 2006: 449, 2009a: 250). He viewed that with the development of forces of production on a global scale, the agrarian question of capital became redundant and the classical agrarian question lost its relevance in the present context of globalisation. To quote him,

> With contemporary globalisation and the massive development of productive forces in (advanced) capitalist agriculture, the centrality of the 'classic' agrarian question to industrialisation is no longer significant for international capital. In this sense, then, there is no longer an agrarian question of capital on a world scale, even when the agrarian question – as a basis of national accumulation and industrialisation – has not been resolved in many countries of the South.
>
> (Bernstein 2004: 202)

Bernstein made a distinction between agrarian question of capital and agrarian question of labour[9] (1996: 25–26) and forcefully argued that, by now, the agrarian question for capital resolved in most of the world and that the only question now was about labour (2006: 450–51). This view was debated in a recent issue of the *Canadian Journal of Development Studies* as well as in other places (e.g. see Akram-Lodhi and Kay 2009). Among those who joined this debate, Philip McMichael figured prominently. Bernstein (2006) argued that the agrarian question of capital was superseded in the current period of globalisation, and therefore, neither classes of predatory pre-capitalist landed property exited nor was it useful to regard today's small farmers as 'peasants'. He also noted that struggles over land might manifest an agrarian question of classes of labour; however, they did not have the same systemic significance as did the agrarian question of capital. On the other hand, Philip

14 B. B. Mohanty

McMichael (2006) criticised the conception of the agrarian question and underscored the role played by the agrarian movements, especially transnational agrarian movements. For him, the new agrarian question is now centred on food and food security which in turn is to be resolved within the realm of political policy and practice. Emphasising on the politicisation of food and agricultural production through the analysis of the political discourse of the global peasant movement, McMichael tried to go beyond the parameters of the classic agrarian question. To him,

> Food is a touchstone for a potentially far more profound political intervention to transcend the depeasantisation scenario embedded in the development narrative . . . the food sovereignty movement at large embodies a strategic transformation of political institutions based on a global moral economy.
>
> (McMichael 2009: 305)

In a more recent debate on food sovereignty in *The Journal of Peasant Studies*, Bernstein (2014) criticised McMichael for overlooking the contrasts and contradictions between and within agrarian classes and putting together too many different categories under the label 'peasants' as a category which was different from and opposed to capitalism. Thus, while McMichael viewed agrarian capitalism in terms of homogenous global food regime, Bernstein looked at capitalism in terms of class dynamics and concrete contradiction between different agrarian classes in the production process (Jansen 2014: 5–6).

There were also many others like Friedmann (2006), Araghi (2009) and Akram-Lodhi and Kay (2010b) who participated in this debate. In response to Bernstein's argument Friedmann (2006: 462) argued that both agrarian question of capital and agrarian question of labour were having long histories and each needs to be understood as part of world-historical changes of accumulation and of the state system. Similarly, Araghi situated the agrarian question within the dynamics of the world-historical system of globalised capitalism. He drew attention to the global political aspect of the agrarian question and emphasised the linkages between the reproduction of the reserve army of labour in the West and agrarian transitions as well as food production in the South. For Araghi the expansion of capitalism implied a general tendency towards dispossession and depeasantisation; yet it also generated peasantisation in particular regions. What distinguished the current phase of the agrarian transition, however, is a quasi-universal tendency

Agrarian transition: from classic to current debates   15

towards dispossession in the context of global overproduction, and a forced under-consumption among the labouring classes in the South. Besides, the gender and ecological dimensions of the agrarian question were highlighted by Bridget O'Laughlin (2009), Tony Weis (2007), Michael Watts (2009) and John Bellamy Foster (2009). Akram-Lodhi (2000) and Akram-Lodhi and Kay (2010b) also noted the relevance of agrarian question in the context of emergence of global capitalism. Akram-Lodhi and Kay (2010b: 280) identified and summarised seven agrarian questions,[10] tracing their roots from the nineteenth-century classic to recent debates in the context of varied effects of globalisation driven by neoliberal capitalism. They concluded,

> Agrarian question offers a sufficiently nuanced account that rigorously yet flexibly captures both the common processes at work in the countryside of developing capitalist countries as well as the substantive diversity, rooted in globally-embedded, historically – informed and country-specific trajectories of variation, which can cumulatively assist in understanding paths of agrarian transition.
> (Akram-Lodhi and Kay 2010b: 280)

To put it succinctly, the impulse to universalise and essentialise the grand classical formulations declined after taking into account fresh empirical data and findings pointing to a wider set of processes that were shaping rural transformation – such as changing production relations, agricultural expansion to new zones, intensification of production technology, new land use patterns for urbanisation, industrialisation and for livelihoods. Bernstein's interpretation of agrarian question and transition and the subsequent debate that it had generated broadened the horizon of understanding of political economy of agrarian change since it has wider implications for Africa, Latin America and Asia. Already a kind of debate surrounding Bernstein's argument was initiated in some of the countries belonging to these parts of the globe (Harriss-White 2008; Moyo 2008; Patnaik 2012; Lerche 2013).

5. The Indian debate

In India, agrarian change was the core of scholarly research and debate for over three decades beginning with the 1960s.[11] The dominant line of inquiry then mainly focused on identifying the nature and the extent of growth of capitalism in Indian agriculture. In the early 1960s the

16   B. B. Mohanty

evidence on signs of capitalist farming was reported by Gupta (1962)[12] and Kotovsky (1964).[13] Though these two studies did not stimulate any wider debate as such (Thorner 1982: 1962), they motivated American economic historian Daniel Thorner to extend their arguments on the emerging capitalist trend in Indian agriculture. Based on his extensive tour in 1953, 1958–59 and 1966–67 through major regions of India and his interaction with agricultural labourers, progressive farmers and large capitalist farmers, Daniel Thorner (1967/1980) indicated the emergence of a burgeoning wave of capitalist agriculture in the Indian countryside. In a paper presented at the conference of European Scholars on South Asia, held at Cambridge in 1968, Daniel Thorner stated,

> Going by what I have seen myself, and by the reports of many other observers, I would say that the number of genuine agricultural capitalist was quite small in the early 1950's, smaller than the proportion suggested by Gupta or Kotovsky; but that it has since been increasing rapidly in the second half of the 1960's. V.K.R.V. Rao was already calling attention to signs of this in 1962. For the first time a class of capitalist farmers has come into being on an all-India scale. It is certainly likely to continue in the proximate future.
>
> (Thorner 1980: 252–53)

Elsewhere he also observed,

> What we are witnessing in India is the emergence of an advanced sector in agriculture that is broadly comparable to the advanced sector in modem industry. This new agriculture has been tested, has proved profitable, and is rapidly expanding. Accordingly, big business in India is campaigning for an open door policy of free entry into agricultural production. The house of Birlas has taken the lead in demanding a shift in Government policy away from cooperative farming and towards corporate farming.
>
> (Thorner 1980: 232, originally appeared in 1967 in *The Statesman*, November 1, 2, 3, 4)

Stated precisely, Daniel Thorner viewed that compared to the situation before the 1960s, the capitalist trend was prominently visible throughout India during the 1960s though the extent of its development was not uniform across different regions and the states. However, his analysis was

Agrarian transition: from classic to current debates 17

largely based on limited empirical evidences and was not well grounded in a theoretical frame (Bagchi 1981).

The subsequent studies made in the late 1960s following the 'green revolution' triggered off a prolonged debate in theoretical and empirical terms on nature of capitalist transition in Indian agriculture known as the 'mode of production debate', which arguably was central to the study of political economy of India's agrarian change. This debate took place mainly in the annals of *Economic and Political Weekly*, and the terminology and framework of the debate was unequivocally Marxist. The works of Marx (particularly *Capital* Vol. III) and Lenin (*The Development of Capitalism in Russia*) were the points of departure in this debate.

The first phase of the Indian debate on mode of production started off with a report by Rudra and his associates (1969) which was based on a survey of 261 farms over 20 acres in size in Punjab (where the green revolution had been an apparent success) in the year 1967–68. Rudra set up a model of the attributes[14] of a capitalist farmer, as distinguished from big farmers, and on the basis of statistical analysis he concluded that the transition to capitalism did not take place in India (Rudra 1970, 1971). Patnaik (1971a, 1971b, 1972), however, challenged this conclusion on the basis of her own extensive fieldwork and criticised Rudra's theoretical assumptions and also statistical procedures he followed in his study. She argued that India was in a transitional phase moving towards capitalism and therefore capitalist accumulation was not evident in its clear form, as it retained some characteristics of pre-capitalist formations. Patnaik noted,

> Ex-colonial countries like India are characterised precisely by a limited and distorted development of capitalism which does not revolutionise the mode of production.
>
> (Patnaik 1971a: A124)

To Patnaik, the prolonged colonial rule influenced capitalist transformation due to large share of surplus transferred outside agriculture with the consequence of undermining primitive accumulation and inhibiting productive investment. It created a labour force that only appeared to be free but was effectively bonded for all practical purposes. She argued that the distinguishing features of capitalist farmers were not just the use of hired labour and marketing of product but the reinvestment of the surplus in expanded agricultural production (1971a: A126). Based on her survey of 66 big farmers carried out in 1969 in the states of Orissa,

18   B. B. Mohanty

Andhra Pradesh, Mysore, Madras and Gujarat, she reported the emergence of a capitalist development. However, she also noted,

> To recognise and analyse the reality of limited capitalist development which is taking place today is very different in my view, from putting forward the thesis that anything like a successful capitalist transformation of Indian agriculture is at all possible. On the contrary, it is necessary to analyse the nature of the capitalist development now taking place, precisely to identify its limits.
>
> (Patnaik 1971a: A130)

Paresh Chattopadhyay (1972a, 1972b) joined this debate at this point. While he agreed with the general terms of Patnaik's critique of Rudra's argument, he also criticised Patnaik's theoretical formulations. He defended Lenin's conception of capitalism as 'the highest stage of commodity production where labour power itself becomes a commodity' and argued that the generation of surplus value and its reinvestment was a logical corollary of this definition. To Chattopadhyay, capitalist relations of production did exist in the countryside. Jairus Banaji (1972) extended his support to Patnaik regarding mainly identification of capitalist development and also to Chattopadhyay pertaining to the specificity of colonial economy. Banaji advanced the thesis that 'colonial modes of production' was having its 'own coherence and laws of development'. Hamza Alavi (1975) supported Banaji's conception of colonial mode of production and argued that neither feudalism of colonial India nor contemporary rural capitalism can be grasped theoretically in all its implications except specifically in the context of the worldwide structure of imperialism into which it is articulated.

The second phase of the debate began with an article by Bhaduri (1973) who took a different position; he characterised Indian mode of production as semi-feudal on the basis of a field survey data from 26 villages of West Bengal in 1970. He identified four[15] prominent features of the semi-feudal production relations and viewed that these relations acted as barriers to the introduction of improved technology. This position on semi-feudalism was supported by Prasad (1973, 1974), Chandra (1974), Sau (1975) and others, who argued differently on this issue using their empirical studies of villages from West Bengal, Bihar and Orissa. The semi-feudalism thesis was severely criticised by the proponents of 'capitalist school' led by Bardhan and Rudra (1978, 1980) and Rudra (1981). However, the semi-feudalism school of thought subsequently

Agrarian transition: from classic to current debates 19

withdrew from the mode of production debate itself after about the middle of the 1970s (Alice Thorner 1982: 2063).

The debate over nature of mode of production also extended to rural class structure. A set of rural classes were proposed by various scholars from Ashok Rudra's drastic duality to Nirmal Chandra's sixfold grouping and the even larger number of class categories used by Joan Mencher (1977) and Utsa Patnaik. Rudra (1978) identified the big landowners and the agricultural labourers as the two agrarian classes which were having antagonistic relations and conflict of interests with each other. On the other hand, Patnaik (1976) presented a class differentiation in terms of 'labour exploitation criterion'. She distinguished between the exploiting classes – landlords and rich peasants – and also between the exploited classes – poor peasants and farm labourers. She further identified two different strata or divisions among the landlords, rich peasants and poor peasants. The caste-based hierarchy among agrarian classes was noticed by Breman (1985), Harriss (1982), Omvedt (1978) and Gough (1989). Broadly, there was limited consensus on the existence of two antagonistic classes – the capitalist farmers and the wage workers – and the mode of production debate reached the paradoxical result of describing Indian agriculture as a capitalist system in which conventional capitalist classes were limited (Elisabetta 2013: 77).

In fact, of the several interesting strands and ideas involved with mode of production debate, only the discourse on the extent of either preservation or destruction of pre-capitalist forms of appropriation by capitalism continued for many years. The mode of production debate tapered off without any broad consensus, as there was little evidence to show that pre-capitalist peasant social formations in India were getting transformed through commercialisation, depeasantisation and proletarianisation and to suggest that a sizeable proportion of cultivable land was under capitalist farming. Moreover, it was obvious that the mode of production debate did not add much to the classical Marxist view of capitalist development and appeared more as an academic dispute within the same interpretive paradigm (Chakrabarti and Cullenberg 2003: 55–56). The role of agriculture in industrialisation which was an important issue in India in the 1960s and 1970s was, by and large, overlooked in this debate (Lerche et al. 2013). Though the debate came to an inconclusive end in the 1980s, it was believed that the introduction of new technology was chiefly instrumental in bringing about a deeper penetration of capital into agricultural production (see e.g. Jodhka 2004; Mohanty 2012).

20   B. B. Mohanty

The neo-classical Lewisian framework[16] on the other hand postulated that predominantly agricultural countries, characterised by unlimited supply of labour, would eventually go through capitalist development because of an inevitable shift of labour from agriculture to the fast-developing modern industrial and other non-agricultural activities; however, this shift was also nowhere visible in agrarian structural change (e.g. see Nayyar 1978; Amjad 1988; Bhardwaj 1989). Similarly, Kalecki's[17] idea of 'intermediate regimes' generated a debate on distinctiveness of class structure in India in the 1970s. Following this model, Raj (1973) considered this development as 'intermediate classes', the term indicating social strata between the proletariat and the bourgeoisie (who are owners as well as users of means of production like small proprietors in agriculture). He argued that these classes represented a phase – in between the two ends of the capitalist transition – that is neither feudalism nor capitalism, and they were in between bourgeoisie and the proletariat – neither capital nor labour. Jha (1980) contested Raj's line of argument and viewed that the intermediate class was not a transitory class; rather, it was the nascent bourgeoisie of early stage of capitalist development.

Stated precisely, agrarian transition was mostly analysed in stereotyped manner within the classical framework of agrarian studies. Neither Marxian nor non-Marxian theories of agrarian transformation, drawing on the historical experiences of developed countries, could indicate a definite path of transformation in India, because complexities were added partly as consequences of colonialism and partly by state-directed development planning in the post-colonial phase. In course of the 1980s, therefore, agrarian change lost its central position in the academic agenda and declining interest became conspicuous in the last two decades (1990s onwards) mainly due to the effect of neoliberal reforms. It raised a variety of new issues and contradictions beyond what the classical theoretical and conceptual framework of agrarian change had anticipated.

Neoliberalism and the newly emerging debate

From the 1990s the influence of global capitalism and neoliberal reforms set in motion a process of agrarian change in India on an unprecedented scale and pace. It marked a shift from the planned slow growth to market-driven rapid growth facilitated by new technology of farm production and substantive changes in government's development policy. The traditional pre-capitalist agrarian formations were transformed first by the colonialism and later by the planned development that

Agrarian transition: from classic to current debates 21

significantly altered both scale and relations of production within and across states; that in turn paved the way for transition to both agrarian and urban-industrial capitalism. Massive acquisition of agricultural land by multinational corporations for non-agricultural purposes and increasing privatisation of natural resources introduced new patterns of urbanisation and industrialisation. Agricultural land came to be used for setting up new industries, townships, megacities, and special economic zones that offered both freedom and tax concessions to private corporate capital and attractive land prices to farmers. The increasing control of agribusiness over input and output flows of agriculture indicated a massive debouching of workforce from the farm sector. In the changing context, land was no longer the source of status and power and nor did it limit the alternative livelihood possibilities of the rural and urban poor. Non-agricultural sectors started growing rapidly, resulting in a perceptible decline in the share of agriculture to gross domestic product (GDP).[18] According to a recent estimate, in more than two-thirds of the states of India, over 40 per cent of rural households were engaged in non-agricultural occupation and their number was steadily rising.[19] Evidence suggested that rural households increasingly diversified their ways of earning a living.[20] It was argued that there was a tendency among the rural people to move away from farming, showing signs of 'vanishing village' (Gupta 2005).

This transition, however, brought out its own contradictions. The available statistics showed that there was growing persistence of small-scale cultivation.[21] Although 'primitive accumulation of capital' had displaced people who lost their means of subsistence because of industrial and urban development, the evidences showed that these displaced farm labourers were not getting absorbed to new capitalist sectors of growth.[22] The trend of increasing rural to urban migration in India over the decades showed a declining trend since the 1990s despite increase in economic inequality.[23] Labour migration took multiple directions and character: rural–urban, rural–rural, urban–rural and also permanent and cyclical. Newer types of agrarian movements, networks and coalitions emerged and gained political influence. Moreover, the demands of electoral democracy created opportunities through many welfare measures and poverty alleviation programmes[24] that generated means of subsistence and alternative sources of livelihood for the poor. It was argued that the process of primitive accumulation tended to survive along with a parallel process of the reversal of the effects of primitive accumulation.

In this context still a new debate was initiated by contribution of some scholars like Partha Chatterjee (2008), who ruled out the possibility

22 B. B. Mohanty

of agrarian transition in India in the near future. Following the framework of transition advanced by Sanyal (2007),[25] he argued that under the present conditions of post-colonial development in the context of globalised economy the narrative of capitalist transition was no longer valid. Challenging Gupta's (2005) hypothesis on the vanishing trend of village and agriculture in India, Chatterjee concluded that such a transition was unlikely to take place in India due to the state interventions in response to 'demand politics' of electoral democracy. According to him, though with the continuing rapid growth of global capitalism more and more primary producers lost their means of production, the government policies and programmes which were launched under the conditions of democratic politics tended to reverse the effect of this primitive accumulation.

Utsa Patnaik (2007: 16) held the view that the development of capitalism in agriculture came to a halt due to changes in the internal relations of production and in the class structure in the agrarian sector under the process of new corporatisation. She argued that new technology and investment brought by the domestic and foreign corporate groups led only to the process of subordination of the peasantry under external capital and not the development of capitalism from within agriculture (because both transnational capitals and domestic corporations were external to the agricultural sector). Yet another alternative view was that India missed the bus for such a transition. Taking Bernstein's lead, Lerche (2013) concluded that agrarian transition in the 'classical' sense was bypassed in India. He also argued that capitalism in Indian agriculture was still deepening and the process of capitalist agrarian accumulation and peasant differentiation was ongoing in a manner not anticipated by the classical model.

For Harriss-White *et al.* (2009), though started very late, agrarian transition was going to be a slow process. Based on evidences from Arunachal Pradesh, they viewed that agriculture serviced little, but agriculture and the agrarian system continued to exhibit non-capital production relations in terms of development of wage labour, investment of surplus in productive technology, commercialisation of input and output markets and the like. John Harris (2013) pointed to the declining trend of landlordism and further argued that semi-feudal surplus extraction and its 'depressor effect' was substantially transformed over large parts of India although agrarian power relations continued to influence agricultural productivity. Like him, Basu and Das (2013) also provided evidences on decreasing control of large landowners at the village level. Having noted these changes in the rural economy

Agrarian transition: from classic to current debates 23

and society, both the analyses, however, did not indicate a fast change towards capitalist transition.

Das (2012), however, in his analysis of forms on subsumption of labour indicated an uneven transition to capitalist development which was partly a product of less-specific outcome of class struggle. He emphasised the crucial mediating role of class struggle in the transition from an underdeveloped capitalism to a developed one. Similarly, in a recent debate on unfree labour and capitalism in India, Tom Brass (2008, 2014) argued that the capitalist transition already took place in India, which contested the views held by Breman(1985), Jodhka (1994, 1995, 1996), Lerche (1995) and many others who said that existence of unfree labour in India signified pre-capitalist relations. In Brass's interpretation, the classical Marxist theory also viewed unfree labour power as compatible with capitalist accumulation. Likewise, Guérin (2013), drawing on a number of case studies, also argued that unfree labour could go hand in hand with capitalism and that it could be initiated and sustained by capital itself in order to accumulate surplus value. Breman (2010) changed his earlier position and argued that debt bondage did not disappear, but still existed on a large scale, even to a greater extent than traditional forms of bondage in agriculture. Breman argued that it is a form of unfree labour that received a strong boost as the capitalist economy rose to dominance.

Most scholars contributing to this debate, however, confined themselves to only certain aspects of agrarian change using limited empirical evidences drawn from specific states or regions in India. The nuances of agrarian change and its complexity, as well as regional specificities and commonalities, were hardly analysed either at theoretical or at empirical levels keeping in view more recent data on many aspects of changing rural economy and society.

It is on this backdrop of the long-drawn debate that an attempt is made in this volume to extend and deepen this discourse on agrarian transition both at theoretical and empirical levels given the larger context of development of contemporary global capitalism.

6. Introduction to the volume

This book presents ten chapters on the general theme of agrarian transition in the context of neoliberal global capitalist development to provide an analytical account of changing agrarian situation in India by critically engaging with major global debates. Though content-wise the ten chapters included in this book are very different from each other in terms of focus, all of them have probed their critical themes of agrarian

24 B. B. Mohanty

transition and have attempted to add new perspectives to the existing discourse on agrarian change. Most of the contributions here have been authored by leading scholars in agrarian studies. Though it is not exhaustive in terms of thematic coverage, this collection of chapters addresses a variety of important issues central to the understanding of agrarian transition, especially in the peripheral world which is overlooked by the existing literature.

The book is divided in three parts. Part I has three chapters that presents core issues of conceptual and theoretical nature raised in the discourse on agrarian transition. Revisiting the earlier contributions on pre-capitalist peasant social formation, and on development of capitalism in agriculture, these three authors have analysed agrarian dynamics and the wide-ranging changes while attempting to explain the specificities of India's agrarian transition.

In the first chapter A Haroon Akram-Lodhi and Cristóbal Kay have revisited the problematic of the agrarian question from the perspective of global value relations, and have assessed the extent to which such a perspective renders reconsideration of the basic tenets of the agrarian question as imperative. Situating the agrarian question and capitalist agrarian transition within Marx's framework of the mode of production, and introducing the famous 'mode of production' debate of the late 1960s and early 1970s, Akram-Lodhi and Kay have argued that Marx's analysis of capitalist agrarian transition was far more nuanced and complex than is commonly suggested; they emphasise the primacy of the conjuncture and the balance of forces rather than a historically inevitable if unpredictable and uneven process. They conclude that the agrarian question continues to have resonance, particularly in countries with large sections of populations engaged in agriculture, such as India.

In the second chapter, Henry Bernstein has posed four categories of key questions: (1) Transition *from* and *to* what? (2) *Where* and *when* it took place? (3) *How* and *why* it happened? (4) Why is agrarian transition still incomplete in certain cases? Bernstein has contextualised the theoretical and historical antecedents of these questions and has tried to explain the dynamics of transition in the Global South, including India. He argues that current complex and diverse agrarian change could not be comprehended adequately by regarding classical notions of transition as false 'predictions', because they are key to framing the central questions of agrarian political economy. He recognises the need to understand the changes in capitalism across all its spaces – from global divisions of labour and flows of capital and commodities

Agrarian transition: from classic to current debates   25

through vastly different national economies to similarly diverse agrarian structures.

The last chapter of the first part is contributed by D. Narasimha Reddy, who has reviewed briefly the changing contours of the analytical debate on the agrarian question and has tried to locate the peasant question in contemporary Asia, with a particular focus on India. Beginning with the basic aspects of the agrarian question, Reddy draws attention to the shifting nature of priority bestowed on these aspects with the changing phases of the debates on the agrarian question. His analysis ends with the review of the changes in the agrarian relations (which subsumes the peasantry question) in contemporary India.

The three chapters in Part II of this book give a detailed account of trajectories of global capitalist development and the emerging changes in the Indian agriculture in the context of neoliberal reforms and their implications for agrarian transition.

In her chapter Utsa Patnaik offers a critical perspective on the question as to whether the peasant populations displaced by emerging capitalism get re-absorbed into more productive occupations within their own countries or whether large-scale out-migration helps to explain rising domestic wages. Patnaik further raises a question: to what extent does the capitalist transformation of domestic agriculture provide the material possibility of industrialisation? She views the specific problems of developing countries as qualitatively different due to their past and present interactions with developed nations. Finally, she explains why the developing countries despite their higher growth rates than today's advanced countries do not succeed in reducing unemployment and poverty.

The main argument of the chapter contributed by D. N. Dhanagare is that India's agrarian crisis, not simply transition, is sponsored by the neoliberal state because of its declining credibility and that the agrarian crisis is deepening with the globalisation process. He has focused on four aspects of the crisis: (1) large-scale out-migration of farmers from agricultural to non-agricultural pursuits for better livelihood alternatives; (2) declining rate of agricultural growth and also in the share of agriculture to the GDP, in addition to poor marketing and credit facilities; (3) steadily mounting use of bonded labour and/or semi-bonded and also increasing contract farming, heightened by agricultural indebtedness, that are resulting in phenomenal rate of farmers' suicides, especially in the green revolution belt since the beginning of the era of new economic reforms; and (4) the decline of the farmers' movement.

In their chapter B. B. Mohanty and Papesh K. Lenka have attempted a state-wise analysis of the impact of global capitalism on peasantry. They argue that the process of agrarian change in India is quite complex and its trend is not uniform across the states. According to them, though agriculture invariably continues to be the major source of livelihood and employment in the countryside even today and though rural economy is dominated by preponderance of small-scale agricultural producers, the signs of disappearance of peasantry are discernible in almost all states. The states with relatively higher or moderate level of capitalist development in agriculture but with greater level of industrial development experience fast disappearance of peasantry compared to the other states. Mohanty and Lenka ultimately conclude that though large-scale disappearance of peasantry has not taken place, the classical Marxist view with regard to conditions of peasantry under capitalism holds true in Indian context.

The last part of this book contains four chapters that focus on regional experiences of agricultural transformation and highlight common processes at work and diversities in region-specific development experiences.

Judith Heyer traces changing gender relations in an OBC (other backward classes) community of Gounders in western Tamil Nadu villages that went through a process of transition from an agrarian to an industrial economy over three decades. She first gives an account of gender relations in what was very much an agrarian economy in 1981–82 and then goes on to show how these changed. She focuses on the role played by female labour, increasing female participation in education, changing marriage arrangements and fertility decline, which was associated with sex ratios that were increasingly unfavourable to women and girls in the context of changing patterns of out-migration from the agricultural sector. Heyer argues that decline in fertility reduced the pressure on agricultural resources and countered the tendency towards proliferation of small and marginal holdings to a certain extent, as did migration to urban areas. However, the insecurities inherent in the non-agricultural economy were also leading people to hold onto their lands. The net effect was an increase in the numbers of small and marginal holdings still, in the farm sector.

The next chapter by Daniel Münster introduces an ongoing ethnographic project situating responses to agrarian crisis in the rural district of Wayanad, Kerala. He looked at alternative agricultures that emerged in response to a protracted crisis of commercial agriculture – a crisis that

Agrarian transition: from classic to current debates   27

has repeatedly caused many smallholders to proclaim that agriculture has 'gone' (*poyi*) from the region. Münster focuses on the crisis: a natural farming movement, the Zero Budget Natural Farming method, which came to Wayanad at a time when the district made headlines for its high incidences of farmers' suicides. Within the larger picture of the political economy of agrarian transition in India, he has argued that agro-ecological movements and protests for food sovereignty, though they operate within dubious ideological idioms, constitute important allies for the creation of a possible agrarian future in India – a future that hinges on a necessary agro-ecological transition.

In the subsequent chapter Santanu Rakshit has attempted to explain the inclusion process of the agricultural sector into the capital-non-capital complex controlled by global capitalism and interventions through different instruments in order to maintain a systematic surplus appropriation process and influence the trajectories of agrarian transition. Rakshit evaluates the nature of output and surpluses, vis-à-vis the emerging exchange processes at the farm level through the lens of socioeconomic class differentiation. He has also explained how 'stressed commerce' impacts the structure and pattern of farm labour and farm-disposable surplus produced by the peasants and the consequences of such stressed commerce on the process of surplus accumulation. Finally, he argues that the emerging process of agrarian transition in West Bengal is quite different in structure and essence from that implied in the classical notion of the transition.

In their chapter Singh and Bhogal point to the economic crisis faced by the small peasantry in the agriculturally advanced state of Punjab. They argue that though the total workforce has increased over time, the proportion engaged in agriculture has been falling and the number of marginal and small holdings has been declining. Their analysis indicates that the farm surpluses of indebted farmers are very low, and significant numbers of marginal and small farmers are effectively bankrupt. Singh and Bhogal noted that low profitability has prompted many small farmers to leave agriculture, and many of them have entered the labour market. More pressingly, a significant number have preferred to take their own lives.

7. Concluding remarks

In the context of changed and still changing global and Indian discourse on agrarian transition, some common points of agreement and disagreement that emerged from chapters included in this book are noteworthy.

28 B. B. Mohanty

First, though not unanimously shared by all the contributors, some contributions have indicated that the classical notion of agrarian transition is still relevant. For example, Bernstein says, 'Much of their (classic notions) approach to framing the central questions of agrarian political economy remains valid, even if some of the answers provided might be found wanting as historical interpretation or applications to contemporary realities or both.' For Bernstein, many of the core elements of the classical debate are still of central relevance for the study of contemporary processes of agrarian change. In their explanation of diversity of capitalist transitions, Akram-Lodhi and Kay write, 'The complex multiplicity of actual forms of capitalist agrarian transition was in fact well understood by Marx himself.'

Second, it is also commonly shared that global changes over the past few decades have generated new kinds of agrarian dynamics and relationships. The neoliberal reforms facilitated deeper penetration of capital as a result of which new patterns of wealth accumulation and class differentiation have emerged and the capitalist investors have a firm grip on land and use of hired labour resulting in deepening the agrarian crisis in the countryside. Patnaik, for instance, notes, 'The tensions unleashed by dominant global financial interests have been implementing their deflationary neo-liberal policies, and in league with the corporates attack on the land resources of the peasantry; these policies and practices aided and abetted by the state, have produced a new global food and livelihoods crisis which is likely to intensify in future.' Likewise, citing a number of instances, Dhanagare has attributed the characteristics of agrarian crisis to neoliberalism, as it serves the interests of corporate industrial capitalism that not only desires but also demands free competition and trade. The experience of Punjab, as indicated by the analysis of Singh and Bhogal, presents a similar picture where the farming sector shows signs of sickness and suffers from declining employment elasticity, falling productivity and shrinking returns resulting in decline of small peasantry. In case of Tamil Nadu, Heyer also noted the declining importance of agriculture and illustrated how the new generation is getting set to move out of agriculture. Münster presented three agrarian responses to this crises in the context of Kerala operating both within and against neoliberalism. The greater entry of private capital into agriculture in the wake of neoliberal reforms has also been stressed by Mohanty and Lenka. However, many of the contributors share the view that the majority in the countryside are still located in, connected to or are dependent in multiple ways on their relationships with rural or agrarian environments.

Agrarian transition: from classic to current debates 29

By and large, it is argued that the effects of neoliberal reforms are quite complex in India given its regional diversity and varied response of socially differentiated categories. Therefore, the process of agrarian transition in India neither is similar to the patterns outlined in the classical model nor does conform neatly to any definite line of arguments expressed in the subsequent global debates on the mode of production in general and agrarian transition in particular. Reddy has argued that the combination of historical and contemporary forces under which capitalism with the Indian characteristics has been developing in Indian agriculture is quite different. Almost a similar line of argument is found in the analysis made by Rakshit. To him, the emergence of socioeconomic differentiation in West Bengal peasantry does not imply that capitalist development is taking place in the classical sense; rather, in the classical sense it appears to have stalled giving rise to a distorted or deviated path resembling primitive accumulation of capital in agriculture. Mohanty and Lenka have also noted the varying regional trends. The analysis made by Heyer and Münster highlights the regional complexities and peculiarities in the context of Tamil Nadu and Kerala, respectively. Münster's account reveals the diverse responses of farmers in the context of Kerala.

Besides these common issues, the collection of chapters carries forward the wider debate on the relevance of the classical agrarian question in the context of neoliberalism. Bernstein's thesis – that the agrarian question is no longer valid in the current phase of globalisation – is contested in Indian context by many contributors. Challenging this view, Patnaik has argued, 'The agrarian question has not ceased to exist in the present era; on the contrary it is more important than ever.' In almost similar line, Reddy argues that the emerging changes in the agrarian conditions in terms of land use, prevalence of tenancy, livelihood of peasantry and the like make it untenable to propose that the agrarian question has been bypassed in India. Akram-Lodhi and Kay too echo the fact that the agrarian question as also the entire debate of agrarian transition has become significant in countries like India.

To sum up, the book brings together contributions from some of the best-known experts in the field of agrarian political economy. These contributions critically evaluate the relevance of classical debate and extend the horizon of contemporary debates in the Indian context linking the national trends with specifications of regional experiences. It questions classic definitions of 'the agrarian question' framed within a narrow political economy and historical materialist tradition, and the book, in fact, reveals broader and inclusive dimensions of agrarian

30 B. B. Mohanty

questions. While acknowledging the importance of classics to understandings of agrarian change, it also recognises some of the limitations of the procrustean orthodox materialist approach that ignored many discursive dimensions of agrarian relations, overlooking the limitations of stereotypical binaries between capital and non-capital, rural and urban, agriculture and industry, accumulation and subsistence and the like.

Finally, it would not be inappropriate to conclude that the contributions in this book widely acknowledge the fact that given the current scale and speed of ongoing changes in the countryside, the agrarian-rural economy of India is moving more clearly along the axis of capitalist development than ever before. Sanyal (2007: 1) rightly commented,

> The search for an alternative to capitalism seems to be over . . . the entire third world is being integrated into one global capitalist network: the triumph of capitalism seems unquestionable, self evident and total. The world . . . is fast embracing capitalism.

Notes

1 It is also cited by Li (2009) and highlighted in ICAS-LDPI Colloquium on 'Agrarian Transformation and Surplus Population in the Global South: Revisiting Agrarian Questions of Labour', held in the International Institute of Social Studies (ISS), the Hague on 3 May 2011. Accessed from http://www.iss.nl/fileadmin/ASSETS/iss/Research_and_projects/Research_networks/ICAS/ICAS_3_May_2011_FINAL_Colloquium_programme.pdf on 10 October 2014.
2 However, Marx acknowledged the enduring existence of peasantry in France though he claimed that the rural percentage of population which was 76 per cent in 1846 was down to 71 per cent in 1861 (see Duggett 1975: 169).
3 Important aspects of this debate are presented systematically in Bernstein (2009b).
4 Emmanuel Le Roy Ladurie criticised Brenner for combining economic and political factors while explaining 'surplus-extracting' classes and 'ruling' classes as if they were one and the same (Wood 2002: 55). Guy Bois, a Marxist of a slightly different stripe, critiqued Brenner's approach on several counts. Bois took exception to the 'voluntarism' of Brenner's 'political Marxism' in reaction to the wave of economic tendencies. He also observed that Brenner's historical materialism neglected mode of production as characteristic of feudalism. Among the other critics, Postan and Hatcher restated their interpretation of overpopulation, technological underdevelopment and dwindling soil fertility for medieval England. Brenner had the last word in the debate in a response to his critics that runs over a hundred pages. For details on this debate, see Aston and Philpin (1985), which presents an anthology of ten articles by number of leading English and continental scholars along with an extensive essay by Brenner himself who reviews the comment of his critics.

Agrarian transition: from classic to current debates 31

5 Bernstein (1994) summarised Byres's key features of different paths of agrarian transition based on the following themes: (1) pre-capitalist agrarian class structure, (2) the characteristics forms of production and class character of transition, (3) effects of agricultural production on investment in farming, (4) contribution of agriculture to industrialisation. Akram-Lodhi and Kay (2010b: 258–62) present seven paths of transition incorporating additional material from Byres (2003) and Bernstein (2010). The Taiwanese/South Korean path is subdivided into (1) Japanese colonial period (first half of the twentieth century) and (2) Taiwanese/South Korean path (1950s, 1960s).

6 Though Byres also indicates about the development of socialism, he was more concerned with capitalism and its diverse forms of development in the countryside. See Byres (1986: 4).

7 Taking Kautsky's lead, Byres (1996: 26) elaborated the agrarian question as 'the continued existence in the countryside, in a substantive sense, of obstacles to an unleashing of accumulation in both the countryside itself and more generally-in particular the accumulation associated with capitalist industrialisation'.

8 While the problematic of production relates to Marx, Lenin and Kautsky, the problematic of accumulation is associated with Preobrazhensky. The last problematic of politics is linked to Engels. For details, see Bernstein (1996) and Akram-Lodhi and Kay (2010b).

9 While the agrarian question of capital relates to the question of the transition to capitalism in which pre-capitalist agrarian classes and social formations are transformed by emerging capitalist social relations of production, agrarian question of labour refers to the failure of capitalism to reproduce its labour force.

10 The seven agrarian questions relate to class forces, path-dependent, decoupled agrarian question of labour, global reserve army of labour, corporate food regime, gender and ecological dynamics. These contemporary questions and their intellectual heritage is explained in detail in Akram-Lodhi and Kay (2010b).

11 However, attempts were also made by sociologists, economists and historians in the 1940s and 1950s to analyse the agrarian change and the rural class structure in India, for example A. R. Desai (1948), Mukherjee (1948), Darling (1947) and M. B. Desai (1948). Mann and Kanitkar's (1921) work on land and labour is one of earlier studies on agrarian issues.

12 As cited in Thorner (1980), based on farm management studies S. C. Gupta (1962) estimated that in states like Uttar Pradesh wage labour contributes largely to agricultural output than family labour on farms with 20 or more acres. As per his estimate a capitalist agriculture was carried out by less than 6 or 7 per cent of all operational holdings amounting to about one-third of the total area under cultivation.

13 Grigory Kotovsky (1964) while analysing the changing class structure of rural India as a result of implementation of land reforms indicated a movement towards capitalist farming. Like S. C. Gupta, he also reported that 25 to 30 per cent of area was cultivated by hired labour.

14 Rudra (1970) used the following five attributes of capitalist farmer: (1) self-cultivation of land rather than giving it out to lease, (2) use of hired labour in a much greater proportion than family labour, (3) use of farm machinery,

32 B. B. Mohanty

(4) market orientation and (5) high rate of return on investment (profit orientation).

15 According to Bhaduri (1973), the following are the main features of semi-feudalism: (1) share cropping; (2) perpetual indebtedness of small tenants; (3) concentration of two modes of exploitation, namely usury and land ownership in the hands of some economic class; and (4) lack of accessibility to market for the small tenants.

16 Arthur Lewis (1954) gave central importance to the movement of labour from agriculture to industry and capital accumulation in the latter. For Lewis, the large agricultural sector of low-income countries is characterised by an unlimited supply of unskilled labourers and low labour productivity. This surplus labour can be employed more productively in industry and he argues that labour productivity will automatically increase in agriculture when surplus labour is removed.

17 Kalecki (1972) used the term 'intermediate regimes' in the analysis of class nature of the state in countries like India, Indonesia and Egypt – which shared three basic features: (1) an unfinished capitalist transition, (2) a strong involvement of the state in the management of the economy (3) the inability of the native upper-middle classes to perform the role of dynamic entrepreneurs on a large scale.

18 As per the data given in Planning Commission Data Tables, the share of agriculture and allied sector to total GDP has come down to 14 per cent in 2012–13 as against 30 per cent in 1990–91 and 36 per cent in 1980–81 at 2004–5 constant prices. For more details, see Government of India (2014a).

19 As per the estimate made by NSS, 33 per cent of rural households were outside agriculture in 1993–94 and 35 per cent in 2000–2002 and 45 per cent in 2011–12. In 2011–12 more than 80 per cent of the states had about 40 per cent of the households as non-agriculture (for details, see NSS 50th, 57th and 68th round).

20 To go by the NSS 68th round (2011–12), over the years, an increasing trend is observed in the proportion of rural workers engaged in 'trade, hotel and restaurant', 'transport, storage and communications' and 'manufacturing'. For more details, see Government of India (2014b).

21 The estimate made by NSS 68th round (2011–12) shows that less than 3 per cent of the rural households were in the highest land-owned class (4.01 ha or more) and 74 per cent belonged to less than 1.00 ha category. See Government of India (2014b).

22 It is reported by many studies that hardly 2 to 3 per cent of the total increased workforce has been employed in the large-scale manufacturing sector in countries like India, Pakistan and Bangladesh (see e.g. Amjad 1988).

23 According to the data furnished by Census of India, the rural-to-urban migration (intra-state by the place of last residence from zero to nine years' duration) which was 18.86 per cent in 1991 decreased to 17.62 in 2001. See Migration Tables D2, Census of India, relevant years.

24 In a recent analysis Dreze and Khera (2013) show the impact of the Public Distribution System on rural poverty, using National Sample Survey data for 2009–10 and official poverty lines. Their estimate shows at the all-India level, the PDS reduced the poverty-gap index of rural poverty by 18 to 22 per cent. Similarly Mahatma Gandhi National Rural Employment

Guarantee Act (MGNREGA), since its inception, generated 13.48 million person-days of employment (MoRD 2013). At the national level, with the average nominal wage paid under the scheme increasing from Rs 65 in FY 2006–7 to Rs 115 in FY 2011–12, the bargaining power of agricultural labour has increased as even private-sector wages have increased (MoRD 2012). It has set a base price for labour in rural areas, improved the bargaining power of labourers and has led to a widespread increase in the cost of unskilled and temporary labour, including agricultural labour.

25 According to Sanyal (2007), the accumulation economy of globalised capital causes dispossession, exclusion and marginalisation through primitive accumulation. In order to legitimise this capitalist order, a broader politico-ideological condition of existence is created. It is in this context, he says, that the developmental face of the state comes into being, which addresses the issue of creating, protecting and monitoring an informal sector to rehabilitate the victims of the capitalist onslaught in a need economy. The two distinct sides – one destructive and one supportive – constitute the structure and modalities of global governance in the current era of capital.

References

Akram-Lodhi, A. H. 1998. 'The Agrarian Question, Past and Present'. *The Journal of Peasant Studies* 25 (4): 134–49.

Akram-Lodhi, A. H. 2000. 'The Agrarian Question in an Age of "New Capitalism"'. In Jan Toporowski (ed.). *Political Economy and the New Capitalism: Essays in Honour of Sam Aaronovitch*. London: Routledge, pp. 114–31.

Akram-Lodhi, A. H. 2007. 'Land, Markets and Neoliberal Enclosure: An Agrarian Political Economy Perspective'. *Third World Quarterly* 28 (8): 1437–56.

Akram-Lodhi, A. H. and C. Kay (eds). 2009. *Peasants and Globalisation: Political Economy, Rural Transformation and the Agrarian Question*. London: Routledge.

Akram-Lodhi, A. H. and C. Kay. 2010a. 'Surveying the Agrarian Question (I): Unearthing Foundations, Exploring Diversity'. *The Journal of Peasant Studies* 37 (1): 177–202.

Akram-Lodhi, A. H. and C. Kay. 2010b. 'Surveying the Agrarian Question (Part 2): Current Debate and Beyond'. *The Journal of Peasant Studies* 37 (2): 255–84.

Alavi, Hamza. 1975. 'India and the Colonial Mode of Production'. *Economic and Political Weekly* 10 (33/35): 1235–62.

Amjad, R. 1988. *Rural Employment Planning: Selected Lessons from the Asian Experience*. New Delhi: Indian Labour Organisation.

Araghi, F. 2009. 'The Invisible Hand and the Visible Foot: Peasants, Dispossession and Globalisation'. In A. H. Akram-Lodhi and C. Kay (eds). *Peasants and Globalization: Political Economy, Rural Transformation and the Agrarian Question*. London: Routledge, pp. 111–47.

Aston, T. H. and C. H. E. Philpin (eds). 1985. *The Brenner Debate: Agrarian Class Structure and Economic Development in Pre-Industrial Europe*. Cambridge: Cambridge University Press.

34 B. B. Mohanty

Bagchi, A. 1981. 'Daniel Thorner's India'. *Economic and Political Weekly* 16 (13): 572–78.

Banaji, Jairus. 1972. 'For a Theory of Colonial Modes of Production'. *Economic and Political Weekly* 7 (5): 2498–502.

Banaji, Jairus. 1980. 'Summary of Selected Parts of Kautsky's The Agrarian Question'. In Harold Wolpe (ed.). *The Articulation of Modes of Production: Essays from Economy and Society*. London: RKP, pp. 45–92.

Bardhan, Pranab and Ashok Rudra. 1978. 'Inter-Linkage of Land, Labour and Credit Relations: An Analysis of Village Survey Data in East India'. *Economic and Political Weekly* 13 (6/7): 367–84.

Bardhan, Pranab and Ashok Rudra. 1980. 'Terms and Conditions of Sharecropping Contracts: An Analysis of Village Survey Data in India'. *Journal of Development Studies* 16 (3): 287–302.

Basu, Deepankar and Debarshi Das. 2013. 'The Maoist Movement in India: Some Political Economy Considerations'. *Journal of Agrarian Change* 13 (3): 365–81.

Bernstein, H. 1994. 'Agrarian Classes in Capitalist Development'. In Leslie Sklair (ed.). *Capitalism and Development*. London: Routledge, pp. 40–71.

Bernstein, H. 1996. 'Agrarian Questions Then and Now'. *The Journal of Peasant Studies* 24 (1/2): 22–59.

Bernstein, H. 2004. '"Changing before Our Very Eyes": Agrarian Questions and the Politics of Land in Capitalism Today'. *Journal of Agrarian Change* 4 (1/2): 190–225.

Bernstein, H. 2006. 'Is There an Agrarian Question in the 21st Century?'. *Canadian Journal of Development Studies* 27 (4): 449–60.

Bernstein, H. 2009a. 'Agrarian Questions from Transition to Globalisation'. In A. H. Akram-Lodhi and C. Kay (eds). *Peasants and Globalisation: Political Economy, Rural Transformation and the Agrarian Question*. London: Routledge, pp. 239–61.

Bernstein, H. 2009b. 'V. I. Lenin and A. V. Chayanov: Looking Back and Looking Forward'. *The Journal of Peasant Studies* 36 (1): 55–81.

Bernstein, H. 2010. *Class Dynamics of Agrarian Change*. Halifax: Fernwood.

Bernstein, H. 2014. 'Food Sovereignty via the "Peasant Way": A Sceptical View'. *Journal of Peasant Studies* 41 (6): 1031–63.

Bhaduri, Amit. 1973. 'A Study of Agricultural Backwardness under Conditions of Semi-Feudalism'. *The Economic Journal* 83 (329): 120–37.

Bhardwaj, K. 1989. 'The Formation of the Labour Markets in Rural Asia'. WEP Working Paper No. 18, ILO, Geneva.

Brass, T. 2008. 'Capitalism and Bonded Labour in India: Reinterpreting Recent (Re-) Interpretations'. *Journal of Peasant Studies* 35 (2): 177–248.

Brass, T. 2014. 'Debating Capitalist Dynamics and Unfree Labour: A Missing Link?'. *The Journal of Development Studies* 50 (4): 570–82.

Breman, Jan. 1985. *Peasants, Migrants and Paupers: Capitalist Production and Labour Circulation in West India*. Delhi: Oxford University Press.

Breman, Jan. 2010. 'The Political Economy of Unfree Labour in South Asia: Determining the Nature and Scale of Debt Bondage', Hivos Knowledge Programme,

Agrarian transition: from classic to current debates   35

accessed from http://www.hivos.nl/content/download/94737/832639/file/The%20long%20road_paper%201.pdf on 18 October 2014.

Brenner, Robert. 1976. 'Agrarian Class Structure and Economic Development in Pre-Industrial Europe'. *Past and Present* 70 (1): 30–75.

Brenner, Robert. 1986. 'The Social Basis of Economic Development'. In J. Roemer (ed.). *Analytical Marxism*. Cambridge: Cambridge University Press, pp. 23–53.

Byres, T. J. 1986. 'The Agrarian Question, Forms of Capitalist Agrarian Transition and the State: An Essay with Reference to Asia'. *Social Scientist* 14 (11/12): 3–67.

Byres, T. J. 1991. 'The Agrarian Question'. In Tom Bottomore, Laurence Harris, V. G. Kiernan and Ralph Miliband (eds). *A Dictionary of Marxist Thought*. Oxford: Blackwell, pp. 9–11.

Byres, T. J. 1996. *Capitalism from Above and Capitalism from Below: An Essay in Comparative Political Economy*. London: Macmillan.

Byres, T. J. 2003. 'Paths of Capitalist Agrarian Transition in the Past and in the Contemporary World'. In V. K. Ramachandran and M. Swaminathan (eds). *Agrarian Studies: Essays on Agrarian Relations in Less-Developed Countries*. London: Zed Books, pp. 54–83.

Byres, T. J. 2009. 'The Landlord Class, Peasant Differentiation, Class Struggle and the Transition to Capitalism'. In A. H. Akram-Lodhi and C. Kay (eds). *Peasants and Globalization: Political Economy, Rural Transformation and the Agrarian Question*. London: Routledge, pp. 57–82.

Chakrabarti, A. and S. Cullenberg. 2003. *Transition and Development in India*. New York: Routledge.

Chandra, Nirmal K. 1974. 'Farm Efficiency under Semi-Feudalism: A Critique of Marginalist Theories and Some Marxist Formulations'. *Economic and Political Weekly* 9 (32, 33 and 34): 1309–32.

Chatterjee, Partha. 2008. 'Democracy and Economic Transformation in India'. *Economic and Political Weekly* 43 (16): 53–62.

Chattopadhyay, Paresh. 1972a. 'On the Question of the Mode of Production in Indian Agriculture: A Preliminary Note'. *Economic and Political Weekly* 7 (13): 39–46.

Chattopadhyay, Paresh. 1972b. 'Mode of Production in Indian Agriculture: An Anti-Kritik'. *Economic and Political Weekly* 7 (53): A185–92.

Chayanov, A. V. 1991. *The Theory of Peasant Co-Operatives*. London: I. B. Tauris.

Chayanov, A. V. 1966. *The Theory of Peasant Economy*. Homewood, IL: The American Economic Association.

Darling, M. L. 1947. *Punjab Peasant Life*. New Delhi: Cosmo Publications.

Das, Raju. 2012. 'Reconceptualising Capitalism Forms of Subsumption of Labor, Class Struggle and Uneven Development'. *Review of Radical Political Economics* 44 (2): 178–200.

Desai, A. R. 1948. *Social Background of Indian Nationalism*. Bombay: Popular Prakashan.

Desai, M. B. 1948. *The Rural Economy of Gujarat: Bombay University Economics Series*. Bombay: Oxford University Press.

36 B. B. Mohanty

Deshpande, R. S. and S. Arora (eds). 2010. *Agrarian Crisis and Farmer Suicides*. New Delhi: Sage.

Dobb, Maurice. 1946. *Studies in the Development of Capitalism*. London: Routledge & Kegan Paul.

Dobb, Maurice. 1976. 'A Reply'. In Rodney Hilton (ed.). *The Transition from Feudalism to Capitalism*. London: New Left Books, pp. 57–67.

Dreze, Jean and Reetika Khera. 2013. 'Rural Poverty and the Public Distribution System'. *Economic and Political Weekly* 48 (45–46): 55–60.

Duggett, Michael. 1975. 'Marx on Peasants'. *The Journal of Peasant Studies* 2 (2): 159–82.

Elisabetta, Basile. 2013. *Capitalist Development in India's Informal Economy*. London: Routledge.

Engels, F. 1950. 'The Peasant Question in France and Germany'. In K. Marx and F. Engels (eds). *Selected Works*, vol. 2. London: Lawrence and Wishart. First published in 1894.

Food and Agriculture Organisation. 2014. *The State of Food and Agriculture: Innovation in Family Farming*. Rome: Food and Agriculture Organization of the United Nations.

Foster, J. B. 2009. *The Ecological Revolution: Making Peace with the Planet*. New York: Monthly Review Press.

Friedmann, Harriet. 2006. 'Focusing on Agriculture: A Comment on Henry Bernstein's "Is There an Agrarian Question in the 21st Century?"'. *Canadian Journal of Development Studies* 27 (4): 461–65.

Gough, Kathleen. 1989. *Rural Change in Southeast India, 1950s to 1980s*. Delhi: Oxford University Press.

Government of India. 2014a. 'Planning Commission Data Tables', p. 43, accessed from http://planningcommission.nic.in/data/datatable/0814/table_42.pdf on 16 October 2014.

Government of India. 2014b. 'Employment and Unemployment Situation in India', NSS 68th Round, Report No. 554(68/10/1).

Guérin, I. 2013. 'Bonded Labour, Agrarian Changes and Capitalism: Emerging Patterns in South India'. *Journal of Agrarian Change* 13 (3): 405–23.

Gupta, Dipankar. 2005. 'Whither the Indian Village: Culture and Agriculture in "Rural" India'. *Economic and Political Weekly* 40 (8): 751–58.

Gupta, Sulekh Chand. 1962. 'Some Aspects of Indian Agriculture'. *Enquiry*, Delhi (cited by D. Thomer 1980, pp. 251–52 and A. Thorner 1982, pp. 1961–68).

Hammen, Oscar J. 1972. 'Marx and the Agrarian Question'. *The American Historical Review* 77 (3): 679–704.

Harriss, J. 1982. *Capitalism and Peasant Farming: A Study of Agricultural Change and Agrarian Structure in Northern Tamil Nadu*. Delhi: Oxford University Press.

Harriss, John. 2013. 'Does "Landlordism" Still Matter? Reflections on Agrarian Change in India'. *Journal of Agrarian Change* 13 (3): 351–64.

Agrarian transition: from classic to current debates 37

Harriss-White, Barbara. 2008. 'Introduction: India's Rainfed Agricultural Dystopia'. *European Journal of Development Research* 20 (4): 549–61.

Harriss-White, Barbara. and J. Heyer (eds). 2015. *Indian Capitalism in Development*. New York: Routledge.

Harriss-White, Barbara, D. K. Mishra and V. Upadhyay. 2009. 'Institutional Diversity and Capitalist Transition: The Political Economy of Agrarian Change in Arunachal Pradesh, India'. *Journal of Agrarian Change* 9 (4): 512–47.

Hazelkorn, Ellen. 1981. 'Some Problems with Marx's Theory of Capitalist Penetration into Agriculture: The Case of Ireland'. *Economy and Society* 10 (3): 284–315.

Jansen, Kees. 2014. 'The Debate on Food Sovereignty Theory: Agrarian Capitalism, Dispossession and Agroecology'. *Journal of Peasant Studies*, accessed from http://www.tandfonline.com/doi/full/10.1080/03066150.2013.852082 on 19 October 2014.

Jha, P. S. 1980. *The Political Economy of Stagnation*. Delhi: Oxford University Press.

Jodhka, Surinder S. 1994. 'Agrarian Changes and Attached Labour: Emerging Patterns in Haryana Agriculture'. *Economic and Political Weekly* 29 (39): A102–6.

Jodhka, Surinder S. 1995. 'Agrarian Changes, Unfreedom and Attached Labour'. *Economic and Political Weekly* 30 (31/32): 2011–13.

Jodhka, Surinder S. 1996. 'Interpreting Attached Labour in Contemporary Haryana'. *Economic and Political Weekly* 31 (21): 1286–87.

Jodhka, Surinder S. 2004. 'Agrarian Structures and Their Transformations'. In Veena Das (ed.). *Oxford Companion to Sociology and Social Anthropology*. Delhi: Oxford University Press, pp. 365–87.

Kalecki, M. 1972. 'Social and Economic Aspects of "Intermediate Regimes"'. In M. Kalecki (ed.). *Selected Essays on the Economic Growth and Socialist and Mixed Economy*. Cambridge: Cambridge University Press.

Kautsky, Karl. 1988. *The Agrarian Question*, vol. 1 (translated by Peter Burgess with Introduction by Hamza Alavi and Teodor Shanin). London: Zwan Publications.

Kelly, P. F. (ed.). 2013. *Migration, Agrarian Transition, and Rural Change in Southeast Asia*. New York: Routledge.

Kotovsky, G. 1964. *Agrarian Reform in India*. Moscow: Progress Publisher.

Lenin, V. I. 1964. *The Development of Capitalism in Russia*. Moscow: Progress Publishers. First published in 1899.

Lerche, Jens. 1995. 'Is Bonded Labour a Bound Category? Reconceptualising Agrarian Conflict in India'. *The Journal of Peasant Studies* 22 (3): 484–515.

Lerche, Jens. 2013. 'The Agrarian Question in Neoliberal India: Agrarian Transition Bypassed?'. *Journal of Agrarian Change* 13 (3): 382–404.

Lerche, Jens, Alpa Shah and Barbara Harriss-White. 2013. 'Introduction: Agrarian Questions and Left Politics in India'. *Journal of Agrarian Change* 13 (3): 337–50.

38 B. B. Mohanty

Lewis, Arthur. 1954. 'Economic Development with Unlimited Supplies of Labour'. *Manchester School of Economic and Social Studies*, 22 (2): 139–91.
Mann, H. H. and N. V. Kanitkar. 1921. *Land and Labour in a Deccan Village*. Delhi: Oxford University Press.
Marx, K. 1965. *Capital*, vol. I, part-VIII. Moscow: Progress Publishers.
Marx, K. 1981. *Capital: A Critique of Political Economy*, vol. 3. Harmondsworth: Penguin Books. First published in 1894.
Marx, K. and F. Engels. 1945. *The German Ideology*. Calcutta: Modern.
McMichael, P. 2006. 'Reframing Development: Global Peasant Movements and the New Agrarian Question'. *Canadian Journal of Development Studies* 27 (4): 470–83.
McMichael, P. 2009. 'Food Sovereignty, Social Reproduction and the Agrarian Question'. In A. H. Akram-Lodhi and C. Kay (eds). *Peasants and Globalisation: Political Economy, Rural Transformation and the Agrarian Question*. London: Routledge, pp. 288–312.
Mencher, Joan P. 1977. *Agriculture and Social Structure in Tamil Nadu: Past Origins, Present Transformation, and Future Prospects*. New Delhi: Allied.
Mohanty, B. B. 2012. 'Agrarian Studies in Indian Sociology'. In B. B. Mohanty (ed.). *Agrarian Change and Mobilisation*. New Delhi: Sage.
MoRD. 2012. 'MGNREGA Sameeksha: An Anthology of Research Studies on the Mahatma Gandhi National Rural Employment Guarantee Act, 2005, 2006–2012', edited and compiled by Mihir Shah, Neelakshi Mann and Varad Pande. New Delhi: Orient Blackswan.
MoRD. 2013. Report to the People, MGNREGA, 2005, Ministry of Rural Development.
Moyo, Sam. 2008. 'African Land Questions, Agrarian Transitions and the State: Contradictions of Neo-Liberal Land Reforms' Dakar, CODESRIA Working Paper Series.
Mukherjee, Ramkrishna. 1948. 'Economic Structure of Rural Bengal: A Survey of Six Villages'. *American Sociological Review* 13 (6): 660–72.
Nayyar, D. 1978. 'Industrial Development in India: Some Reflections on Growth and Stagnation'. *Economic and Political Weekly* 13 (31–33): 1265–78.
O'Laughlin, B. 2009. 'Gender Justice, Land and the Agrarian Question in Southern Africa'. In A. H. Akram-Lodhi and C. Kay (eds). *Peasants and Globalisation: Political Economy, Rural Transformation and the Agrarian Question*. London: Routledge, pp. 190–213.
Omvedt, Gail. 1978. 'Towards a Marxist Analysis of Caste'. *Social Scientist* 6 (2): 70–76.
Patnaik, U. and S. Moyo. 2011. *The Agrarian Question in the Neoliberal Era: Primitive Accumulation and the Peasantry*. UK: Fahamu/Pambazuka.
Patnaik, Utsa. 1971a. 'Capitalist Development in Agriculture – A Note'. *Economic and Political Weekly* 6 (39): 123–30.
Patnaik, Utsa. 1971b. 'Capitalist Development in Agriculture: Further Comment'. *Economic and Political Weekly* 6 (52): 190–94.

Agrarian transition: from classic to current debates 39

Patnaik, Utsa. 1972. 'On the Mode of Production in Indian Agriculture; A Reply'. *Economic and Political Weekly* 7 (40): 145–51.

Patnaik, Utsa. 1976. 'Class Differentiation within the Peasantry: An Approach to Analysis of Indian Agriculture'. *Economic and Political Weekly* 11 (39): 82–101.

Patnaik, Utsa. 2007. 'New Data on the Arrested Development of Capitalism in Indian Agriculture'. *Social Scientist* 35 (7/8): 4–23.

Patnaik, Utsa. 2012. 'Some Aspects of the Contemporary Agrarian Question'. *Agrarian South: Journal of Political Economy* 1 (3): 233–54.

Prasad, Pradhan. 1973. 'Production Relations: Achilles' Heel of Indian Planning'. *Economic and Political Weekly* 8 (19): 869–72.

Prasad, Pradhan. 1974. 'Reactionary Role of Usurers' Capital in Rural India'. *Economic and Political Weekly* 9 (32, 33 and 34): 1305–8.

Raj, K. N. 1973. 'The Politics and Economics of "Intermediate Regimes"'. *Economic and Political Weekly* 8 (27): 1189–98.

Reddy, D. N. and S. Mishra (eds.). 2009. *Agrarian Crisis in India*. New Delhi: Oxford University Press.

Rudra, Ashok. 1970. 'In Search of the Capitalist Farmer'. *Economic and Political Weekly* 5 (26): 85–87.

Rudra, Ashok. 1971. 'Capitalist Development in Agriculture: Reply'. *Economic and Political Weekly* 6 (45): 2291–92.

Rudra, Ashok. 1978. 'Class Relations in Indian Agriculture – III'. *Economic and Political Weekly* 13 (24): 998–1004.

Rudra, Ashok. 1981. 'Against Feudalism'. *Economic and Political Weekly* 16 (52): 2133–46.

Rudra, Ashok, A. Maiid and B. D. Talib. 1969. 'Big Farmers of the Punjab: Some Preliminary Findings of a Sample Survey'. *Economic and Political Weekly* 4 (39): 143–46.

Sanyal, Kalyan. 2007. *Rethinking Capitalist Development: Primitive Accumulation, Governmentality and Post-Colonial Capitalism*. New Delhi: Routledge.

Sau, Ranjit. 1975. 'Farm Efficiency under Semi-Feudalism: A Critique of Marginalist Theories and Some Marxist Formulation – A Comment'. *Economic and Political Weekly* 10 (13): A18–21.

Sen, Asok. 1984. 'The Transition from Feudalism to Capitalism'. *Economic and Political Weekly* 19 (30): 50–66.

Sweezy, P. 1976. 'A Critique'. In Rodney Hilton (ed.). *The Transition from Feudalism to Capitalism*. London: New Left Books, pp. 33–56.

Thorner, A. 1982. 'Semi-Feudalism or Capitalism? Contemporary Debates on Classes and Modes of Production in India'. *Economic and Political Weekly* 17 (49, 50 and 51): 1961–68, 1993–99 and 2061–66.

Thorner, Daniel. 1966. 'Chayanov's Concept of Peasant Economy'. In Daniel Thorner, Basile Kerblay and R. E. F. Smith (eds). *A. V. Chayanov on the Theory of Peasant Economy*. Homewood, IL: The American Economic Association, pp. xi–xxiv.

Thorner, Daniel. 1980. *The Shaping of Modern India*. Delhi: Allied Publishers.

40 B. B. Mohanty

Watts, M. J. 2009. 'The Southern Question: Agrarian Questions of Capital and Labour'. In A. H. Akram-Lodhi and C. Kay (eds). *Peasants and Globalisation: Political Economy, Rural Transformation and the Agrarian Question*. London: Routledge, pp. 262–87.

Weis, T. 2007. *The Global Food Economy: The Battle for the Future of Farming*. London: Zed Press.

Wood, E. M. 2002. *The Origin of Capitalism: A Longer View*. London: Verso.

Wood, E. M. 2009. 'Peasants and the Market Imperative: The Origins of Capitalism'. In A. H. Akram-Lodhi and C. Kay (eds). *Peasants and Globalisation: Political Economy, Rural Transformation and the Agrarian Question*. London: Routledge, pp. 37–56.

World Bank. 2007. *World Development Report 2008: Agriculture for Development*. Washington, DC: The World Bank.

Part I

Agrarian transition: theoretical discourse

Chapter 1

Back to the future?
Marx, modes of production and the agrarian question

A. Haroon Akram-Lodhi and Cristóbal Kay

1. The agrarian question, capitalist agrarian transition and historical puzzles

It has been almost 150 years since a specifically agrarian political economy emerged, originating in Karl Marx's (1976, orig. 1867) analysis of the genesis of capitalism, and the processes by which the core characteristics of capitalism came to be established: a system that is on the one hand exploitative and inhumane in its construction of the differential material interests of capital and labour while being a system that is, because of its capacity to develop the material forces of production, a necessary precondition of a more economically prosperous and more socially humane society.[1] This is the terrain of what Karl Kautsky later called 'the agrarian question', which he defined when he asked 'whether, and how, capital is seizing hold of agriculture, revolutionising it, making old forms of production and of property untenable and creating the necessity for new ones' (Kautsky 1988: 12, orig. 1899). Terence J. Byres (1991) has argued that in order for agriculture to no longer pose any obstacles to capitalist transformation, the agrarian question must be 'resolved' through some form of successful 'agrarian transition'. Byres's definition of a capitalist agrarian transition was the occurrence of 'those changes in the countryside of a poor country necessary to the overall development of capitalism and its ultimate dominance in a particular national social formation' (Byres 1996: 27).

Marx's concern with the process of capitalist development, through a resolution of what we now call the agrarian question and some form of capitalist agrarian transition, was shared by the key figures of classical historical materialism in the late nineteenth century: Engels (1950, orig. 1894), Lenin (1964, orig. 1899) and Kautsky (1988), among others, who viewed it as a two-sided process. Marx had argued that capitalist agrarian transition saw the exclusion of the direct producer from the

44 A. Haroon Akram-Lodhi and Cristóbal Kay

land through outright forced dispossession. This was necessary because capitalist agrarian transition required the development of a market in land, which in turn necessitated dispossessing rural labour, which in turn created a waged labour force. In other words, capitalist agrarian transition required the commodification of land and labour. What Engels, Lenin and Kautsky brought to the discussion was a second side of capitalist agrarian transition: a process of differentiation within a peasantry that was internally stratified into distinct socioeconomic groups, commonly labelled 'small'/'poor', 'medium' and 'large'/'rich'. Engels, Lenin and Kautsky can be distinguished by their differing perspectives on the drivers of this process of agrarian class formation. Engels argued that capitalist agrarian transition required the elimination of the small peasant, who could be owners of land, tenant workers of land, or both, and who used primarily family labour in on-farm production. The small peasant was eliminated by the middle and large peasants, who required, to differing degrees, waged labour for their farms and for whom the principal source of waged labour lay in an ever-more-steadily floundering, and then disappearing, small peasantry, whose termination provided the labour force necessary for the capitalist agrarian transition to be completed. By way of contrast, for Lenin landless waged labour was the remnants of both small and middle peasant farmers, and it was the elimination of the middle peasants that was key to the process of exclusion and social polarisation in the villages. For Kautsky, the process of capitalist agrarian transition was connected to the concentration of landholdings by the large peasants as the centralisation of capital in agriculture drove agrarian transition. In this light, the survival of small peasants was, for Kautsky, not a function of their economic efficiency but rather reflected the penury within which they lived, and their willingness to overwork themselves and complement that work with marginal sources of off-farm and non-farm income in order to survive. Agrarian political economy thus approaches capitalist agrarian transition as a process of the commodification of land and labour through the dispossession of the smallholder from the land, as a consequence of either forced displacement or the dispossession created by peasant class differentiation and the exclusionary implications of the normal, everyday workings of land, labour and product markets. During the current period of neoliberalism David Harvey (2003) encapsulates both collectively, if imperfectly, in the very popular concept of 'accumulation by dispossession'.

What then can be made of what Byres terms 'historical puzzles' (1996: 15): contemporary agrarian transitions that do not result in the full development of capitalist social relations of production and where a multiplicity of contrasting social forms might not even resolve the agrarian question (Byres 2003)? For almost two decades Henry Bernstein has argued that the agrarian question as one in which capital–labour relations coalesce and solidify has been rendered redundant; the current phase of capitalist development has resulted in the agrarian question, to paraphrase Marx, melting into air. This chapter does not share that perspective. It will go 'back to the future': situating the agrarian question and capitalist agrarian transition within Marx's understanding of the mode of production, and introducing the famous 'mode of production' debate of the late 1960s and early 1970s, it is argued that Marx's analysis of capitalist agrarian transition was far more nuanced and complex than is commonly suggested, emphasising the primacy of the conjuncture and the balance of forces rather than a historically inevitable if unpredictable and uneven process. For this reason, and notwithstanding the significant transfigurations that can be witnessed within actually existing global capitalism, the agrarian question continues to have resonance, particularly in countries with large agrarian populations, such as India, or countries where the demand for food is outstripping its supply, such as parts of sub Saharan Africa, and in some places, contemporary East Asia (Akram-Lodhi and Kay 2009).

2. Modes of production and the transition to capitalism

In the canonical works on the agrarian question, the transformation of pre-capitalist social relations of production into capitalist social relations of production that were sketched out by Marx in *Capital* and analysed in much further detail by Engels, Lenin and Kautsky appeared to be a linear process, in which the new forms of social relations and organisation undermined old forms of social relations and organisation in such a way as to speed the demise of the latter, older form of social relations and organisation. As a consequence, history can appear to be a unilinear sequence of stages, in which one mode of production decays as it is replaced by another mode of production. This linearity, which many read into Marx and suggest that he was a precursor of modernisation theory, can be traced back to the classic definition of a mode of production that was offered by Marx in the preface to *A Contribution to the Critique of Political Economy*:

> In the social production of their life, men enter into definite relations that are indispensable and independent of their will; these

46 A. Haroon Akram-Lodhi and Cristóbal Kay

relations of production correspond to a definite stage of development of their material forces of production. The sum total of these relations of production constitutes the economic structure of society – the real foundation, on which rises a legal and political superstructure and to which correspond definite forms of social consciousness. The mode of production of material life determines the social, political and intellectual life process in general. It is not the consciousness of men that determines their being, but, on the contrary, their social being that determines their consciousness. At a certain stage of their development, the material productive forces in society come in conflict with the existing relations of production, or – what is but a legal expression for the same thing – with the property relations within which they have been at work before. From forms of development of the productive forces these relations turn into their fetters. Then begins the epoch of social revolution.

(Marx 1983b: 159–60, orig. 1859)

This passage has several implications for an understanding of capitalist agrarian transition. First, it indicates that a mode of production is defined as a specific correlation of two components: the forces of production and the relations of production. The forces of production consist of the means of production, and in capitalism, labour power, or commodified labour. Relations of production are a consequence of the economic ownership and hence substantive control of the forces of production. The agrarian question is thus about the process by which the forces and relations of production that together constitute the capitalist mode of production are established: about the character of a capitalist agrarian transition that resolves the agrarian question.

A second implication of the passage is that it says that the economic 'base' defines other aspects of the social 'superstructure': 'social, political and intellectual life'. So the material conditions of the process of production within the agrarian question shape the sociopolitical ramifications of the agrarian question. A third implication of the passage is that it says that at some point the development of the forces of production become constrained by the structure of the relations of production. It is at this point that social transformation begins: that a new mode of production begins to undermine and replace an old mode of production, a process that involves not only a reorganisation of the relations of production but also the social, political and intellectual superstructure. So the passage suggests that the relations of production which structure both labour processes and surplus labour appropriation develop both out of and as a result of other, older modes of production. Thus, a capitalist agrarian transition that transforms pre-capitalist farming and agriculture and in so doing resolves the agrarian question must develop out of and as a result of a pre-capitalist agrarian question. A clear implication is, as suggested, that history is a sequence of stages and that, in a historical and developmental sense, the old and the new modes of production stand in a sequential relationship to the other.

However, seeing history as a series of stages is an extremely functionalist view of history and indeed led to a widespread discounting of the utility of a historical materialist approach to capitalist agrarian transition. Moreover, it places such an emphasis on the structure of capitalism as to discount the agency of social actors that clearly shaped the history of the development project in the latter half of the twentieth century. In the 1960s, a way of getting round this seeming impasse drew on the French Marxist tradition, paying particular attention to the theories of Louis Althusser and Etienne Balibar (Althusser and Balibar 1970; Anderson 1980), and how they were applied by the historical materialist anthropologists Pierre-Philippe Rey and Claude Meillassoux (Rey 1971, 1973, 1975; Meillassoux 1980; Bloch 1983). The Althusserian school argued that Marx's analysis of the mode of production was an abstract theory and that actual economic and political systems in societies, which they called 'social formations', involved more than one mode of production. In trying to understand the operation of multiple modes of production within a social formation, the critical issue was that of reproduction: how do different components of different modes of production intermingle, interact and interlock to sustain the operation of a social formation over time, for, as Althusser (1971: 123) wrote, 'the ultimate condition of production is . . . the reproduction of the conditions of production'.

The emphasis on the conditions of the reproduction of the social formation was because the process of capitalist agrarian transition was not seen to be an abstract and timeless one but is rather a historical event: one mode of production cannot instantaneously replace another, and so there must be a period in which there is an articulation of modes of production, during which time the new mode of production slowly comes to first dominate and then undermine the old mode of production. Rey, heavily influenced by Rosa Luxemburg (1951), in particular believed that the process of articulation within a social formation could be itself stable, persisting for a very long time. If such was the case, when trying to understand social formations characterised by some forms of pre-capitalism, it was not possible to understand one mode of production in isolation from another: the methods, means and mechanisms by which modes of production articulate created what we now call 'historical puzzles' and defined the unique character of the social formation.

In this light the stubborn persistence of the social formations that characterise many contemporary developing capitalist countries might be explained by the character of the articulation of the pre-capitalist and the capitalist modes of production. During the period of imperialism capital entered into what were primarily agrarian social formations in the South, often through the intermediary of merchant's capital and the process of commodity exchange. In so doing, the law of value was imposed: the idea that the exchange value of commodities, their monetary price, must ultimately reflect the socially necessary labour time necessary for the production of the commodities. The imposition of the law of value initially took place through the process of circulation, and had the effect of starting to undermine and break down the relations of production of the prevailing pre-capitalist mode of production in the social formation. However, as capital sought to appropriate the surpluses of labour, it worked within existing pre-capitalist labour processes. So while the conditions needed for the reproduction of the capitalist mode of production may have been put in place, the changes to the labour process necessary to finally dispense with the pre-capitalist mode of production would not have been completed. In this way, historical puzzles were created.

Rey (1971) offered a clear example of this in a detailed and groundbreaking case study of Congo-Brazzaville. The entry of capital into a developing social formation created the beginnings of a class of wage labourers who were necessary for the full maturation of capitalist social relations of production. However, this process witnessed workers entering into a capitalist mode of production from initially non-capitalist divisions of labour. They were thus used to working within non-capitalist labour processes, relations of production and ideologies. Moreover, this class of waged labour required food, and a capitalist agrarian transition that could resolve the agrarian question and establish capitalist social relations of production in agriculture had not occurred. So in the interim the capitalist mode of production's workforce had to obtain basic foods from the prevailing pre-capitalist mode of production, drawing peasants into the process of exchange and establishing them as petty commodity producers, but in a way that did not expose them to the full force of the market imperative and the law of value because of their continuing ability to self-provide, while reinforcing the social power of pre-capitalist dominant classes that appropriated food and agricultural commodities from the direct producers for consumption by the waged labour force. Indeed, as the social power of pre-capitalist dominant classes was reinforced by the needs of capital, they increasingly resisted the establishment of a complete set of capitalist social relations of production because these were not in their material interest. So the full fruition of capitalism was blocked; capitalist labour processes could combine with pre-capitalist ideologies; capitalist relations of production could combine with a non-capitalist division of labour; different forms of the division of labour could coexist; and indeed the different possible forms of individualised and socialised labour could be identified in one and the same worker (Taylor 1979). Capitalist and pre-capitalist modes of production articulated in a way that did not resolve the agrarian question but indeed perpetuated it over a prolonged period of time.

The Althusserian argument of French anthropologists was thus that capitalist development had been inhibited by pre-capitalist modes of production, as a result of the inherent strength of the pre-existing pre-capitalist mode; the weakness of the capitalist impulses that had been implanted into the developing capitalist country under imperialism; or the way in which pre-capitalist modes of production in fact meet the reproduction needs of the capitalist mode of production. In this way the nature of the pre-capitalist mode of production inhibited a capitalist agrarian transition, giving rise to highly combined and uneven development.

The debate on the articulation of modes of production reached perhaps its apogee in India in the 1960s and 1970s (Thorner 1982). While not couched in the language of French Marxism, in a wide ranging if in the end somewhat inconclusive debate the central question that was asked was whether the relative backwardness of India's agriculture was caused by the dominance of capitalist social relations of production or by the absence of capitalist social relations of production. In other words, was the specific process of capitalist agrarian transition or the lack of a process of capitalist agrarian transition inhibiting India's agricultural development? In this polarised debate, Chattopadhyay (1972a, 1972b) argued that the widespread presence of commodity production and waged labour indicated that Indian agriculture was largely capitalist, even if it was in transition. Patnaik (1971, 1972) on the other hand argued that the waged labour that was present in Indian agriculture was not free because of limited employment choices and because of continuing landlord power that constrained its substantive freedom. Moreover, she followed Banaji (1972, 1977) in arguing that agricultural surpluses were not being reinvested for the purpose of capital accumulation, and so the behaviour of agricultural producers was evidently not dominated by capitalist market imperatives and the law of value. So, for Patnaik, Indian agriculture was not capitalist.

The Indian mode of production debate re-emphasised the need to excavate the content of the underlying social relations of production rather than focus on the more superficial and apparent juridical content of the legal status of workers and peasants. At the time, it is this which unknowingly paralleled the much earlier work of the so-called Agrarian Marxists led by Lev Kritsman in the Soviet Union in the 1920s (Cox and Littlejohn 1984), work that was not available until after the protagonists in the debate had moved on to other areas of investigation, who in extensive empirical research had tried to understand the real content of the social relations of production in a rural Russia undergoing a transition to socialism. The Agrarian Marxists sought to do this by uncovering, following Marx, the modes and mechanisms by which the surplus product was produced, controlled and appropriated (Marx 1981: 927, orig. 1894). So, consistent with the Indian debate, the key characteristic needed to evaluate a capitalist agrarian transition was the way in which the surplus product was produced and controlled, in part because it was the surplus product that permitted an elementary process of capital accumulation. A key issue in understanding a capitalist agrarian transition would then be to understand how a predominant form of surplus appropriation, which characterised a specific and unique mode of production, was transformed into another predominant form of surplus appropriation that was characteristic of another, qualitatively superior mode of production. A key question resulted from this: was it possible to identify the critical variables in the process of transformation in modes of surplus appropriation?

The answer emerged out of a debate that had earlier taken place, in the first three decades of the development project, but which re-ignited in the mid-1970s, as the Indian mode of production debate wound down. In 1950 an exchange took place between Maurice Dobb and Paul Sweezy about the transition from feudalism to capitalism in Europe that had important implications for the understanding of the agrarian question and capitalist agrarian transition. Economic historians analysing the transition from feudalism to capitalism in Europe usually focused on two key questions. First, why did serfdom decline in some regions and persist in others? Second, why did landlord–tenant relations emerge in some regions and an owner–occupier, petty commodity producing small peasantry in others? In the case of England, Sweezy had argued, in a critique of Dobb, that feudalism ended because of the expansion of trade,

Back to the future? 51

which greatly increased commodification and so prepared the ground for the capitalism that later emerged (Dobb 1963; Sweezy 1976). However, Sweezy never offered a convincing explanation of the origin of capitalism, while his emphasis on the process of exchange rather than the terms and conditions governing production was deemed by many to be non-materialist. Dobb prepared the terrain for such a materialist explanation.

In *Studies in the Development of Capitalism*, first published in 1946, Dobb had argued that feudalism ended in England because of the conflictual social relations that existed between lords and peasants: class struggle allowed peasants to free themselves from their feudal obligations and allowed some of them to transform themselves into embryonic capitalists. Later, Rodney Hilton substantially elaborated Dobb's argument, providing the archival evidence of the character of the transition (Hilton 1990). Hilton showed that the demands of lords for the agricultural surpluses of the peasants led the peasants to improve their production techniques, which in turn encouraged the emergence of simple commodity production, which had been hindered by feudalism. Hilton also documented the character of peasant resistance to the appropriations of landlords, and its role in bringing about the transition to capitalism (Hilton 1976).

In 1976 the Dobb–Sweezy debate (Sweezy *et al.* 1976) was reopened by Robert Brenner, who more systematically examined the transition to capitalism in Western Europe and produced what is without doubt the most rounded explanation of it within historical materialism (Brenner 1977; Aston and Philpin 1985). Although influenced by Dobb and Hilton's emphasis on the social relationships between the appropriators and the appropriated, and agreeing that the downfall of feudalism had to be found with the social relations of feudalism itself, Brenner did not like the implicit assumption of Dobb and Hilton that within the interstices of feudalism lay the basis of capitalism waiting to be unleashed. Like Sweezy, Brenner believed that feudalism was a tenacious mode of production, but Brenner went further than Sweezy in arguing that it was the social property relations of feudalism that resulted in its collapse.

In feudalism surplus appropriation was the basis by which the dominant landlord class reproduced itself. Surplus appropriations from the peasantry were carried out through the mechanism of rent and backed up by coercion. Production was organised through the institution of serfdom to fit the needs of surplus extraction by the lords. Peasant ownership of land was by and large excluded. Social property relations thus resulted in lords and serfs not having to rely on the market.

52 A. Haroon Akram-Lodhi and Cristóbal Kay

Reproductive strategies, focused not on accumulation but on familial consumption, were the logical outcome of such social property relations. So for Brenner pre-capitalist feudal social relations of production could not develop the forces of production because lords ultimately used force to appropriate the agricultural surplus of the peasantry, not having to rely upon markets. Lords could increase their incomes by making peasants work harder and longer, or reducing their incomes, but there was neither incentive nor need to systematically improve efficiency, labour productivity and competitiveness.

So the material benefits of heavy surplus appropriation gave no incentive for the dominant classes to innovate, while the peasantry lacked both the incentive and the means to invest. As a result, productivity dropped and an exhaustion of peasant production emerged. The class structure of feudalism thus precipitated a crisis of productivity and threatened the basis of subsistence for the rural population. This crisis broke down the inhibiting effect of the lords' coercive capacity among the peasantry. Conflict was the result, which took the shape of struggles over the control of surpluses and possession of the means of production. These struggles occurred from the fourteenth century to, in some parts of Europe, the eighteenth century and beyond (Sweezy et al. 1976; Aston and Philpin 1985; Brenner 1986; Hilton 1990). The outcomes of these struggles were regionally specific and based on the prevailing balance of class forces. In some areas, such as France, the direct producers took control of the land. Freed of the burden of surplus extraction, they could invest to overcome productivity decline. As output increased and surpluses accrued, the gains to be had from the pursuit of efficient market-oriented competitive strategies became clear. The law of value became binding, market imperatives were imposed and capital accumulation was fostered. In other areas, such as England, the crisis meant that both landlords and peasants had to become more competitive in the market and more productive on the land: in the lords' case, in order to increase the rents that they were paid, and in the tenants' case in order to keep and indeed enhance their access to land. Those who were not competitive were driven off the land, either by coercive and exclusionary dispossession or through the normal workings of market imperatives, the emerging law of value and a resulting process of 'market-led enclosure' (Akram-Lodhi 2007). As serfs became separated from the land, they had to rely on the market for subsistence. With a growing demand for subsistence goods and lacking access to secure surpluses, individual landlords started to move directly into agricultural production. Falling under the sway of market relations and the law of value meant having to compete, which entailed both labour-productivity enhancing specialisation and innovation. Those who were competitive and more productive increasingly commodified their output, facilitating the emergence over time of agrarian capitalism in England, with landlords, capitalist tenants and waged labour. Agrarian production responded and capital accumulation in agriculture began. Again, agriculture was transformed. In yet other areas in Europe, the result was the emergence of new, commercially based tenancy arrangements. In all these instances, then, the law of value was imposed on the countryside.

The key to capitalist agrarian transition in Europe was thus an economic crisis in the pre-capitalist mode of production that the social property relations of that mode could not resolve. So Brenner argued that capitalism emerged because of the relationships between lords and peasants trying to best reproduce themselves within the conditions that they faced. But it was not markets and trade, which had existed for millennia, which fostered change and social transformation. Rather, in the genesis of agrarian capitalism the structure of social relations brought about stagnation and eventual decline, fostering class struggles that gave rise to social transformation. Eventually, pre-capitalist property relations and labour processes were subordinated and integrated into the value relations of the capitalist mode of production (Brenner 1986; Wood 2009). The roots of the crisis lay in the fetters to development engendered by the structure of social property relations, which spurred change and promoted agrarian capital accumulation (Carling 1991).

The importance of Brenner's argument for contemporary readings of the agrarian question and capitalist agrarian transition is that Brenner is systematically able to uncover 'the mechanisms linking structural features of the mode of production to its dynamics. . . . Development and underdevelopment are the product of class structures which are themselves the outcome of a historical process' (Brewer 1990: 231). In reconciling structure and agency in the explanation of historical puzzles, Brenner rigorously reasserted the centrality of class structure, class relationships and class struggle as the central dynamic variable in understanding processes of agrarian change. In this reassertion, Brenner was able to highlight the importance of the specificity of the conjuncture in producing substantive diversity in processes of change along with the differential uniformity of the outcomes that were generated. In other words, Brenner offered an analytical approach that seemingly explained Byres's historical puzzles. What is far less well understood is that the complex multiplicity of actual forms of capitalist agrarian transition was in fact well understood by Marx himself.

3. Marx, primitive accumulation and the historical context

As is well known, for Marx the possibility of transcending capitalism lay in the hands of the class that it created: the proletariat, a class free from the ownership of the means of production and free to sell its labour power for the best wage that it could obtain, was capable of eradicating class society and ending exploitation. This then was the starting point for Marx's analysis of the agrarian question: if small-scale peasant producers combined elements of being petty capitalists and labour, how could the complete development of the capitalist mode of production, and the concomitant creation of a working class, take place? That Marx had a clear understanding of petty commodity production is clear without doubt, for he wrote that it would be witnessed

> where the peasant owns the land he cultivates, or the artisan owns the tools with which he is an accomplished performer. . . . This mode of production presupposes the fragmentation of holdings, and the dispersal of other means of production. As it excludes the concentration of these means of production, so it also excludes co-operation, division of labour within each separate process of production, the social control and regulation of the forces of nature, and the free development of the productive forces of society. It is compatible only with a system of production and a society moving within narrow limits.
>
> (Marx 1976: 927–28)

Marx's answer to the question of how the working class was established was to carefully consider the relationship between small-scale pre-capitalist peasant farming, petty commodity production and the emergence of agrarian capital. This was evident as early as the *Grundrisse* (Marx 1973, orig. 1939–41), which elaborates a variety of ways in which transitions from pre-capitalism to capitalism occur.

In these discursive notes small-scale pre-capitalist peasant farming often appears in the guise sketched out in many of Marx's writings over a 30-year period, including his famous journalism on India (Marx 1977, orig. 1852 and 1853), in which the peasantry is essentially seen as being, for lack of a better phrase, a remnant that will be dragged into modernity by the capitalist mode of production. He could be brutal in his judgement of this kind of peasant society, noting, for example, that 'small-scale landownership creates a class of barbarians standing half outside society' (Marx 1981: 949, orig. 1894), but this was, in part, because of its implications for the establishment of capitalism, a historically progressive force: 'agricultural smallholding, by its very nature, rules out the development of the productive powers of social labour' (Marx 1981: 943) and thereby impedes the development of capitalism. This perspective – that Marx viewed the small-scale pre-capitalist peasantry as a structural impediment to the full fruition of the capitalist mode of production – is very widely held. It is also, in our view, false.

Marx's most fully developed analysis of the development of capitalism in agriculture is that which he worked out later in his life and which was published as the first volume of *Capital* (Marx 1976). Bernstein (2006: 449) reminds us that here the class basis of the emergence of capitalist farming within England was explored in detail, through the use of the concept of so-called primitive accumulation, which is used to explain how capital initially comes into existence. There, Marx wrote that

> in the history of primitive accumulation, all revolutions are epoch-making that act as levers for the capitalist class in course of formation; but this is true above all for those moments when great masses of men are suddenly and forcibly torn from their means of subsistence, and hurled onto the labour-market as free, unprotected and rightless proletarians. The expropriation of the agricultural producer, of the peasant, from the soil is the basis of the whole process. The history of this expropriation assumes different aspects in different countries, and runs through its various phases in different orders of succession, and at different historical epochs. Only in England, which we therefore take as our example, has it the classic form.
>
> (Marx 1976: 876)

In Marx's 'classic' example, which came, in many ways, to be seen as a *sui generis*, serfdom in England had all but disappeared by the end of the fourteenth century. Feudal lords remained, but their 'might . . . depended . . . on the number of peasant proprietors' (Marx 1976: 878): free, and generally comparatively prosperous, pre-capitalist peasant farmers who controlled their land and cultivated it with their own labour, but whose social and material reproduction relied heavily on access to common lands. At the start of the sixteenth century the feudal lords began 'forcibly driving the peasantry from the land' as well as

56 A. Haroon Akram-Lodhi and Cristóbal Kay

the coercive 'usurpation of common lands' (Marx 1976: 878). 'So-called primitive accumulation . . . is nothing else than the historical process of divorcing the producer from the means of production', creating

> free workers, in the double sense that they neither form part of the means of production themselves . . . nor do they own the means of production, as would be the case with self-employed peasant proprietors.
>
> (Marx 1976: 874)

Primitive accumulation in England used dispossessory enclosures by predatory feudal lords, later supported by the state, to reconfigure the social relations of production in order to physically exclude a prosperous yeomanry from the land and create a propertyless class of rural waged labour that faced a class of capitalist tenant-farmers, beneath the dominant landlord class (Tribe 1981). Primitive accumulation is in this sense not accumulation at all; it is rather the conversion of the pre-capitalist means of production into capital and the consequent establishment of both the capital–labour relation and the law of value.

For many casual readers of Marx it often appears that the outcome of the introduction of capitalist social relations of production into agriculture must seemingly inevitably be the emergence of agrarian capital and agrarian wage labour. Indeed, in *Theories of Surplus Value* it appeared he was unequivocal:

> The . . . peasant who produces with his own means of production will either gradually be transformed into a small capitalist who also exploits the labour of others, or he will suffer the loss of his means of production and be transformed into a wage-labourer. This is the tendency in the form of society in which the capitalist mode of production predominates.
>
> (Marx 2009, orig. 1863)[2]

But note the critical provisions that Marx has made in the previous quotes: 'the history of this expropriation assumes different aspects in different countries, and runs through its various phases in different orders of succession, and at different historical epochs'; 'this is the tendency'. As ever, while Marx offered precise analytical clarity in order to reveal underlying laws of motion, he clearly believed that there could be multiple and differential ways by which a set of capitalist social relations of production could be established or consolidated in agriculture.

Back to the future? 57

This was to be expected because the establishment or consolidation of capitalist social relations of production in agriculture was not a one-time event but, as has already been discussed, a complex and contradictory historical process. As Marx noted, 'The entry of capital into agriculture as an independent and leading power does not take place everywhere all at once, but rather gradually and in particular branches of production' (Marx 1981: 937). While 'supremacy and subordination in the *process of production* supplant an earlier state of *independence*' (Marx 1976: 1028–29, emphasis in original),

> capital subsumes the labour process as it finds it. For example[:] . . . a mode of agriculture corresponding to a small, independent peasant economy. If changes occur in these traditional established *labour processes* after their takeover by capital . . . in themselves these changes do not affect the character of the actual labour process, the actual mode of working.
>
> (Marx 1976: 1021, emphasis in original)

Marx called this the formal subsumption of labour to capital: formal in the sense that while the labour process carries on much as it did prior to the entry of capital, the control of the means of production by capital, and hence the means of subsistence, means that labour is compelled to undertake waged labour, which facilities capital accumulation. Marx contrasted formal subsumption with the real subsumption of labour: the labour process itself is transformed by capital as it establishes completely capitalist social relations of production, labour regimes and the law of value in order to produce capital accumulation.

Marx did not stop there, however. He also wrote that the modes and mechanisms by which capital subsumes labour in the establishment of the capitalist mode of production can produce 'certain hybrid forms, in which although surplus labour is not extorted by direct compulsion from the producer, the producer has not yet become formally subordinate to capital' and the law of value (Marx 1976: 645). It is these hybrid forms, we propose, that are witnessed in the early stages of capitalist agrarian transition as historical puzzles emerge: petty commodity production becomes slowly, differentially and highly unevenly subordinated to market imperatives and the law of value. It is in the interstices of these hybrid forms, we propose, that, among other forms of labour regimes, unfree labour, defined as commodified labour that the worker cannot 'dispose of . . . as his own commodity' (Brass and van der Lindon

58 A. Haroon Akram-Lodhi and Cristóbal Kay

1997: 59), can be found within the capitalist mode of production, which means that it is thus completely consistent with it (Banaji 2003).

Hybrid forms of labour subsumption in peasant production are witnessed because of the 'contradictory unity' (Bernstein 1991: 418) embodied within small-scale peasant farms as capitalism consolidates and petty commodity production becomes established under it:

> The independent peasant or handicraftsman is cut up into two persons. As owner of the means of production he is capitalist; as labourer he is his own wage-labourer. As capitalist he therefore pays himself his wages and draws his profit on his capital; that is to say, he exploits himself as wage-labourer, and pays himself, in the surplus-value, the tribute that labour owes to capital.
>
> (Marx 2009)

So while peasants may be dispossessed as capitalism develops, capital can also subsume peasant labour through formal or hybrid forms that may, apparently, consolidate the peasantry. Those who are not conversant in agrarian political economy tend to miss this important aspect of Marx's analysis. The peasantry would outwardly appear unchanged even as capital produced a fundamental transformation in its social characteristics: there would be an ephemeral yet substantive separation of means of production and labour within the peasant farm. Indeed, we suggest, this is precisely what transforms small-scale pre-capitalist peasant farms into small-scale petty commodity producers under capitalism (Gibbon and Neocosmos 1985; Bernstein 1991).

The transformation of the social characteristics of the peasantry belies their apparent resilience in the face of capitalism. Peasants survive, but their poverty is created because of coping mechanisms that are employed by petty commodity producers under capitalism:

> The smallholding peasant's exploitation is not limited by the average profit on capital, in as much as he is a small capitalist; nor by the need for rent, in as much as he is a landowner. The only absolute barrier he faces as a petty capitalist is the wage that he pays himself, after deducting his actual expenses . . . and he often does so down to a physical minimum.
>
> (Marx 1981: 941–42)

Kautsky grasped this essential insight into petty commodity production under capitalism, evocatively writing that for peasant farmers 'profit

Back to the future? 59

did not mean his barns were full; it meant their stomachs were empty'
(Banaji 1980: 70).

So 'smallholding and petty landownership . . . production . . .
proceeds without being governed by the general rate of profit' (Marx
1981: 946), which can foster socioeconomic stratification and peasant
class differentiation as

> the custom necessarily develops, among the better-off rent paying
> peasants, of exploiting agricultural wage-labourers on their own
> account. . . . In this way it gradually becomes possible for them to
> build up a certain degree of wealth and transform themselves into
> future capitalists. Among the old possessors of the land, working for
> themselves, there arises a seed-bed for the nurturing of capitalist
> farmers, whose development is conditioned by the development of
> capitalist production.
>
> (Marx 1981: 935)

So Marx clearly recognised that the process of capitalist development in agriculture can create both peasant dispossession by displacement, or the enclosures of so-called primitive accumulation
of which he wrote about in *Capital*, and peasant dispossession by
differentiation (Akram-Lodhi 2007; Arraghi 2009: 118), which is
driven by the value relations and market imperatives of capitalism to
exploit labour, improve productivity and cut the costs of production
(Wood 2009).

Formal, real and hybrid forms of subsumption of labour to capital:
clearly, in trying to understand the content of the relations of production there was manifest complexity, as was witnessed in the context of
the developing capitalist countries of Asia, Africa and Latin America
throughout the twentieth century. In order to unpack this complexity,
Marx had written that

> the specific economic form in which unpaid surplus labour is
> pumped out of the direct producers determines the relationship of
> domination and servitude. . . . On this is based the entire configura-
> tion of the economic community arising from the actual relations
> of production, and hence also its specific political form. It is in
> each case the direct relationship of the owners of the conditions
> of production to the immediate producers – a relationship whose
> particular form naturally corresponds always to a certain level of
> development of the type and manner of labour, and hence to its

60 A. Haroon Akram-Lodhi and Cristóbal Kay

social productive power – in which we find the innermost secret, the hidden basis of the entire social edifice.

(Marx 1981: 927)

Indeed, it was this emphasis on uncovering the 'hidden basis' of the dynamics of surplus labour appropriation that guided the empirical research of the Agrarian Marxists.

In this light a letter Marx composed in 1881 appears somewhat less remarkable than that which is sometimes claimed (Shanin 1983). Rather, the four drafts and final text of the letter to Vera Zasulich resemble *The Eighteenth Brumaire of Louis Bonaparte* (Marx 1967, orig. 1852), demonstrating how Marx applied his materialist political economy to the analysis of the messy and complex set of actual social and economic conditions governing the possible fate of the Russian peasantry (Marx 1983a, orig. 1925). The context was clearly stipulated: a formally independent but internationally weak state, with a dominant small-scale peasant population, which was nonetheless rapidly industrialising under the auspices of an interventionist state, and with industry under the control of the state or non-Russians. It is, in many ways, a remarkably contemporary setting, made all the more so because Marx explicitly situates the fate of the Russian peasantry within the context of global economic processes: the Russian commune was 'linked to a world market in which capitalist production is predominant' (Marx 1983a: 102). He stresses the specificity of the economic structure: a 'type of capitalism fostered by the state at the peasant's expense' (Marx 1983a: 104). In so doing, Marx argued that in this setting the Russian commune was not threatened by the irresistible economic logic of the law of value and the capital–labour relation per se but was rather threatened by oppression by the state and by 'capitalist intruders whom the state has made powerful at the peasant's expense' (Marx 1983a: 105).

So Marx identified a set of 'powerful interests' seeking to subordinate the rural commune and the peasantry: 'overburdened by state exactions, fraudulently exploited by intruding capitalists, merchants, etc., and the landed "proprietors", it is also being undermined by village usurers' (Marx 1983a: 114). In this messy and complex setting, two different resolutions of the agrarian question were identified by Marx as being possible. The first would see the dominant class coalition – the 'new pillars of society' – largely eliminate the peasantry, converting them 'into wage-labourers' or, a small number, into 'a rural middle class' (Marx 1983a: 116), thus completing the real subsumption of labour and the transition to a fully capitalist mode of production.

Back to the future? 61

The second resolution of the agrarian question in the letter to Zasulich would see the agricultural commune gradually transforming itself into 'an element of collective production on a national scale' (Marx 1983a: 106). This could occur, according to Marx, because of the corporate specificities of the commune. These specificities included the fact that membership of the commune was not based on kinship, that all members of the commune received a private house and garden and that the arable land itself had never been private property but was allocated and reallocated to individuals who were allowed to individually appropriate the product of the land for their own subsistence (Marx 1983a: 108). This 'dualism' (Marx 1983a: 104), according to Marx, gave the commune a set of social relations that articulated the positive and progressive features of capitalism with a set of features derived from an archaic but historically adaptable structure. It was, in our view, clearly an example of a 'hybrid form': subordinate to an emerging capitalist mode of production that was not yet supreme (Marx 1976: 1027). This opened up the possibility that the commune could 'reap the fruits with which capitalist production has enriched humanity without passing through the capitalist regime' (Marx 1983a: 112), creating, in a sense, a new form of historical puzzle.

But in order for the second path of transition to take place, the collective tendencies within the commune would have to gain a dominant logic over private interests, and this required, in turn, a working-class revolution that succeeded in creating a countervailing force to the anti-commune stresses fostered by emergent capital. Moreover, hypothesised Marx, following the revolution new technologies could also be introduced to sustain the position of small-scale peasant farming. Finally, the deepening of democratic processes arising out of the revolution would be essential to the survival of the commune. Thus, Marx argues in the letter, 'To save the Russian commune there must be a Russian revolution' (Marx 1983a: 116).

This letter is more than a historical footnote, for consistent with Marx's underlying logic it shows that multiple resolutions of the agrarian question facing small-scale petty commodity-producing peasants located and operating within a dominant capitalist economy were possible. Indeed, Marx writes repeatedly in the drafts of the letter that the analysis of *Capital* is 'expressly restricted to the countries of Western Europe' (Marx 1983a: 117) and that it is wrong to place all agrarian transformations 'on the same plane' (Marx 1983a: 107, footnote c). This intellectual flexibility and this willingness to confront messy realities are possibly the most important analytical legacies that should be borne in

62 A. Haroon Akram-Lodhi and Cristóbal Kay

mind when contemplating the contemporary salience of the agrarian question and contemporary processes of capitalist agrarian transition. For, as Marx writes in the letter, the agrarian commune's 'innate dualism admits of an alternative: either its property element will gain the upper hand over its collective element; or else the reverse will take place. Everything depends upon the historical context in which it is located' (Marx 1983a: 120–21).

4. The agrarian question, substantive diversity and the balance of class forces

In this light, then, does the agrarian question have contemporary relevance? In our view the answer is clearly 'yes'. On a global scale capital continues to undermine peasant petty commodity production through the application of the law of value in order to facilitate market-led enclosures that change the land, labour and capital intensity of agricultural production. This is principally done to increase the production of cheap food that fuels capitalist development by increasing the rate of surplus value and hence enhancing profitability (Akram-Lodhi 2012). However, if this is the case it would not appear to suggest that the agrarian question of capital has been resolved, as suggested by Bernstein. Rather, it appears that in seeking to facilitate the further reorganisation of global agriculture capitalism promotes some form of capitalist agrarian transition by seeking to enclose and convert property into capital, currently through the phenomenon that we know as land grabbing. This in turn suggests that the agrarian question and processes of capitalist agrarian transition on a global scale remain central to understanding current factors and forces propelling the capitalist world economy.

However, in an era of neoliberal globalisation, forms of labour subsumption can be multiple and varied, outright dispossession continues even as peasant class differentiation takes place and thus the specificities of the historical context explain not only the differences posited by Engels, Lenin and Kautsky but also the nature, timing and pace of capitalist agrarian transition that is subject to substantive diversity and differential uniformity in its outcomes. It is for this reason that most contemporary agrarian political economists propose that no uniform path of capitalist agrarian transition need necessarily be identified. Rather, while both the contemporary understanding and the arguments of classical historical materialists place dispossession and differentiation, the establishment or otherwise of capital–labour relations and the imposition of the law of value as the central *explicatus* of capitalist

Back to the future? 63

agrarian transition, these processes are explained in turn by the balance of forces – class conflict remains the central driver of capitalist agrarian transition.

Notes

1 This chapter draws heavily on parts of Akram-Lodhi and Kay (2010a, 2010b) but goes significantly beyond those earlier papers.
2 The references taken from *Theories of Surplus Value* are taken from a website that does not offer pagination. But entry of a fragment of the quote into the website's search engine will take the reader directly to the quote.

References

Akram-Lodhi, A. H. 2007. 'Land, Markets and Neoliberal Enclosure: An Agrarian Political Economy Perspective'. *Third World Quarterly* 28 (8): 1437–56.

Akram-Lodhi, A. H. 2012. 'Contextualising Land Grabbing: Contemporary Land Deals, the Global Subsistence Crisis and the World Food System'. *Canadian Journal of Development Studies* 33 (2): 119–42.

Akram-Lodhi, A. H. and C. Kay. 2009. *Peasants and Globalisation: Political Economy, Rural Transformation and the Agrarian Question*. London: Routledge.

Akram-Lodhi, A. H. and C. Kay. 2010a. 'Surveying the Agrarian Question (Part 1): Unearthing Foundations, Exploring Diversity'. *The Journal of Peasant Studies* 37 (1): 177–202.

Akram-Lodhi, A. H. and C. Kay. 2010b. 'Surveying the Agrarian Question (Part 2): Current Debates and Beyond'. *The Journal of Peasant Studies* 37 (2): 255–84.

Althusser, L. 1971. *Lenin and Philosophy and Other Essays*. London: New Left Books.

Althusser, L. and E. Balibar. 1970. *Reading Capital*. London: New Left Books.

Anderson, P. 1980. *Arguments within English Marxism*. London: New Left Books.

Arraghi, F. 2009. 'The Invisible Hand and the Visible Foot: Peasants, Dispossession and Globalisation'. In A. H. Akram-Lodhi and C. Kay (eds). *Peasants and Globalisation: Political Economy, Rural Transformation and the Agrarian Question*. London: Routledge.

Aston, T. H. and C. H. E. Philpin (eds). 1985. *The Brenner Debate: Agrarian Class Structure and Economic Development in Pre-Industrial Europe*. Cambridge: Cambridge University Press.

Banaji, J. 1972. 'For a Theory of Colonial Modes of Production'. *Economic and Political Weekly* 7 (52): 2498–502.

Banaji, J. 1977. 'Modes of Production in a Materialist Conception of History'. *Capital & Class* 3: 1–44.

64 A. Haroon Akram-Lodhi and Cristóbal Kay

Banaji, J. 1980. 'Summary of Selected Parts of Kautsky's *The Agrarian Question*'. In H. Wolpe (ed.). *The Articulation of Modes of Production*. London: Routledge, pp. 45–92.

Banaji, J. 2003. 'The Fictions of Free Labour: Contract, Coercion and So-Called Unfree Labour'. *Historical Materialism* 11 (3): 69–95.

Bernstein, H. 1991. 'Petty Commodity Production'. In T. Bottomore, L. Harris, V. G. Kiernan and R. Miliband (eds). *A Dictionary of Marxist Thought* (2nd edition). Oxford: Blackwell.

Bernstein, H. 2006. 'Is There an Agrarian Question in the 21st Century?'. *Canadian Journal of Development Studies* 27 (4): 449–60.

Bernstein, H. 2009. 'Agrarian Questions from Transition to Globalisation'. In A. H. Akram-Lodhi and C. Kay (eds). *Peasants and Globalisation: Political Economy, Rural Transformation and the Agrarian Question*. London: Routledge.

Bloch, M. 1983. *Marxism and Anthropology*. Oxford: Oxford University Press.

Brass, T. and M. van der Linden. 1997. *Free and Unfree Labor: The Debate Continues*. Bern: Peter Lang.

Brenner, R. 1977. 'The Origins of Capitalist Development: A Critique of Neo-Smithian Marxism'. *New Left Review* (first series) 104: 25–92.

Brenner, R. 1985. 'The Agrarian Roots of European Capitalism'. In T. H. Aston and C. H. E. Philpin (eds). *The Brenner Debate: Agrarian Class Structure and Economic Development in Pre-Industrial Europe*. Cambridge: Cambridge University Press, pp. 10–63.

Brenner, R. 1986. 'The Social Basis of Economic Development'. In J. Roemer (ed.). *Analytical Marxism*. Cambridge: Cambridge University Press, pp. 23–53.

Brewer, A. 1990. *Marxist Theories of Imperialism: A Critical Survey* (2nd edition). London: Routledge.

Byres, T. J. 1991. 'The Agrarian Question'. In T. Bottomore, L. Harris, V. G. Kiernan and R. Miliband (eds). *A Dictionary of Marxist Thought* (2nd edition). Oxford: Blackwell.

Byres, T. J. 1996. *Capitalism from Above and Capitalism from Below: An Essay in Comparative Political Economy*. Houndmills, Basingstoke and London: Macmillan.

Byres, T. J. 2003. 'Paths of Capitalist Agrarian Transition in the Past and in the Contemporary World'. In V. K. Ramachandran and M. Swaminathan (eds). *Agrarian Studies: Essays on Agrarian Relations in Less-Developed Countries*. London: Zed Books, pp. 54–83.

Carling, A. 1991. *Social Division*. London: Verso.

Chattopadhyay, P. 1972a. 'On the Question of the Mode of Production in Indian Agriculture: A Preliminary Note'. *Economic and Political Weekly* 7 (13): A39 and A41–46.

Chattopadhyay, P. 1972b. 'Mode of Production in Indian Agriculture: An "Anti-Kritik"'. *Economic and Political Weekly* 7 (53): A185–92.

Cox, T. and G. Littlejohn (eds). 1984. *Kritsman and the Agrarian Marxists*. London: Frank Cass.

Dobb, M. 1963. *Studies in the Development of Capitalism*. London: Routledge & Kegan Paul.

Engels, F. 1950. 'The Peasant Question in France and Germany'. In K. Marx and F. Engels (eds). *Selected Works*, vol. 2. London: Lawrence and Wishart. First published in 1894.

Gibbon, P. and M. Neocosmos. 1985. 'Some Problems in the Political Economy of "African Socialism"'. In H. Bernstein and B. Campbell (eds). *Contradictions of Accumulation in Africa: Studies in Economy and State*. Beverly Hills, CA: Sage Publications.

Harvey, D. 2003. *The New Imperialism*. Oxford: Oxford University Press.

Hilton, R. H. 1976. 'Introduction'. In Paul Sweezy *et al.* (eds). *The Transition from Feudalism to Capitalism*. London: Verso, pp. 9–30.

Hilton, R. H. 1990. *Class Conflict and the Crisis of Feudalism* (revised edition). London: Verso.

Kautsky, K. 1988. *The Agrarian Question*, 2 volumes. London: Zwan Publications. First published in 1899.

Lenin, V. I. 1964. *The Development of Capitalism in Russia*. Moscow: Progress Publishers. First published in 1899.

Luxemburg, R. 1951. *The Accumulation of Capital*. London: Routledge & Kegan Paul.

Marx, K. 1967. *The Eighteenth Brumaire of Louis Bonaparte*. Moscow: Progress Publishers. First published in 1852.

Marx, K. 1973. *Grundrisse*. Harmondsworth: Penguin Books. First published between 1939 and 1941.

Marx, K. 1976. *Capital*, vol. I. Harmondsworth: Penguin Books. First published in 1867.

Marx, K. 1977. 'The Future Results of British Rule in India'. In D. McLellan (ed.). *Karl Marx: Selected Writings*. Oxford: Oxford University Press. First published in 1852 and 1853.

Marx, K. 1981. *Capital*, vol. III. Harmondsworth: Penguin Books. First published in 1894.

Marx, K. 1983a. 'Marx-Zasulich Correspondence: Letters and Drafts'. In T. Shanin (ed.). *Late Marx and the Russian Road: Marx and 'the Peripheries of Capitalism'*. London: Routledge & Kegan Paul. First published in 1925.

Marx, K. 1983b. 'A Contribution to the Critique of Political Economy'. In E. Kamenka (ed.). *The Portable Karl Marx*. Harmondsworth: Penguin Books. First published in 1859.

Marx, K. 2009. 'Theories of Surplus Value', accessed from http://www.marxists. org/archive/marx/works/1863/theories-surplus-value/index.htmon 19 June. Written in 1863.

Meillassoux, C. 1980. 'From Reproduction to Production: A Marxist Approach to Economic Anthropology'. In H. Wolpe (ed.). *The Articulation of Modes of Production: Essays from Economy and Society*. London: Routledge, pp. 189–201.

Patnaik, U. 1971. 'Capitalist Development in Agriculture: A Note'. *Economic and Political Weekly* 6 (39): A123–24 and A126–30.

Patnaik, U. 1972. 'On the Mode of Production in Indian Agriculture: A Reply'. *Economic and Political Weekly* 7 (40): A145–51.

66 A. Haroon Akram-Lodhi and Cristóbal Kay

Rey, P. P. 1971. *Colonialisme, néo-colonialisme et transition au capitalisme* [Colonialism, Neo-Colonialism and the Transition to Capitalism]. Paris: Maspero.

Rey, P. P. 1973. *Les alliances de classes*. Paris: Maspero.

Rey, P. P. 1975. 'The Lineage Mode of Production'. *Critique of Anthropology* 3: 27–79.

Shanin, T. 1983. 'Late Marx: Gods and Craftsmen'. In T. Shanin (ed.). *Late Marx and the Russian Road: Marx and 'the Peripheries of Capitalism'*. London: Routledge & Kegan Paul.

Sweezy, P. 1976. 'A Critique'. In P. Sweezy *et al.* (eds). *The Transition from Feudalism to Capitalism*. London: Verso, pp. 33–56.

Sweezy, P., M. Dobb, C. Hill, R. Hilton, G. Lefebvre, K. Takahashi, G. Procacci, J. Merrington and E. Hobsbawm. 1976. *The Transition from Feudalism to Capitalism*. London: Verso.

Taylor, J. 1979. *From Modernisation to Modes of Production*. Houndmills, Basingstoke, and London: Macmillan.

Thorner, A. 1982. 'Semi-Feudalism or Capitalism? Contemporary Debates on Classes and Modes of Production in India'. *Economic and Political Weekly* 17 (49): 1961–68.

Tribe, K. 1981. *Genealogies of Capitalism*. London and Basingstoke: Macmillan.

Wood, E. M. 2009. 'Peasants and the Market Imperative: The Origins of Capitalism'. In A. H. Akram-Lodhi and C. Kay (eds). *Peasants and Globalisation: Political Economy, Rural Transformation and the Agrarian Question*. London: Routledge.

Chapter 2

Revisiting agrarian transition

Reflections on long histories and current realities

Henry Bernstein

1. Introduction: some key questions about agrarian transition

Some key questions concerning concepts of agrarian transition and their applications follow:

1   Transition *from* what? Transition *to* what? A subsidiary question here is, how do we know when a transition is complete?
2   Where and when did agrarian transition take place? This question can be addressed exclusively in terms of countries/'national' economies, or framed in world-historical terms of the formation and development of a capitalist world economy and its effects for transition (or lack of it) in different places at different times. A subsidiary question is, how long did various transitions take?
3   How and why? This is the always testing question of cause(s) and mechanism(s). Materialist political economy seeks to explain agrarian transition through class relations and dynamics, contradictions and struggles. Can this be done adequately through an exclusive focus on rural classes: classes of pre-capitalist landed property and peasant farmers, and (emergent) capitalist landed property, agrarian capital and agricultural wage labour, or does it require the consideration of non-rural classes: (emergent) industrial capital and wage labour? There are also important forces that can be active in both the countryside and beyond, in both pre-capitalist conditions and transitions from them, notably merchant capital and states.
4   Why is agrarian transition *incomplete* where and when that is deemed the case? How is agrarian change in conditions of incomplete transition characterised and investigated? To what extent is this a matter, as commonly stated, of the 'persistence' of the peasantry?

68   Henry Bernstein

Of course, these questions interconnect closely. Here I aim to map some of their markers, both theoretical and historical, through ways in which they have been posed and answered.[1] Along the way I have been struck by how much certain historical experiences have influenced, in different ways, conceptions of agrarian transition, whether explicitly or implicitly: those of England (the 'original' transition), the United States and the Soviet Union. India is a compelling instance of the fourth type of question because of its size, importance and diversity – the largest country of the South without a completed agrarian transition? – and because of the rich literature and debates about its agrarian structures and processes of change, including in the recent decades of neoliberal 'reform'. Aspects of this are dealt with in other chapters in this volume by those far more qualified than I am to do so.

2. Transition from what to what?

Pre-capitalist to capitalist agriculture

The 'classic' agrarian transition centres on the development of capitalist agriculture which is held to drive the development of the productive forces. This is usually associated with economies of scale on large farms organised by agrarian capital and employing wage labour, but may also be exemplified by capitalist forms of agricultural petty commodity production (see section 4). Capitalist agriculture emerges from some or other type of pre-capitalist agrarian structure, typically (or stereotypically) 'feudal' in the case of Europe (and Japan). There have also been important debates about forms of 'feudalism' created by colonial rule, notably in parts of Latin America, and of 'semi-feudalism' as the legacy of colonialism elsewhere. For example, the Indian 'mode of production' debate of the 1960s and 1970s was framed by such questions as

> what is agricultural 'capitalism' particularly in an ex-colonial country? How is 'feudalism' and 'semi-feudalism' to be conceptualised? In what way if any do prevalent landlord–tenant relations constrain productive investment? And how do they shape the contours of capitalist accumulation in the post-independence period?
>
> (Patnaik 1990: 2)

The reference to experiences of colonialism is crucial as they (re-) shaped, at different times and in different ways in the history of world capitalism, both 'internal' and 'external' dimensions of the 'initial conditions' of transition, in the countries of the South[2] – those countries where agrarian transitions are often regarded as incomplete until now. It could also be inferred that transition became a question in any meaningful sense in the South only with independence from colonial rule, with its initial conditions shaped by the interactions of (indigenous) pre-capitalist social forms and colonial processes of commodification ('colonial capitalism').

V.K. Ramachandran (2011) points towards conceptions of a 'thwarted', 'stalled' or otherwise incomplete transition to capitalist agriculture – for long a topic of debate in India as in much of the South – in which *combinations* ('articulations') of capitalist and 'pre-capitalist' elements, rather than their mere coexistence, signal, or might even explain, the slow and incomplete nature of transition.

Agriculture to industry

In several seminal works Byres (1991, 1996) clarified three meanings of the agrarian question (AQ) in classical materialism:

1   The challenges confronting socialist and communist parties of alliances with rural classes in countries undergoing a transition to industrial capitalism (notably Engels 1970 on late nineteenth-century France and Germany);[3]
2   The (variant) forms and effects of capitalist development in agriculture or, somewhat differently, 'the development of agriculture in capitalist society' (in the title of the first part of Kautsky 1988);
3   The creation of an accumulation fund for industrialisation which, in its initial stages at least, has to come from some mechanism of net transfer of an agricultural 'surplus'.

These can be summarised as the problematics of politics (AQ1), production (AQ2) and accumulation (AQ3) (Bernstein 1996). The radical extension of the meaning of agrarian transition in Byres is his insistence on AQ3: industrialisation via an accumulation fund from agriculture is central to his notion of successful agrarian transition. In effect this enlarges (and transforms) the question of 'transition to what?' from agriculture to industry. He has applied, explored and elaborated the schema outlined, especially concerning AQ2 and AQ3, through historical analyses of England, the Netherlands, France, Prussia/Germany, the United States, Japan, Korea and Taiwan (see section 2), and considered their

70 Henry Bernstein

implications for countries of the South so far lacking a completed 'agrarian transition' (see also Byres 2003, and sections 2 and 4).[4]

A notable feature of his work is that his formulation of AQ3 can disconnect it, in certain historical circumstances, from the inherited logic of the 'classic' AQ2 as the prior development of capitalist agriculture:

> We can have a form of agrarian transition, a resolution of the agrarian question in our third sense, such that the agrarian question appears to be resolved in neither the Engels nor the Kautsky-Lenin sense. If, however, the agrarian question is so resolved, in this third sense, in such a way that capitalist industrialisation is permitted to proceed, then, *as the social formation comes to be dominated by industry and by the urban bourgeoisie, there ceases to be an agrarian question* with any serious implications. There is no longer an agrarian question in any substantive sense.
>
> (Byres 1991: 12, emphasis added)

This is especially clear in his East Asian cases: Japan (Byres 2003: 188) and Korea and Tawian after 1945 (Byres 2003: 203), and indeed, in his view, the agrarian transition of the United States also departed from the development of capitalist agriculture through the formation of agrarian capital and wage labour (Byres 2003: 187–88).[5]

How do we know when agrarian transition is complete?

Byres (2003) presented statistical data on the sectoral composition of the labour force in a wide range of countries at different times as an approximate means of identifying when their transition was completed or otherwise. Those data are organised by proportions of employment in agriculture (A), industry (I) and services (S). His Table 1 lists 18 'fully industrialised countries': 12 in Western Europe, 4 originally 'settler' countries (the United States, Canada, Australia and New Zealand), Japan and the Soviet Union. From this Byres derives a profile of stages ('eras'): (1) the 'pre-capitalist', where upwards of 80 per cent of labour is employed in farming, to (2) early industrialisation where a typical profile of labour force composition in A/I/S is 50/30/20 per cent, (3) further industrialisation with a typical profile of A/I/S of 30/40/30 per cent and (4) mature industrialisation with ranges in A/I/S of 2 to 12/25 to 38/58 to 72 per cent (derived from Byres 2003, Table 1, and excluding the Soviet Union).

He then uses this schema to consider the 'broad contemporary record of structural change' in four main regions of the contemporary (or recent) South. With the exceptions of Taiwan and the Republic of Korea, on the criterion of proportion of the labour force in industrial employment, none of the countries in those regions have moved beyond early industrialisation; while in most of them the proportion of the labour force in agriculture has fallen, often significantly so, with such 'release' of labour from agriculture absorbed much more by employment in services than in industry. In short, the failure of the countries of the South to complete an agrarian transition is read off from the proportions of their labour force in *industrial* employment. This is the essential marker of their (incomplete) transformations of agriculture (AQ2) even when some of them, especially in Central and South America, and also Southern Africa, show relatively low, and declining, proportions in agricultural employment (IFAD 2011: 256).

Byres's method of comparing *countries at different times*, above all within different phases (as well as locations), of the development of the capitalist world economy abstracts from both how earlier industrialisation changes the conditions of (aspiring) 'latecomers' and the (changing) dynamics of imperialism, including its global divisions of labour. It also suggests a need to consider changes in capitalist industry (and its capital and employment intensity) over the long period he surveys – which might also advise lowering the proportion of total labour force in industrial employment as a threshold (see further later).[6] Very different paths and patterns of agrarian change today are acknowledged by Byres but subsumed under a negative: the failure to complete agrarian transition in the sense of AQ3 which, in effect, covers most places in the history of world capitalism to the present day.

Byres's conception of transition and its applications point towards two further questions. First, do the East Asian experiences indicate the possibility, at least, of the *development of the productive forces in 'peasant' farming* in such instances of industrialisation *without* capitalist farming (*and* without significant peasant differentiation)?[7] Second, is it possible that a capitalist transformation of agriculture can occur, 'classic' agrarian transition (hence 'resolution' of AQ2), *without* leading to full industrialisation ('resolution' of AQ3). Might a sufficiently dramatic decline in agricultural employment without commensurate growth in industrial employment serve as a rough proxy for this? There are some serious candidates for further investigation of this question in particular cases, especially in Latin America.

72 Henry Bernstein

Given Byres's rich comparative history of transition from (pre-capitalist) agriculture to industry, this brief introduction of his ideas has already strayed deep into the terrain of the places and times (and timings) of successful transition, the topic of the next section.

3. Agrarian transition: where and when?

The English transition

The transition from feudalism to capitalism, especially in England, has demonstrated a particular potency because it is generally regarded as the first agrarian transition and was the one most familiar to Marx, the principal basis of his sketch of primitive accumulation (Marx 1976, Part 8). In some ways that transition, and its centrality to continuing debates about the *origins* of capitalism, casts a long shadow over conceptions and investigation of agrarian transition in other times and places. This is not the occasion to rehearse its arguments of theory and evidence, but some points can be made about its continuing legacies.[8]

First, it is worth noting differences of emphasis on the formation of *capitalist landed property* as the hallmark of that original transition, notably by Robert Brenner (1976, in line with his theorisation of 'social property relations'), and on the formation of *agrarian capital*, especially through differentiation of the peasantry, by Byres (2006, 2009) and Heller (2011). In both instances, the principal point is that the emergence and development of capitalist social relations generated the growth of the productive forces in agriculture.

Second, the potency of, and continuing interest in, the 'original' agrarian transition is also due to the common (if again contested) argument that it established the conditions of capitalist industrialisation.

Third, did the decline of feudalism ('feudal mode of production') in England, or Western Europe more generally, necessarily give rise to capitalism? Or might the two processes have been quite discrete or distinct (as argued by Federici 2004)? If so, what are the implications for conceptions of agrarian transition?

This connects with a fourth and further kind of complexity concerning the characterisation of ('pre-capitalist') agrarian structures, their classes and dynamics that provide the (notional) historical starting point or initial conditions, as noted earlier: transition from what? If this is not as straightforward as might once have appeared in debate of the original transition from feudalism to capitalism, then it becomes the more necessary to confront it in considering transition in subsequent places and times of the development of capitalism, not least those shaped by different experiences of colonialism (and indeed by industrial capitalism already established elsewhere).

A fifth kind of issue then concerns how well processes of successful agrarian transition in the past are able to illuminate later (including current) challenges of transition – and the dangers that lurk in some such 'uses of history' (on which see Byres 1996: 418–19). In effect, investigation and analysis of transition can be both *retrospective*, that is in historical debates, and *prospective*, that is aiming to identify the opportunities of, and obstacles to, agrarian transition when and where it has not occurred or is deemed 'incomplete' in some sense or other: when history has not (yet) repeated itself (with whatever variations). The shift from retrospective to prospective, or their combination, is fraught with difficulties for well-known reasons. One is a danger of teleological reasoning, especially perhaps when the prospective is framed as a desirable goal, the object of intent, politics and policy.[9]

'Internal' and 'external' dynamics

Schematically, there are two approaches in Marxist and *marxisant* debate of the origins of capitalism. One locates it in the English (more broadly Western European) transition from feudalism to capitalism, as we have seen, and the other in the emergence of a 'world system' from the fifteenth or sixteenth century. Do these two approaches tend to generate different kinds of questions about the subsequent development of capitalism in other places and times?

Concerning the English transition, both Brenner and Byres apply an 'internalist' problematic, that is one

1 limited to the dynamics and struggles of classes internal to the countryside;
2 in particular, and discrete, social formations;
3 in which agriculture and industry provide the demand for each other's growing mass of commodities (with the supply of food staples the most strategic element in agricultural growth): the development of the home market.

Prima facie, this internalist problematic may be relatively more plausible in the moment and place of the first (English) transition and its (unique) historical circumstances.[10] For Brenner it is also a

74 Henry Bernstein

methodological principle against well-known arguments of the origins and development of capitalism as 'world system' (Brenner 1977). Indeed, once the transition to capitalist agriculture was complete in England (in the sixteenth century, in his account), industrialisation was likewise endogenous: it followed seamlessly some two centuries later, apparently independently of whatever was happening elsewhere in the emerging world economy. By contrast Byres recognises that

> the full picture requires that we note the extent to which the unleashing of the accumulation crucial to capitalist industrialisation, in certain instances depended upon . . . 'external sources of accumulation', or, more precisely 'colonial surplus appropriation' . . . one or other of: access to captive colonial markets, cheap food from colonies, and investible surplus appropriated from colonies.
>
> (Byres 2003: 189, quoting Byres 1996: 423)

The other side of this coin is that 'contemporary developing countries do not, of course, have any such advantage' (Byres 2003).

I would emphasise these observations much more strongly: not only are the 'internal' conditions and prospects of agrarian transition in both senses noted – internal to rural social/class structure and to individual social formations/countries – shaped by their interactions with forces external to the countryside (e.g. industrial, commercial and financial capital) and to national economies (forms of international economic exchange and integration) but those *external forces change over time.*

A more substantive question then for contemporary developing countries that lack the advantage enjoyed by some previous cases of (successful) agrarian transition/industrialisation is how their 'internal dynamics' interact with, and are shaped by, 'external forces' beyond their countrysides and beyond their territorial boundaries. Moreover, those forces have a differential nature, weight and power of determination in the different times, as well as places, of the development of capitalism on a world scale,[11] with crucial (if variant) effects for the mechanisms, duration, rhythms and speed, as well as completion/non-completion of agrarian transition ('resolution' of AQ2, AQ3 or both). In short, investigation of the places and times of successful (and incomplete) transition requires a number of additional 'determinations', in Marx's term, to assess adequately the circumstances of different transitions across the history of capitalism.

To conclude, it is striking that among the historical experiences that Byres considers in some detail, it seems that

1   the only clear cases of *capitalist* transformation of agriculture (AQ2) were the English transition (and perhaps that of the Netherlands) which commenced some five centuries ago, followed by the lagging Prussia and France in the nineteenth century;
2   the United States in the nineteenth century did not entail a capitalist transformation of agriculture in the sense of large-scale agrarian capital and wage labour (AQ2) to industrialise (AQ3);
3   likewise Japan from the late nineteenth century and post-war Korea and Taiwan which were *the only cases of completed transition in the capitalist world in the twentieth century.*

This connects with the subsidiary question here: how long did various transitions take? This requires, of course, decisions about when transition is deemed to have started and finished in the various places where it was completed. Byres's answer to the latter question has been discussed, while answers to the former tend to be more elusive. For example, as observed earlier, should any meaningful notion of transition, and assessment of its prospects, be dated only from the moment of independence from colonial rule in Asia and Africa? Nonetheless, it is evident that European transitions were generally more leisurely enjoying the world historical luxury, as it were, of centuries to complete the capitalist transformation of agriculture and to channel its outcomes into industrialisation. The American and Japanese transitions of the nineteenth century were of relatively shorter duration, while the major twentieth-century transitions (AQ3), both capitalist (Taiwan and Korea after 1945) and state socialist (the Soviet Union), were extremely compressed, a matter of decades.

4. Agrarian transition: how and why?

Byres continues to deploy the internalist problematic of the original English transition in his comparison of agrarian transition(s) from then until now.[12] There are four principal mechanisms of that problematic derived from the English transition.

First is the capitalist transformation of agriculture which Byres replaced with a 'substantive diversity' of paths of agrarian transition which led to industrialisation (AQ3), among his most innovative contributions.

76 Henry Bernstein

Second, dispossession of the peasantry which 'releases' labour for industrialisation is especially close to the heart of debate about the original (English) agrarian transition: where did the (first) industrial proletariat come from? It is a long way from there and then (during an early phase of the emergence of a capitalist world economy) to current conditions of global capitalism, where the magnitude of the reserve army of labour, and the compound crises of its social reproduction, is so central an issue. One index of this, indicated by Byres (2003) and emphasised earlier, is the declining proportion of the labour force employed in agriculture without any commensurate rise in industrial employment.

A third mechanism, especially important for the internalist view and noted earlier, is the development of the home market. This, of course, has tremendous resonance for theories of the development of underdevelopment and dependency, now reprised as 'anti-globalisation', and their advocacy of world market 'de-linking', import-substituting industrialisation 'inner-directed' development, food (and other) 'sovereignty' and so on. At the same time, historical experience problematises this emphasis on the home market, and any implicit view it harbours of industrialisation = home market + exports ('surplus' to domestic demand). This downplays the centrality of international trade to British industrialisation at one end of the historical spectrum, and at the other end export-led industrialisation in the transitions of Taiwan and Korea.

Agricultural 'surplus' and the industrial accumulation fund

This fourth mechanism is the most central dynamic uniting the historical cases that Byres addresses, and also the strongest in a conceptual sense. Whatever the substantive diversity of different paths of transition, they must all produce the same effect to register their success: the transfer of an agrarian surplus for industrialisation. Here we can detect the long shadow of another, less immediately obvious, historical experience, namely that of the Soviet Union, and the model of 'socialist primitive accumulation' of Preobrazhensky (1965), the most explicit formulation of AQ3, whose inspiration Byres acknowledges. Preobrazhensky's concern was how an accumulation fund for industry in the Soviet Union could be achieved from a mostly *peasant* (*vs* capitalist) agriculture – and without the sources of primitive accumulation available to the industrialised capitalist countries from their colonial and other imperialist exactions. This gives the central sense of agrarian transition as transfer or *extraction* of an agricultural surplus for industrialisation, whether agriculture has undergone capitalist transformation *or not*: Byres's interpretation of the East Asian cases, and indeed of the United States (discussed earlier). In these instances, as already noted, the need for AQ2 *qua* transition to capitalist agriculture might disappear altogether.

In theory, an industrial accumulation fund might be derived from agriculture by various mechanisms of 'transfer'/extraction classified roughly (and normatively) as more or less 'virtuous' and 'vicious'. The former includes the 'immanent' (or 'spontaneous') investment of agrarian profits and rents in industry ('productive' investment) – the historical exception? – while the latter centres on coercive transfers, via some or other means of the taxation of agrarian profits and rents, or of peasant farmers, in both instances requiring the agency of a strong ('developmental') state. One should ask here too whether there might be, and have been, significant sources of (early) industrial accumulation other than agriculture, answers to which could embrace merchant capital (in some of its multifarious forms) in particular historical circumstances.[13]

Byres's East Asian cases, together with the proposals of Preobrazhensky's *New Economics*, highlight the preoccupation of agrarian transition as prospective *and* (or hence?) requiring a *political* programme to implement it, the outcomes of which in turn depend on the agency and balance of contending class forces and their consequences for state effectiveness in pursuing that programme.[14] Indeed, a strong state to effect that crucial transfer from agriculture to industry becomes increasingly central as Byres's historical sequence of (successful) agrarian transitions proceeds, and as manifested in the highly 'compressed' transitions of the Soviet Union and post-war Taiwan and Korea.[15]

Also apposite here is the question noted earlier: can capitalist transformation of agriculture, 'classic' agrarian transition ('resolution' of AQ2), occur without leading to full industrialisation ('resolution' of AQ3)? And might this be indicated when the proportion of total labour force employed in agriculture falls beneath 20 per cent, say? This further highlights Byres's central mechanism of the mobilisation (or otherwise) of the agricultural 'surplus' for industrial accumulation, a familiar concern in India with, on the external side, 'surplus drain' from its colonial origins through to, or resumed under, current neoliberal globalisation (Patnaik 2012); and on the 'internal' side, the social and political strength of landlordism and tenancy, and other, often connected ('interlocked'), forms of 'semi-feudal' exploitation of peasants/small farmers (Bhaduri 1973), terms of trade between agriculture and industry, and the (non-)taxation of agricultural profits and rents (Mitra 1977; Byres 1979), or the otherwise spontaneous (virtuous) productive investment

78 Henry Bernstein

of agricultural profits and rents in industry, if highly limited in practice (Lerche forthcoming).

5. Agrarian transition in the south: completed, transcended 'stalled'?

Completed?

Concerning the *prospects* of further agrarian transitions in the South, the 'strongest variant' of Byres's argument, in his term, applies to China and India – 'giant economies' (2003: 209) with vast potential domestic markets which reflect their 'gigantic' demographic profiles. Suffice it to say that China is a very strong candidate for a completed transition despite the proportion of its labour force engaged in agriculture, perhaps around 40 per cent today. Among the key features of the case for a (completed) transition 'with Chinese characteristics' are (1) the miniscule scale of most of its farming, which displays extraordinary labour intensity, to be sure, but combined with very high levels of (external) inputs – irrigation, improved seeds, massive applications of chemical fertiliser – to produce extremely high yields, and (2) the magnitude of 'rural labour beyond the farm' in its industrial and urban economy more generally.[16] By contrast, the application of the transition schema to India, it seems, continues to represent more of a (frustrated) hope rather than an expectation, let alone a prediction of agrarian transition. Otherwise, Byres suggests that the transition thesis remains valid for 'a variety of other economies, in Latin America, Asia and the Middle East: those economies in which industrialisation has made some limited progress, at least' (Byres 2003: 209). To this I would add that, as for China, some might be considered to have completed the transition in the sense of AQ3 when, as advised earlier, the proportion of their total labour force in industrial employment is relaxed as a threshold for 'completion'.[17]

Transcended? ('bypassed'?)

The dominant tendency in agrarian political economy today is an intense focus on neoliberal globalisation: the centrality of corporate agribusiness both 'upstream' and 'downstream' of farming in shaping a new 'global food system', and its effects in subordinating farmers in the South (and the North, in some versions), especially small ('peasant') farmers – hence by extension suppressing agrarian transition understood as any properly national path of development. Key themes include

Revisiting agrarian transition 79

unequal international trade in agricultural commodities; the impact of the speculations of finance capital on the volatility of food prices; imposition of environmentally destructive ways of farming, processing and transporting food, including growing 'chemicalisation' and fossil fuel dependence; the dangers of genetically modified organisms, both seeds and livestock; land grabbing and further dispossession of small farmers, not least to promote the large-scale production of biofuel feedstocks and so on. These contemporary dynamics are often conceptualised as a new wave of primitive accumulation, or 'enclosure' on a world scale, and specifically 'accumulation by dispossession' in David Harvey's term (Harvey 2003) taken up in accounts of global land grabbing. This political economy of a 'new agrarian question' (McMichael 2006) is both radical in the intensity of its opposition to neoliberal globalisation and populist in its celebration of 'peasant resistance' and advocacy of 'the peasant way' (*La Via Campesina*), 'food sovereignty' and the like, as the only viable alternative to corporate agribusiness and its depredations both social and ecological.

This is not the occasion to engage with this tendency and its literatures, which I have done elsewhere (most recently, Bernstein 2014). Rather I want to propose a different thesis about globalisation derived from a recognition, summarised earlier, that the 'classic' agrarian question was (1) the agrarian question of capital (2) within national social formations – and indeed, for Byres, above all the agrarian question of (emergent) industrial capital (and the states that promoted it) centred on the growth of the domestic (national) market. This is, in effect, a 'closed economy' model of transition strongly influenced, one suspects, by the (near) autarchy of Soviet industrialisation in considering the prospects of 'national development' in newly independent Asia and Africa, as much as by the projection of an internalist view of the original English transition.

The alternative thesis proposes that (1) the productive forces of capitalist agriculture and (2) the internationalisation of agricultural production, markets, technologies, finance and so on have now reached a point at which there is *no longer an agrarian question of capital on a world scale*; however, much agrarian transition in its inherited sense might remain unfinished business (stalled) in many (most?) countries of the South. The effect of contemporary 'globalisation' is that

> the intersectoral linkages of agriculture and industry at the core of the ('internalist') problematic of agrarian transition/ industrialisation . . . (are) now mediated by the (differential)

effects of the circuits of international capital and world markets, for each sector in *any* capitalist economy (central or peripheral) . . . modern imperialism has extended the determinants of industrialisation far beyond the prospects of agrarian transition in landscapes inhabited exclusively by [agrarian] classes.

(Bernstein 1996: 42–43)

In effect, the circuits of global economy are now *internalised* in national economies. What makes an economy national – how national economy is constituted and functions – is a familiar and long-debated issue, which itself changes shape historically, so to speak, within the capitalist world economy at different times. My thesis properly requires further exploration and specification, of course, and has sometimes been misunderstood, with reference to two of its components: the end of the agrarian question *for global capital* (e.g. by Goodman and Watts 1997; Patnaik 2011; Moyo *et al.* 2013; Oya 2013), and the possibility – but *not* inevitability – of other sources of industrial accumulation, including foreign investment (Byres 2003; Moyo *et al.* 2013; Oya 2013).

However, the thesis does *not* claim that

1   the (very different) agrarian structures and class dynamics of the countries of the South are determined exclusively, and in the same fashion, by their locations in the global capitalist economy;
2   the end of the agrarian question/agrarian transition for global capital means the end of the development of capitalism in agriculture, in all its substantive diversity, including the (further) development of (indigenous) classes of agrarian capital, nor then of the contradictions of class formation in the countryside and beyond;
3   the current global nature of agriculture does not generate or intensify pressures on the reproduction of many or most small farmers ('peasants'), nor the importance of political responses this generates;
4   trajectories of agrarian change in today's global capitalist economy do not generate new contradictions, or intensify older ones, for example, the ecological contradiction between capital and nature, and the pervasive crises of reproduction of classes of labour in contemporary conditions of employment, of the production and reproduction of the reserve army of labour.[18]

Stalled but dynamic?

In a careful assessment of my thesis of the end of the agrarian question of (global) capital in relation to India during the reform period, Jens Lerche (2013: 400) wrote that

> the conclusion could be that the agrarian question has been 'bypassed', as suggested by Bernstein. However, I would argue that it is preferable to state that only the 'classical' agrarian transition [as formulated by Byres, HB] has been bypassed, as such a formulation allows for a continued investigation into the actual processes of agrarian change that clearly *are* taking place in India.

Indeed, and this takes us back (or forwards!) to grappling with more and less dynamic processes of agrarian change that are taking place today. As always, they require further concrete investigation informed by questions such as

1   what is happening with aggregate agricultural production, and more specifically (labour) productivity in farming (which links with [2]))? How is this affected by (changing) forms of social relations and of the organisation of production in farming? How is this affected by the incorporation of farming in circuits of capital and markets upstream and downstream of farming, both domestic and international (also linking with [2])?

2   in turn, how does this affect the reproduction/welfare of different classes of farmers? Rural classes of labour (linking with [3])? In what ways (if any) does an agricultural 'surplus' contribute, directly and/ or indirectly, to industrial accumulation (and markets for industrial goods)? What sorts of inter-relations between agriculture and industry affect the prospects of farming? Of different classes of farmers and rural classes of labour (linking with [3])?

3   what conditions of exploitation and oppression in the countryside – and in urban sectors/areas, for example through labour migration – inform the political ideas and practices of different classes of farmers and rural classes of labour? What political actions and movements do they generate? How does the analysis by socialist parties of conditions of exploitation and oppression in the countryside inform their programmes, positions and practices concerning agrarian, and related, questions?

82 Henry Bernstein

And we could, and should, add: what kinds of state policies and practices affect the processes outlined and their effects for different classes? These questions are familiar and correspond with the frameworks of agrarian transition proposed by Ramachandran (2011, concerning AQ2) and Byres (concerning AQ3), albeit extending the 'determinations' they focus on beyond the countryside and beyond the national. They inform a number of valuable recent surveys and analyses of agrarian change in India that draw on national data sets, their regional disaggregations and more local (including more qualitative) case studies (inter alios Ramachandran and Rawal 2010; Basole and Basu 2011a; Ramachandran 2011; Basu and Das 2013; Harriss 2013; Lerche 2013, 2014; Reddy and Shaw 2013; see also Shah and Harriss-White 2011; Harriss-White 2012).

Here I offer a final, and fundamental, contention: that the research questions so briefly sketched need not, and should not, be framed with any reference to social relations and dynamics outside capitalism, notably the ('persistent') 'pre-capitalist', as an explanation of stalled transition. This points to the pervasive and highly charged 'peasant question' in considerations of agrarian transition, and of agrarian change more generally.

It is now sometimes noted that an inherited motif of the problematic of the 'classic transition', namely the disappearance of the peasantry in the course of capitalist development (AQ2), has been replaced more recently by claims and debates concerning its persistence in twenty-first century capitalism. On one hand, the 'disappearance' of the peasantry as an intrinsic component of capitalist agrarian transition expressed an *expectation*, or more strongly a *prediction*, attributed in 'stereotypical' fashion to Marx and Lenin by both followers and critics. On the other hand, there are various explanations of 'persistence', a term that itself suggests (pre-capitalist?) continuities. These include a current wave of more and less radical populism, already alluded to, that applauds various scales and forms of peasant 'resistance' to capitalism, including the revival of peasantries (and formation of 'new peasantries' for Ploeg 2008): peasants as 'capital's other', exemplars of an alternative modernity to global capitalism and a world-historical subject capable of transcending it (see further Bernstein 2014).

In the face of the massive literature on these issues of peasant disappearance, persistence and revival ('re-peasantisation'), and the intensity of its contestations, for present purposes I can only take a shortcut, as it were, and invoke Marx's observation, from a different context, that 'frequently the only possible answer is a critique of the question and the only solution is to negate the question' (1973: 127). The question I wish to negate is, 'disappearance or persistence?', which entails dispensing with the term 'peasant' itself and its applications to the contemporary worlds of capitalism. Analytically, I have long proposed to replace notions of peasants with a theorisation of agricultural petty commodity production in capitalism, needed to (re-)frame in contemporary conditions 'the original questions of class formation and class differentiation in agriculture' (Patnaik 1990: 4).[19] There is not the space here to reprise the argument (see Bernstein 2010), other than to note that attention to the tendency to differentiation of petty commodity producers creates a different approach to class formation and dynamics in the countryside than that centred on disappearance or persistence of the peasantry. Thus,

1 emergent capitalist farmers are those able to accumulate productive assets and reproduce themselves as capital on a larger scale, engaging in *expanded reproduction* in farming;
2 petty commodity producers reproduce themselves as capital on the same scale of production, and as labour on the same scale of consumption (and generationally) – simple reproduction;
3 poor or marginal farmers struggle to reproduce themselves as capital, hence to reproduce themselves as labour from their own farming, and are subject to a *simple reproduction squeeze* (Bernstein 1978).

Should poor/marginal farmers be considered farmers (or peasants) at all, or are they better understood as workers, as a particular (and large) formation within 'classes of labour' in the South? Classes of labour comprise 'the growing numbers . . . who now depend – directly *and indirectly* – on the sale of their labour power for their own daily reproduction' (Panitch and Leys 2000: ix, my emphasis). They have to pursue their reproduction in conditions of growing income insecurity (and 'pauperisation') as well as employment insecurity and the downward pressures exerted by the neoliberal erosion of social provision for those in 'standard' wage employment who are shrinking as a proportion of classes of labour in most regions of the South, and in some instances in absolute terms as well (and whose wages often support wider networks of kin, urban and rural). Poor and marginal farmers understood as classes of labour might not be dispossessed of *all* means of reproducing themselves, recalling Lenin's warning against 'too stereotyped an understanding of the theoretical proposition that capitalism requires the free, landless worker' (1964: 181). But nor do most of them possess *sufficient* means to

84 Henry Bernstein

reproduce themselves, which marks the limits of their viability as petty commodity producers.

Like patterns of the commodification of small-scale farming, patterns of differentiation also display massive variation. The *tendency* to differentiation that can be identified theoretically from the contradictory unity of class places in petty commodity production is not – and cannot be – evident in identical *trends*, mechanisms, rhythms or forms of class differentiation everywhere (Bernstein 2010). This is because 'many determinations' (Marx 1973: 101) mediate between the tendency and particular concrete circumstances and local dynamics. Importantly, those determinations include rural–urban connections of both capital and labour: the former what I term '(agrarian) capital beyond the countryside', the latter 'rural labour beyond the farm' supplied not only by fully 'proletarianised' landless rural workers but also by marginal farmers or those too poor to farm as a major component of their livelihood and reproduction (see note 16).

Both categories of labour, which typically have very fluid social boundaries, can be employed locally on the farms of neighbours (capitalist and petty commodity producers), or seasonally in more distant zones of capitalist farming and well-established petty commodity production, sometimes in other countries, or in towns and cities within their countries or, again, internationally. 'Footloose labour' in the resonant term of Jan Breman (1996) is a massive fact of social life in the rural zones of today's South and expresses the ways in which their types of farming and its contributions to reproduction are differentiated by capitalist class dynamics.

In short, poor farmers experience most acutely the contradiction of reproducing themselves as petty commodity producers, as both labour and capital, and may reduce their consumption to extreme levels in order to retain possession of a small piece of land or a cow, to buy seeds, or to repay debts, hence are likely to accept the most arduous, precarious and dangerous work for the lowest wages – 'in the course of the most ferocious economic struggle for existence, the . . . [small farmer] who knows how to starve is the one who is best adapted', as Chayanov (1991: 40) put it in the 1920s.

6. Conclusion

This chapter has taken a more circuitous route than was anticipated, in part due to a desire to interrogate inherited notions of agrarian transition, to locate different experiences of transition in the world history of capitalism and the implications of their interpretations for exploring

Revisiting agrarian transition 85

and understanding contemporary processes of agrarian change. In doing so, it has no doubt attempted to take on too much, hence too schematically, and got too big (and ungainly) while leaving out a great deal. For example, although the centrality of the politics of the agrarian question, whether as 'responses from below' or indeed 'from above', has been signalled, it has been left hanging. Nor have I explored complexities of class analysis indicated by Etienne Balibar who put it this way: in a capitalist world, class relations are '*one determining* structure, covering *all* social practices, without being the *only* one' (as quoted by Therborn 2007: 88, emphases in original). In sum, class relations are *universal but not exclusive* determinations of social practices in capitalism. They intersect and combine with other social differences and divisions of which gender is the most widespread, and which can also include oppressive and exclusionary relations of race and ethnicity, religion and caste.[20]

The challenges to analysis that the diversity and complexity of current agrarian change present cannot be grasped adequately by regarding inherited notions of transition as simply false 'predictions', hence discarding what they offer to inform investigation of current realities, above all concerning class formation, class struggle and how, and how much, accumulation (and what kinds of accumulation) proceeds. In short, much of their approach to framing the central questions of agrarian political economy remains valid, even if some of the answers provided might be found wanting as historical interpretation or applications to contemporary realities or both. Indeed, this is simply to recognise the demand of grasping how capitalism changes across all its spaces from global divisions of labour and flows of capital and commodities, through vastly different national economies to similarly diverse countrysides and agrarian structures.

Notes

1 In particular, resuming a conversation with my long-standing co-worker and friend T. J. (Terry) Byres, in what, it seems, is now dubbed the 'Bernstein–Byres debate' (Oya 2013). The very ambition of Byres's intellectual project casts a strong light on the challenges that notions of agrarian transition present. In using his work as a springboard in this chapter, I am uncomfortable with the violence that my schematic summaries inflict on his many theoretical and empirical subtleties and his careful qualifications, perhaps strengthened in Byres (2003). There is no substitute for reading the original.

2 Utsa Patnaik (1990: 3) noted the 'great variations in the initial socio economic conditions and in the trajectories of subordination among the colonised countries'.

86 Henry Bernstein

3 By extension AQ1 *qua* politics of agrarian transition can be extended to encompass all instances of struggles between contenting classes of 'precapitalist' and capitalist landed property, (emergent) agrarian capital, (emergent) industrial capital, and labour (both peasant and proletarian), typically mediated by states – and especially when agrarian transition, whether as intrinsic objective or (instrumental) condition of industrialisation, is a major state preoccupation and goal.

4 Not least India on which he also made many seminal contributions. Bernstein (1994) provided a tabular summary of Byres's main historical cases, adapted by Akram-Lodhi and Kay (2010) with additional material from Byres (2003) and Bernstein (2010).

5 'Surplus was appropriated not via the wage relation but via price relations' – in sum, the terms of trade version of the agricultural sources of industrial accumulation. Post (2011) provides a different interpretation of the nineteenth-century United States that insists on the capitalist character of its agrarian transition outside the zones of plantation slavery.

6 'Clearly, capitalist industrialisation, to the extent that it is proceeding, is absorbing a significantly smaller share of the labour force than in the past' (Byres 2003: 200). There can be a number of reasons for this.

7 Byres acknowledges this in his East Asian cases; on Japan and Taiwan, see also Karshenas (1996).

8 Note Utsa Patnaik's view that 'the claim that today's developed countries underwent successful agricultural revolution' is 'downright false', the 'myth of successful agricultural revolution in today's advanced countries' (2012: 237–38), and on English agriculture before and during the first industrial revolution, Patnaik (2011: 20–27).

9 In an essay on eighteenth- and nineteenth-century capitalist estate production, Jairus Banaji (2010: 347) observed: 'It is not obvious that there are "national" "paths of transition", and it seems more useful therefore to concentrate on trajectories of accumulation. . . . Whether those were also transitions, and if so, to what exactly, can obviously only be established once we have clear descriptions or reconstructions of the different trajectories themselves.' He concluded: '"Trajectories of accumulation" is a more flexible concept' than 'transition' 'in the sense that the chronological spans are variable, different trajectories can be at work simultaneously, and the outcome is not predetermined' (Banaji 2010: 348). If this is sound advice on doing historical research (and against 'reading history backwards'), it applies all the more to investigation of current dynamics of agrarian change.

10 Albeit vigorously contested by Patnaik (note 8, also Patnaik 2012).

11 For substantive illustration see Bernstein (2010, Chapters 5 and 6).

12 He explains this approach as necessary to establish the diverse paths of his historical case studies (2003: 189), the details of which following an internalist problematic may, however, still be open to question (Bernstein 1996).

13 Banaji (2010) argues against inherited views of merchant capital as engaged solely in secondary and derivative activities in the development of capitalism, hence often seen as predatory. Barbara Harriss-White (2008) has long documented and proposed the 'productive' functions that merchant capital can play in Indian agriculture, summarised in a useful survey essay (Jan and Harriss-White 2012). Basole and Basu (2011b) consider the role of

Revisiting agrarian transition 87

merchant capital in organising informal small-scale manufacturing ('putting-out'), and in a different vein, see Dipankar Gupta's account of 'how merchant producers operate' in India (2009, Chapter 4).

14 Thus pointing towards the politics of the agrarian question (AQ1) more broadly (note 3).

15 Indeed, for Byres the state is the principal (exclusive?) agency 'external' to agrarian class structure in effecting successful transition, presumably on behalf of (emergent) industrial capital against the entrenched powers of 'the agrarian interest' – above all, landed property (and merchant capital) – but also relevant to the highly charged issue of taxation (and oppression) of the peasantry when that constitutes the principal source of extraction by the state of agricultural 'surplus'.

16 According to Li et al. (2012) 50 per cent of farmers in China cultivate only from 0.03 to 0.11 ha of arable land, and less than 3 per cent cultivate more than 0.67 ha. And its official statistics count as farmers 'those formally registered by the government as rural residents', including some '150 million people registered as peasants who work away from home in industry and services . . . and another 150 million who work off-farm near home', many in local industry (Huang et al. 2012, 142). To these observations can be added China's extraordinary rates of economic growth and importance in the global economy – for all the contradictions lurking in them, this would be very surprising for a country yet to complete its transition.

17 Prominent among candidates for successful completion of AQ2 (and AQ3?) is Brazil, surely – an agricultural superpower, with massive corporate agribusiness that is technically and financially sophisticated and active globally. (Brazil also pioneered biofuels in the production of ethanol from sugarcane). A rather different candidate is South Africa, whose 'minerals revolution' (diamonds and gold) in the last third of the nineteenth century, that key moment in modern imperialism, preceded its more generalised transition to capitalist agriculture and to manufacturing industry. One can also note from the South African case how much the growth of its capitalist agriculture from the 1930s to the 1980s was supported by state subsidies – a reverse flow from that at the centre of Byres's agrarian transition (AQ3); substantial direct and indirect subsidies (in infrastructure, including irrigation, 'soft' credit and other 'institutional rents') were also strategic at key moments of the growth of capitalist farming (and agribusiness) in Brazil in the past 60 years. At the same time, of course, South Africa today presents an especially stark instance, among many, of the crises of reproduction of classes of labour.

18 On the contradiction between capital and nature, James O'Connor (1998); see the remarkable project of Jason Moore on capitalism as 'world ecology' (inter alia 2010, 2011, and his analysis of 'Nature and the transition from feudalism to capitalism', 2003), also Tony Weis (2010); on reinserting labour and its reproduction at the centre of agrarian political economy, see Tania Murray Li (2011).

19 Harris-White (2012: 144–45) nicely observes that petty commodity production is 'as modern a kind of capitalism as the corporation' (144–45), '(re) created as an outcome of contradictory processes of capitalism' (128–29).

20 See further Bernstein (2010) on the intrinsic complexities of the economic and political sociology of class, and on the additional determinations

88 Henry Bernstein

needed to move from the former to the latter. To quote again from Harriss-White (2012), who refers to 'relations of caste, gender, ethnicity, religion, locality, and generation reworked as social structures of modern capitalism' (123–24) and observes that 'capitalism hardly ever undresses to its bare essentials, but is almost always clothed in non-class social structures and relations' (125).

References

Akram-Lodhi, H. and C. Kay. 2010. 'Surveying the Agrarian Question (Part 2): Current Debates and Beyond'. *Journal of Peasant Studies* 37 (2): 255–84.

Banaji, J. 2010. *Theory as History. Essays on Modes of Production and Exploitation.* Leiden and Boston: Brill.

Basole, A. and D. Basu. 2011a. 'Relations of Production and Modes of Surplus Extraction in India: Part I – Agriculture'. *Economic and Political Weekly* 46 (14): 41–58.

Basole, A. and D. Basu. 2011b. 'Relations of Production and Modes of Surplus Extraction in India: Part II – "Informal" Industry'. *Economic and Political Weekly* 46 (15): 63–79.

Basu, D. and D. Das. 2013. 'The Maoist Movement in India: Some Political Economy Considerations'. *Journal of Agrarian Change* 13 (3): 365–81.

Bernstein, H. 1978. 'Notes on Capital and Peasantry'. *Review of African Political Economy* 10: 60–73.

Bernstein, H. 1996. 'Agrarian Questions Then and Now'. In H. Bernstein and T. Brass (eds). *Agrarian Questions. Essays in Appreciation of T. J. Byres.* London: Frank Cass.

Bernstein, H. 2010. *Class Dynamics of Agrarian Change.* Halifax, NS: Fernwood.

Bernstein, H. 2014. 'Food Sovereignty via "The Peasant Way": A Sceptical View'. *Journal of Peasant Studies*, accessed on 8 January 2014.

Bhaduri, A. 1973. 'Agricultural Backwardness under Semi-Feudalism'. *The Economic Journal* 83 (329): 120–37.

Breman, J. 1996. *Footloose Labour. Working in India's Informal Economy.* Cambridge: Cambridge University Press.

Brenner, R. 1976. 'Agrarian Class Structure and Economic Development in Pre-industrial Europe'. *Past and Present* 70: 30–75.

Brenner, R. 1977. 'The Origins of Capitalist Development: A Critique of Neo-Smithian Marxism'. *New Left Review* 104: 1–50.

Brenner, R. 2001. 'The Low Countries in the Transition to Capitalism'. *Journal of Agrarian Change* 1 (2): 169–241.

Byres, T. J. 1979. 'Of Neo-Populist Pipe-Dreams: Daedalus in the Third World and the Myth of Urban Bias'. *Journal of Peasant Studies* 6 (2): 210–44.

Byres, T. J. 1991. 'The Agrarian Question and Differing Forms of Capitalist Agrarian Transition: An Essay with Reference to Asia'. In J. Breman and S. Mundle (eds). *Rural Transformation in Asia.* Delhi: Oxford University Press.

Byres, T. J. 1996. *Capitalism from Above and Capitalism from Below: An Essay in Comparative Political Economy*. London: Macmillan.

Byres, T. J. 2003. 'Structural Change, the Agrarian Question and the Possible Impact of Globalisation'. In J. Ghosh and C. P. Chandrasekhar (eds). *Work and Well-Being in the Age of Finance*. New Delhi: Tulika Books.

Byres, T. J. 2006. 'Differentiation of the Peasantry under Feudalism and the Transition to Capitalism: in Defence of Rodney Hilton'. *Journal of Agrarian Change* 6 (1): 17–68.

Byres, T. J. 2009. 'The Landlord Class, Peasant Differentiation, Class Struggle and the Transition to Capitalism: England, France and Prussia Compared'. *Journal of Peasant Studies* 36 (1): 33–54.

Chayanov, A. V. 1991. *The Theory of Peasant Co-Operatives*. London: I. B. Tauris.

Engels, F. 1970. 'The Peasant Question in France and Germany'. In K. Marx and F. Engels (eds). *Selected Works*. Moscow: Progress Publishers.

Federici, S. 2004. *Caliban and the Witch: Women, the Body and Primitive Accumulation*. New York: Autonomedia.

Friedmann, H. 1980. 'Household Production and the National Economy: Concepts for the Analysis of Agrarian Formations'. *Journal of Peasant Studies* 7 (2): 158–84.

Gibbon, P. and M. Neocosmos. 1985. 'Some Problems in the Political Economy of "African Socialism"'. In H. Bernstein and B. K. Campbell (eds). *Contradictions of Accumulation in Africa. Studies in Economy and State*. Beverly Hills, CA: Sage Publications.

Goodman, D. and M. Watts. 1997. 'Agrarian Questions: Global Appetite, Local Metabolism: Nature, Culture, and Industry in *Fin-de-siècle* Agro-food Systems'. In D. Goodman, and M. Watts (eds). *Globalizing Food: Agrarian Questions and Global Restructuring*, London: Routledge, pp. 1–32.

Gupta, D. 2009. *The Caged Phoenix. Can India Fly?* New Delhi: Penguin/Viking.

Harriss, J. 2013. 'Does "Landlordism" Still Matter? Reflections on Agrarian Change in India'. *Journal of Agrarian Change* 13 (3): 351–64.

Harriss-White, B. 2008. *Rural Commercial Capital. Agricultural Markets in West Bengal*. New Delhi: Oxford University Press.

Harriss-White, B. 2012. 'Capitalism and the Common Man: Peasants and Petty Production in Africa and South Asia'. *Agrarian South* 1 (2): 109–60.

Harvey, D. 2003. *The New Imperialism*. Oxford: Oxford University Press.

Heller, H. 2011. *The Birth of Capitalism. A Twenty-First Century Perspective*. London: Pluto.

Huang, P. C. C., G. Yuan and Y. Peng. 2012. 'Capitalisation without Proletarianisation in China's Agricultural Development'. *Modern China* 38 (2): 139–73.

IFAD. 2011. *Rural Poverty Report 2001. New Realities, New Challenges: New Opportunities for Tomorrow's Generation*. Rome: IFAD.

Jan, M. A. and B. Harriss-White. 2012. 'The Three Roles of Agricultural Markets: A Review of Ideas about Agricultural Commodity Markets in India'. *Economic and Political Weekly* 47 (52): 39–52.

90 Henry Bernstein

Karshenas, M. 1996. 'Dynamic Economies and the Critique of Urban Bias'. In H. Bernstein and T. Brass (eds). *Agrarian Questions. Essays in Appreciation of T. J. Byres*. London: Frank Cass.

Kautsky, Karl. 1988. *The Agrarian Question*. 2 volumes. London: Zwan Publications. First published in 1899 in German.

Lenin, V. I. 1964. *The Development of Capitalism in Russia. The Process of the Formation of a Home Market for Large-Scale Industry*. In *Collected Works*, vol. 3. Moscow: Progress Publishers.

Lerche, J. 2013. 'The Agrarian Question in Neoliberal India: Agrarian Transition Bypassed?'. *Journal of Agrarian Change* 13 (3): 382–404.

Lerche, J. 2014. 'Regional Patterns of Agrarian Accumulation in India'. In B. Harriss-White and J. Heyer (eds). *Indian Capitalism in Development*. London: Routledge.

Li, T. M. 2011. 'Centering Labor in the Land Grab Debate'. *Journal of Peasant Studies* 38 (2): 281–98.

Li, Xaoyun, Qi Gubo, Tang Lixia, Zhao Lixia, Jin Leshan, Guo Zhenfang and Wu Jin. 2012. *Agricultural Development in China and Africa. A Comparative Analysis*. London: Routledge.

Mamdani, M. 1987. 'Extreme but Not Exceptional: Towards an Analysis of the Agrarian Question in Uganda'. *Journal of Peasant Studies* 14 (2): 191–225.

Marx, K. 1973. *Grundrisse*. Harmondsworth: Penguin Books.

Marx, K. 1976. *Capital*, vol. 1. Harmondsworth: Penguin Books.

McMichael, P. 2006. 'Reframing Development: Global Peasant Movements and the New Agrarian Question'. *Canadian Journal of Development Studies* 27 (4): 471–83.

Mitra, A. 1977. *Terms of Trade and Class Relations*. London: Frank Cass.

Moore, J. W. 2003. 'Nature and the Transition from Feudalism to Capitalism'. *Review* 26 (2): 97–172.

Moore, J. W. 2010. 'The End of the Road? Agricultural Revolutions in the Capitalist World-Ecology, 1450–2010'. *Journal of Agrarian Change* 10 (3): 389–413.

Moore, J. W. 2011. 'Transcending the Metabolic Rift: A Theory of Crises in the Capitalist World-Ecology'. *Journal of Peasant Studies* 38 (1): 1–46.

Moyo, S., P. Jha and P. Yeros. 2013. 'The Classical Agrarian Question: Myth, Reality and Relevance Today'. *Agrarian South* 2 (1): 93–119.

O'Connor, J. 1998. *Natural Causes. Essays in Ecological Marxism*. New York: Guilford Press.

Oya, C. 2013. 'The Land Rush and Classic Agrarian Questions of Capital and Labour: A Systematic Scoping Review of the Socioeconomic Impact of Land Grabs in Africa'. *Third World Quarterly* 34 (9): 1532–57.

Panitch, L. and C. Leys. 2000. 'Preface'. In L. Panitch and C. Leys (eds). *The Socialist Register 2001*. London: Merlin Press.

Patnaik, U. 1976. 'Class Differentiation within the Peasantry: An Approach to Analysis of Indian Agriculture'. *Economic and Political Weekly* 11 (39): A82–101.

Patnaik, U. 1990. 'Introduction'. In U. Patnaik (ed.). *Agrarian Relations and Accumulation: The 'Mode of Production' Debate in India*. Delhi: Oxford University Press, pp. 1–10.

Patnaik, U. 2011. 'The Agrarian Question in the Neoliberal Era'. In U. Patnaik and S. Moyo (eds). *The Agrarian Question in the Neoliberal Era. Primitive Accumulation and the Peasantry*. Dar es Salaam: Pambazuka Press.

Patnaik, U. 2012. 'Some Aspects of the Contemporary Agrarian Question'. *Agrarian South* 1 (3): 233–54.

Ploeg, J. D. van der. 2008. *The New Peasantries. Struggles for Autonomy and Sustainability in an Era of Empire and Globalisation*. London: Earthscan.

Post, Charles. 2011. *The American Road to Capitalism: Studies in Class Structure, Economic Development and Political Conflict, 1620–1877*. Leiden and Boston: Brill.

Preobrazhensky, E. 1965. *The New Economics*. Oxford: Clarendon Press.

Ramachandran, A. K. 2011. 'The State of Agrarian Relations in India Today'. *The Marxist* 27 (1–2): 51–89.

Ramachandran, V. K. and V. Rawal. 2010. 'The Impact of Liberalisation and Globalisation on India's Agrarian Economy'. *Global Labour Journal* 1 (1): 56–91.

Reddy, B. and A. Shaw. 2013. '"New Landlords". "Too Poor to Farm" or "Too Busy to Farm"'? *Economic and Political Weekly* 48 (38): 65–69.

Shah, A. and B. Harriss-White. 2011. 'Resurrecting Scholarship on Agrarian Transformations'. *Economic and Political Weekly* 46 (39): 13–18.

Therborn, G. 2007. 'After Dialectics. Radical Social Theory in a Post-Communist World'. *New Left Review* (ns) 43: 63–114.

Weis, T. 2010. 'The Accelerating Biophysical Contradictions of Industrial Capitalist Agriculture'. *Journal of Agrarian Change* 10 (3): 315–41.

Chapter 3

Contours of the agrarian question

Towards political question of 'the peasantry' in contemporary India

D. Narasimha Reddy

1. Introduction

For almost half a century now, the 'agrarian question' has been one of the extensively researched and debated areas in the political economy, as could be evidenced from a number of meticulously documented reviews of the same from time to time (e.g. Thorner 1982; Patnaik 1990; Byres 1991, 1995, 1996, 1999; Akram-Lodhi and Kay 2010). Yet the results of the debate is more frustrating largely because the diversity of conditions across space and the dynamic changes over time are too wide to fit into any linear notions of change. It is especially so when it comes to the question of peasantry in contemporary social formations in the developing world. The resulting disaffection may force some to abandon the analysis as inappropriate (Chatterjee 2008) in the context of rapid structural changes in developing countries of the globalised world. Nonetheless, the debate does indicate that the analytical framework of the agrarian question in its dynamic sense still holds the promise of 'puzzle solving' rather than throwing up merely more puzzles. This chapter is a modest attempt to review briefly the changing contours of the analytical debate on the agrarian question and to locate the peasant question in contemporary Asia, with a focus on India.[1] It is essentially teleological in nature, though it draws heavily from the contributions like that of Henry Bernstein who are, by and large, averse to such a method. Since it is essentially in the form of a simplified review, the contents are bound to be too familiar. The chapter begins with the basic aspects of the agrarian question and draws attention to the changing nature of priority bestowed on these aspects with the changing phases of the debates on the agrarian question. It ends with the review of the changes in the agrarian relations (which subsumes the peasantry question) in contemporary India.

Before reviewing the 'aspects' or 'meanings' of the agrarian question, it would be helpful to begin with a clarificatory statement. Marx's account of the agrarian question deals with 'primitive accumulation' in England that dispossessed yeomen peasantry through state-supported predatory enclosures by landlords, which created capitalist tenant-farmers and wage labourers, and the development of capitalism in agriculture. Marx's model of development of capitalism in agriculture was the *classic* agrarian question but 'was soon subject to various, and increasing, theoretical, historical, and political complexities and tensions' (Bernstein 2006). It is in the analysis of the development of capitalism in agriculture elsewhere like Prussia, Russia and America earlier, and in developing countries later, that the agrarian question acquires different meanings and shifting focus. It is the seminal work of Byres (1991) that identified several different meanings of the agrarian question in classic Marxism, but the task of streamlining these aspects was left to Bernstein (1996), and these efforts have brought considerable clarity to the limitations and the potential of the agrarian question as a framework of analysis of the contemporary agrarian context.

2. Aspects of agrarian question

There are three aspects[2] or meanings of agrarian question as discerned by Byres (1991) and elaborated by Bernstein (1996). The first aspect concerns the other European countries where, unlike the classic case of England, the agrarian question is traced, paradoxically, not to the development of capitalism in agriculture but as to how the development of industrial capitalism and the industrial working class could form a class along with the peasantry. Here, it was a political concern which prompted investigation of the agrarian question in terms of the industrial working class looking for alliances with peasantries in countries where it was still a large social force. 'Byres took Engels' *The Peasant Question in France and Germany* (1894) as the key focus of this "explicitly political" formulation of the agrarian question' by adding the facts that industrialisation in mainland Europe was not consequent on the development of capitalism in agriculture as a source of accumulation for industrial development as in England, and that the development of industrial capital in mainland Europe could stimulate the peasantries to join forces for struggles for social transformation (Bernstein 1996). This proposition has come to be known as the *political* aspect of the agrarian question 1 (AQ1) with the origins associated with Engels (1894) (Bernstein 1996).

The second aspect of the agrarian question (AQ2) is concerned with the explicit development of capitalism in agriculture. This dimension

94 D. Narasimha Reddy

of the agrarian question is associated with Kautsky's *The Agrarian Question* (1899) and Lenin's *The Development of Capitalism in Russia* (1899). Kautsky's engagement was on the explanation of the differences between development of capitalism in agriculture and industry, while Lenin's concern was to demonstrate that capitalism could be and actually was developing in Russia, including in agriculture. This aspect of the agrarian question has come to be known as the 'production' dimension or agrarian question 2 (AQ2) (Bernstein 1996). The third aspect of the agrarian question has its origin to Preobrazhensky's *New Economics* (1926) concerned with the primary accumulation for socialist industrialisation following the Russian Revolution. The issue was one of transfer of 'surplus' from a peasant agriculture to industrialisation. Byres paid special attention to this dimension considering this as central to the agrarian question, and rechristened the process of transfer of surpluses from agriculture to capitalist industrial development as 'agrarian transition'. This dimension of agrarian question has come to be known as the 'accumulation' aspect or agrarian question 3 (AQ3) (Bernstein 1996).

In identifying the three aspects of the agrarian question, there is no assumption of their exclusivity. On the contrary, there is a clear awareness of their interdependence, especially between AQ2, in analysing the development of capitalism in agriculture and characterisation of the nature of the capitalism, and AQ1 in assessing the nature of class relations and the political strategies in mobilising the exploited for struggle. One can argue, as some have done with justification, that appropriate characterisation of mode of production is 'an issue of politics because its resolution determines their strategy and tactics; the questions of identifying who is the "enemy"; who to form alliance with; and how to progress the struggle' (Shah 2013). However, for the purpose of this analysis 'the production' (AQ2) and 'the political' (AQ1) are treated separately for two reasons. One, unlike in the classical case of Kautsky and Lenin or unlike in the 1960s' and 1970s' debate in India when the proof of existence of capitalism in agriculture was itself an important aspect of the agrarian question, in the contemporary context especially since the onset of the present economic globalisation, the existence of capitalism per se may not be any longer in question. Second, it is the existence nature of capitalism, which is changing, that becomes critical for the resolution of the agrarian question politically.

The main objective of restating these three dimensions is to track the debates on the agrarian question in the past 50 years with the help of the framework of these dimensions and to locate the contemporary 'peasant question' in the analytical space of the agrarian question. *Over the years, the shifts in the agrarian debate are such that on some of the aspects enumerated earlier, there is a tendency towards settled conclusions, while on others, there is no such consensus.* The attempt here is to run through the debates under each one of these three aspects and to identify as to which aspect is central in the contemporary context of countries where large peasantries survive. We shall begin with the second aspect (AQ2), which is about the development of capitalism in agriculture, then move on to the third aspect (AQ3), which is on agrarian transition through accumulation from agriculture for the development of industrial capitalism, and then turn to the first aspect (AQ1), namely the political dimension by contextualising the state of contemporary peasantry.

3. Agrarian question and the development of capitalism in agriculture

For quite some time, development of capitalism in agriculture (AQ2) was an aspect widely debated across all the developing countries. Of all the contexts, perhaps, the debate on the 'modes of production in Indian agriculture' during the 1960s and 1970s was the one that had drawn the participation of the largest number of Marxist scholars from India and abroad. Though their contributions raised wide-ranging issues, including political aspects, the core of the debate was on the development of capitalism in Indian agriculture. There is no attempt here to review this extensive literature. We draw here from the major findings of this first phase of the debate in the 1960s and 1970s based on an earlier comprehensive review (Thorner 1982, in parts), and from some of the recent papers revisiting the issue with the hope of 'resurrecting scholarship on agrarian transformation' (Shah and Harriss-White 2011). Though the debate included proponents of capitalism, pre-capitalism, semi-feudalism, colonial and post-colonial modes, there did emerge by the early 1980s certain broad agreement that capitalism dominated Indian agriculture as it had already been seen to dominate industry, though the capitalism that was developing in India was not the classical capitalism subject to the Marxist laws of motion, since India's capitalism had emerged in a particular colonial setting. Growth of capitalist farming in India was accompanied by the transformation in the relations of production and forms of exploitation which was not the same as in the classical capitalist development elsewhere. Servitude, bonded labour and unfree labour had largely declined, and farming by employing wage labour became the main form of surplus extraction. Yet there persisted master–servant types of behaviour, extra economic constraints and usury.

96 D. Narasimha Reddy

There were still areas where feudal and semi-feudal relations of production persisted (Thorner 1982). The recent stock taking on the progress in the development of capitalism in Indian agriculture shows there were important structural changes in the wake of globalisation (Lerche *et al.* 2013). There has been a steep decline in the share of agriculture in the national product and also decline in the labour force in agriculture. By the middle of the last decade, the share of small and marginal farms reached about 85 per cent, and marginal farmers alone with an average size of less than 1 ha accounted for 63 per cent of holdings. There has been growth of productive forces and growth in agricultural production, but unevenness has aggravated regional differences. Under the neoliberal reforms, public investment in agriculture and subsidies to the farming experienced decline. The penetration of capital and the spread of market forces under the spell of globalisation have brought Indian agriculture increasingly into the fold of the present imperial capitalist expansion.

There was a certain convergence between Marxists who held different positions on development of capitalism in agriculture. These include Marxists who insisted on the internal development of capitalism in agriculture based on their findings on the indicators of increasing employment of wage labour and reinvestment of surpluses in developing productive forces in agriculture (Patnaik 1990); those Marxists who insisted on the entry of capitalism in agriculture as a part of the process of colonial mode of production (Banaji 1972; Frank 1973); and those Marxists who theorised on semi-feudal and semi-colonial relations of production since capitalism in India entered at the imperialist phase without any internal transformation (Rao 1984). There is yet another major intervention on the nature of post-colonial capitalism in the era of globalisation, which shows the spread and morphing of productive forces and production relations that subserve the imperial interests (Sanyal and Bhattacharyya 2009). It explains the division of the entire economy into the 'accumulative economy', which functions through normal capitalist accumulation, and the 'need economy' outside the circuits of capital proper. The post-colonial economies continue to operate through specific forms of 'primitive accumulation' which is a permanent rather than an initial (as in Marx) feature of capitalism. Much of the need economy is resident in self-employment in agriculture. Thus, the existence of exploitative exclusion is a part of the existing form of post-colonial capitalism, and there is no question of any further 'transition' to capitalism as conceived in the agrarian question. All these contributions converge that there is capitalist development in Indian

Contours of the agrarian question   97

agriculture, but the basic difference arises on the nature of capitalism in agriculture. Here too, they all agree, and there is inconvertible evidence as well, that capitalism in Indian agriculture is not, and will not be, the same as the classic capitalist transition in the English or European agriculture. A recent review of agrarian question concludes that there exists capitalism in Indian agriculture, but the development varies based on different regional class relations (Shah and Harriss-White 2011). Thus, the agrarian question, as a question of development of capitalism in Indian agriculture (certainly elsewhere too), is a resolved question. But what is to be resolved relates to the specification of widely varying agrarian relations that have implications for political action which elevates it into the other agrarian question, namely AQ1. We shall come back to it after examining AQ3.

4. Agrarian question and the development of capitalist industrialisation through agrarian surplus

We shall now turn to the third proposition of agrarian question (AQ3) to which Byres (1991) attached considerable importance and formulated it as the agrarian transition, meaning the role of agriculture in capitalist industrialisation 'with or without the full development of capitalism in agriculture'.

Byres begins by what he calls as a 'barest outline that might connect with analysis of contemporary Asia'. Aware of substantial diversity, he is, nonetheless, optimistic that the history of successful transitions does not exhaust the possibilities in contemporary circumstances and hopes that there may be yet other paths. He discerns six paths of transition by adding three to the already familiar three. Briefly these six paths are:

1   The English Path: This is the classical path wherein the transition takes place in the shift of land from feudal landlords to capitalist tenants, who, by employing wage labour, facilitate accumulation from agriculture, which serves as a source of capitalist industrial development.
2   The Prussian Path: This is referred to as 'capitalism from above', since the feudal landowners, by undertaking investments in agriculture, reduce peasants into wage labourers, while appropriated surpluses serve as the source of capital for industrial development.
3   The American Path: This is described as 'capitalism from below', since the petty commodity producers, the peasants, under state

98 D. Narasimha Reddy

protection, emerge as those producing for profit and reinvestment in the development of capitalist agriculture, which also serves as the source of investment for the market and the industry.

4   The French Path: In this case, serfdom disappears because of the class struggle and peasant resistance prevails against the enclosure type of development. French peasantry survives side by side with capitalist transformation in the northern parts. But there is no evidence of the contribution of agricultural surplus to industrial development. The emphasis is on the 'transition from below'.

5   The Japanese Path: Following the Meiji restoration, the tenants, in this case were exploited by landlords through high rents and the state acted as the main agency of accumulation through taxation of agriculture for industrial investment.

6   The Taiwanese and South Korean Path: Land reforms of the 1940s made peasants free from rents; but through ruthless state taxation, primary accumulation was carried on for industrialisation.

While trying to apply these alternative paths to the Asian context, Byres rules out the English Path, since nowhere in Asia is there any sign of such a possibility of the emergence of the landlord class. He rejects the relevance of the Japanese Path, which was uniquely characterised by its landlord class. The Taiwanese–South Korean Path was influenced by Japanese colonialism, which produced its own image of the landlord class that has no parallels in other Asian countries. While studying other Asian countries, specifically India, Byres recognises pockets of successful capitalist transformation in the North-West and elsewhere, but predominantly, this transformation accrued through the peasant route, that is capitalism from below. Such transition could come through peasant struggles and action against 'landlords'. Byres expects a variety of positive actions in favour of the peasants by the Indian state too. Like the French example, he suggests that capitalist transformation in agriculture may spread slowly. According to him, 'It is perfectly conceivable that non-capitalist forms will persist in the countryside in large parts of the Indian social formation for a long time to come.'

In spite of his inspiring observation on the need for 'struggles and action against landlords', Byres's (1991) search for alternative paths of transition for Asian countries in general, and India in particular, ends up with an open question rather than an answer, because of certain self-imposed limitations. The first limitation is the sense in which 'AQ' is used, that is seeing the process of capitalist transition as a process of agriculture serving as a source of primary accumulation through either rents

Contours of the agrarian question 99

or taxes or adverse terms of trade. Byres's view gives an impression as if that agrarian transition was merely a process of primary accumulation for industrialisation, and once the social formation comes to be dominated by industrial and urban bourgeoisie, 'there ceases to be an agrarian question with any serious implications' (Byres 1991: 12). In the analysis of Bernstein (1996), the AQ gets divided into AQ of capital (AQ2 and AQ3) and AQ of labour (AQ1). The capital question according to him, is resolved through the inflow of international capital into developing countries. And what remains is the labour question (AQ1) that remains to be resolved within the national boundaries. Utsa Patnaik, in her self-introspective assessment of the 'modes of production debate in India', provides a very incisive explanation as to what is wrong with a post-colonial country like India expecting to accumulate for industry from the already-ruined and retarded agricultural sector (Patnaik 1990). Here it would be sufficient just to summarise her explanation. First, the trajectory of development of an ex-colonial country like India will not be the same as that of the 'Western' capitalist countries. Second, there is a qualitative break between colonial and post-colonial production relations relating to accumulation. Even as the colonial revenue-cum-rent pauperised the peasantry through forced 'commerce', the surplus transferred abroad and invested in industry sparked off industrialisation there and left behind only retardation in the colonies. Third, the task of domestic primary accumulation in countries like India is far higher than that in others in the absence of an external sector, as in the case of capitalist countries. Finally, the agriculture–industry linkage has to be conceptualised in a radically different manner today. The task of the home market is much more important than primitive accumulation. Though it might have had relevance in many countries in Europe, the post-colonial experience of most of the developing countries like India hardly suggests the possibility of accumulation of agricultural surpluses as the basis of industrial investment, the kind of transition conceived under AQ3. It is this fact that prompted some to argue that there are only two (AQ1 and AQ2) aspects, not three, to the agrarian question (Lerche 2013).

5. Agrarian question and politics of agrarian classes, mobilisation and struggles

With two of the three aspects of the agrarian question, namely the development of capitalism in agriculture associated with the work of Kautsky and Lenin (AQ2) and the transition to capitalist industrialisation through surpluses from agriculture associated with the work

100 D. Narasimha Reddy

of Preobrazensky (AQ3), seen as settled questions,[3] the third aspect, namely political dimension of agrarian question (AQ1), remains a live and challenging puzzle. Since the nature of capitalism in the agrarian periphery, as much as in its imperial whole, has been subject to change, more so since the beginning of globalisation, the nature of agrarian relations in the periphery is bound to reflect the external neoliberal influences as much as the internal historical specificities. Nonetheless, the complexity and gravity of the centrality of agrarian relations in a social formation are bound to be influenced by the magnitude of the presence of the peasantry. Therefore, in the politics of agrarian question, existence of peasantry becomes central. Unlike certain misleading notions that resolving the agrarian question implies 'disappearing peasantries', the politics of agrarian question is very much about the existence of peasantry.

Though there has been a general decline in the presence of the peasantry across the world, there are regions where they have a substantial presence, and the issue of 'politics' of agrarian question as the question of peasantry continues to be critical. In an insightful article Bernstein (2001) clears the misconstrued notion of associating Marxian analysis of development of capitalism in agriculture with the 'vanishing peasantries' and shows how though there are only three regions with substantial dominance of peasantry, they do matter much. Bernstein (2001) explains the historical context in which Marx was referring to peasantry as 'anachronistic' and 'backward'. For Marx or Classic Marxism, the peasantry was emblematic of the world's past, past represented by feudal, autocratic and parasitic land control, with the peasant denied of advantages of scale, ability to develop productive forces and the technological division of labour. It is characterised by materialist and social backwardness that generates reactionary culture and politics, localism and stagnation that creates 'a hermetic cultural space' of custom of 'rural idiocy' and the small scale that contests the project of social ownership and production vested in the proletariat. However, with the spread of capitalism, the constitution and reproduction of peasantries could be seen through the social relations, the dynamics of accumulation and division of labour, and could be analysed within the theoretical categories and methods of Marx and other classical Marxists without the assumptions of 'backwardness' and 'anachronism'. He takes issues with Hobsbawm who dismissively declared: 'Only three regions of the globe remained essentially dominated by their villages and fields: sub-Saharan Africa, South and Continental South-east Asia, and China' (Hobsbawm 1994, quoted in Bernstein 2001), implying it was only small

Contours of the agrarian question 101

minority and therefore one could take it as signalling the death of peasantry. It was left to Bernstein (2001: 25) to point out that ' "admittedly" these regions of "peasant dominance" comprised half the world's population in the 1990s. The "death of the peasantry" is thus somewhat exaggerated'. Even in 2005, about 46 per cent of the world's population lived in rural areas and the largest concentration was in Asia, especially India, China, Bangladesh, Indonesia and Pakistan which together accounted for about two-thirds of world's rural population (Proctor and Lucchesi 2012). India with a rural population of 842 million, more than that of China (725 million), has the world's largest proportion of rural population and would remain so even by 2030. Though agricultural dependence of rural population is declining, it is still likely to be an important source of livelihood, security, social status and self-respect for substantial proportion of especially poor peasants. With it, the peasant question and therefore the land question are likely to be dominant within the politics of agrarian question in these regions.

Bernstein (2001) goes on to trace the trajectory of the peasantry in the capitalist era till the recent globalisation phase. A brief summary of the same is presented here as a cursory analysis of the peasantry in the post-colonial period. By the end of colonial era, social formations in the imperialist periphery were capitalist in terms of production relations in the historical sense. Majority of peasants in Africa and Asia could be seen as petty commodity producers within capitalism. However, class differentiation of 'peasants' as a tendency as in the case of other petty commodity producers acquires certain distinctive complexities and contradictions. First, peasants today are not exclusively engaged in farming but combine agricultural production with a range of other economic activities. There does exist differentiation as 'poor peasants' with survival strategies into wage labour and other petty activities, 'middle peasants' with diversification of sources of income and the 'rich peasants' with diversified accumulation strategies ranging from crop trading, money lending, rural transport, agricultural machinery renting, village shops and bars. Second, rural labour markets become pervasive and most of the middle and rich peasants depend upon hired labour. The class lines may not be clearly drawn between buyers and sellers of labour, showing some complications like some small and middle peasants selling as well as hiring labour, and with the boundaries between poor peasant and rural proletariat blurred. Third, if poor peasantry is part of the reserve army of labour for the rich and middle peasants, then all classes of peasantry are likely to have links of different kinds with the urban centres. In the era of globalisation poor peasants are experiencing simple

102   D. Narasimha Reddy

reproduction squeeze but there is no uniform linear definitive 'demise of peasantry'. Immiserisation of peasantry and pressure on industrial and urban employment may result in 're-peasantisation' in some instances. One manifestation is the growing number of the reserve army of labour that straddle the city and countryside in their pursuit of means of livelihood in which informal self-and-wage employment may be a major part. The peasant struggles could take several forms, of which two are more visible. One form is the mobilisation of agricultural workers and poor peasants against violence of landed property, agrarian capital and the state. This includes fighting against all forms of 'tied' labour, relations based on personal dependence, debt bondage and patronage of any form of 'deproletarianisation' that denies positive freedom. The second form of struggle is for improving access to land by the landless workers and peasants against the parasitic forms of appropriation by landlordism and merchants' and usurers' capital, state-supported industrial accumulation by the 'bureaucratic capital' or privileged sectors of capitalist farming at the expense of petty producers. However, the results of one part of these struggles of petty producers and workers against capital and state policies and practices which involve redistribution of land are seen as ambiguous. Doubts are expressed about the success of struggles for land since such a success may consolidate petty property in the ways detrimental to workers' interests, when agrarian interest is defined by rich peasant ideology and rich peasant leadership encompassing rural ('peasant' or 'farmer') organisations and movements.

The *aforementioned account could be seen as a classic and succinct restatement of the agrarian question in terms of the political aspect* (AQ1) with the centrality of 'peasantry', whoever they are and wherever they are (Bernstein 2001). But what is puzzling is within a span of five years, Bernstein (2006) turns the whole argument upside down by stating that the 'the agrarian question of capital has been superseded in the current period of globalisation'. If he is referring to the 'capital' as 'accumulation' question (AQ3), one need not be surprised. But what he actually means is the agrarian question with centrality to peasant struggles (AQ1) is superseded! He argues that because of earlier 'peasant wars', 'more or less comprehensive land reforms were pursued for different purposes, by different social and political forces, through more or less radical means, and with various outcomes. Due to land reforms and other dynamics of capitalist restructuring and accumulation in the post-war period, and with all the variation indicated, I suggest that predatory landed property had largely vanished as a significant economic and political force by the end of the 1970s. This was one marker of the end of the agrarian question of

Contours of the agrarian question 103

capital on a world scale'[4] (Bernstein 2006). Further, he goes on, 'Land reforms in the name of "land to the tiller", a slogan shared across a wide ideological spectrum, seldom led to comprehensive redistribution in terms of who received land, except in the most dramatic instances of social revolution' (Bernstein 2006: 452–53). That inequalities persisted, reforms were halted and many deserving did not get access to land could not be considered as arguments against struggles for access to land by the land poor and the landless labour. But Bernstein goes on to conclude: 'At this point, on the verge of considering globalisation and its effects for agrarian question, I advance another argument: that from the end of the 1970s (if not earlier), it makes little sense – at least from the view point of political economy – to refer to "peasants" in the world(s) of contemporary capitalism. In short, if there are *agrarian questions of labour in the 21st century, they have little connection with any "peasant question" constituted in the earlier epochs – the different times and places – of the formation of modern capitalism on a world scale*, or indeed with the "classic" agrarian question of capital' (Bernstein 2006: 453–54, emphasis in original). He argues that the *political economy of agriculture in modern capitalism shows that by the time they attained independence from the colonial rule, most of Asia and Africa are permeated by generalised commodity production. Non-rural and non-indigenous sources of agrarian capital expanded.* Different types of agrarian capital including capitalist and petty commodity production, among different peasantries, are likely to be combined in activities across sectors, including non-agricultural sectors, in simple or expanded reproduction of farming enterprises. The once 'pure' agricultural labour and petty commodity producers diversify, and agriculture is not entirely synonymous with nor reducible to farming but is getting increasingly integrated with other activities. There is no denying of these processes. These are all familiar processes with varying degrees of difference across regions. But these developments in no way would suggest that agrarian question could no longer have the dimension of land relations, peasantry and peasant struggles!

In the light of the drastic pronouncement on the irrelevance of peasant dimension to the twenty-first-century agrarian question (Bernstein 2006), it would be instructive to examine how different the ground realities of agrarian conditions in the context of India are, where it may be difficult to imagine that the agrarian question or the land and peasant question is suspended. It is not surprising that there are several critical responses to the conclusion of Bernstein (2006) that there is no agrarian question of capital, and with that the political question of peasantry as well would have no place in the twenty-first

104 D. Narasimha Reddy

century (e.g. Akram-Lodhi and Kay 2010; Moyo *et al.* 2013; Banerjee 2014). Akram-Lodhi and Kay (2010: 279) argue why the twenty-first-century 'circumstances are precisely the wrong time to doubt the continued salience of the agrarian question, and that in contrast, it has assumed a new relevance, albeit in a variety of forms and in different circumstances. The renewed relevance of the agrarian question is witnessed in postsocialist representation through decollectivisation; semi-proletarianisation and fragmentation without full proletarianisation as livelihood strategies reconfigure; the remarkable stability in the absolute number of peasant farmers over the last 40 years; the continued importance of smallholder food production to rural livelihoods in much of the South'. There may be politics in the United Nations declaring 2014 as the 'International Year of the Peasantry', but there is also substantial peasantry in the world with several questions on their present and future. What follows is a summary account of the evidence brought out by some of the recent studies with specific reference to the agrarian question in India.

Agrarian question and the Indian context

One of the cautions sounded in approaching the agrarian conditions in India relates to the diversity. There are regions which are agriculturally dynamic with better resource endowments and developed productive forces, while many regions still are very backward in terms of resource endowments and resource development, which reflects in the form of diverse forms of agrarian relations. It is necessary for the debates in India to analyse not only the different meanings of the agrarian question but also the plurality of agrarian questions. 'Agrarian capitalism in India may develop not only at different speeds but also in different regionally specific ways, based on different regional class relations' (Lerche *et al.* 2013: 343). Though there has been penetration of capitalism in agriculture, the Indian agriculture has not yet been experiencing classical agrarian transition (Lerche 2013), but only a generalised commodity production with varying degrees of persistence of non-proletarian relations. Though land reforms abolished the *zamindari* and reduced landlordism, more benefits were derived by a class of rich farmers. The benefits of state-supported green revolution, which was scale neutral but not resource neutral, were more in favour of the rich capitalist farmers, resulting in increased inequalities in the countryside. Semi-feudal landlordism has largely gone, except in some parts of the country, but surplus appropriation by the rich

Contours of the agrarian question 105

peasant is not necessarily through rent or interlocked labour markets but by capitalist profit, trading profit and usurious interest – all of which continue in different degrees (Basu and Das 2013; Harriss 2013; Lerche 2013). There has also been increase in land concentration, and the landholdings represent a pear-shaped distribution. The process of class differentiation and polarisation has been considerably slowed down due to the steady incorporation of the Indian economy into global capitalist system. Land may no longer be so important as a basis for status and local power, but still regional power based on land ownership is well established. There has been loosening of ties of dependence on the rich, but the poor peasantry exercise little leverage over political space. Keen observers of rural India point out 'that for all the evidence of the "declining power of caste hierarchies" and reduced significance of the village, landed power remains a major factor in Indian politics and society' (Harriss 2013). For small and marginal farmers, agricultural income alone does not provide the livelihood needs but has to be supplemented from non-agricultural sources (Basole and Basu 2011).

As observed earlier, agrarian relations in India do not reflect clearly the classic capitalist differentiation of the peasantry into capitalist farmers and wage labourers. Yet there exist two complex but clearly differentiated groups, one at the top of the hierarchy who are generally called as rich peasants and the other group of poor peasants and agricultural labourers at the bottom. Development of capitalism in agriculture in the context of land ceilings on the one end and the landlessness or tiny holdings on the other would make the rich peasant to diversify beyond agriculture to accumulate and the poor peasant to seek supplementary sources of livelihood in non-agriculture. Multiple activities at both the ends would make the class configuration purely in terms of agricultural activities more complex. The broader narratives of these two polar groups would make the complexity apparent.

The rural assetless workers are partially proletarianised with a foothold in agriculture but no longer depend entirely on large landowners for employment. They supplement their earnings from petty trade, non-agricultural work and migration (Harriss 2013). The poor Indians in 'rural areas are no longer simple peasants or rural wage labourers, but people who have complex livelihoods involving both forms of work; tilling their small plots of land and now, dependent on migrant wage labour, on working in the rural non-farm economy and on petty commodity production and trade in the capitalist economy to reproduce their household' (Shah and Harriss-White 2011: 17). This group may

106 D. Narasimha Reddy

not be a class of labour but 'classes of labour' pursuing different types of employment and degrees of self-employment (Lerche 2010). Equally complex is the upper end of the classes. The remnants of landlords and rich capitalist peasants found increasing opportunities for accumulation outside agriculture as much as in agriculture, and more so since the neoliberal reforms. Though the extent of land under their control may not have increased much, their diversification into non-farm activities, including speculative trading activities, input dealerships, agricultural machinery leasing, lucrative political positions, 'gate keeping', overwhelms their farming income. In many parts of the country for these dominant peasants land is not so much a source of income as of sociopolitical influence and power. They invest heavily in education to secure positions for their family members through public employment in India and abroad. They hold positions of power in local governments and have axes to grind in public works contracts. They pass as rich peasants often with apparently no visible direct exploitative relations with the poor peasantry and other rural labour.

In this diffused class configuration, the peasant struggles often take the form of struggles for land, employment in non-farm activities, basic securities like food and shelter or just to defend against encroachments on their livelihoods, displacement and dispossession. Land reforms with the core demand of 'land-to-the-tiller' has been one of the major demands of the poor peasantry and the basis for political mobilisation of the peasantry by most of the Left parties. Though most of the Left parties see land reforms and land-to-the-tiller still as an 'unfinished agenda of land reforms in India', there are two types of doubts, expressed, surprisingly both from the Left-leaning intellectuals. The first one questions the very relevance because redistributive land reforms by giving access to small parcels of land would perpetuate petty commodity production that would not give rise to any improvement in the productivity of the land and in the incomes of the poor peasants and labourers (Bernstein 2006; Harris-White 2012). This argument is countered by pointing out that in the wake of shift in the agrarian question of capital, it is not the land productivity that matters but the social justice to the poor peasantry that holds the demand alive and relevant (Lerche 2013).

The second type of doubt is in the nature of scepticism on land reforms with a focus on land-to-the-tiller, and it comes from the interpretation of the estimation of the magnitude of the growing inequality in land ownership (from the Gini coefficient of 0.73 in 1992 to 0.76 in 2003–4), the magnitude of the landless households (42 per cent or

59.6 million) and the potential additional ceiling surplus land of about 15 million acres (Rawal 2008), which if distributed among the landless households comes to about 0.35 acre to each household (Lerche 2013), and thus a land-to-the-tiller reform now would amount to a 'subsistence reform' (Harriss 2013). Nonetheless all these authors are, on the considerations of social justice, strong votaries of redistributive land reforms agenda of political mobilisation of the peasantry. However, Harriss (2013) observes that though there can be strong case for continuing to press for redistributive land reform, 'there is little sign of political mobilisation to make claim for it, even on the part of the CPI (M)'.

On the question of the limitation of the land, it may be necessary to draw attention to the availability of additional land for redistribution. Even the limited success of redistributive land reforms in India shows that the ceiling surplus land is only one of the sources of additional land available, and the other sources include 'cultivable' government land, and the so-called Bhoodan land (which of course was only a small proportion compared to the other two sources). It is the government land that could be brought under plough, if allotted to the poor peasants, which is supposed to be several multiples of ceiling surplus land, but there was never any earnest attempt to properly estimate the extent of such land. Wherever government land was used long with ceiling surplus, there was substantial improvement in the land access to the land poor. For instance, Andhra Pradesh is one state where the land distribution to the rural landless and land poor amounts to about 12.5 per cent of the total cultivated area in the state, and in extent it is only next to West Bengal and Jammu and Kashmir. Of the 12.5 per cent of the area distributed, only about 2.5 per cent is ceiling surplus land, and the rest is mostly government land (Reddy 2013). An official assessment of the potential for redistributive land reforms in the state observes that 'the existing laws and programmes still offer significant scope for linking land with the landless. Government officials with substantial grass-roots and land revenue department experience reveal that concerted efforts to fully and effectively implement existing laws and programme, could substantially enhance the rural poor's access and rights to rural land' (GoAP 2002). Recently, there were efforts in the state to identify and distribute government land to the poor because of political initiative of the previous government (Rajasekhar 2012). According to the state officials involved, one estimate was that about 19 million acres of 'waste' land was available in the state which could be utilised for redistribution (Raju et al. 2006).

6. Globalisation and peasant mobilisation strategies

Globalisation and neoliberal reforms have opened up agriculture, and every agricultural activity has been exposed to the larger global market forces. There is a view that one of the major means of accumulation is through that of the emergence of corporate food system (Wilkinson 2009). In the wake of these changes there have been voices appealing to change in the strategy of agrarian mobilisation. There have emerged global farmers' organisations appealing to the need for mobilisation against the global corporate control over agriculture (Borras *et al.* 2008). There is resonance of these voices at the national level appealing that neoliberal globalisation is fusing local and global markets through domestic and multinational corporations resulting in growing dispossession of peasantry and therefore the peasant emancipator struggles should be against the global capital control on the agricultural input and commodity markets (Basu and Das 2013). Examining the issue in the Indian context, Lerche (2013) observes that there is little evidence on the ground of the main contradiction being between 'the peasantry' and the international corporate food regime and concludes that the doomsday scenario presented by some in terms of 'corporate food regime' has not materialised, at least in the Indian context. On the contrary, the neo-colonial system of exploitation that has penetrated into agriculture makes peasant struggles an important aspect of agrarian question (Moyo *et al.* 2013).

The other issue emerging in the context of overlapping livelihoods across sectors beyond agriculture is on rethinking towards combined struggles of peasant and petty commodity producers (Srivatsava 1989). Lerche (2013) proposes that if agricultural and non-agricultural labour and petty commodity producers are all part of the capitalist class relations, then there is need to consider their struggles as part of a whole, against their exploitation by dominant capitalist classes, as opposed to viewing them as sector specific. There is a growing recognition for the need to think through new strategies, especially in the light of the experience of increasing schism between the ideological stances and clearly laid-down strategies on the one hand and the ground-level practices of most of the Left parties on the other (Shah and Harriss-White 2011; Lerche *et al.* 2013).

Bernstein's global assessment of agrarian question, which prompts him to believe that agrarian question of capital (which includes peasant question) has lost its relevance after 1970s, reminds us that whatever

Contours of the agrarian question   109

that was sought to be done even in terms of redistributive land reforms in India had made a beginning only in the 1970s. The social dimensions of agrarian society in India are too complex to imagine that mere entry of capital would bring about homogenous class differentiation. 'There is no "agrarian question" in India to which the issue of caste, tribe, gender and other forms of social exclusion and discrimination based on hierarchies of status are not intrinsic' and 'no fundamental transformation of conditions of poverty and oppression in Indian society is possible without a resolution of its agrarian question' (Ramachandran 2011: 79). The change in the land use from agriculture to nonagriculture resulting in active speculative market in land, the livelihood concerns of the peasantry in the context of acquisition of vast stretches of land for non-agricultural use (Banerjee 2014), rapid increase in the exploitative tenancy in parts of the country and the tendency towards concentration of land in the lax adherence to the tenets of land reforms legislation would make it untenable to propose that the agrarian question has been bypassed in India. The semi-feudal markers of capitalism at its entry in the imperial phase into Indian agriculture; the caste hierarchies with deep roots of extra economic coercion and exclusion; political dominance of rich farmer lobbies in alliance with the commercial and corporate capital; the state power subordinated to the rural political oligarchies; the exposure to neoliberal market penetration and the globalisation unleashing primitive accumulation and a processes of dispossession; and exposure of the poor peasantry and labour to informal multiple livelihoods are all a combination of historical and contemporary forces under which capitalism with the Indian characteristics has been developing in Indian agriculture. These are as much part of the larger processes of capitalist development of which development of capitalism in agriculture and the struggles of the poor peasantry in alliance with those similarly situated would continue to be part of the agrarian question.

Notes

1 Originally it was conceived as a larger project covering Asia, but that part remains to be completed. I am grateful to the comments of B. B. Mohanty, Judith Heyer, Jens Lerche, Barbara Harris-White and other participants in the International Seminar on Agrarian Transition in India held at Pondicherry University during 28–30 January 2014.
2 There is an attempt to extend it to six (Akram-Lodhi and Kay 2010) and preference for two (Lerche 2013), but here it is confined to (Byres 1991 and Bernstein 1994, 1996) propositions of three.

110 D. Narasimha Reddy

3 That AQ3 is resolved outside the national boundaries through entry of foreign capital is contested by citing continued primitive accumulation in agriculture through money lending, output and input trading (Lerche 2013) and other forms of secondary exploitation (Banerjee 2014). However, these forms of accumulation in agriculture could hardly be taken as the major source of capitalist industrial development. Further, there is no contestation of the development of capitalism in agriculture (AQ2), hence the proposition here that AQ2 and AQ3 may be taken as resolved questions.

4 The irony is that an earnest initiation of even the 'unfinished' agenda of redistributive land reforms in India began only in the 1970s.

References

Akram-Lodhi, A. H. and C. Kay. 2010. 'Surveying the Agrarian Question (Part 2): Current Debates and Beyond'. *The Journal of Peasant Studies* 37 (2): 255–84.

Banaji, J. 1972. 'For a Theory of Colonial Modes of Production'. *Economic and Political Weekly* 7 (52): 2498–502.

Banerjee, Arindam. 2014. 'Peasant Classes, Accumulation and Agrarian Crisis in India: Locating Land Question within the Agrarian Question'. Paper presented at the conference on 'The Return of the Land Question: Dispossession, Livelihoods, and Contestation in India's Capitalist Transition', coorganised by the Faculty of Arts and the Australia India Institute, University of Melbourne, the Institute of Development Studies, Kolkata, and the Indian Institute of Management, Kolkatta (IDSK, 4–6 March 2014).

Basole, A. and D. Basu. 2011. 'Relations of Production and Modes of Surplus Extraction in India: Part I – Agriculture'. *Economic and Political Weekly* 46 (14): 41–58.

Basu, Deepankar and Debarshi Das. 2013. 'The Maoist Movement in India: Some Political Economy Considerations'. *Journal of Agrarian Change* 13 (3), July: 365–81.

Bernstein, H. 1994. *Agrarian Question: Essays in Appreciation of T. J. Byres*. London: Frank Cass.

Bernstein, H. 1996. 'Agrarian Questions Then and Now'. *The Journal of Peasant Studies* 24 (1–2): 22–59.

Bernstein, H. 2001. 'The "Peasantry" in Global Capitalism: Who, Where and Why? In L. Paxitech and Colin Leys (eds). *Socialist Register*. Kolkata, India: K. P. Bagchi.

Bernstein, H. 2006. 'Is There an Agrarian Question in the 21st Century?'. *Canadian Journal of Development Studies/Revue canadienne d'études du développement* 27 (4): 449–60.

Borras, S. M., M. Edelman Je and C. Kay (eds). 2008. *Transnational Agrarian Movements Confronting Globalisation*. Oxford: Wiley-Blackwell.

Contours of the agrarian question 111

Bryceson, D. F. C. Kay and J. Mooij (eds). 2000. *Disappearing Peasantries? Rural Labour in Africa, Asia and Latin America*. London: The Intermediate Technology Group.

Byres, T. J. 1991. 'The Agrarian Question and Differing Forms of Capitalist Agrarian Transition: An Essay with Reference to Asia'. In Jan Breman and Sudipta Mundle (eds). *Rural Transformation in Asia*. New Delhi: Oxford University Press.

Byres, T. J. 1995. 'Political Economy, Agrarian Question and Comparative Method'. *Economic and Political Weekly* 30 (10): 507–13.

Byres, T. J. 1996. *Capitalism from Above and Capitalism from Below: Essays in Comparative Political Economy*. London: Palgrave Macmillan.

Byres, T. J. 1999. 'Rural Labour Relations in India: Persistent Themes, Common Processes and Differential Outcomes'. *The Journal of Peasant Studies* 26 (2–3): 10–24.

GoAP. 2002. 'Increasing the Rural Poor's Access and Rights to Rural Land: Operational Manual', A.P. Rural Poverty Reduction Project, Society for Elimination of Rural Poverty, Department of PR and Rural Development, Government of Andhra Pradesh, Hyderabad.

Harriss-White, B. 2012. '"Capitalism and the Common Man" Peasants and Petty Production in Africa and South Asia'. *Agrarian South: Journal of Political Economy* 1 (2): 109–60.

Harriss, John. 2013. 'Does "Landlordism" Still Matter? Reflections on Agrarian Change in India'. *Journal of Agrarian Change* 13 (3): 351–64.

Hobsbawm, Eric. J. 1994. *The Age of Extremes: The Short Twentieth Century, 1914–1991*. London: Michael Joseph.

Lerche, J. 2010. 'From "Rural Labour" to "Classes to Labour": Class Fragmentation, Caste and Class Struggle at the Bottom of the Indian Labour Hierarchy'. In B. Harriss-White and J. Heyer (eds). *The Comparative Political Economy of Development*. London: Routledge.

Lerche, J. 2013. 'The Agrarian Question in Neoliberal India: Agrarian Transition Bypassed?'. *Journal of Agrarian Change* 13 (3): 382–404.

Lerche, Jens, Alpa Shah and Barbara Harriss-White. 2013. 'Introduction: Agrarian Questions and Left Politics in India'. *Journal of Agrarian Change* 13 (3): 337–50.

Moyo, Sam, Praveen Jha and Paris Yeros. 2013. 'The Classical Agrarian Question: Myth, Reality and Relevance Today'. *Agrarian South: Journal of Political Economy* 2 (1): 93–119.

Patnaik, U. 1990. *Agrarian Relations and Accumulation: The Mode of Production Debate in India*. New Delhi: Oxford University Press.

Proctor, Felicity and Valerio Lucchesi. 2012. *Small-Scale Farming and Youth in an Era of Rapid Rural Change*. London: International Institute of Environment and Development.

Rajasekhar, B. 2012. 'Land Para-Professionals as Last Mile Solutions to Land Issues of the Poor'. SERP website accessed on 6 December 2012.

Raju, K., K. Akella and K. Deininger. 2006. 'New Opportunities for Increasing Access to Land: The Example of Andhra Pradesh'. Paper presented at MoRD and World Bank Workshop on 'Land Policies for Sustainable Growth and Poverty Reduction', January 2006, New Delhi.

Ramachandran, V. K. 2011. 'The State of Agrarian Relations in India Today'. *The Marxist* 27 (1–2): 51–89.

Rao, R. S. 1984. 'In Search of a Theory of Agrarian Relations'. In R. S. Rao (ed.) (1995). *Towards Understanding Semi-Feudal Semi-Colonial Society*, Hyderabad: Perspectives.

Rawal, V. 2008. 'Ownership Holdings of Land in Rural India: Putting the Record Straight'. *Economic and Political Weekly* 43 (10): 43–48.

Reddy, D. Narasimha. 2013. 'Rural Poor and Access to Land: Andhra Pradesh Experience of Administrative Initiatives in Augmenting Land Resources of Scheduled Castes'. Working Paper 5, S. R. Sankaran Chair, National Institute of Rural Development, Hyderabad.

Sanyal, K. and R. Bhattacharyya. 2009. 'Beyond the Factory: Globalisation, Informalisation of Production and the New Locations of Labour'. *Economic and Political Weekly* 44 (22): 35–44.

Shah, Alpa. 2013. 'The Agrarian Question in a Maoist Gorilla Zone: Land, Labour and Capital in the Forests and Hills of Jharkhand, India'. *Journal of Agrarian Change* 13 (3): 424–50.

Shah, Alpa and Barbara Harris-White. 2011. 'Resurrecting Scholarship on Agrarian Transformations'. *Economic and Political Weekly* 46 (39): 13–18.

Srivastava, R. 1989. 'Interlinked Modes of Exploitation in Indian Agriculture during Transition: A Case Study'. *Journal of Peasant Studies* 16 (3): 493–522.

Thorner, A. 1982. 'Semi-Feudalism or Capitalism? Contemporary Debate on Classes and Modes of Production in India'. *Economic and Political Weekly* 17 (49, 50 and 51): 1961–68, 1993–99, 2061–86.

Wilkinson, J. 2009. 'Globalisation of Agribusiness and Developing World Food Systems', accessed from http://www.monthlyreview.org/090907wilkinson.php on 27 February 2014.

Part II

Global capitalism, neoliberalism and changing agriculture

Chapter 4

Capitalist trajectories of global interdependence and welfare outcomes

The lessons of history for the present

Utsa Patnaik

1. Introduction

A frequently heard statement in the Indian context, especially from those in or connected with its government, is that the persisting problems of India's peasant agriculture show that it is too 'inefficient' to compete globally. On the theoretical plane, it has been argued that in the era of globalisation the classical 'agrarian question' no longer exists. The problem of transformation of the social relations of production within the agrarian sector of a developing country towards capitalist production, assumed to be necessary for raising productivity and for mobilising the agricultural surplus for development, has become quite otiose since free, large capital inflows have eased the constraint of resource mobilisation for developing country governments. It is also argued by many that displacement of small peasant producers from land owing to increasing demands for industry, residential construction and commercial activities by the corporate sector is to be expected and is a necessary part of accumulation. The population subsisting on agriculture should largely shift away to other more-paying activities according to this view, and the corporate sector should enter agriculture directly to raise the technological level.

There are a number of implicit assumptions which underpin these diverse arguments, which are not always spelt out but are taken for granted as being correct. The first assumption is that land productivity today is much higher in agriculture of the developed countries compared to that of developing ones since by now after two centuries of capitalist growth, the technological level in the former has been raised, making the industrial nations' agricultural production more 'efficient' compared to peasant production. The assumed successful capitalist transformation in today's advanced countries and resulting rise in productivity enabled them to meet the wage goods and raw materials requirements of their industrialisation either entirely from their own agriculture or partially through exchange between the countries making up today's advanced nations, so interaction with other parts of the world was not essential for their industrialisation. In short, in this view any role for the colonies is ignored.[1]

The most important inference which follows is that the small peasant population evicted and displaced from agriculture by the emerging capitalists seeking to establish a larger scale of production was absorbed productively sooner or later into other faster-growing sectors, especially industry. Such 'primitive accumulation of capital' involving the grabbing and centralising of peasant property into fewer hands, while it may have been painful for its victims, eventually turned out to be for the greater good for it was the essential precondition for the transition to a far more productive and advanced economic system. So goes the accepted understanding.

It is usually taken for granted that today's developing nations will follow the same or similar trajectories of development as today's advanced nations did, with a reduction in the share of the primary sector both in the nation's output and in its employment. Labour and population would face displacement from agriculture, but with the much faster expansion of the secondary and tertiary sectors characteristic of what Simon Kuznets had called 'modern economic growth', displaced populations would be re-absorbed into the latter sectors along with a fast rate of urbanisation of the population.

However, the assumptions underlying the view sketched above turn out to be untenable when we study the actual history of the development of industrial capitalism. Nations build up their own mythical origins and history no less than do communities. The scenario sketched earlier does serious violence to what actually happened in history because it ignores the specific nature of the exploitative interaction between today's advanced and today's developing nations, an interaction without which capitalist industrialisation at the core would hardly have been possible. This exploitative interaction is sought to be re-created in new forms in the current era, and this very fact makes it impossible for developing countries, to follow the past growth trajectory of the advanced countries.

In this chapter I propose to take up first, from a critical perspective, the question of whether the peasant populations displaced by emerging capitalism did get re-absorbed entirely into more productive occupations within their own countries or whether large-scale out-migration helps to explain rising domestic wages. Second, was it the capitalist transformation of domestic agriculture which provided the material possibility of industrialisation, considering Britain as the first industrialising nation? Next, I take up the question of the ways in which the specific problems of developing countries today are qualitatively quite different precisely as a result of their past and present interaction with developed nations. Developing countries, even when they experience much higher rates of growth than today's advanced countries ever did, not only do not succeed in reducing unemployment and poverty but actually see an intensification of these problems.

2. There was 'primitive accumulation', but no 'agricultural revolution' preceding industrialisation

Two separate processes of economic and social change tend to get mixed up when we talk of agricultural revolution preceding industrial revolution in England in the eighteenth century or in the other European countries somewhat later. The first is the displacement of the small peasantry through land enclosures and other means, and the second is the rise in productivity which is supposed to have resulted from the larger-scale capitalist production which followed such displacement of peasants. The first is a part of the process of primitive accumulation of capital, which Marx famously described as follows:

> The capitalist system presupposes the complete separation of the labourers from all property in the means by which they can realise their labour. As soon as capitalist production is once on its own legs, it not only maintains this separation but reproduces it on a continually extending scale. The process, therefore, which clears the way for the capitalist system, can be none other than the process which takes away from the labourer the possession of his means of production; a process that transforms, on the one hand, the social means of subsistence and of production into capital, on the other, the immediate producers into wage labourers. The so-called primitive accumulation, therefore, is nothing else than the historical process of divorcing the producer from the means of production.
>
> (Karl Marx, *Capital*, Vol. 1, Part VII, Chapter XXVI)

This process of primitive accumulation certainly did occur not only in the eighteenth century through enclosures but also into the nineteenth century as regards Ireland, where tenant farmers were evicted on a mass scale during and after the great famine of 1846–47 (Slicher van Bath

118 Utsa Patnaik

1963). It led to the formation of a large propertyless underclass, potentially an army of manufacturing workers, but in fact only a fraction of this class was actually re-absorbed into productive employment within national economic boundaries. Marx's insight was that capital requires the formation and expansion of a 'reserve army of labour' which keeps down wages, so that it leads necessarily to the accumulation of wealth by the minority at one pole and to misery and deprivation of the majority at the other pole. This insight has been attacked as a wrong prediction by citing the rise in working-class living standards which took place in industrial Europe. In the long run however, Marx has been proved to be more correct than his myopic critics, once his system is opened to include global flows of labour and capital (for estimates of such flows, see Kenwood and Loughheed 1971; Bhattacharya 2006). Capitalist accumulation did generate an expanding reserve army, but heavy out-migration of the unemployed to the New World based on seizure of land and resources from indigenous populations continuously reduced the metropolitan reserve army of labour and allowed a rise in working-class bargaining power. In the current era of globalisation, no such open frontiers exist, even for advanced country populations. The share of wages in national income is constant or shrinking in developing countries and in industrial nations alike.

The second process, the formation of larger-scale capitalist farms, is supposed to have raised productivity to a sufficient extent to meet the expanding wage goods and raw materials needs of industrialisation. It is this second process which did not actually take place although it is wrongly assumed to have occurred. Consider the most important food staple and the wage good of the labouring poor, wheat for making bread. Detailed research by economic historians shows that the output per head of grain actually declined in Britain during the second half of the eighteenth century when the maximum enclosures and productivity rise were supposed to be taking place, and while recovering a little in 1850, still remained below the level of 1700 (see Table 4A.1). A non-inflationary growth path was not possible and rapid food price inflation took place during the Napoleonic Wars, 1793–1815, pushing the labouring poor to starvation and causing food riots even as the factory system grew and prospered (Chambers and Mingay 1971).

The problem did not arise from the prevailing Corn Laws alone, which restricted the import of cheaper corn (wheat) from abroad. The basic problem arose because output growth was very slow despite all capitalist enclosures that it fell below the accelerating population growth rate. The Corn Laws simply aggravated further the basic problem of inflation in food prices owing to domestic supply shortage, by not allowing duty-free imports until domestic prices reached very high levels. The most important political economy issue for 50 years in Britain was the agitation for cheaper bread, and hence for free imports of cheaper foreign corn, an agitation which united the manufacturers and fledgling working class. David Ricardo's *Essay on the Influence of a low price of Corn on the Profits of Stock* (1815) argued for free corn imports even while maintaining silence on the raising of tariffs against imports of Asian textiles. This prolonged agitation itself is a telling indictment of the failure of 'agricultural revolution' to provide its wage goods requirements.

In 1988 I wrote a paper titled 'Was there an Agricultural Revolution in England?' in which I presented the argument given above and made detailed calculations, which showed a one-eighth to nearly one-fifth decline in per capita corn output depending on the population series adopted.[2] More recently, a similar conclusion has been reached by a number of economic historians researching agricultural growth in Britain, and a debate has taken place between them and the upholders of the earlier standard view of successful agricultural revolution (Overton 1996a, 1996b; Allen 1998, 1999; Brunt 1999; Turner et al. 2001). Table 4A.1 shows their estimates, which corroborate the decline in per capita output by one-fifth between 1700 and 1820. While per worker output within agriculture did rise, the rise was not enough to maintain at least the same per head output for the population, thus violating the essential condition of success in meeting wage good needs.

The reason industrialisation could proceed without being hampered by agricultural failure lay in colonial imports which did not have to be paid for by Britain in the sense that these imports created no external liability for the British economy since local producers were 'paid' out of taxes they themselves contributed to the state. In India the colonial state guided and operated from Britain, extracted taxes from peasants and artisans and used a portion of tax revenues to purchase their products, including exported crops like wheat. Even when wheat was purchased from temperate lands like the European Continent and the United States, in the earlier period – the eighteenth century – direct re-exports of tropical colonial goods paid for a large part of these imports. Later from the nineteenth century onwards, the exchange earnings of colonies which exported to these lands were appropriated and used to pay for a large part of temperate imports into the metropolis through a continuation of the multilateral payments system (Saul 1960), which in essence functioned on the basis of colonial transfers. The exact mechanism of colonial exploitation and appropriation of foreign exchange

120   Utsa Patnaik

earnings has been discussed elsewhere (Patnaik 1999, 2006). There is little doubt that other European countries would show a similar failure of their agricultural revolution and a similar dependence on their colonies, particularly the Netherlands which controlled Java and which had even larger dependence on re-exports of tropical goods to pay for its temperate imports, than did Britain (Maddison 2006).

Interestingly in Japan too we find that early industrial transition was marked by domestic rice shortages, and only the deliberate extraction of rising tax-financed rice imports from its colonies, Korea and Taiwan, permitted it to maintain about the same level of availability for its population by the 1930s as in the 1870s (Penrose 1940; Hayami and Ruttan 1970). Per head consumption of rice and average calorie intake fell in Japan's colonies (Grabowski 1985).

W. A. Lewis (1978) very clearly articulates the common misconception that there was higher productivity in Britain, here taken as representing the industrial nations in general, as compared to the tropics; and he makes this allegedly higher yield the entire basis for explaining higher wages: 'The yield of wheat by 1900 was 1600 lbs. per acre as against the tropical yield of 700 lbs. of grain per acre' (Lewis 1978, *The Evolution of the International Economic Order* : 14).

But there is a fallacy in the comparison Lewis makes, because 'productivity' has no meaning without a uniform time dimension being clearly specified, which he fails to do. Over one year, an acre of land in Britain may well have produced 1600 lbs of wheat, but it could produce nothing else since there was only one growing season in cold temperate lands. In the tropics crops can be produced all the year round. Over the same one year, an acre of land in the tropics produced not only 700 lbs of grain but also a second crop – either another crop of grain or cotton or jute or vegetables, plus often, a third crop of gram or lentils. The term 'crop rotation ' in temperate lands refers to crops grown over *successive years*, while the same term in tropical lands refers to crops grown in *successive seasons* within the same year. Despite all technical change in the advanced countries, by 2007 India, with much less cultivated area than the United States, produced annually a larger total tonnage (818.7 million ton) of cereals, root crops, oil crops, sugar crops, fruits and vegetables than the United States (644.2 million tons). As for China, its even more intensive cultivation developed over centuries, and consequent high land productivity was legendary. By 2007 China produced over 1275 million tons from a cultivated area even smaller than in India and about one-third of that of the United States. Compared to physical output tonnage per hectare of cultivated land in the United States, in India

Capitalist trajectories of global interdependence 121

it was nearly 40 per cent higher and in China it was three times higher (see Table 4A.3).

True, technical change in Northern agriculture meant higher output per worker or per labour day, but this was achieved only by substituting dead labour – machinery – for living labour, machinery which required large inputs of fossil fuels to run. The 'energy balance' or the amount of energy embodied in all the inputs required to produce the energy obtainable from a unit of final output to this day is more unfavourable in temperate lands.

Not only W. A. Lewis but most other writers completely ignore the growing import dependence of today's advanced countries on cheap primary imports from tropical lands, used for diversifying their consumption baskets and output structure. They show little awareness of the tremendously important role re-exports of tropical goods played in boosting the global purchasing power of exports from these countries. Global patterns of specialisation of production were deliberately engineered, were maintained by force exercised through direct political control under colonialism and were very far from the model of voluntary specialisation and exchange leading to mutual benefit, expounded in David Ricardo's fallacious theory of comparative advantage.

Ricardo's theory using a two-country, two-commodity model states that trade takes place because even when the cost of production of both goods is lower in one country than the other, provided the relative cost of production is different, both trading parties benefit from specialisation and exchange in the sense of consuming more of one good for no lower consumption of the other good. Relative cost is the number of units of a good which a country can produce by withdrawing labour from the production of one unit of the other good. I have pointed out elsewhere that the fallacy in this theory arises from the assumption 'both countries produce both goods'. This assumption is essential for defining relative cost at all, but the assumption is not true, since a temperate country has never produced and cannot ever produce tropical crops. Say Britain or Germany imports Indian rice/tea/cane sugar and exports spinning machines. The relative cost, namely number of units of rice/tea/cane sugar producible by reducing machine output by one unit and diverting the labour released to these goods, can be obtained for India. But such relative cost does not exist for Britain and Germany which have zero output of rice/tea/cane sugar since these simply cannot be produced at all. Where the assumption is not true, there is no mutual benefit from trade. Specialisation and trade did indeed take place in which cold temperate lands imported tropical products and

122 Utsa Patnaik

exported machine-made goods, but such trade had nothing to do with comparative advantage and mutual benefit. It had to do with the fact that tropical lands are highly bio-diverse and can produce crops which are desired by temperate advanced countries for consumption or as raw material, which they could never produce, and which they sought to acquire through establishing political control. At least three-fifths and up to three-quarters of world trade in 1876–1913 was in primary products (see Table 4A.2) and about four-fifths of this in turn were crops which could only be produced in warmer climes (Kenwood and Loughheed 1971; Davis 1979).

Far from benefitting the developing country, specialisation and export of primary products became positively harmful because it always led to a decline in the land and resources devoted to food grains, the basic staple the local population required, and because food grains too were exported. Very often the colonial masters taxed the population so heavily as to force a shift in local consumption towards inferior food staples (millets, potatoes) while the superior grains (wheat, rice) were exported to the metropolis. Not only did nutritional standards see decline, but also colonised populations were periodically plunged into famine (Dutt 1970; Grabowski 1985; Patnaik 2003b).

Few theories have done as much harm to rational thinking as Ricardo's logically incorrect theory of comparative advantage which embodies a particular type of material fallacy – the 'converse fallacy of accident' or the converse of Aristotle's A *dicto simpliciter ad dictum secundum quid* (from a proposition taken in a general sense to a specific case). A highly specific assumption is made – 'both countries produce both goods' to draw the inference that trade, following specialisation, is mutually beneficial to both parties, and then this inference is improperly treated as a general one, applied even where the assumption is not satisfied.[3] Trade patterns which were actually the result of military conquest, setting up of plantations using slave or unfree labour set to producing export crops for metropolitan centres, have been sanitised and rationalised as being 'mutually beneficial' for slaves and masters alike. Fiction and apologetics replace intellectual honesty in economic analysis. My paper 'Ricardo's Fallacy' (2006) points out that the material fallacy is supported and compounded by a verbal fallacy since Ricardo's repeated talks of 'growing wine', a term which makes no sense.

W. Arthur Lewis (1978) too ignores real economic history in the same manner by developing a modified Ricardian theory to say that because of allegedly higher land productivity in temperate lands – an incorrect statement of fact, as we have already seen – the 'product wage' was

Capitalist trajectories of global interdependence 123

higher for the English and European out-migrants generally and lower for the 'Chinese coolies' and this is why the Australian ended up with a much higher standard of life than Chinese coolies did. The same argument would be applied to explain the higher wage of white settlers in South Africa or in Canada.

The real reason for higher wage in Australia or South Africa than in China was very different. Britain appropriated the entire Australian land mass relegating its original inhabitants to the same fate as it had the Amerindians, while it followed an equally exclusionist policy vis-à-vis the indigenous black population in South Africa, appropriating their best lands and relegating them to 'homelands'. These vast areas permanently grabbed through a process of primitive accumulation were used for exporting Britain's criminal underclass and later for settling emigrants. It is easy enough to understand the strong impetus to emigrate from Britain, a country which could not feed its people at the same level by 1850 as it had in 1700. To fill the consumption gap Britain colonially exploited Ireland so severely that it caused a massive famine, carrying off one-eighth of the Irish population in 1846–47 and initiating a long period of demographic collapse. The high product wage of emigrants from Europe was not because of high productivity in England or other European countries, but because of land grabbing and resource grabbing on a scale never seen before in history. The human cost was very high especially in the Americas.[4]

To sum up, the failure of capitalist agriculture in Northern countries has not been recognised at a conceptual level, and a large part of the reason is that this failure did not constrain their industrial expansion. But this lack of constraint itself arose solely from the forcible access they acquired to tropical lands with their superior productivity and bio-diversity. They also acquired access to temperate colonies – of which only Ireland remained by the twentieth century, the only region in Europe to have halved its population over less than a century after the colonial exploitation induced the shock of the great famine of 1846–47.

As advanced countries enjoyed more and more diversified imports-based consumption baskets, the availability of food grains for third-world populations declined. This inverse relation between primary exports and decline in food grains output/availability can be established very firmly on the basis of the historical data (Patnaik 2003b, 2007a). Nutritional decline and in extreme cases famines were the result – this is the most important adverse impact of export-oriented growth and it is a result in present-day India and China as well: both countries have seen deteriorating average nutrition in the past 15 years accompanying high gross domestic product (GDP) growth.

124 Utsa Patnaik

The reason is not far to seek. Land is not a product of human labour – in Karl Marx's striking formulation, 'the price of land' is an irrational category. The 'price of land' can only be the capitalised value of the product of the land or of the income to be drawn from the land. Land, not being itself a product of human labour, cannot be augmented at will, it cannot be 'produced'. Greater external demands on a developing country's limited land simply mean that less is available for satisfying the needs of the local population. And if the purchasing power of local populations can be restricted through heavy taxation and measures of fiscal compression, so much the better for the advanced countries which can then access the productive capacities of these foreign lands simply through the market, which responds only to purchasing power and not to needs. Indian and other developing country lands then produce more and more products for filling up supermarket shelves in the North at the expense of less and less food and basic staples for their own populations.

3. Capitalist industrialisation was based on the export of unemployment

All the early industrialising countries overcame the problem of growing unemployment inherent in their capitalist growth and technical change, simply by exporting their unemployment abroad, an option which is not open in any serious way to today's large labour surplus economies like India and China. The export of unemployment took place through colonisation and imperialism and appeared in multifarious forms. The most direct form of export of unemployment was the physical migration of population. The precondition for this was the seizure of enormous tracts of land by the West Europeans from indigenous peoples in the Americas, South Africa and Australia, and their permanent occupation by the in-migrants. 'Land' in this context means not just crop land but includes all the natural fauna, the rich water, timber and mineral resources of these occupied regions. Some 50 million Europeans emigrated permanently in the century after 1820, led by Britain whose population that year was 12 million and which saw 16 million persons emigrating in the next nine decades – about half the population increment each year left the country (Kenwood and Lougheed 1971). To match this rate between Independence in 1947 and now, over 700 million Indians would have needed to have emigrated abroad.

Unemployment was also exported by industrialising countries through flooding the subjugated already-populous tropical colonies with cotton

Capitalist trajectories of global interdependence 125

textiles and other manufactured goods under discriminating commercial policy which kept these markets compulsorily completely open to imports, while the home market was protected from their handicraft manufactures for nearly 150 years.[5] While employment and wages rose in the industrialising country with output expanding at about double the rate of domestic absorptive capacity, the other side of the coin was that in the colonies manufactures employment went down sharply resulting in de-industrialisation.

As the unwilling recipients of the export of unemployment from today's advanced countries, India the former colony and China the former semi-colony, had ended up by the mid-twentieth century with mass poverty and with significantly tertiarised economies – a higher share of services and lowered share of both agriculture and industry in GDP – namely compared to their initial states. They inherited very high levels of unemployment and underemployment, which became a matter of serious concern as they sought to pursue an independent path of national development. The choice of techniques question was much discussed in the early decades, the 1950s and 1960s, and it was recognised in both countries that industrialisation with employment generation meant 'walking on two legs', to borrow Mao Zedong's words – capital-intensive heavy industries and intermediate goods production had to be built up from scratch or expanded; there had to be a simultaneous thrust for expansion in labour-intensive segments of manufacturing including small-scale and village industry; and for all this to occur in a non-inflationary way, agricultural growth had to accelerate to provide the required wage goods and raw materials. This was the rationale for giving priority-sector status to small-scale industry and agriculture in India as regards credit.

However, though the fastest expanding segments of manufacturing output in the first 15 years of Indian independence logged 9 per cent annual growth rate, the associated employment growth was only 3 per cent. It was already very clear and widely recognised that no visible net shift of the workforce out of agriculture could be expected even at such high manufacturing growth rates. Subsequently, the elasticity of employment with respect to manufacturing output has been falling steadily and especially sharply after liberalisation in the 1990s. Maintaining competitiveness by firms in a trade- and investment-open economy entails adopting the latest technology, and the loss is in terms of employment generation. In addition, the thrust of neoliberal reforms is always towards retrenchment of labour and 'downsizing' with a total ignoring of the impact of this on aggregate demand and hence on the inducement to invest. The combination of the two factors has led to near-zero impact

126 Utsa Patnaik

of manufacturing growth on employment, while for organised industry there is absolute job loss, as is well established by now.

It was amply clear from the 1960s that industrialisation even at a high rate could not make any substantial dent in the unemployment and livelihood problem, especially for the rural millions. While there was never any conscious strategy of mobilising labour for capital formation in India, an expansionary fiscal stance up to the 1980s including expanding rural development expenditures and a system of market intervention via state procurement or commodity board procurement of crops at prices covering production costs were together conducive to maintaining reasonably buoyant levels of activity and inducing private investment, so that employment in rural India was expanding faster than the labour force up to the early 1990s. True, the inequality of distribution of assets and incomes was not addressed and actually worsened slowly over time, but absolute decline of real incomes or decline in nutritional standards did not take place except briefly in the mid-1960s.

In the late 1970s and early 1980s a number of studies were carried out, many under International Labour Organization auspices, which correctly argued that there was scope in poor developing countries for more intensive cultivation and greater labour absorption within agriculture and sideline activities. The intensity of cultivation was substantially lower in India compared to East Asia in terms of both material input use and labour use per unit area, and yields were capable of being raised. This technical slack could be taken up provided price–cost conditions were created to make it profitable to invest in cultivating intensively.

From the 1980s onwards, however, the entire theoretical discourse was radically altered by the incessant pushing by international financial institutions of conservative neoliberal dogmas which advocate expenditure deflation and fiscal austerity no matter how high unemployment might be, and which represent a reversion to pre-Keynesian theory.

The impact of neoliberal reforms from 1991 has been extremely adverse on rural employment and incomes because it has entailed contraction not only in public investment but also in development expenditures generally, lowering the level of activity and affecting the inducement to invest of farmers. Current discussion on unemployment reveals total amnesia regarding all previous literature on the impossibility of industrialisation alone, leading to notable labour shifts out of the primary sector. Many economists opine that it is high time the Indian labour force started shifting out of agriculture and into the secondary sector, as though it is a question of subjective wishes and not objective constraints, which are far more binding today than earlier. The prospects for labour

Capitalist trajectories of global interdependence   127

absorption in agriculture and in industry have been worsened greatly by the public investment reducing, development expenditure deflating and labour-retrenchment policies which are at the core of economic reforms, and which are supported in the main by the same economists who argue for industrialisation and more free trade as the solutions to unemployment. They choose to ignore the contradiction: how public investment and expenditure deflation, fiscal austerity, downsizing and reduction in public utilities employment can possibly be compatible with expanding aggregate demand and maintain the inducement to invest in agriculture and industry is a question which does not exercise their minds. Nor can it be seriously maintained that India is in a position to export unemployment in the manner today's advanced countries had done.

4. Globally capitalist accumulation produces poverty at one pole and riches at the other

Global interdependence in the past produced in today's developing countries falling nutritional standards and even famine, on the one hand, and promoted underemployment and unemployment on the other. Global interdependence in the current era has been producing exactly the same outcomes, from the moment the attempt to follow autonomous development trajectories was given up by governments in developing countries under the onslaught of the hegemonic dogmas of finance capital. Leading advocates of high growth in advanced and developing countries alike have tried to obfuscate and mask these adverse welfare outcomes by putting forward fallacious theories, but these negative welfare outcomes are so obvious and so blatant that all they succeed in doing through their apologetics is to intellectually discredit themselves. It is a little difficult to explain away over 160,000 farmer suicides in India since trade liberalisation started in 1997 (see Nagaraj 2008), as a positive result of high growth. It is more than a little difficult to explain declining per head energy (calorie) intake and similarly declining average protein intake in India, as a positive effect of 'dietary diversification'. It is hardly a credible proposition, which is officially put forward and continues to be reiterated, that over the same period that agricultural incomes became stagnant and unemployment rose in India,[6] rural and urban poverty, as officially estimated, registered substantial decline.

The truth of the matter is that capitalist accumulation has never taken place within closed economic systems. The historical conditions for the industrial transformation of today's advanced nations lay in the primitive accumulation they practiced vis-à-vis other nations and regions,

128 Utsa Patnaik

through direct seizure of resources by means of force. Without primitive accumulation on this scale, their poorly endowed temperate lands were incapable of meeting the wage good and raw material needs of their own industrial growth. This resulted initially in decimation of entire populations and subsequently in their enthrallment and exploitation producing declining nutrition and famine. The labour displacement caused by the mechanisation associated with industrial transformation far exceeded any notion of a normal reserve army of labour, and only their ability to export unemployment staved off acute social and political tensions. At the other pole de-industrialisation and unemployment resulted in the global South.

After half a century of decolonisation we find once more that a new phase of primitive accumulation has been launched with a more sophisticated ideology, under which developing country elites are offered integration with the global elite provided they collaborate with the economic and educational policies which will betray the interests of their own people and will once more subordinate the national interest to global capital. Rosa Luxemburg's (1951) brilliant insight in *The Accumulation of Capital*, that capitalist expansion at the core was always at the expense of destruction of the small-scale production of the peasant and the artisan not only within the core countries but at the global level, remains as true today as it was a century ago. While the main emphasis in her work was on the question of creation of markets for realising surplus value – which was indeed very important – this paper has stressed the question of past and continuing appropriation of resources. Since the advanced countries today are even more dependent on the qualitatively superior productive capacity of tropical lands, they make increasing demands on these lands to produce, apart from traditional tropical exports, a new range of perishable products from fruits and vegetables to flowers. This produces a decline in the food grains growth rate and it falls below the population's growth rate, resulting in falling per capita output of food grains.

As Table 4A.5 documents, with its great 'success' in global integration, the per capita cereal supply in India (namely output available for uses of all kinds after adjusting the gross domestic output for net exports and change in stocks) by 2011 – a good harvest year – had fallen substantially below the level not only of Africa as a whole but also of the poorest countries in the world, the least developed countries. Cereal supply is identically equal to the demand for all uses, both direct demand for consuming as food and indirect demand for consuming as animal products raised on feed cereals, and other uses (seed, processing, fuel). The annual direct and total demand in India had fallen to 152 kg and 176.5 kg,

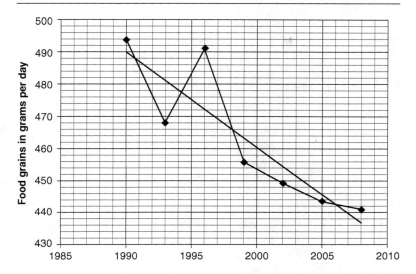

Figure 4.1 Food grains availability per capita during economic reforms period, India

Source: *Economic Survey 2012–13*, Ministry of Finance, Government of India.

respectively, the lowest in the world and about the same level as 60 years ago at Independence. Figure 4.1 shows the steep decline in per capita food grains availability during the period of economic reforms, from an official Indian government source – availability roughly measures direct consumption as food since seed, feed and so on are excluded. Availability has declined faster than output because income deflation and targeting have resulted in the dual problem of a large build-up of unsold public stocks (Patnaik 2003a), and very large exports which totalled nearly 40 million tons over two years, 2013 and 2014. Four decades of successful effort to raise domestic per capita supply and demand has been wiped out in two decades of trade liberalisation and reforms.

It is not surprising that poverty has risen substantially in the sense that the percentage of persons unable to reach official nutritional standards through their monthly spending has gone up (see Table 4A.2). The official claim is that poverty has reduced, but this claim is based on an incorrect procedure for measuring poverty in which the definition of 'poverty line' adopted by the Planning Commission has been changed after the initial estimate and de-linked from the official nutrition norms.

There is a serious problem with this official estimation procedure, namely, *the standard against which poverty is being measured is not kept constant over time or space.* So successive poverty estimates cannot be compared, no valid inference can be drawn regarding the direction of change and official claims of poverty reduction are not true. Consider an example: we are told that the percentage of failed students in a school has declined sharply from 30 to 10 between 1973 and 2005, so we infer that academic performance has 'improved' for we take it for granted that the pass mark must be unchanged to allow such a comparison. But then we find out that in fact the pass mark has been steadily lowered over time, from say 50 out of 100 in 1973 to 25 out of 100 in 2005. By the latter date, say two-fifths of students could not reach the original 50 per cent pass mark and this figure exceeds the school's failure percentage in 1973. It is clear the inference of academic 'improvement' is not true; rather the opposite inference of worsening is true.

Similarly in official poverty estimates, a certain standard was set in the initial year that those persons were to be considered 'non-poor' who through their MPCE (monthly per capita expenditure) on all goods and services could obtain at least 2400 (kilo)calories energy per day in rural and 2100 calories in urban areas, and these MPCEs were called the 'poverty lines'. But for all later years the standard was steadily lowered as a consequence of changing the definition of 'poverty line', which was simply the original poverty line adjusted upwards by a price index without ever asking the question as to whether this poverty line allowed people to obtain the same level of nutrition as before. In fact under the new definition the poverty line underestimated the sum required to maintain the same nutrition level and the underestimation became cumulative as time passed. By 2005 in some states in India, the nutrition accessible at the official underestimated poverty line was as much as 1000 calories per day below the official nutrition norm. Just as the definition of 'passing the examination' in 2010 is changed from meeting the original 50 marks standard to obtaining only 25 marks, the definition of a rural/urban person who is 'non-poor' is effectively changed from one who could afford at least 2400/2100 calories in 1973 to one who can afford 1820/1795 calories by 2010. It is obvious that comparison over time is not valid.

If we use the correct procedure of applying the same standard for measuring poverty over space and time, we find that the percentage of persons in poverty, while it changed, did not change very much between 1973 and 1993–94. But over the economic reforms period 1993–94 to 2009–10, poverty rose sharply in both rural and urban areas (Patnaik 2010, 2013). The percentage of all rural persons unable to reach the initial official 2200 calories daily nutrition norm rose from 58.5 to as high as 75.5 per cent, while the percentage of all urban persons unable to

Capitalist trajectories of global interdependence 131

reach the official 2100 calories daily nutrition norm rose from 57 to 73 per cent (see Table 4A.4). China follows the same procedure of updating a 1985 nutrition norm-based rural poverty line of 205 yuan per annum by a price index, giving by 2011 a grossly underestimated poverty line of only 1274 yuan or 3.5 yuan a day which would not have bought a single kilogram of rice leave alone meeting all living costs. Since the World Bank's global dollar poverty lines are based on taking the median of the poorest countries' national currency rural poverty lines and adjusted for purchasing power parity (Reddy and Pogge 2002), they similarly represent large underestimates by now. Actual poverty in the Global South is much higher than claimed in its reports.

Nassau Senior, professor of political economy at Oxford University, had opposed the bill shortening the 11-hour working day in English factories to 10 hours, and advocated the longer working day. He argued that capitalists made their profits 'in the last hour' and all profits would disappear if the hours worked was reduced to ten. Karl Marx mercilessly attacked Senior's theory of 'the last hour' as blatant anti-working-class apologetics pretending to be legitimate academic work. Today in India and China alike, poverty reduction is being falsely claimed by lowering the standard by which it is measured. The adverse welfare outcome, whatever the intent might be, is very clear since despite all food crises, the existing system of public distribution of food in India is undermined by continued targeting with the object of eventually throwing the poor to the mercies of the market. Like Senior's 'last hour', we have the Indian and Chinese equivalent in the absurd daily official poverty lines which were supposed to meet all essential daily food and non-food expenses for one person, whereas these paltry sums would hardly have bought a single bottle of water. Such apologetics parading as academic work needs to be thoroughly critiqued at the theoretical level by all those still committed to academic values.

Capitalism can never ameliorate the condition of the masses because its functioning at the global level is predicated on the growth of riches at one pole and the promotion of unemployment and hunger at the other. Recognition of this is necessary for active intervention to stabilise livelihoods and ensure that basic needs of the mass of a population are not compromised in the pursuit of profit by a minority. The agrarian question has not ceased to exist in the present era; on the contrary, it is more important than ever. The tensions unleashed by dominant global financial interests implementing their deflationary neoliberal policies, combined with the corporate attack on the land resources of the peasantry aided and abetted by states, have produced a new global food and livelihood crisis which is likely to intensify in future.

Appendix

Table 4A.1 Annual per capita output of wheat, England and Wales, in bushels and in kilograms

	Net output (million bushel)	Net output (million kg)	Population (million)	Per capita (kg)
1700	29.2	743.53	5.29	140.55
1750	34.03	866.218	6.2	139.71
1800	40.03	1019.2	9.16	111.27
1820	53.29	1356.47	12.071	112.37
1850	88.48	2252.22	17.603	127.95

Source: Turner et al. (2001).

Table 4A.2 Share of primary products in world trade 1876–80 to 1913, percentage

Year	Values in current prices	Values in 1913 prices
1876–80	63.5	61.8
1886–90	62.3	62.3
1896–1900	64.3	67.7
1906–10	63.2	64
1913	62.5	62.5

Source: Kuznets (1967).

Table 4A.3 Land productivity in China, India and the United States, 2007

	Arable area (000 ha)	Food crop output (000 ton)	Output per hectare (ton)	Index, United States = 100
China	109,365	1,275,047	11.66	309
India	158,114	818,698	5.18	137
United States	170,428	644,203	3.78	100

Source: Food Balance Sheets/Supply Utilisation Accounts, United Nations Food and Agriculture Organisation, Rome.

Table 4A.4 Trends in rural and urban poverty measured directly and by the official method

Rural	1973	1983	1993–94	2004–5	2009–10	2011–12
Direct poverty line, Rs	49	100	268	575	1075	1350
Official poverty line, Rs	49	86	206	415	645	816
Direct poverty percentage	56.4	56	58.5	69.5	75.5	70
Official poverty percentage	56.4	45.7	37.1	28.3		
Revised official poverty percentage			50.1	41.5	33.8	25.7

Urban	1973	1983	1993–94	2004–5	2009–10	2011–12
Direct poverty line, Rs	57	147	398	1000	2000	2380
Official poverty line, Rs	57	118	285	539	830	1000
Direct poverty percentage	49.2	58.8	57	64.5	73	68
Official poverty percentage	49.2	42.2	32.6	25.7	20.9	13.7

Note: Direct poverty line is the monthly per capita expenditure (MPCE) at which the rural/urban nutrition norms of 2200/2100 calories can be obtained, as observed from the NSS data on spending and nutrition. Official poverty line is the poverty lines by the Planning Commission, which takes the 1973–74 MPCE at which the rural/urban nutrition norms could be accessed and brings these forward to later years by using consumer price indices.

Table 4A.5 Cereal supply and utilisation 2011 selected countries/regions

Country/region	Total production (million ton)	Net import and stock change (million ton)	Total supply (million ton)	Per capita in kg/annum			Feed (kg)	Share in total supply			Population (million)
				Total production (kg)	Total supply (kg)	Food (direct) (kg)		Food/ total %	Feed/ total %	Other/ total %	
India	235.3	−19.7	215.5	192.7	176.5	152.1	9	86.2	5.1	0.02	1221.2
Least developed countries	152.4	14.8	167.2	197	216.2	148.4	26.9	38.7	12.5	5.6	773.5
Africa	153.8	65.5	219.2	158.3	225.7	150.5	40.5	66.67	17.94	3.26	971.2
China	451.9	0.6	452.5	330.2	330.7	152.5	121.7	46.12	36.8	8.36	1368.4
South America	148.6	−21.5	127.1	217.5	351.6	178.4	119	50.74	33.85	3.93	398
Russian Federation	91.4	−17.7	73.7	637.5	514.1	149.5	254.7	29.07	49.54	0	143.4
European Union	293.1	−14.5	278.6	577.6	549.1	124.9	330.5	22.74	60.18	4.54	507.4
United States	384	−58.8	325.3	1219.5	1032.9	105.8	396.3	10.24	38.37	42.1	314.9
World	2345.6	−27.4	2318.2	340.6	336.6	147.2	118.9	43.7	35.3	9.9	2345.6

Source: United Nations Food and Agriculture Organisation, Rome (faostat3.fao.org/faostat-gateway/go/to/download/F/FO/E, accessed October 10, 2014).

Capitalist trajectories of global interdependence 135

Notes

1 The literature is large; the 'Brenner debate' (Aston and Philpin 1985) encapsulates the completely Eurocentric thesis of internal successful capitalist agricultural transformation. W. A. Lewis (1978) explicitly states that today's industrial nations had all the resources they needed within their own countries.

2 The paper was presented in a seminar in the School of Oriental and African Studies, London, in June 1992. It has circulated for two decades among Indian students; a revised version presented to the Indian History Congress in May 2010 has been published (Patnaik 2011) in Moosvi (2011).

3 Whatever Ricardo's own position may have been, the subsequent use made of his theory leads to apologetics. The trade in wine and cloth between Portugal and England was not owing to 'comparative advantage' which was not even definable for England which could not produce grape wine, but resulted from Britain's naval and diplomatic dominance over Portugal allowing it to extract the Methuen Treaty in 1703 giving non-agricultural market access (Boxer 1973: 170).

4 Over nine-tenths of the indigenous population of the Central American civilisation was destroyed over the century following Spanish conquest and the settling of Hispania (Parry 1973: 210).

5 It is a notable fact that leading historians of industrialisation and technical change in advanced countries (Hobsbawm 1968; Landes 1969) make no mention of these crucial discriminatory commercial policies in their writings though they were in operation for over a century.

6 The 2009–10 National Sample Survey Report on Unemployment shows a substantial rise in unemployment rates compared to the 1993–94 report.

References

Allen, R. C. 1998. 'Agricultural Output and Productivity in Europe, 1300–1800', University of British Columbia, Department of Economics Discussion Paper (98–14).

Allen, R. C. 1999. 'Tracking the Agricultural Revolution in England'. *The Economic History Review* 52 (2): 209–35.

Aston, T. H. and C. H. E. Philpin (eds). 1985. *The Brenner Debate*. Cambridge: Cambridge University Press.

Bhattacharya, S. 2006. 'International Flows of Un-Free Labour'. In K. S. Jomo (ed.). *Globalisation under Hegemony – The Changing World Economy*. Delhi: Oxford University Press, pp. 195–226.

Boxer, C. R. 1973. *The Portuguese Seaborne Empire 1415–1825*. Harmondsworth: Pelican.

Brunt, L. 1999. 'Estimating English Wheat Production in the Industrial Revolution', *University of Oxford Discussion Papers in Economic and Social History*, No. 29, June.

Chambers J. D. and G. E. Mingay. 1971. *The Agricultural Revolution 1788–1850*. London: Batsford.

136 Utsa Patnaik

Davis, R. 1979. *The Industrial Revolution and British Overseas Trade*. Leicester: Leicester University Press.

Dutt, R. C. 1970. *The Economic History of India Vol. 1: Under early British Rule 1757–1837, Vol. 2: In the Victorian Age 1837–1900* (first published London, 1902 and 1904). Delhi: Government of India, reprinted 1970 by arrangement with Routledge & Kegan Paul.

Grabowski, R. 1985. 'A Historical Re-Assessment of Early Japanese Development'. *Development and Change* 16 (2): 235–50.

Hayami, Y. and V. W. Ruttan. 1970. 'Korean Rice, Taiwan Rice, and Japanese Agricultural Stagnation: A Case Study of Economic Imperialism'. *Quarterly Journal of Economics* 84 (4): 562–89.

Hobsbawm, E. J. 1968. *Industry and Empire – An Economic History of Britain since 1750*. London: Weidenfeld and Nicholson.

Kenwood, A. G. and L. Loughheed. 1971. *The Growth of the International Economy 1820–1960*. London: Allen and Unwin.

Kuznets, S. 1967. 'Foreign Trade: Long-Term Trends'. *Economic Development and Cultural Change* 15 (2), Part II (January): 1–140.

Landes, D. 1969. *The Unbound Prometheus: Technological Change and Industrial Development in Western Europe from 1750 to the Present*. Cambridge: Cambridge University Press.

Lewis W. A. 1978. *The Evolution of the International Economic Order*. Princeton, NJ: Princeton University Press.

Luxemburg, Rosa. 1951. *The Accumulation of Capital* (translated by Agnes Schwarzschild). London: Routledge & Kegan Paul.

Maddison, A. 2006. *The World Economy, vol. 1: A Millennial Perspective, vol. 2: Historical Statistics*. Paris: OECD Publishing.

Marx, Karl. 1965. *Capital, vol. 1*. Moscow: Progress Publishers.

Moosvi, S. (ed.). 2011. *Capitalism, Colonialism and Globalization: Studies in Economic Change*. Delhi: Aligarh Historian's Society and Tulika Books.

Nagaraj, K. 2008. *Farmers' Suicides in India: Magnitudes, Trends and Spatial Patterns*. Madras Institute of Development Studies, accessed from www.macroscan.org.

Overton, M. 1996a. 'Re-Establishing the English Agricultural Revolution', *Agricultural History Review* 44 (1): 1–20.

Overton, M. 1996b. *The Agricultural Revolution in England*. Cambridge: Cambridge University Press.

Parry, J. H. 1973. *The Spanish Seaborne Empire*. Harmondsworth: Pelican.

Patnaik, U. 1999. 'Tribute Transfer and the Balance of Payments in the Cambridge Economic History of India Volume II'. In U. Patnaik (ed.). *The Long Transition – Essays on Political Economy*. Delhi: Tulika.

Patnaik, U. 2003a. 'Food Stocks and Hunger – Causes of Agrarian Distress', *Social Scientist* 31 (7–8): 15–41.

Patnaik, U. 2003b. 'On the Inverse Relation between Primary Exports and Domestic Food Absorption under Liberalised Trade Regimes'. In J. Ghosh and C. P. Chandrasekhar (eds). *Work and Welfare in the Age of Finance*. Delhi: Tulika Books, pp. 256–86.

Patnaik, U. 2006. 'The Free Lunch – Transfers from Tropical Colonies and Their Role in Capital Formation in England during Industrial Revolution'. In K. S. Jomo (ed.). *Globalisation under Hegemony – The Changing World Economy*. Delhi: Oxford University Press.

Patnaik, U. 2007a. *The Republic of Hunger and Other Essays*. Delhi: Three Essays Collective, and Monmouth: Merlin Press.

Patnaik, U. 2007b. 'Neo-Liberalism and Rural Poverty in India'. *Economic and Political Weekly* 42 (30): 3132–50.

Patnaik, U. 2010. 'Trends in Urban Poverty under Economic Reforms, 1993–4 to 2004–5'. *Economic and Political Weekly* 45 (4): 42–53.

Patnaik, U. 2011. 'The "Agricultural Revolution" in England and Its Cost for the English Working Class and the Colonies'. In Shireen Moosvi (ed.). *Capitalism, Colonialism and Globalisation*. Delhi: Aligarh Historian's Society and Tulika Books.

Patnaik, U. 2013. 'Poverty Trends in India 2004–5 to 2009–10: Updating Poverty Estimates and Comparing Official Figures'. *Economic and Political Weekly* 48 (40), October 5: 43–58.

Penrose, E. F.1940. 'Rice Culture in the Japanese Economy'. In E. B. Schumpeter (ed.). *The Industrialisation of Japan and Manchukuo 1930–1940*. New York: Macmillan.

Reddy, S. G. and T. W. Pogge. 2002. 'How Not to Count the Poor', accessed from www.socialanalysis.org.

Saul, S. B. 1960. *Studies in British Overseas Trade*. Liverpool: Liverpool University Press.

Slicher Van Bath, B. H. 1963. *The Agrarian History of W. Europe A.D. 500–1800*. London: Edward Arnold.

Turner, M. E., J. V. Beckett and B. Afton. 2001. *Farm Production in England, 1700–1914*. Cambridge: Cambridge University Press.

Chapter 5

Declining credibility of the neoliberal state and agrarian crisis in India: some observations

D. N. Dhanagare

Let me first of all highlight the basic features of a neoliberal state within the broad theoretical framework of neoliberalism. Then, with some data one can establish linkages between micro-processes and macro-level forces working at global and at nation-state levels. We can then spell out why we consider the Indian state as a neoliberal state, especially since the advent of economic liberalism in the 1990s. It is then possible to understand and explain the agrarian crisis, not just transition, in India today by relating it to declining credibility of the neoliberal Indian state.

Broadly, the theory of neoliberal capitalism would view the state as an institution that acts as a custodian of individual private property, and upholds rule of law – especially the law protecting the sanctity of property as a fundamental right; it also facilitates and promotes free market economy and trade. With robust optimism, it exudes exemplary confidence in the efficiency of market mechanisms to ensure a fair allocation of scarce resources. Further, it subscribes to desirability of the global regime for free trade (including international trade) and free capital mobility (Hay 2007: 53–54), with the state to intervene only as a facilitator/custodian of free market. In fact the term 'neoliberal' is the term used as prefix for global capitalism that marks the 'second coming of the nineteenth century *laissez-faire* capitalism' (Munster and Strumpell 2014: 3). Such a notion creates an impression that contemporary theory of neoliberalism is reaffirmation of Adam Smith's utopian idea of *laissez-faire* economy operating within nation-state boundaries. It therefore logically follows that in legal framework of a neoliberal state, all contracts would be honoured and business transactions would have a built-in 'safety valve' so that capital accumulation through profit maximisation would be possible; the same is attributed to entrepreneurial skills, initiative and hard work. Naturally, such a theory of neoliberalism would propound ideas that (1) 'economic prosperity is a precondition

Declining credibility of the neoliberal state 139

for poverty alleviation and that (2) 'trickle-down effect' of economic development through free market offers the lasting solution to problems of any welfare state'. In a nutshell, therefore, the forces of neoliberal economy constantly peep into politics and expect the state to act as a conduit of neoliberal regime (see Clark 1991).

It is obvious why any neoliberal state acts as the champion of privatisation of key economic sectors and endeavours assiduously for deregulation – through cutting notorious bureaucratic red tape. The neoliberal state thus paints a glossy picture of free competition that achieves maximum consumer satisfaction and yet promises to reduce tax burden (Harvey 2010: 65). It is almost axiomatic that a neoliberal state would sing the tune of globalisation and readily agree to dance to the rhythm of world market (Dhanagare 2014: 82–86). Success or failure in work, or in business enterprise, is explained in terms of absence or presence of entrepreneurial skills and initiative and not attributed to any systemic property of the neoliberal state.

The consequences of neoliberalism and its impact on the state are not far to seek; the state views national sovereignty over production, marketing and capital investment movement as something to be willingly subjected to the laws of global market economy. Aihawa Ong has characterised 'neoliberalism' as an 'economic tsunami that attacks nation-state space conceived of as an inert receptacle for market driven forces and effects' (Ong 2007: 4). Theorists of neoliberalism are often suspicious of democratic system founded on the principle of majority rule usually perceived as a threat to free market economy and as that could subvert capitalism, and the individual right to property and liberty. The rule by majority is seen as an obstacle to quick decision making. Neoliberals seldom feel comfortable with 'isms' of any kind; they fear fascism, communism and socialism, and also they are as apprehensive about authoritarian populism as they are about majority rule. Their fear is that ideologically committed regimes may impose limits to democratic governance otherwise manageable by money power. Democratic regimes are easy to pressurise for truncating or eliminating market competition – or 'market fundamentalism'. For neoliberals the state ought to intervene as the praetorian guard of free market economy and resort to undemocratic measures when necessary. In fact, many tend to view the neoliberalism in actual working of – what are known as – the Breton Woods institutions (e.g. the World Bank, International Monetary Fund [IMF] and WTO) (Goldman 2006); therefore, a nation-state ought to remain subdued to focusing on the these unaccountable institutions like the Federal Reserves, IMF and WTO. No wonder that neoliberals admire

140 D. N. Dhanagare

state intervention with repressive measures for denying the very freedom that they proclaim to uphold (Harvey 2010: 69; also see Dhanagare 2014: 91–94).

Our discussion in this chapter is aimed at focusing on the impact of the neoliberal Indian state on agricultural sector leading to what we consider as 'agrarian crisis'. Section 1 spells out how the Indian state has functioned in reality in relation to the global economic order in general and institutions like World Bank and IMF in particular both before and after the neoliberal reforms began in India in 1991. This is followed by a critical assessment of the performance of the agricultural sector, presented in Section 2, where we compare the agricultural sector's performance in terms of its contribution to gross domestic product (GDP) with that of other sectors. The shift from growing cereals to cash crop production, rising need of farmers for loans, lack of minimum support remunerative prices for farm produce and rising debt burden on farmers are all leading to farmers' eviction from farm to non-farm economy and/or to suicides. These developments have been demonstrated with data in Section 3. In Section 4 we have attempted to reveal how the Indian state's emphasis on promoting contract farming is actually legitimising debt bondage and increased use of bonded labour; this is done using the findings of a study on Punjab. Discussion in Section 5 explains why agricultural marketing, its policy and institutional practices in the neoliberal state are controlled by the state bureaucracy and the way it functions to serve the interests of the corporate companies at the cost of farmers. How this policy is again reinforcing the use of bonded labour, when legally it is abolished, is elaborated in Section 6. Finally, we have summed up the basic features of agrarian crisis in India resulting from the declining credibility of the neoliberal state.

1. Neoliberal state in reality

In actual functioning and governance a neoliberal state often diverges from the theory of neoliberalism, going outside the limits of its logic and ethics. It also constantly adapts to situations and pressures of circumstances. In some cases, for example, (1) in order to restore and balance the class power twists, neoliberal states can even reverse neoliberal theory when necessary to create good business environment for profitable capital investment. Sometimes political stability requires full respect for law and justice that are supposed to be 'class neutral'. At other times, urgency of such needs can be class specific and hence biased; for example, the treatment of labour and environment is considered by the neoliberal

Declining credibility of the neoliberal state 141

state simply as commodities. When conflict of interest arises with rules and laws, a neoliberal state unfailingly sides with 'good business climate' and indifferent (at times even hostile) to collective rights of workers, their quality of life and/or to the capacity of environment to regenerate itself. (2) The neoliberal state also has a bias in favour of the integrity and solvency of financial institutions. One has to recall the way the United States came to rescue the private banking and insurance sectors when their excessive indiscrete transactions precipitated financial crisis and general economic slowdown. Consequently, the US government had to dole out billions of dollars to put the free market economy back on its wheels (see Roy and Denzau 2007: 128–31). In contrast, issues like human welfare and environmental safety are relegated or side-tracked. (3) Under the pretext of deficit cutting, a neoliberal state can also impose certain tariffs on one industry to favour another although the real purpose could be to generate electoral funds, as President Bush did in the United States, or to assuage feelings of domestic industries. In general, the neoliberal state can either ban imports or restrict import quotas of specific commodities in the interest of a healthy competitive market (Roy and Denzau 2007 122–26; also Harvey 2010: 70–73). One can even expect political interventions by the neoliberal state to serve business interests in geopolitically sensitive areas-such as the Middle East and West Asia, often leading to divergence between theory and practice of neoliberalism.

Several developmental states in Asia, South Asia in particular, have been promoting public sector and planning to work in tandem with their domestic industrial corporate business groups. In the Nehruvian era of development planning, for instance, the Indian state and its 'mixed capitalist economy' attempted to harmonise interests of private and public sectors. At times it preferred collaboration with, or take-overs by, foreign multinational companies to achieve faster economic growth and higher rates of capital accumulation and to generate new employment opportunities. On and off such developing nation-states pay comparatively greater attention to social sector's needs in general, and in post-colonial state in particular, whose economic growth had been stunted during colonial period; such states have to invest massive proportions of their national resources in infrastructural development (Amin 1982: 205–9). More egalitarian policies like inclusive access to educational opportunities, housing and health care services, denied to marginalised sections of society during the colonial period, are given top priority. In the 1980s, for instance, before India announced its policy of new economic reforms, its neoliberalism even facilitated competition

142 D. N. Dhanagare

among corporates, and free and open export market to help leading business houses to compete in the international market. Such bold initiatives helped India's integration with the global economy. India's performance as a neoliberal state since 1991, however, needs a closer scrutiny. After signing the Dunkel Draft of trade agreement and joining the World Trade Organisation (WTO) in 1994, India has shown its inclination to accelerate the process of her economic integration. However, quite contrary to expectations, India's overall annual growth rate of over 8 per cent during 1996–2004 declined to around 4.5 per cent in 2004–13. The growth rate, expected by the World Bank in 2014–15, is between 4.5 and 5.0 per cent. Experts thus say that India continues to score poorly in the World Bank's Risk Perception Index for 2014 since on the zero (0) to 100 scale India's score – a meagre 31 – is lower than the world average of 55. Shockingly enough India trails even the lower-middle countries' average of 43 and is also far behind Russia, China, Brazil and South Africa, which scored 71, 69, 58 and 45, respectively (Singh 2013: 18). Similarly, even using parameter of the 'Ease of Doing Business Index' of the World Bank, India ranked 132 among 185 countries for the year 2013 (Singh 2013: 18). India almost willingly submitted itself to the new regulatory institutions that are now defining new rules, as also conditions, for joining up capital market, and also for membership of the WTO, IMF, or Foreign Trade Agreement (FTA) and thereby conforming to their conditionalities.

The emerging new international institutions drew the new developmental states in South Asia into the neoliberal ambit. Therefore, to avoid their ham-handed treatment, the Stiglitz Commission suggested a number of strong measures for reforming global regulations for capital and market liberalisation (Stiglitz 2010: 106–14). Similarly, the role of international institutions – like the Bretton Woods institutions – such as the Asian Development Bank and WTO has been critically reviewed by the Stiglitz Commission to ensure fairness in free market competition and to protect the interests of developing countries in South Asia (Stiglitz 2010: 129–32 and 141–51). However, the dilemma of developing nation-states is that, on the one hand, they are by no means convinced that neoliberalism is the only option for them (Harvey 2010: 72), and on the other hand, neoliberal capitalist states, like India, have even facilitated the diffusion of the new financial institutions and have adopted a policy of deregulation in major sectors of their economies. In India, for example, recently one of the cabinet ministers in the UPA-II government, Jayanti Natarajan, in charge of the Ministry of Environment and Forestry (until 2013), was summarily removed

Declining credibility of the neoliberal state   143

from the Union Cabinet because her ministry was stalling proposals for foreign direct investment (FDI) of several corporate companies by not giving clearance. It is noteworthy that soon after Natarajan's removal from the Union Cabinet, as many as 70 projects worth Rs 1500 billion were approved by the Ministry of Environment within a week after her removal (Mohan 2014: 10). This confirms that the international regulatory institutions did influence not only the functioning but also neoliberal policies of India to create facilitating environment for world trade and capital flows in finance market primarily to serve the interest of transnational corporate groups.

What has been India's record of economic growth like since 1991? For the first time the Congress government at the centre, led by then prime minister P. V. Narasimha Rao, distanced itself from the Nehruvian democratic socialism and proclaimed India's entry into the global market by endorsing Dunkel Draft and joining WTO. The Indian government took several measures for structural adjustments – such as disinvestment in public-sector undertakings, privatisation of banks and the insurance sector, permitting competition in media, telecommunication and electronic industries, reforms in labour and taxation laws and protecting intellectual property rights. It would be interesting to critically assess the ups and downs that the Indian economy experiences since the 1990s. Likewise, what is the perception of stakeholders from different sectors of Indian economy, about its trajectory of economic growth and development? Examining some selected parameters would enable us to find out whether the Indian economy is advancing and stabilising itself or is sliding down under the global regime and whether the credibility of the Indian state and its neoliberal policies is rising or declining?

2. Agricultural sector as compared to other sectors

A study conducted by the Institute of Applied Manpower Research (New Delhi) has revealed several facts about the conditions prevailing in the agricultural sector. During the decade-long rule of the United Progressive Alliance (UPA) government (from 2004 to 2014), some 15 million workers, including farmers, either have been rendered jobless or have been pushed out of the farm sector to become casual/informal labourers. The world's fourth-largest economy – India –neither has been able to achieve sizeable growth in the non-agricultural sector nor has generated employment opportunities required to absorb the surplus population from the farm sector. The study has further noted that 15 million workers have shifted out of the agricultural sector into the manufacturing and services sectors, leading to a decline in agriculture's share in total employment from 57 to 53 per cent during 2005–10, and some 18 million workers have been added to the workers employed as casual/contract labour in the construction sector because the government has made massive investment in infrastructure development (Sethi 2013: 9). Out of a total of 44 million employed in the construction industry in India, 42 million (nearly 95 per cent) are informal workers without any social security. Thus, the growth in the construction sector is accompanied by casualisation and informalisation of labour mostly evicted from the agricultural sector.

Such a declining trend in India's economy in general, and in the agricultural sector in particular, is further confirmed by the NSSO data (Table 5.1) for 2000–2012.

The data in Table 5.1 show that during 2000–2012 jobs in all the sectors *increased* in India by a meagre 2.2 per cent per year. Particularly the agricultural sector, which used to provide work to nearly 58 to 60 per cent of the working population, has practically stagnated; rather, it has steadily *plummeted* during the period of 13 years (1999–2012). Based on a comparative data on jobs that the NSSO report-2011–12 released recently (contrasted with NSSO report of 1999–2000), one can say that during this period of sustained growth, the bulk of increase

Table 5.1 Sector-wise availability of jobs*

Sector	Jobs in 2011–12 (million)	As share of total (percentage)	Annual change since 1990–2000 (percentage)
Agriculture	224	48	–0.001
Manufacturing	60	13	4
Construction	50	11	17
Trade, hotel	53	11	4
Transport, storage communication	23	5	6
Other services	53	11	4
All	468	100	2.2

Source: NSSO Reports 456 (1999–2000) and 554 (2011–12). These figures have been taken from Verma (2014: 1).

*Obviously some sectors have been left out in the source while presenting the data on selected sectors in this table.

Declining credibility of the neoliberal state 145

has been in retail trade, construction industry and personal services in which only low-paid transitory, but tough jobs became available. The construction sector has had a phenomenal increase in jobs from 16 million to 50 million at the rate of 17 per cent per year. In rural areas jobs on construction sites increased from about 9.4 million in 1999–2000 to 37.2 million in 2011–12, that is by almost 300 per cent during the 13-year period (Verma 2014: 1). This suggests that construction projects provided the second-largest job opportunities in rural areas after agriculture. However, this is in no way a spillover effect of the construction boom in urban India. Rather public works of the central government under the Employment Guarantee Act or MGNREGA account for most of the growth in construction work in rural areas. The other side of the growth story is that real wages have increased by 61 per cent; however, price inflation has tended to neutralise the wage hikes (Verma 2014: 1).

The dismal performance in India's agricultural sector is further confirmed by the statistics on the share of agriculture in GDP as compared to that of Industry and service sectors. In 1950–51 the agricultural sector used to contribute to the extent of 51.88 per cent of the total GDP; however, this share of the agricultural sector has gradually declined to just 14 per cent in 2011–12 (Table 5.2). On the other hand, the service sector's share in the total GDP has increased from 11.10 per cent in 1950–51 to 66.77 per cent in 2011–12 (Jawandia 2012: 6). In spite of this declining share of the agricultural sector in the GDP, the union agriculture minister Sharad Pawar claimed in his interviews to media that Indian agriculture has done extremely well during the UPA-II regime, as wheat and sugar exports from India have touched a new high in world trade. In Maharashtra, experts in agricultural economics say that the

Table 5.2 Share of agricultural sector in GDP to industry and service sectors (percentage)*

Sector	1950–51	1980–81	2011–12
Agriculture	51.88	35.69	14.01
Industry	34.63	22.11*	19.22
Service and others	13.49*	42.20	66.77
Total	100.00	100.00	100.00

Source: Jawandia (2012: 6).

*These figures have been corrected/adjusted on the basis of other sources.

146   D. N. Dhanagare

contribution of the agricultural sector to GDP has come down to just 12 per cent, which is lower than the national average of 14 per cent. The declining trend in agriculture has also been confirmed recently by an expert, according to whom the share of agriculture in the GDP declined from 30 per cent in 1991 to 14.4 per cent in 2011–12 (Singh 2013: 18). However, this decline is not accompanied by any corresponding reduction in the share of agriculture in employment.[1] One of the reasons why performance in agricultural growth has been dismal is that the government of India, as also the state governments, has no consistent policy either for agricultural prices or for marketing, or even for import and export of farm produce. Consequently, farmers seem to have lost faith in the ability of the Indian state and government agencies to offer reasonable support prices for their farm produce and efficient marketing facilities. For example, minimum support prices (MSP) announced by the central and the state governments for various crops every year have not attracted farmers to sell their produce and reap benefits of MSP. For instance, in Uttar Pradesh, where the Samajwadi Party's government had announced MSP, only 14.10 per cent of farm produce (all crops included) was sold to government agencies. Therefore, farmers sold their produce to local traders, middlemen and moneylenders who dominate the local markets and multiply their profits year after year (Table 5.3).

A survey conducted by the Giri Institute of Development Studies, Lucknow (Uttar Pradesh), to find out the 'income and consumption

Table 5.3 Agencies where farmers from Uttar Pradesh prefer to sell their farm produce

Agencies to which sold	Share of farm produce (percentage)
Wholesaler	28.30
Village trader	25.70
Government agency	14.10
Kisan Mandis (agricultural market yards meant for farmers to sell their produce)	13.93
Cooperative society	5.58
Consumers	2.33
Moneylenders	0.52
Agro-processing units	0.30

Source: Parashar (2012: 12).

Declining credibility of the neoliberal state 147

levels of U.P. farmers' collected data from a sample of about 4000 farm households randomly selected from 9 agro-climatic zones covering 24 districts, 42 blocks and 84 villages. The survey findings show that farmers, under normal circumstances, retain around 20 per cent of their crop output for themselves (i.e. family consumption). However, nearly 72 per cent of their produce is sold in the market though farmers do not get any fair value for the farm produce. This clearly shows that less than 20 per cent deal with the government agencies and cooperative societies (that are registered and at times financially supported by the government). An overwhelming majority of Uttar Pradesh farmers do not seem to trust the credibility of these agencies. They prefer to sell their produce to wholesale dealers and/or local traders more than moneylenders-turned traders.

Farmers are generally practical enough to choose the best marketing option for their produce that will fetch them better price barring exceptions of distress sales, that is they prefer prices remunerative enough not only to cover the costs of farm production but also to yield some profit. This rationality is fully justified since production is rising steadily, particularly after farmers started using chemical fertilisers and new seed varieties. Moreover, costs increase exponentially with inflation as also with rising transportation costs and fuel prices. For instance, per acre cost of cotton cultivation was Rs 5000 in 2001–2, but it rose to Rs 24,000 per acre a decade later in 2010–11, because prices of seeds have increased phenomenally. A decade ago the indigenous variety of cotton seeds used to cost Rs 9 per bag of 450 grams. If, ten years later, the same farmer decided to use a hybrid seed variety, then he had to pay Rs 1600 for a bag of 750 grams (Jawandia 2012: 6). Similarly, now cash crop-oriented farmers are no longer just the 'Chayanovian peasants', but are now inclined to experiment, take risk and replace production of food grains by cash crop production, involving quantum jump in production costs. For example, if a farmer grows wheat in Maharashtra, or paddy in Kerala, then his per acre production cost is within the range of Rs 8000 to Rs 10,000. But if he switches over to cultivation of cotton, or grapes, vanilla (in Kerala) or bananas, then per acre costs would range between Rs 0.04 and Rs 0.14 million. The risk in the latter case is then four to five times higher than the risk involved in producing traditional crops. In anticipation of profits farmers take loans from either banks or familiar moneylenders for switching over to cash crops. However, farmers' movements have been protesting against the government for not declaring remunerative prices for farm produce; consequently, this is adding to debt burden on farmers.

148   D. N. Dhanagare

The credit supply to farmers in India is either through the nationalised or cooperative banks and primary credit societies, though most farmers have no easy access to these agencies. Corruption in banks is simply rampant. Local private moneylenders then are left free to fleece farmers by charging exorbitant rates of interest on loans given to farmers. Interestingly enough, the banks charge between 9 and 14 per cent as interest per annum on farm loans. However, the same banks charge just 7 per cent interest rate on loans for purchasing cars and other luxury consumer goods. Consequently, farmers have been getting increasingly drawn into a debt-trap, while input dealers (retail merchants of Bt seeds or suppliers of genetically modified seed varieties and traders of fertilisers and pesticides) are not only getting superrich but also becoming new moneylenders; the net result is that small-time moneylenders, who are often part-time farmers in rural India, have also been committing suicide out of sheer desperation.

3. Farmers' suicides and the response of the state

The period between 1997 and 2009 witnessed farmers' suicides that India never had in the past century. In the states of Andhra Pradesh, Chhattisgarh, Karnataka, Madhya Pradesh and Maharashtra (five states), there were 0.24 million suicides by farmers during that period. If we add figures for 2010–11, then the total number of suicides committed by farmers was 256,000 over the 13-year period. But the first seven years account for 53 per cent of those suicides, while in the remaining six years, 118,000 suicides were committed. This means that in the second half of this period as many as 17,200 farmers committed suicides a year.[2] In Maharashtra state alone during 2001–10, there were 47,670 farmers' suicides, which were three times higher than that in West Bengal. However, the state and central governments have been insensitive to the problem of the affected victims' families. The then union agriculture minister Sharad Pawar neither has reported to have visited families of the victims as a token of sympathy nor has even made any public statement about farmers' suicides.

The worst affected has been the Vidarbha region – the largest cotton-growing belt in Maharashtra state where most of these suicides have taken place. In 2006, the prime minister of India visited some places in Yawatmal district of Vidarbha from where the largest numbers of farmers' suicides were reported. The Indian prime minister wanted to find out facts and offer sympathies to the victims' families. However, neither

Declining credibility of the neoliberal state 149

Sharad Pawar (the then union agriculture minister) nor Vilasrao Deshmukh (the then chief minister of Maharashtra, now deceased) had the courtesy to accompany the prime minister during his visit. Of course, Sharad Pawar could manage to secure a relief package of Rs 22 billion from the central government for the benefit of affected families. However, very little information is available about the actual disbursement of this relief grant. Cumbersome procedures that a victim's family has to follow for getting such a relief grant (Rs 100,000 per case in Maharashtra) has been open to bureaucratic red tape. In some states there are as many as 42 indicators of entitlement for relief for the victim's family. The family is required to fill up information pertaining to these indicators and the victim's family is expected to furnish satisfactory proofs failing which the family stands disqualified. Fed up with such queries, not few families give up their attempt to secure relief. This in turn opens the floodgates for misappropriation of relief funds. Malpractices range from forging signatures of beneficiaries to demanding a commission from them for releasing the relief grant.

Here it is then perfectly legitimate to raise a question: on whose side is the state? Whether the state is protecting the interests of farmers and their families affected by suicides or on the side of those usurious moneylenders and corrupt staff in government (who are often hand in glove with local politicians), banks and cooperative credit societies who compel farmers to commit suicide? In a shocking case of a farmer's suicide in Buldhana district from the Vidarbha region in Maharashtra, the affected family registered a complaint against the moneylender who had charged excessive interest rate and committed fraud that had forced the farmer to commit suicide. However, then chief minister Vilasrao Deshmukh prevented the police from registering an FIR in such a criminal case against the moneylender who happened to be the father of then sitting Congress member of legislative assembly. But when the case was pursued by the victim's family, the ex-chief minister was censured by the Supreme Court for his utterances and action of preventing arrest of the moneylender concerned. After this censure Deshmukh was moved to the rural development portfolio in a cabinet reshuffle at the centre. But the Supreme Court had imposed a fine of Rs 1 million on Deshmukh, but it was paid by the Maharashtra government. Thereafter, at a seminar held in Mumbai Justice Ganguli, one of then sitting judges of the Supreme Court bench, said that 'the shift of Deshmukh from Heavy Industries to Rural Development Ministry [was] a shameful act on the part of the Union Government'. How could a person who thought farmers are lazy in Vidarbha area and are committing suicide because they

150   D. N. Dhanagare

have no other option continues to be a union cabinet minister, that too holding charge of the rural development portfolio (which Deshmukh did till his death)?[3]

4. Promotion of contract farming or of debt bondage?

Recently, the Reserve Bank of India's (RBI) executive director – Deepak Mohanty – suggested that the Indian government ought to exempt fruits and vegetables from agricultural procurement laws as an incentive to improve food productivity. He argued that rising incomes are impacting consumption patterns of people that have shown inclination for increased intake of proteins and vegetables; this led to higher costs of these items. Moreover, wage labour constitutes a major part of the costs of cultivation; also preponderance of small and marginal landholders prevents mechanisation of farm operations as they find costs unaffordable. Similarly, rural employment schemes like Mahatma Gandhi National Rural Employment Guarantee Act (MGNREGA) and growing bargaining power of labour have not only hiked labour wages but also accelerated inflation.[4] Therefore, to curb inflation and control wages, RBI has now recommended contract farming in India.

In advocating contract farming as a panacea, the RBI officials did not think of its impact on small and marginal farmers, who often work as part-time hired labourers during off season. With the Indian state policy favouring FDI, corporate companies are seizing this opportunity to invest in contract farming; if given free hand, they would entice farmers to sign legal agreements. At any rate, unable to compete with contract companies, most small and marginal farmers will be forced to join contract farming; it would entail proletarianisation of small-time producers; they will opt either to sell out their farmland and migrate to cities, or to join the ranks of farm labour and manage to survive on low wages; they will borrow money even for their family subsistence and get trapped in debt bondage. This is the likely impact of contract farming as a method of controlling farm wages recommended by RBI.

Likewise, certain other side effects of contract farming have been neither carefully studied nor even anticipated by RBI officials. Some results of an important study of the 'Effects of Contract Farming Practices on the Farmers in General, and Their Effectiveness in Bringing about Equity in Hoshiarpur Region of Punjab' in particular are worth taking note of in this context. This study has highlighted the fact that a multinational company (MNC) called PepsiCo, a company involved in

Declining credibility of the neoliberal state   151

contract farming, and a large cooperative establishment like Marketing Federation (Markfed) have been aiming at their profit maximisation by imposing certain exploitative terms and conditions on farmers in the draft contract agreement, leaving very little negotiating space for farmers in fixation of prices of farm produce. Similarly, farmers have no right to deciding the terms and conditions of the contract document they sign. The contract agreement between PepsiCo and Markfed and the farmers safeguarded the interests of the corporate companies but did not protect the farmers' rights and interests (Singh 2009: 22–39).

This empirical study focused on Punjab and Haryana farmers who had contracted with corporate companies to grow tomatoes, potatoes, and *Basmati* rice. The farmers were obliged to sell their produce only to their respective contracting companies – PepsiCo and Markfed that were authorised to penalise the farmers who failed to honour the contract. From the stage of sprouting seeds and tender plants, the crop was treated as the *exclusive* property of the contracting company; in the event of any loss or crop failure, the companies could terminate the contract unilaterally; then farmers could sell their produce in the open market. When entire *Basmati* crop failed in 2006 due to the infested seeds supplied by Markfed, the contract risk was not shared by the companies. The same year, an entire project for tomato had to be given up as the contract did not provide for any risk-sharing (Singh 2009: 42). Over the years enormous cost escalation of seeds, fertilisers and pesticides has added to the financial burden, woes and miseries of the contracted farmers. Moreover, contracting companies were delaying payments of purchases in the past, adding to livelihood hardships of small holders. The contract farming companies often involved middlemen traders (especially for export and import), which made no difference to then existing marketing system, and the real producer was at the receiving end. The most important finding of the Punjab study of contract farming is that it encouraged leasing out practices of agricultural landowners. For instance, non-resident Indians owning land or those in service but could not manage self-cultivation, as also those owning small farms but could not face competition with the big corporate companies, were tempted to lease out their farmlands to rich farmers. Thus, contract farming induced 'reverse tenancy' (i.e. small-holding farmers leasing out to rich farmers who became de facto tenant of small landowners); such a practice finally led to irreversible dispossession of small owners (i.e. 'depeasantisation'). Thus, the Punjab experience with contract farming has shown that (1) the contract farming denies equal opportunity to different classes of farmers, (2) that the gap between the rich and the poor

152   D. N. Dhanagare

farmers widens further and (3) that the rich farmers too have to face asymmetrical relationship vis-à-vis the contracting corporate companies (Singh 2009: 42–43).

Not only the contract farming but also FTAs – between India and the European Union – have been the least beneficial to Indian farm producers. As Indian economy got integrated with the global market after the neoliberal economic reforms were introduced in the 1990s, India's trade policy significantly shifted in favour of bilateral trade. The main change is discernible in India's increasing engagement with FTAs as compared to unilateral trade liberalisation through WTO. The FTA between two or more partners has today become a more effective tool of promoting trade liberalisation. This shift has had a significant impact on India's agricultural sector. While the Indian government has been more aggressive in liberalising trade in other sectors, it has been more cautious about committing itself in respect of agricultural trade, because the Indian government is keen to protect the interests of its own large agricultural population, though ironically by reducing tariff rates (specially on imports), and because the bulk of small and marginal farmers, who do not receive remunerative prices, has to compete with imported goods sold at reasonable rates due to tariff reduction. Consequently, a sizeable section of agricultural labourers is living below poverty line[5] as reduced import tariffs have lowered wages. Paradoxically India has achieved food self-sufficiency, necessary to provide food security to the poor and marginalised groups, but India is an exporter of food grains that brings no substantial benefit to the farm producers, while imported cheap raw materials are supplied to domestic industries (Singh and Sengupta 2009: 1).

This study by Roopam Singh and Ranja Sengupta has revealed that exports and imports of agricultural commodities/farm produce in 2007–8 of India's cotton were 10.20 per cent of total exports but cotton imports, being 34.59 per cent of total agricultural imports, were over three times higher. Thus, cotton imports were allowed by India to serve the interests of certain industries at the cost of farmers. Similarly, India's exports of rice (including *Basmati*) were 9.51 per cent + 5.57 per cent (= 15.08 per cent) of total agricultural exports, while, paradoxically, India's rice imports (including *Basmati*) were 17.73 per cent + 5.76 per cent (= 23.49 per cent) of the total agricultural imports, that is one and half times higher than rice exports (Roopam Singh 2009: 10). Notwithstanding these paradoxes, India's then union agricultural minister Sharad Pawar, at a cultural film festival (award function) recently held in Macao, made a tall claim that India was the top exporter of wheat and the second-largest exporter of rice![6] This clearly shows how the Indian state relegated the interests of farmers in agricultural trade and chose to prioritise higher imports over exports to suit the interests of Indian industries.

5. Agricultural marketing in a neoliberal state

In India institutional mechanism evolved over the years for marketing of agricultural produce betrays all principles of free market economy that are integral to theory of neoliberalism. In December 2000 the Government of India-Ministry of Agriculture appointed an expert committee to draft a Model Act for the state agricultural produce marketing. It came out with the Model Act (Development and Regulation Act 2003) that aimed at regulating marketing of agricultural and horticultural produce by setting up market yards and constituting Market Committees district-wise; however, the act kept the controls in the hands of director/managing director of such committees to be nominated by the state government. Such committees had representatives of farmers and traders, who were also nominated by the government. These committees issue licences to weighmen, coolies and others to operate inside the market yards. Government also retained powers to dissolve such committees (Government of India 2003: 7–79). But the state governments seldom allowed to safeguard farmers' interests and in reality allowed traders free hand.

It is important to note that the structure of agricultural marketing committees and their regulation through the Model Act was modelled after the Maharashtra Agriculture Produce Marketing (Regulation) Act 1963 amended in 2005 that provided for full control of the state director with power to issue licences for exports and imports, and to levy and collect fees for marketing and taxes (Government of Maharashtra 2005: 1–5); such state intervention violates free economy under neoliberalism. Similar provisions of state control over agricultural marketing were replicated in regulating the contract farming practices in Andhra Pradesh (Government of Andhra Pradesh 2005: 3–14) and also in Punjab and Haryana where state government also amended (in 2007) the Punjab Agricultural Produce Market Rules – 1962 – in order to regulate contract (Government of Haryana 2007). Compared to the provisions for agricultural marketing in other states, Haryana rules appeared to be caring for the interests of contracting farmers.

Another instance of the declining credibility of the Indian state is that it claimed to have written off loans of farmers to the tune of Rs 23.76 billion during 2009–10. However, the government seldom mentions that it had waived off Rs 8 billion worth of loans given to industries during the same period, and the total industrial loans written off during 15 years (1995–2010) amounted to Rs 5700 billion. It is an irony that the Indian government's rules in the name of rural people, by seeking legitimacy primarily from the rural electorate, sacrifices their interests at the altar of industrial groups and corporate companies who give electoral funds to political class liberally!

It is true that India's nationalised banks are instructed to ensure that at least half of their loans are given to the agricultural sector. However, procedures of processing and sanctioning loan applications, and actual disbursement of loans, remain in shrouded mystery. The National Capital Region (NCR), that is Delhi a metropolitan megacity, is full of concrete jungle with the least of farming. However, according to the data released by the National Bank for Agriculture and Rural Development (NABARD), metropolitan Delhi has more farmers practising agriculture than in Madhya Pradesh, Uttar Pradesh, Karnataka and West Bengal. Delhi-based 'farmers' were allotted Rs 220.77 billion in agricultural loans in 2009 at a mere 5 per cent interest rate, whereas in most other states banks charged an annual interest rate between 9 and 13 per cent on agricultural loans. The loan amount disbursed in Delhi was the second highest in the country, except Punjab where farmers, during the same year, received Rs 270 billion in loans. Even farmers in Uttar Pradesh (Rs 210 billion), Madhya Pradesh (Rs 134.3 billion) and Haryana (Rs 149.15 billion) received much less total amounts of loans though the numbers of cultivators in these states far exceed those in Delhi (Vikram 2010: 1–3).

The high level of loan disbursement for agricultural purposes in Delhi is inexplicable as the NCR has a mere 39,000 ha of farm land. However, records show that just 26,785 ha cover the net cropped area in the NCR of Delhi. The available figures then suggest that Rs 8.06 million worth of loan per hectare was sanctioned by NABARD to farmers in Delhi metropolitan area. However, NABARD supplied agricultural credit for buying inputs like fertilisers and new seed varieties, for installing well, or drip irrigation for horticulture, aquaculture, floriculture, and also sericulture, in addition to purchasing agricultural equipment (for details, see Vikram 2010). Owners of farm houses, cropping up in the elitist Delhi posing themselves as (fake) 'farmers', have often managed loans at cheaper rate which is the worst scams in Delhi, because some of them managed loans through Kisan Credit Cards.

It must be emphasised here that discriminatory rates of interests are charged for farmers seeking agricultural loans at 9 to 13 per cent interest per annum. On the contrary, luxury goods like imported cars can be purchased by securing bank loan at a meagre 7 per cent interest. In the economically backward region of Marathwada in Maharashtra, loans have been given for purchasing 146 Mercedes cars at a cost of Rs 0.63 billion, of which Rs 0.42 billion came from nationalised banks; especially the State Bank of India was in the lead.[7]

6. Use of bonded labour in a neoliberal economy

When social institutions fail to assert themselves effectively, it is a symptom of the declining credibility of the neoliberal state. An uninterrupted use of bonded/slave labour system in India is a striking example of how the neoliberal state has so far failed to prevent labour vulnerability not only in the agrarian but also in the urban industrial sector as both sectors are thriving on illegal use of bonded labour.

Despite the Slavery Abolition Act 1842, use of bonded/slave labour was rampant in Kerala, where the upper-caste Namboodiri Brahmin landlords were treating their untouchable labour as bonded labour, practically bordering on slavery. The practice of slave labour continued unabated as an unresolved agrarian question even after India's Independence. Studies from Rajasthan, Bihar, Gujarat and also Punjab and Haryana have revealed the widespread use of bonded labour (Breman 1974; Tripathi 1989; Jodhka 1994, 1995). After India's independence, the Bonded Labour (Abolition) Act 1976 was passed by the Indian government and made it obligatory for all the state governments to implement the law in letter and spirit. Such a progressive step was in coherence with the general prohibition of forced labour and slavery in Article 23 of the Indian Constitution. However, the traditional system of bonded/slave labour continued through advancing payments of wages to the needy, followed by perpetual obligation to work (often with other family members) without payment till the outstanding debt is fully repaid, which is the most common modus operandi. Whether it is *Kamaiya* system or *melha* arrangement in Chhattisgarh, *sumangali* system in Tamil Nadu in which young girls are sold in prostitution by paying a bride-price or the system in Odisha where entire household is employed by contractors in Kendu leaf production for the Forest Department by advancing certain amounts, in each of these systems indebtedness is the primary source through which men, women, young girls or children are drawn into a debt trap and in perpetual bondage (CEC 2008: 8–15) adding to labour vulnerability.

156   D. N. Dhanagare

When the Bonded Labour (Abolition) Act 1976 came into force, all such labour regardless of the extent of indebtedness was supposed to be freed; the act summarily terminated all such debtor–creditor relationships, written or oral contracts, with local or migrant labour, whether individual or group or family bondage. Using bonded labour has been forbidden and is now punishable under the law. The state has to constitute 'vigilance committees' and to rehabilitate bonded labourers (CEC 2008: 38–59). Notwithstanding such legislative measures, India still has the highest number of bonded labourers as documented by Kara (2012: 9–10) across all industries in the entire South Asia region (Table 5.4).

According to Kara, in relation to size of population, Nepal has the highest number of bonded labourers followed by India and Bangladesh. The average outstanding debt is the highest in India, while the average duration of loan was longest in Pakistan. Average highest rate of interest on loan was 62 per cent per annum in India. Reasons for taking loans included (1) family consumption 24 per cent (of the total reasons mentioned), (2) starting income-generating activity (17 per cent), (3) wedding ceremony (12 per cent), (4) repayment of previous loan (15 per cent), (5) medical treatment (12 per cent), (6) funeral rites (8 per cent), (7) house renovation or repairs (10 per cent) and others (2 per cent) (Kara 2012: 11–12).

Another study of extensive use of bonded labour is conducted in India more recently by John (2014). This study has highlighted the fact that in the brickkiln industry the use of bonded labour is quite common

Table 5.4 Summary statistics on bonded labour cases documented, 2011

Countries	Number of bonded labourers	Average initial debt ($)	Average outstanding debt ($)	Average aggregate duration of bondage	Average duration of each loan	Number of loans taken	Average interest rate percentage
India	327	162	282	6.5	2.5	2.6	62
Nepal	76	153	254	5.5	1.4	4.0	56
Bangladesh	71	169	277	5.7	1.6	3.5	51
Pakistan	30	151	266	6.8	2.4	2.8	60
Total or average	504	161	276	6.3	2.2	2.9	59

Source: Kara (2012: 9–10).

throughout India. It is estimated that one brickkiln unit, with a capacity of providing 3 to 4 million bricks per season, employs 250 workers on an average. Estimates of the number of functioning brickkiln units in India vary from 50,000 to 100,000. It is then safe to estimate that employment in brickkilns in India varies from 12.5 million to 25 million every season. These estimates of labour employed in the brickkiln industry are much below the NSSO data for 2009–10, which suggests that the construction industry employed as many as 44 million (John 2014: 16–18). Indian authorities generally admit the extensive use of bonded labour in the brickkiln industry, an integral part of the construction industry, though debt bondage or 'slave labour' has been totally abolished 38 years ago in India by the Bonded Labour (Abolition) Act 1976. This legislation conformed with the ILO Forced Labour Convention 1930, and also the United Nations (UN) Slavery Convention of 1926 and also the UN Supplementary Convention of 1956 (CEC 2008: 7–8). Therefore, the use of bonded/semi-slave labour in India's brickkiln units is the most contemporary form in which slavery has re-emerged right in the face of all kinds of statutory provisions abolishing or banning that simply exist in the law books but are seldom implemented.

A study of brickkiln labourers in Punjab showed that most (86 per cent) of the workers came from within Punjab itself and only 14 per cent of them were migrant workers – but mostly bonded labourers from Chhattisgarh, Rajasthan and Uttar Pradesh. Moreover, some 97 per cent were Dalits, 94.4 per cent of whom belonged to the *Pathari* caste from Punjab (John 2014: 21–23). Significant is the fact that Punjab has the highest percentage of the scheduled castes (31.9 per cent) in its total population and that most of the Dalit *Patharis* are landless, as just 2.34 per cent of them own some small patches of agricultural or parched land. This recent study has further highlighted that a brickkiln unit or contractor, who supplies contract labour to kilns, never recruits an individual worker but only the worker's family, which invariably includes husband, wife, brothers and children. On an average women are officially reported to work for 10 hours a day though nearly 50 per cent of women brick workers worked 12 hours a day. Taken together, a family produces 500 to 800 bricks a day, and at the piece rate a family is paid Rs 432 per 1000 bricks (John 2014: 24–25). If an average family of five members prepares/produces, for example, 800 bricks every day and receives Rs 350 for that work, then it receives only Rs 70 as wages per person per day. Thus, the wage rate, paid by pieces, works out to be far below the wage rate prescribed by the Minimum Wages Act of 1948 and also below the rate in Employment Guarantee Scheme (EGS) such as

158   D. N. Dhanagare

MGNREGA scheme in which wages range between Rs 120 and Rs 200 per day (John 2014: 25–26). None of these brickkiln workers receives any social security benefits – like safety, pension, provident fund or any maternity benefits admissible to brickkiln units in Punjab under the Factory Act 1947; they do not receive any identity cards either.[8] The bonded and semi-slave labour manages its survival on below subsistence wages, and their employers go scot-free. Such violations go undetected and unpunished in India today 23 years after India entered the era of neoliberal reforms (in 1991), but an overwhelming majority of bonded labourers, primarily landless labourers, are the products of agrarian crisis marked by vulnerabilities – income poverty, absence of social security or assets and even minimum livelihood resources, let alone insurance and pension benefits (CEC 2008: 79–86).

It is not that the crisis has gripped only the agricultural sector. The rural infrastructure development in the country is full of challenges in governance despite massive investment by the state. Development of power and electricity, roads, irrigation as well as of water supply and sanitation in rural areas is of vital importance to the agricultural sector. Data presented in Table 5.5 on investments in rural infrastructure (projections for the 11th Five-Year Plan) show how India's rural landscape has remained neglected affecting farmers adversely.

The hefty investment in upgrading rural infrastructure was aimed at providing electricity to as many as 125,000 villages and 23 million households, connecting 66,802 habitations with all-weather roads, providing irrigation facilities to 10 million additional hectares and so on. The private and public sectors were to share 27 and 73 per cent of these investments, respectively. Such optimistic projections for investment

Table 5.5 Investment in rural infrastructure: projections for the 11th Five-Year Plan (rupees in billion at 2006–7 prices)

Sectors	Projected investment
Electricity	340
Roads	413.47
Telecommunications	160
Irrigation (including watershed)	2573.44
Water supply and sanitation	907.01
Total	4393.92

Source: Haldea (2013: 11).

Declining credibility of the neoliberal state   159

assumed that economic neoliberal reforms will usher in rapid economic growth in the industrial sector and eliminate the 'licence raj', and would also pave the way for speedy development of rural infrastructure. However, as Haldea (2013: 13–14) has put it, 'Old barriers of licence raj were simply replaced by the "contract raj", new bureaucratic patronage networks and barriers in decision making; that led to "crisis of credibility" of India's neoliberal state' (Haldea 2013: 84–88).

The general trend visible in political economy of India since the beginning of neoliberal economic reforms suggests that the sites and trajectories of these reforms reveal unevenness of neoliberal transformations in India across different regional spaces, periods and sections of people. The picture at the macro and micro levels can be summed up as follows:

1   The growth in the agricultural sector is declining rapidly – its current share standing at between 14.5 and 16.5 of the GDP, whereas employment in the farm sector has declined only marginally from 56 to 54 per cent.

2   The Indian state policies entailed massive transfer of assets and resources from the rural to urban areas, from agriculture to industry and from poor to the rich. India's policy framework simply conforms to the regulatory institutions like World Bank, WTO, and IMF.

3   Rise in the power of the corporate groups is due to favourable treatment in import–export policies (and tariff rates) as also encouragement for FDI in industry. Experiences and social arrangements with neoliberal capitalism are significantly uneven across sectors of Indian economy. For instance, in the information technology (IT) hubs like Bangalore and Hyderabad or the automobile manufacturing units controlled by the Tata group in Maharashtra and in Gujarat, production relations may not be very different from what may be found in Chicago, Manchester, Frankfurt or Shanghai; however, experiences with the way corporates are penetrating contract farming sector in Punjab or in the Brickkiln units in India are vastly different.

4   Almost all sectors – transport, telecommunication, civil aviation, banking, insurance and even higher education – are being opened to privatisation; on the contrary social sectors, like health care, education up to the age of 14 (under the RTE Act), right to work and social security to the unorganised workers remain neglected. Even in Indian public-sector undertakings (e.g. telephone industries), 'neoliberalism has ushered in a lethal combination of opportunistic

160 D. N. Dhanagare

pricing tactics, official veniality, and the absence of deregulation allowing the prevailing business environment to become a no-holds barred jungle' (Subramanian 2014: 100).

5 To facilitate people's participation in democratic functioning, the authority of village panchayats is deliberately undermined, though ironically the Indian government repeats the rhetoric of its commitment to 'democratic decentralisation' and 'empowerment of Panchayat institutions' in which bureaucracy and the political class work hand in glove.

6 A dominant policy of market fundamentalism, being intrinsic to the theory of neoliberalism, is steadily on the rise. Consequently, all symptoms of agrarian crisis are evident in contemporary India.

7. Features of the agrarian crisis

In conclusion, the agrarian crisis in India may be summarised as follows:

1 The 2011 Census and also agricultural censuses show that number of farmers are steadily decreasing and so is the contribution of the agricultural sector to the GDP.

2 Farmers in large numbers are committing suicides because of low prices of their farm produce, resulting in indebtedness among farmers. The Indian government justifies the low 'Minimum Support Price' (MSP) for Procurement, stating that industries have to be supplied cheap raw materials, that India's low-cost economy cannot afford to declare higher MSPs to farmers and that food security for the poor required the government to raise adequate food stocks for supply through the Public Distribution System, and also agricultural subsidies are siphoned off by those industries that produce the inputs, like seeds and fertilisers (Joshi 2010: 203–4).

3 Large-scale migration of rural population to towns and cities is taking place because, subjected to vagaries of monsoons, agriculture, in the absence of irrigation facility and assured electricity supply, cannot provide any guarantee of livelihood in rural areas.

4 The Indian state has been adopting populist policies of providing subsidised electricity, and cheap supply of grains (rice at Rs 3 per kg and wheat Rs 2 per kg) through the Public Distribution System's outlets but lacks an efficient distributive network to supply good quality of food stuffs that the poor and needy are entitled to.[9]

5 Above all, the political will required for the purposeful governance is nearly absent today apart from the fact that the political class,

preoccupied chiefly with utilising public funds and resources for personal gains, seems to be flourishing day by day.

Thus, all the characteristics of agrarian crisis in India could be attributed to the policy of neoliberalism that serves the interests of corporate industrial capitalism, to ensure free competition and trade. The agrarian crisis remains because the Indian state has neither desire nor ability to resolve it the near future.

Notes

1 According to economist Arvind Panagaria (2014: 16) India's overall growth rate which was 9.4 per cent in the last quarter of 2009–10 has plummeted to 4.6 per cent in the first half of the 2013–14 financial year.
2 These figures were quoted by P. Sainath (Rural Affairs Editor, *The Hindu*) in his keynote address at a seminar organised by the Department of Sociology, Pondicherry University, on 'Farmers' Suicides in India' on 10 and 11 February 2011.
3 The details of this case and Justice Ganguli's remarks were reported extensively in the media. See *The Times of India* (Mumbai ed.), 8 February 2011, p. 9.
4 These observations were made by the RBI official Deepak Mohanty while delivering the annual Lalit Doshi Memorial Lecture at St. Xavier's College in Mumbai. The report appeared in *The Times of India* (Pune edition), 14 January 2014, p. 14.
5 After the Indian Parliament passed the bill (now act) on Minimum Food Security (2014), it would be safe to estimate that nearly 100 per cent of the agricultural labourers, living below the poverty line, will now be entitled to secure benefits envisaged in the act.
6 The Indian agricultural minister's interview, conducted at the film/cultural festival in Macao, was telecast by most of the Marathi channels on television in India in February 2014.
7 These details have been taken from P. Sainath's Keynote address delivered at a seminar held in Pondicherry University on 10–11 January 2011.
8 These revealing data and facts about the living conditions of brickkilns have been presented by J. John in his recently published article: see John (2014: 25–26).
9 On 18 April 2014 the author met Sharad Joshi, leader of the farmers' movement in Maharashtra. In the interview Joshi told him that poor people holding ration cards, and declared to be beneficiaries under the Food Security Programme, were being told that such a supply/facility of cheap food grains will be available only till the end of the polling for the 16th Parliamentary elections (held in May 2014) in India. Thereafter, there would be no guarantee of continuation of the scheme and that people will be required to buy their normal rations at the normal rates in their rationing shops under the Public Distribution System.

References

Amin, Samir. 1982. 'Disarticulation of Economy within "Developing Societies"'. In Hamza Alavi and Teodor Shanin (eds). *Introduction to the Sociology of Developing Societies*. London: The Macmillan Press Ltd., pp. 205–9.

Breman, Jan. 1974. *Patronage and Exploitation – Changing Agrarian Relations in South Gujarat, India*. Berkeley: University of California Press.

Centre for Education and Communication (CEC). 2008. *Labour Vulnerability and Debt Bondage in Contemporary India*. New Delhi: The Information and Feature Trust (TIFT).

Clark, S. (ed.). 1991. *The State Debate*. London: The Macmillan Press Ltd.

Dhanagare, D. N. 2014. *The Missing Tradition – Debates and Discourses in Indian Sociology*. New Delhi: Orient BlackSwan.

Goldman, Michael. 2006. *Imperial Nature: The World Bank and Struggle for Social Justice in the Age of Globalisation*. New Haven, CT: Yale University Press.

Government of Andhra Pradesh. 2005. *Abstract Gazette Notification* (regarding Amendment to Rule 73 Agricultural Produce and Livestock Market Act 1966 and adding Form 11-A to regulate Contract Farming), Hyderabad, 29 September 2005.

Government of Haryana. 2007. *Haryana Government-Agriculture Department – Notification about Contract Farming*, 9 August 2007, Chandigarh.

Government of India. 2003. *Model Act – The State Agricultural Produce Marketing*, New Delhi.

Government of Maharashtra. 2005. *The Maharashtra Agricultural Produce Marketing (Regulation) Act 1963* (as amended in 2005), Mumbai.

Haldea, Gajendra. 2013. *Infrastructure at Crossroads: The Challenges of Governance*. New Delhi: Oxford University Press.

Harvey, David. 2010. *A Brief History of Neoliberalism*. Kolkata, India: Update Publications.

Hay, Colin. 2007. 'The Genealogy of Neoliberalism'. In Ravi K. Roy, Arthur T. Denzau and T. D. Willet (eds). *Neoliberalism – National Regional Experiments with Global Ideas*. London: Routledge, pp. 51–70.

Jawandia. V. 2012. 'Super India's Development at the Cost of "Bharat"'. *Daily Sakal* (a Marathi Daily, Pune), 81 (355), 25 December 2012, p. 6.

Jodhka, Surinder. 1994. 'Agrarian Changes and Attached Labour: Emerging Patterns in Haryana Agriculture'. *Economic and Political Weekly* 29 (39): A102–7.

Jodhka, Surinder. 1995. 'Agrarian Changes, Unfreedom and Attached Labour'. *Economic and Political Weekly* 30 (31–32): 2011–13.

John, J. 2014. 'Brick Kilns and Slave Labour: Observations from Punjab'. *Labour File* 9 (1–2): 16–26.

Joshi, Sharad. 2010. *Down to Earth*. New Delhi: Academic Press.

Kara, Siddharth. 2012. *Bonded Labour – Tackling the System of Slavery in South Asia*. New York: Columbia University Press.

Mohan, Vishwa. 2014. '70 Projects Worth Rs. 1.5 Lakh Crores Okayed after Natarajan's Departure'. *The Times of India* (Pune ed.), 14 January 2014, p. 10.

Munster, Daniel and Christian Strumpell. 2014. 'The Anthropology of Neoliberal India – An Introduction'. *Contributions to Indian Sociology* 48 (1): 1–16.

Ong, Aihawa. 2007. 'Neoliberalism as a Mobile Technology'. *Transactions of the Institute of British Geographers* 32 (1): 3–8.

Panagaria, Arvind. 2014. 'A Tale of Two Prime Ministers'. *The Times of India* (Pune ed.), 11 January 2014, p. 16.

Parashar, B. K. 2012. 'Most U.P. Farmers Reaping MSP Benefits'. *The Hindustan Times* (Chandigarh ed.), 10 December 2012, p. 12.

Roy, R. K. and A. T. Denzau. 2007. 'The Neoliberal Shift in US Fiscal Policy from the 1980s to the 1990s'. In R. K. Roy, Arthur T. Denzau and Thomas D. Willett (eds). *Neoliberalism – National Regional Experiment with Global Ideas.* London: Routledge, pp. 117–34.

Sethi, Nitin. 2013. 'Study: 15 Million Workers Shifted Out of Agriculture'. *The Times of India* (Pune ed.), 8 February 2013, p. 9.

Singh, N. K. 2013. 'No Real Wiggle Room for Now'. *The Hindustan Times* (Delhi ed.), 25 October 2014, p. 18.

Singh, Roopam. 2009. *Effectiveness of Contract Farming Practices for Agricultural Development and Equity* – (A Case of Hoshiarpur District in Punjab). New Delhi: Consortium for Trade and Development (CENTAD).

Singh, Roopam and Ranja Sengupta (eds). 2009. *The EU-India FTA in Agriculture and Likely Impact on Indian Women.* New Delhi: Centre for Trade and Development (CENTAD).

Stiglitz, Joseph E. 2010. *Global Crisis – The Way Forward* (The Stiglitz Commission Report). New Delhi: Orient BlackSwan.

Subramanian, Sanjay. 2014. 'From Monopoly Power to Deregulated Market: The Travails of a State-Owned Firm'. *Contributions to Indian Sociology* 48 (1): 73–102.

Tripathi, S. N. 1989. *Bonded Labour in India.* Delhi: Discovery Publishing House.

Verma, Subodh. 2014. 'Between 2000 and 2012, Jobs Grew by a Mere 2 per cent Per Year', *Sunday Times of India*, 9 February 2014, p. 1.

Vikram, K. 2010. 'Fake Farmers in Loan Scam'. *Mail Today* 3 (341): 1–4.

Chapter 6

Neoliberal reforms, agrarian capitalism and the peasantry

B. B. Mohanty and Papesh K. Lenka

Understanding of agrarian change in India started with the analysis of relationship between capitalism and peasantry. Though peasant farming was a characteristic feature of Indian agriculture for long, the question of survival of peasantry under capitalist development has been an issue of enduring controversy. Recently, it assumed greater significance in the context of economic reforms in the 1990s intended to bring about major changes in the macroeconomic policy framework of the planned economy to globalise agriculture after the signing of the Agreement on Agriculture under the Uruguay Round of Negotiations of GATT (subsequently the WTO) by introducing reforms particularly in the spheres of production and marketing. This was supposed to accelerate capitalist agriculture leading to promotion of exports and rapid agricultural growth. However, the available empirical evidence on the response of peasantry to the emerging trend of capitalist development is limited and largely inconclusive.[1] Hence, an attempt is made in this chapter to analyse the level of capitalist[2] growth in Indian agriculture in the context of neoliberal reforms and its consequent impact on the existence of peasantry[3] across major states.

The chapter is divided into four sections. Section 1 provides an account of classical and contemporary theoretical debates at the global level and the recent Indian debates on permanence and disappearance of peasantry under capitalism. The trend of capitalist growth in Indian agriculture across major states in terms of cropping pattern, use of purchased inputs, growth of output and capital formation is presented in Section 2. Analysis of changes in landholding, size of rural and agricultural workers, rural population and patterns of rural to urban migration is made in Section 3 to examine the response of peasantry. Section 4 recapitulates the findings of the study and draws conclusion.

1. The theoretical debate

The development of capitalism in agriculture and its impact on peasants has been the core of scholarly research in agrarian studies well over a century. The major focus revolves around the continuing debate over agrarian transition. One of the central themes of this debate is related to the question of survival and death of peasantry, which is known as 'peasant question'. The intellectual origin of this question goes back to the late nineteenth-century debate between Marxism and Neo-populism.

Though Marx did not make a systematic analysis of the development of capitalism in agriculture and maintains somewhat ambivalent position about peasantry[4] and somewhere viewed against peasantry,[5] he indicates in Volumes I and III of *Capital* the conditions of peasantry both in pre-capitalist and capitalist societies and explains the manner in which they are exploited by capital and transformed into wage labourers and capitalist farmers. With the development of capitalist mode of production, Marx says that the mass of the people are expropriated from land and agriculture. To quote him, 'It transforms feudal landed property, tribal property, and small peasants' property in mark communes, whatever may be their legal form, into the economic form corresponding to the requirements of capitalism' (1867/2007, III: 723).

Put it somewhat differently, Marx's analysis suggests that small-scale peasant producers are obstacles to the development of capitalist mode of production in agriculture. Based on his historical experience in England, Marx explains how the capitalist method of farming destroyed the peasantry and led to a kind of agricultural production characterised by the formation of agrarian capital and wage labour. He says, 'The capitalist system presupposes the complete separation of the labourers from all property in the means by which they can realise their labour. As soon as capitalist production is on its own legs, it not only maintains this separation, but reproduces it on a continually extending scale. The process, therefore, that clears the way for the capitalist system, can be none other than the process which takes away from the labourer the possession of its means of production; a process that transforms, on the one hand, the social means of subsistence and of production into capital, on the other, the immediate producers into wage-labourers' (1906, I: 785–86). Engels (1894/1977: 460) also notes, 'The small peasant, like every other survival of the past mode of production, is hopelessly doomed. He is a future proletarian.'

Building on the foundation laid by Marx, both Lenin and Kautsky develop a much more elaborated analysis of peasantry in the context of capitalist development. Lenin notes that the development of capitalism in agriculture would lead to differentiation of peasantry which would ultimately result in depeasantisation. According to him, 'The old peasantry is not only "differentiating", it is being completely dissolved, it is ceasing to exist, it is being ousted by absolutely new types of rural inhabitants-types that are the basis of a society in which commodity economy and capitalist production prevail' (1964, III: 174). Lenin argues that capitalism requires 'freeing of small producers from the means of production' and linked the proletarianisation of the peasantry to the growth of a home market. He further argues that the 'depeasantised' rural peasantry would be re-absorbed into the urban manufacturing sector, which ultimately implies that the peasant is bound to become a member of industrial proletariat. He states, 'One cannot conceive of capitalism without an increase in the commercial and industrial population at the expense of the agricultural population . . . this phenomenon is revealed in the most clear-cut fashion in all capitalist countries' (1964, III: 40). Though Kautsky (1976 as in Banaji) indicates uniqueness of the peasant economy under capitalism, he thinks that it would be premature to conclude that the process of concentration/dispossession is not the general direction. He also holds the view that the general direction towards proletarianisation is much the same in agriculture as in industry.

The classical Marxist's thesis on dissolution of peasantry was challenged by versions of peasant essentialism inherent in agrarian populism. The most important opposition came from Chayanov (1966), who formulated a theory known as 'peasant mode of production', arguing that peasant production was an economic system in its own right with laws of production and reproduction that enabled it to outcompete agrarian capitalism. Chayanov developed the theory of demographic differentiation in opposition to the theory of class differentiation in agriculture. Subsequently, many narratives were constructed to validate 'persistence of peasantry' thesis and falsify the classical conception of capitalism in agriculture.[6] However, it is argued that these narratives misunderstood the classical Marxist viewpoints both in theoretical explanation and in empirical application (Bernstein 2003: 5).

Though the debate on permanence and disappearance of peasantry lost its importance in the 1980s due to evidence on persistence of peasantry from different parts of the world, it generated renewed interest recently in the context of emergence of new relations of production under the neoliberal global capitalist development. Eric Hobsbawn (1994: 289) writes, 'The most dramatic and far-reaching social change

Neoliberal reforms, agrarian capitalism and peasantry 167

of the second half of this century, and the one which cuts us off for ever from the world of the past, is the death of the peasantry.' Bernstein (1994) states that a vast majority of peasants has already been converted to petty commodity producers within capitalism. In a lecture on *Farewells to the Peasantry* he says, 'It is likely that in this current phase of imperialism, most poor peasants confront an increasing simple reproduction "squeeze", as indeed do the great majority of the poor in both South and North. Together with the landless rural proletariat, poor peasants form part of an expanding reserve army of labour in the countryside and in the cities and towns of large areas of the imperialist periphery' (2003: 13–14). Araghi (1995) also argues that the pace of depeasantisation is accelerated with the ongoing transformation of the world economy since the early 1970s. He notes, 'Depeasantisation has been a major global process of our time' (1995: 395). Similarly, while Friedmann (2006: 462) points to 'the present massive assault on the remaining peasant formations of the world', McMichael (2006: 476) states that the corporate food regime dispossess peasants as a condition for the consolidation of corporate agriculture, what Harvey (2005) terms as 'accumulation by dispossession'.

On the other hand, there is a contrary view that emphasises persistence of peasantry thesis. Vanhaute (2012: 319) writes, 'After five centuries of capitalism, two centuries of industrialisation and three decades of neo-liberal globalisation, self-provisioning family farming continues to be a major mode of livelihood in the twenty-first century world. A large part of world food production remains in the hands of small-scale sustainable farmers, outside the control of large agribusiness companies or supermarket chains.' Similarly, Van der Ploeg (2010) argues that farming is increasingly being restructured in a peasant-like way and the reconstitution of peasantry is strategic to future world food security. He says, 'Today's peasantries are actively responding to the processes that otherwise would destroy, by-pass, and /or entrap them. Through these responses, which often are multidimensional and multilevel, considerable parts of the world's agriculture are becoming more peasant-like' (2010: 21).

Viewed thus, while the disappearance thesis is premised on the idea that capitalism leads to the dissolution of peasantry as individuals become wage workers in urban and industrial areas and capitalist farmers in the countryside (Johnson 2004), the permanence thesis, by contrast, argues that peasant societies do not abide by the laws of individualistic capital and have development logic of their own that results in the survival of peasantry and conditions of its reproduction (Araghi 1995). However, the long debate on dissolution and survival of peasantry is mainly based on the experience of the industrially advanced countries of the West. Not only in the old nineteenth-century debate but also in recent global debate, India was rarely a case in point despite the recent phenomenal changes in its agrarian economy and society.

Analysis of relationship between capitalism and peasantry in India began in the 1960s following the introduction of the green revolution, which triggered off the most important debate ('mode of production debate') over the nature and extent of the growth of capitalism in Indian agriculture. It continued in the 1970s extending into the 1980s. Based on texts of Marx and Lenin, the contributors to the debate tried to identify the necessary and sufficient conditions of capitalism in agriculture and the rural class structure. However, it died down without a broad consensus as there was 'little' evidence to suggest that peasant agriculture would transform through proletarianisation. Though the recent neoliberal reforms and global capitalist development have brought rapid transformation in terms of growth of agricultural output, greater entry of private capital, migration and diversification of rural economy, rare attempts have been made to revisit this debate in the context of these changes. However, recently Dipankar Gupta (2005) and Partha Chatterjee (2008) advanced two different lines of argument related to the permanence and disappearance thesis of the peasantry. Gupta (2005) indicates a vanishing trend of the peasantry and village. He notes that 'the town is not coming to the country, in as much as the country is reaching out to the town, leaving behind a host of untidy rural debris'; 'from rich to poor, the trend is to leave the village'. Chatterjee (2008) contests this view. He says, 'Gupta is too hasty in this conclusion. He has noticed only one side of the process which is inevitable story of primitive accumulation. He has not . . . considered the other side which is the field of governmental policies aimed at reversing the effects of primitive accumulation.' He further states, 'The passive revolution under conditions of electoral democracy makes it unacceptable and illegitimate for the government to leave these marginalised populations without the means of labour to simply fend for themselves. . . . Hence whole series of governmental policies are being, and will be, devised to reverse the effects of primitive accumulation . . . as far as I can see, peasant society will certainly survive in India in the 21st century' (2008: 62).

Both the lines of argument, however, are hypothetical, lack substantial empirical evidence and overlook the regional diversities and specificities. Rare attempts have been made to substantiate this debate further.

2. Growth of capitalism in agriculture

Needless to say, Indian agrarian economy witnessed a series of changes during British raj days. The agricultural modernising endeavour of British raj through the introduction of new land tenures, commericalisation of agriculture and suffocation of village industries gradually turned the economy upside down from plenty of land and scarcity of labour to plenty of labour and scarcity of land, setting a process of depeasantisation that led to the unusual growth in size of rural proletariat (Moore 1967; Stokes 1978; Dhanagare 1983). It was rightly observed by Scott (1976) that capitalism was imposed under colonialism by transforming land and labour into commodities for sale. The isolated segments of rural areas were connected with the wider economy at the levels of both labour and product. However, though the changed conditions laid the foundation for the growth of capitalism in the countryside, it could not pick up rapid momentum due to wide prevalence of landlordism, backward productive technology and the influence of a host of primordial factors.

After independence agricultural modernisation experienced a paradigm shift. Emphasis was laid on agricultural growth as well as 'distributive' justice. Land reforms were given a top priority in policy agenda to ensure social justice and augment agricultural growth by optimum utilisation of small holdings. From the 1960s 'scale-neutral' green revolution technology backed by subsidised credit, fertiliser and other inputs was introduced in the water-rich regions for food crops like rice and wheat, which was later extended to non-food crops from the 1980s. Though the impact of green revolution on equity was debatable, it set the trend for agricultural growth by enhancing productivity. The emerging conditions of production led to a debate over the growth of capitalism in agriculture. By and large, it was viewed that the introduction of the new technology was instrumental in bringing about a deeper penetration of capital into agricultural production, and there was a clear-cut trend towards capitalist mode of production (Mohanty 2012). The disagreement rather was how to characterise the kind of Indian capitalist development (Thorner 1982: 2063).

The changes in the post-reform period more distinctively indicate the dominance of capitalism in agriculture. An analysis of available data on more recent changes in agriculture clearly reveals this trend.

Shift in cropping pattern

There has been a marked change in cropping pattern over the past two decades, leading to a significant diversification of crops (Table 6.1).

Table 6.1 Changes in cropping pattern (percentage of gross cropped area)

States	Triennium	Food grains	Oilseeds	Fibres	Sugarcane	Other crops
Haryana	1990–93	67.0	10.6	8.8	2.6	10.9
	2003–6	66.6	10.9	9.0	2.2	11.3
Himachal Pradesh	1990–93	87.7	2.1	–	0.2	10.0
	2003–6	84.1	1.7	–	0.3	13.8
Punjab	1990–93	75.4	2.3	9.1	1.4	11.8
	2003–6	78.8	1.1	6.3	1.2	12.6
Uttar Pradesh	1990–93	79.0	6.7	0.1	7.3	6.9
	2003–6	78.7	4.3	–	8.2	8.7
Bihar	1990–93	88.4	2.3	1.6	1.4	6.2
	2003–6	86.3	1.7	1.6	1.1	9.3
Odisha	1990–93	68.4	9.6	0.9	0.4	20.7
	2003–6	62.0	3.7	1.0	0.2	33.1
West Bengal	1990–93	74.0	6.2	6.2	0.2	13.4
	2003–6	68.5	7.0	6.3	5.8	12.4
Gujarat	1990–93	39.9	26.4	10	1.1	22.6
	2003–6	34.8	26.7	16.2	1.7	20.6
Madhya Pradesh	1990–93	73.5	18.6	2.4	0.2	5.4
	2003–6	67.8	22.9	2.4	0.2	6.6
Maharashtra	1990–93	65.7	12.2	12.8	2.1	7.3
	2003–6	55.9	14.6	12.8	1.9	14.8
Rajasthan	1990–93	63.8	17.3	2.5	0.1	16.2
	2003–6	60.0	21.2	2.0	–	16.7
Andhra Pradesh	1990–93	56.7	24.5	6.2	1.4	11.1
	2003–6	54.2	22.5	8.6	1.7	13.0
Karnataka	1990–93	59.0	22.7	5.1	2.2	11.0
	2003–6	60.8	21.4	3.4	1.7	12.6
Kerala	1990–93	19.1	0.8	0.3	0.2	79.5
	2003–6	9.9	0.1	0.1	0.1	89.6
Tamil Nadu	1990–93	57.3	18.6	3.7	3.3	17.0
	2003–6	61.8	12.6	2.2	4.5	18.8
India	1990–93	68.9	13.3	4.7	2.0	11.1
	2003–6	63.8	13.8	4.9	2.1	15.4

Source: Bhalla and Singh (2010).

Though food grains continued to account for a large proportion of gross cropped area, their total share declined, indicating a trend towards gradual increase in cultivation of non-food crops across the states. However, contrary to all-India pattern, states like Punjab and Haryana experienced marginal growth in the area under food grains because they were comparatively more profitable crops due to high yields combined with subsidised inputs and a remunerative price (Bhalla and Singh 2012: 41). The share of fruits, vegetables, condiments and spices increased significantly in most of the states. The area under condiments and spices covers about 90 per cent of the cropped area in Kerala as against the area under food grains which is only about 10 per cent. The area under oilseeds also increased noticeably, particularly in Madhya Pradesh and Uttar Pradesh, despite the reduction in custom duties on both refined and crude edible oils in 2008, which facilitated more demand for foreign oil in the Indian market. In a nutshell, there is a shift towards higher-value crops. The striking feature of the emerging cropping pattern in the post-reform period is that farmers started integrating their agricultural activities with floriculture, horticulture, viticulture and food processing, in tune with economic change (Jadhav 2006; Mohanty 2009). During the Eleventh Plan period 1.67 million hectares of land was brought under horticulture/high-valued horticulture crops under the provision of National Horticulture Mission which covered 18 states (Government of India, 2013a: 183). The analysis made by Jha et al. (2009) also reveals that agricultural diversification, as measured by increase in the percentage of non-food crops, has grown, and there have been significant changes in the pattern of agricultural diversification at the regional level. Within a region, smaller sub-regions or pockets of specialisation in certain crops and crop groups have emerged. It is reported by Kannan and Sundaram (2011) that oilseed crops like sunflower, rapeseed and mustard, sesamum and coconut registered more than 4 per cent growth in areas in different states. While onion registered high growth rate in Gujarat, Karnataka and Maharashtra, potato emerged to be the major crop along with rapeseed, mustard and sesamum in West Bengal and coconut in Tamil Nadu.

In addition, as estimated by Bhalla and Singh (2012), there is a consistent rise in cropping intensity over the years invariably in all the states, indicating signs of intensive cultivation. In agriculturally advanced states like Punjab and Haryana, the cropping intensity has gone up to 200 per cent. The agriculturally backward states like Odisha and Bihar also experienced a steep rise in cropping intensity. Compared with pre-reform period, the cropping intensity has become higher both at all-India and at state levels in post-reform period.

The past two decades have also witnessed a spread of contract farming by national and multinational companies in Punjab, Maharashtra and Karnataka, which serves an important tool for commercialisation of agriculture following the emergence of WTO in 1995.[7] Initiatives have been taken by government agencies like the National Bank for Agriculture and Rural Development to promote contract farming.[8] As on 14 November 2014, as many as 25 private-sector companies were involved in this kind of farming activities in Punjab, Haryana, Tamil Nadu, Karnataka, Gujarat and Maharashtra, covering a variety of commercial crops (GOI 2014). Though it is advocated that contract farming is beneficial to small peasants (Gulati *et al.* 2008), the evidence is that contracting farms prefer large farmers due to their capacity to supply farm produce in bulk, capability to follow the stringent quality parameters and abide high input costs and associated high risk (Singh 2002, 2009). The experience in India and elsewhere shows how contract farming accelerates land dispossession of small farmers through debt accumulation, increases disparities between large and small farmers, and between the landed and the landless, and widens rural social differentiation (Korovkin 1992; Little and Watts 1994; Singh 2002). It is also argued that the expansion of contract farming promotes export-orientated agriculture at the expense of subsistence agriculture harming food security (Shiva 1991; Little and Watts 1994).

Mechanisation and use of purchased inputs

The post-reform period has experienced a rapid process of mechanisation of agricultural practices (Table 6.2). The use of tractors has gone up remarkably in agriculturally advanced states such as Punjab, Haryana and Uttar Pradesh. In the remaining states also, there is a rising trend of tractorisation. Similarly, between 1992 and 2005 there is a phenomenal growth in the number of pump sets in most of the states.

Major crops are largely under the coverage of high-yielding varieties (HYVs) across the states[9] as a result of which farmers become increasingly dependent on production of new seed varieties. As the supply of varieties of hybrid seeds could not be adequately met by the public sector, the private sector gradually emerged in the 1980s in response to the growing demand for HYV seeds and dominated the seed market by the 1990s (Shiva and Jafri 1998; Revathi and Murthy 2005). Since 1991, 100 per cent foreign equity was allowed in the seed industry (Reddy and Mishra 2009: 20). During the Tenth Five-Year Plan, private seed supply had overtaken the seed sourcing from public sources. The share of the

Neoliberal reforms, agrarian capitalism and peasantry 173

Table 6.2 Use of agricultural machinery (No./0000 ha)

States	Tractors		Pump sets	
	1992	*2005*	*1992*	*2005*
Andhra Pradesh	52	85	101	148
Bihar	19	130	89	117
Gujarat	70	150	67	92
Haryana	444	549	143	155
Himachal Pradesh	45	130	4	20
Karnataka	37	60	58	79
Kerala	9	10	88	196
Madhya Pradesh	24	130	47	107
Maharashtra	50	60	66	62
Odisha	4	28	6	19
Punjab	508	704	170	170
Rajasthan	90	184	54	88
Tamil Nadu	52	102	212	210
Uttar Pradesh	201	397	132	191
West Bengal	12	34	54	119
India	86	167	79	111

Source: Bhalla and Singh (2012).

private sector in seed production in 2006 was 58 per cent, as against the public sector share of 42 per cent.[10] As a result of the privatisation of seed industry, there is an increase in the supply of commercial seeds and the private sector has taken over some of the business of the state seed corporations (Pal 2009: 98).

Agriculture has increasingly become dependent on hired labour, particularly in the agriculturally advanced states. It is estimated (Table 6.3) that in Andhra Pradesh, Maharashtra and Tamil Nadu hired labour constitutes as much as 60 to 70 per cent of the total human labour. In many other states like Punjab also, the share of hired labour is high. Its share is relatively low in some states, which may be attributed to the use of machines by the rich peasants (Das 2012). True, a significant part of this labour is contributed by attached labourers/unfree labourers in Tamil

Table 6.3 Per hectare share of hired labour and market purchased inputs (2008–11)

States	Hired labour*	Purchased inputs**
Andhra Pradesh	66.4	78.5
Bihar	59.6	76.2
Gujarat	48.7	73.7
Haryana	39.0	60.6
Himachal Pradesh	3.9	41.4
Karnataka	62.5	71.8
Kerala	79.3	86.4
Madhya Pradesh	39.0	60.7
Maharashtra	61.4	67.9
Odisha	38.7	46.6
Punjab	65.3	78.5
Rajasthan	17.5	48.6
Tamil Nadu	69.2	77.4
Uttar Pradesh	33.1	61.8
West Bengal	49.0	64.8

Source: Government of India (2011).

Note: Figures are (unweighted) averages for the crops grown in particular provinces.
*Percentage to the cost of total human labour; **percentage to the total operational cost of cultivation.

Nadu, Maharashtra, Gujarat and Haryana (Breman 1996; Lerche 2007; Guérin 2013). However, in a series of recent articles Brass (2008, 2014) has interpreted that the classical Marxist theory recognises the association of unfree labourers with capitalism.

In addition, in a majority of states agricultural practices heavily relied on market purchased inputs (Table 6.3). In Punjab, Tamil Nadu and Andhra Pradesh, per hectare share of market purchased inputs to total operational cost comes to about 80 per cent. Only few states like Rajasthan and Odisha report less than 50 per cent share of market purchased inputs. According to the National Sample Survey Organisation's (NSSO) survey (2005) nearly half of the farmers purchased seed off-farm in almost all the agriculturally advanced states. Though increasing

Neoliberal reforms, agrarian capitalism and peasantry 175

dependence on market purchased inputs necessitates availability of credit facilities, there has been a sharp decline in the share of the formal sector in rural credit in the post-reform period.[11] The share of public-sector banks in rural credit has fallen continuously from the peak of 15 per cent in 1987 to 8 per cent in 2006 (Shah *et al.* 2007: 1357). The 'targeted priority lending' or 'directed credit' to agriculture was put on the back burner at the recommendation of the Narasimham Committee (1992) on financial reforms. It is estimated (Ramachandran 2011) that due to reforms the cross-subsidisation declined and big farmers and corporations obtained very large and high proportion of formal sector loans. The reforms with respect to storage and agricultural marketing intensified further privatisation and concentration of incomes in the hands of big farmer-trader and corporate interest.

Growth of agricultural output and gross capital formation (GCF)

The all-India compound annual growth rate in the indices of area, production and yield of the major crops during the past two decades indicates significant progress towards increasing production, yield levels and crop diversification.[12] The state-wise analysis shows a rising trend of total value of output of agriculture from Rs 3828 billion in 1999–2000 to Rs 4257 billion in 2005–6 (at 1999–2000 prices) at all-India level. Almost all the major states follow this pattern excepting minor variations here and there (Table 6.4). The estimates made by Bhalla and Singh (2009) of the annual compound growth rate of value of agricultural output show this as having increased at the rate of 3 per cent per annum in 1990–93 over 1980–83, but at only 2 per cent in 2003–6 over 1990–93. However, Vaidyanathan (2006: 4011) argues, '[r]igorous statistical tests on official time series do not provide strong corroboration of a progressive deceleration of agricultural growth'. Overall GCF in agriculture (including the allied sector) almost doubled in the past ten years and registered a compound average annual growth of 8 per cent. Rate of growth of GCF accelerated to 10 per cent in the Eleventh Plan (2007–12), compared with growth of 3 per cent during the Tenth Plan (2002–7).[13]

The share of private investment in agriculture (in 1999–2000 constant prices) increased from 66 per cent in 1989–90 to 80 per cent in 2003–4. In 2004–5 prices, the share increased from 80 per cent in 2004–5 to 82 per cent in 2008–9 (Dev 2012). On the contrary, the growth in public-sector investment in agriculture which continued up

176 B. B. Mohanty and Papesh K. Lenka

Table 6.4 Total value of output agriculture (at 1999–2000 prices) (rupees in billions)

States	1999–2000	2005–6
Andhra Pradesh	281	340
Bihar	142	149
Gujarat	167	295
Haryana	143	158
Himachal Pradesh	22	37
Karnataka	290	295
Kerala	128	163
Madhya Pradesh	232	218
Maharashtra	437	541
Odisha	114	135
Punjab	223	240
Rajasthan	203	238
Tamil Nadu	188	174
Uttar Pradesh	565	572
West Bengal	343	368
Total	3828	4257

Source: Government of India (2008).

to 1980–81 declined year after year, and the recent level (1989–90 to 2000–2001) of public investment is less than three-fourths of the level attained during 1980–81 (Chand 2009: 46).

Stated precisely, the rapid growth in commercial agriculture led to increasing control of private sector establishing a new link between agriculture and industry. Along with the traditional agriculturally advanced states like Punjab and Haryana, industrially progressive states like Maharashtra and Gujarat also experience a rapid transformation in agriculture on capitalist lines. Kautsky rightly observed, 'Capital does not confine itself to industry. When it is strong enough it invades agriculture' (Banaji 1976: 4–5). The rest of the states also exhibit a similar pattern, although the pace of change is relatively slow. Das (2012: 195) aptly writes,

In India, necessary conditions for capitalism exist, which are empirically verifiable. These include: commodity production;

commodification of land and other means of production confronting labour as capital; and a class of numerically expanding and legally 'free' labourers, forced to work for a wage because they do not own sufficient means of production. Agricultural production is dominantly capitalist.

The same could be said about another study made by Lerche (2013), which also notes that capitalism in Indian agriculture is deepening and the process of capitalist agrarian accumulation and peasant differentiation are ongoing.[14]

3. Impact on peasantry

Differentiation and proletarianisation

The cumulative impact of the agrarian changes has accelerated the process of differentiation among the peasantry in the countryside. Statewise analysis of the distribution of size-classes of land cultivated by households across the states in terms of area as well as number indicates a rising trend of differentiation among the peasantry over the past two decades in many states (Table 6.5). The size class-wise distribution of land cultivated by households between 1993–94 and 2011–12 shows a sharp rise in landlessness among the rural households. The proportion of landless rural households is significantly higher in agriculturally developed states of Tamil Nadu, Punjab and Haryana. The industrially developed states like West Bengal, Gujarat and Maharashtra also record a high percentage of landlessness. Almost all the states invariably indicate a continuous rising trend of landlessness. Comparatively the number of landless rural households is less in Himachal Pradesh.

The analysis made by Rawal (2008) using household-level data from the 48th and 59th rounds (1992 and 2003–4) of the NSSO provides additional facts on rising inequality in landownership. It reveals that more than 40 per cent of the households in rural India are landless and as much as 15 million acres are in ownership holdings of more than 20 acres. The Gini coefficient of ownership of land other than homestead is reported to have increased from 0.73 to 0.76 over this period. States that are particularly noteworthy in this context are Punjab, Haryana, Gujarat, Maharashtra, Karnataka and Andhra Pradesh. However, in few states like Kerala and West Bengal, as per the estimate, a very small amount of land remains under large holdings. As per Rawal's more recent estimate (2013), the Gini coefficient of land cultivated by households at

Table 6.5 Size class-wise distribution of land cultivated by households (percentage)

States	Size classes	Number		Area	
		1993–94	*2011–12*	*1993–94*	*2011–12*
Andhra Pradesh	Landless	49	61	0	0
	Marginal and small	42	32	46	53
	Medium and semi-medium	8	6	45	36
	Large	0	0	10	10
Bihar	Landless	37	46	0	0
	Marginal and small	56	50	58	67
	Medium and semi-medium	6	4	33	32
	Large	0	0	9	2
Madhya Pradesh	Landless	25	38	0	0
	Marginal and small	47	44	27	38
	Medium and semi-medium	27	17	59	54
	Large	2	1	14	9
Gujarat	Landless	46	53	0	0
	Marginal and small	37	36	28	37
	Medium and semi-medium	16	11	56	52
	Large	1	1	17	11
Haryana	Landless	52	60	0	0
	Marginal and small	28	25	22	32
	Medium and semi-medium	19	15	60	63
	Large	2	0	18	5
Himachal Pradesh	Landless	13	21	0	0
	Marginal and small	84	78	81	94
	Medium and semi-medium	3	1	19	6
	Large	0	0	1	0

States	Size classes	Number		Area	
		1993–94	2011–12	1993–94	2011–12
Karnataka	Landless	38	48	0	0
	Marginal and small	45	37	33	32
	Medium and semi-medium	16	14	53	55
	Large	1	1	14	12
Kerala	Landless	69	53	0	1
	Marginal and small	30	47	80	85
	Medium and semi-medium	0	0	20	11
	Large	0	0	0	4
Maharashtra	Landless	43	50	0	0
	Marginal and small	39	37	30	39
	Medium and semi-medium	16	13	54	56
	Large	1	0	15	5
Odisha	Landless	35	41	0	0
	Marginal and small	58	54	64	71
	Medium and semi-medium	7	5	34	28
	Large	0	0	2	0
Punjab	Landless	62	74	0	0
	Marginal and small	21	16	18	26
	Medium and semi-medium	15	10	56	59
	Large	2	1	25	15
Rajasthan	Landless	19	29	0	0
	Marginal and small	48	48	18	27
	Medium and semi-medium	30	21	53	62
	Large	4	1	28	10

(Continued)

180   B. B. Mohanty and Papesh K. Lenka

Table 6.5 Continued

States	Size classes	Number		Area	
		1993–94	*2011–12*	*1993–94*	*2011–12*
Tamil Nadu	Landless	63	79	0	0
	Marginal and small	33	19	62	71
	Medium and semi-medium	3	1	33	29
	Large	0	0	4	1
Uttar Pradesh	Landless	23	35	0	0
	Marginal and small	66	60	53	67
	Medium and semi-medium	10	5	44	31
	Large	0	0	3	2
West Bengal	Landless	42	65	0	0
	Marginal and small	56	34	78	81
	Medium and semi-medium	2	1	21	18
	Large	0	0	0	0

Source: Rawal (2013).

all-India level increased from 0.74 in 1993–94 to 0.78 in 2011–12.[15] The increasing inequality in distribution of land is attributed to the process of primitive accumulation as well as the market-driven class differentiation (Das 2012: 186n).

Besides, looking at the successive reports of *Rural Labour Enquiry* between 1993–94 and 2004–5 on distribution of agricultural labour households without cultivated land (Table 6.6), it is found that in states like Punjab and Haryana almost all the agricultural labour households are landless and the proportion of landlessness has gone up phenomenally in these states in the past one decade. While in Haryana it has gone from 85 per cent in 1993–94 to 97 per cent in 2004–5, Punjab experienced an increase from 95 to 97 per cent during this period. The industrially developed states like Gujarat and Maharashtra also report a rapid rise in landlessness of the agricultural labour households. The rising magnitude of landlessness among the agricultural labour households signifies an increasing separation of capital and wage labour as a consequence of capitalist expansion.

Table 6.6 Agricultural labour households without cultivated land (percentage)

States	1993–94	2004–5
Andhra Pradesh	58.1	69.8
Bihar	62.2	70.1
Gujarat	60.9	67.5
Haryana	85.0	97.0
Himachal Pradesh	27.7	27.2
Karnataka	52.4	61.8
Kerala	75.7	48.7
Madhya Pradesh	43.3	53.9
Maharashtra	57.8	63.5
Odisha	42.0	42.1
Punjab	94.6	97.0
Rajasthan	48.2	55.3
Tamil Nadu	75.1	85.5
Uttar Pradesh	37.9	43.4
West Bengal	50.7	56.6
India	56.9	61.7

Source: Rural Labour Enquiry, Relevant Issues.

Increasing mechanisation gradually reduced the demand for more agricultural labourers, which ultimately resulted in decline of their earnings (Narayanamoorthy and Deshpande 2001). A recent report released by the International Labour Organization (ILO) indicates that real wages in India have declined in a majority of states shrinking the purchasing power of wage earners. As per the report, India's real wages fell 1 per cent, while labour productivity grew 7.6 per cent between 2008 and 2011. An analysis made by Gulati et al. (2013: 6) shows that real farm wages grew at an annual rate of 3.7 per cent during the 1990s, but they grew at a lower rate of 2.1 per cent per annum during the 2000s (2001–2 to 2011–12); noticeably they fell by (–) 1.8 per cent per annum from 2001–2 to 2006–7. It is also pointed out that the two states, namely Gujarat and Haryana, stand out with low growth of real farm wages throughout the entire period, despite the fact that during the 2000s they registered high rate of growth in agriculture and Gujarat

182 B. B. Mohanty and Papesh K. Lenka

has also registered almost 10 per cent growth per annum (Gulati *et al.* 2013: 13).

This apart, the available census data report that in several states the proportion of agricultural labourers has grown in the past two decades with a corresponding decline in the number of cultivators, which clearly reveals the process of proletarianisation of small or marginal peasants (Table 6.7). States like Punjab, Odisha and Haryana which report a declining trend in the number of agricultural labourers between 1991 and 2011 also experience a decline in the number of cultivators, indicating a shift of workforce from agriculture. Growth in the ratio of

Table 6.7 Rural cultivators and agricultural labourers (percentage to total rural main workers)

States	Cultivator		Agricultural labour		Percentage of agricultural labourers to cultivators	
	1991	2011	1991	2011	1991	2011
Andhra Pradesh	33.5	24.5	47.5	51.9	142.0	212.5
Bihar and Jharkhand	47.8	30.6	40.2	44.2	84.2	144.2
Gujarat	46.1	38.5	30.7	35.4	66.5	92.0
Haryana	49.6	42.7	23.4	18.2	47.2	42.7
Himachal Pradesh	68.6	50.2	3.5	3.6	5.1	7.3
Karnataka	43.8	38.7	35.9	31.8	82.1	82.3
Kerala	15.1	9.8	30.6	15.4	202.6	157.9
Maharashtra	46.3	42.1	36.6	39.4	79.2	93.6
Madhya Pradesh and Chhattisgarh	61.1	47.0	27.0	37.7	44.3	80.2
Odisha	49.4	37.3	31.4	27.3	63.7	73.2
Punjab	42.8	33.7	30.8	21.1	71.8	62.8
Rajasthan	71.1	59.6	11.5	12.8	16.3	21.5
Tamil Nadu	32.8	23.0	44.7	40.8	136.5	177.3
Uttar Pradesh and Uttaranchal	63.0	45.4	21.5	26.2	34.1	57.8
West Bengal	38.0	24.8	32.2	34.2	84.9	138.2
India	48.4	37.7	31.6	32.9	65.4	87.3

Source: Primary Census Abstract, Relevant Years.

Neoliberal reforms, agrarian capitalism and peasantry 183

agricultural labourers to cultivators is conspicuous in many states. At all-India level the percentage of agricultural labourers to cultivators has gone up to 87 per cent in 2011 as against 65 per cent in 1991. Among the states Andhra Pradesh and Tamil Nadu experience a higher ratio of agricultural labourers.

Depeasantisation

The number of non-cultivating peasant households in rural India has increased significantly. To go by the NSS data (48th and 59th rounds), non-cultivating peasant households increased from 30 per cent in 1991 to 37 per cent in 2002 at all-India level.[16] Barring few states like Haryana, Kerala and Punjab, in all other states there is a significant growth of them. However, the argument that this increase led to the growth of landlordism (Vijaya 2012) in the countryside is contested. Harriss (2011) notes on the basis of NSS data that in most of the country landlordism has unquestionably declined. The share of leased-in land in the total operated area, according to his estimate, declined from 10.7 per cent in 1960–61 to just 6.5 per cent in the kharif (summer) season of 2002–3. Moreover, the recent analysis of NSS data also clearly indicates the growth of non-cultivating households over the years in almost all the states (Table 6.8). In Tamil Nadu, Punjab, Haryana, West Bengal and Andhra Pradesh, a large majority of rural households do not cultivate land. For example, the proportion of households that did not cultivate any land in Tamil Nadu was about 80 per cent in 2011–12. This evidence demonstrates the declining trend of peasantry.

An analysis of changes in the size of rural workers engaged in agriculture, rural main workers and rural population provides firm evidence on the gradual process of depeasantisation. At all-India level, the number of cultivators which was 48 per cent in 1991 came down to 38 per cent in 2011, indicating a consistent decline over the years (Table 6.7). Almost all the states experienced a sharp decline in the number of cultivators. It is more prominent in states like Punjab, Haryana, Uttar Pradesh, Bihar and Tamil Nadu. There is also a gradual shift of rural labour force from agriculture to non-agriculture, and the trend is more or less common to all the states in the past two decades (Figure 6.1). True, agriculture continues to absorb a large majority of population. Nevertheless, a significant decline of workforce in agriculture is reported in agriculturally advanced states of Punjab, Haryana and Tamil Nadu. Among the states, Kerala has experienced a substantial decline of agricultural labour force in the past two decades, and only about 25 per cent of its rural workforce

Table 6.8 Rural households (%) that did not cultivate any land

States	1993–94	2011–12
Andhra Pradesh	49.5	61.2
Bihar	37.5	45.7
Madhya Pradesh	24.9	38.3
Gujarat	46.3	52.7
Haryana	51.5	60.4
Himachal Pradesh	13.3	21.3
Karnataka	38.3	47.9
Kerala	69.4	52.7
Maharashtra	43	49.7
Odisha	35.4	40.5
Punjab	61.5	73.5
Rajasthan	18.9	29.4
Tamil Nadu	63.4	78.9
Uttar Pradesh	22.9	35
West Bengal	41.6	65
India	38.7	48.5

Source: Rawal (2013).

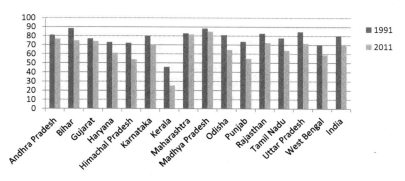

Figure 6.1 Rural workforce in agriculture (%)
Source: Primary Census Abstract of India, Relevant Years.

was in agriculture in 2011. Furthermore, the NSS data (68th round) on household self-employment in agriculture also demonstrate the vanishing sign of peasantry.[17] In states like Kerala, Tamil Nadu and West Bengal, less than 20 per cent of the households have self-employment in agriculture, and a large majority of them across the states are self-employed outside agriculture.

Changes in the number of rural main workers reveal a clear-cut trend towards increasing migration of workers from rural to urban areas. The number of rural main workers which was 78 per cent to total main workers in 1991 has decreased gradually to 68 per cent in 2011 at all-India level (Figure 6.2). The rapid decline of rural workers is noticed in states like Kerala, Tamil Nadu, Punjab, Haryana, Gujarat, Maharashtra and Karnataka. The trend of this change is relatively low in agriculturally backward states of Odisha, Bihar, Rajasthan and Madhya Pradesh. The data furnished by NSSO also indicate higher rate of migration from rural to urban areas in Gujarat, Maharashtra, Tamil Nadu, Andhra Pradesh, Haryana and Karnataka. Relatively less migration is reported in backward states like Bihar, Odisha and Uttar Pradesh.[18] Absence of rapid migration from rural to urban areas across the states (despite rising trend of proletarianisation of peasantry) could be attributed to few recently launched poverty alleviation programmes.[19]

Though decline in rural population as an indicator of depeasantisation has its limitations (Johnson 2004), it provides supplementary information for interpreting the pace of disappearance of peasantry. The changes in the size of rural population (Figure 6.3) reveal that though the majority of population across the states continues to be rural, there is significant decline in rural population, particularly in

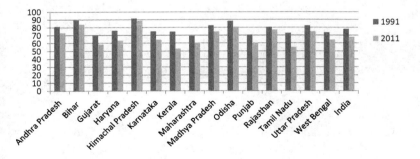

Figure 6.2 Rural main workers (%)
Source: Primary Census Abstract of India, Relevant Years.

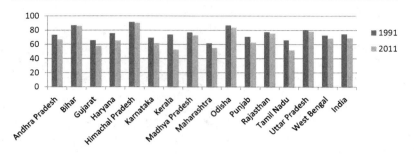

Figure 6.3 Rural population (%)
Source: Primary Census Abstract of India, Relevant Years.

Kerala, Tamil Nadu, Maharashtra, Gujarat, Haryana and Punjab. On the other hand, in states like Himachal Pradesh, Bihar and Odisha, the proportion of rural population comes to more than 80 per cent and the rate of decline is insignificant.

In sum, though the process of impoverishment and proletarianisation of peasantry is common to almost all the states, the process of depeasantisation is more discernible not only in agriculturally advanced states like Punjab, Haryana and Tamil Nadu but also in few other industrially advanced states like Maharashtra and Gujarat.

4. Conclusion

The process of agrarian change in India is complex, and its trend is not uniform across the states. Though agriculture invariably continues to be the major source of livelihood and employment in the countryside and the rural economy is dominated by small-scale agricultural producers, signs of gradual disappearance of peasantry are evident in most states. Almost all the states move in the similar direction although the pace varies. Analysis of the relationship between the level of capitalist development in agriculture and response of peasantry indicates that the states with a higher level of capitalist development show signs of fast disappearance of peasantry (Table 6.9). However, some states with a medium and low level of capitalist development like Maharashtra and West Bengal also indicate signs of fast disappearance of peasantry. This is mainly attributed to their greater industrial development, which provides scope for the absorption of surplus rural labour. A state like Andhra Pradesh (despite its greater level of capitalist development) does not indicate a fast disappearance of peasantry because of its relatively less industrial

Table 6.9 Level of capitalist development and response of peasantry

Particulars	Distribution of states		
	High	*Medium*	*Low*
Relative level of capitalist development in agriculture	Gujarat, Tamil Nadu, Punjab, Andhra Pradesh and Haryana	Karnataka, Madhya Pradesh, Rajasthan, Bihar and Maharashtra	Odisha, Kerala, Himachal Pradesh, West Bengal and Uttar Pradesh
Relative ranks in industrial development	Maharashtra, Gujarat, Tamil Nadu, Uttar Pradesh and West Bengal	Karnataka, Andhra Pradesh, Madhya Pradesh, Rajasthan and Haryana	Bihar, Punjab, Odisha, Kerala and Himachal Pradesh
Response of peasantry	*Signs of fast disappearance*	*Signs of moderate disappearance*	*Signs of slow disappearance*
	Gujarat, Tamil Nadu, Kerala, Punjab, Maharashtra, West Bengal and Haryana	Karnataka and Andhra Pradesh	Madhya Pradesh, Rajasthan, Uttar Pradesh, Odisha, Bihar and Himachal Pradesh

Note: All the selected 15 states are classified into three categories such as top-ranking five, medium-ranking five and bottom-ranking five, based on each indicator identified for assessing the level of capitalist development and disappearance of peasantry. Ranking order for capitalist development is drawn on the basis of four indicators: area under non-food crops, share of hired labour, market purchased inputs and use of tractor. States indicating top ranks in two or more indicators and without having bottom ranking in any of the remaining indicators are treated as having a higher level of capitalist development. Similarly, states showing medium ranks in two or more indicators are categorised as having medium level of capitalist development. The states experiencing bottom ranking in two or more indicators are considered as signs of lower level of capitalist development. Similarly, the rate of disappearance of peasantry is analysed in terms of four indicators: rate of decline in rural population, rural main workers, rural labour force in agriculture and increase in share of households that did not cultivate any land. States with higher ranks with two or more indicators without bottom ranking in any of the remaining indicators are considered as having signs of fast disappearance of peasantry. States showing medium ranks in two or more indicators are classified as having moderate signs of disappearance of peasantry. The states indicating lower ranks in two or more indicators are categorised as having signs of slow disappearance of peasantry. Ranks orders of states in terms of rate of industrial development are assessed in terms of shares in total manufacturing (organised and unorganised sectors) in gross state domestic product, as drawn in Papola et al. (2011: 29).

development as a result of which surplus labour in agriculture moves to non-agricultural occupations in rural areas. States with a low level of capitalist development such as Odisha, Himachal Pradesh and Uttar Pradesh largely signal a slow process of disappearance of the peasantry. Although the relationship between the level of capitalist development and disappearance of peasantry is complex due to large regional variations in terms of sociodemographic and historical conditions, the broad pattern reveals that inroad of capitalism threatens the existence of peasantry across the states. Moreover, under the changed conditions, as argued by Bernstein (1996, 2006), it may not be appropriate to call the small farmers as peasants. Rather, they may be categorised as petty commodity producers (Bernstein 1992: 32).[20] To Bernstein, given the prevalence of rural–urban links which include regular migration in search of wage employment, poor peasants form a part of an expanding reserve army of labour in the countryside and in the cities and towns along with the landless rural proletariat (2003: 13–14).

To sum up, though the analysis lends support to Gupta's (2005) hypothesis on the vanishing signs of peasantry, it shows the regional variations. Marx himself admits that the process of transition to capitalism is not uniform across societies and regions. While explaining the process of primitive accumulation, he notes, 'The history of this expropriation, in different countries, assumes different aspects, and runs through its various phases in different orders of succession, and at different periods. In England alone, which we take as our example, has it the classic form' (1906: 787). The effect of welfare measures may have slowed down the process of extinction of peasantry, but they have not been able to reverse the effect of primitive accumulation, as argued by Partha Chatterjee (2008). It would be appropriate to conclude that though the disappearance of peasantry has not taken place on a large scale, the classical Marxist view with regard to the condition of peasantry under capitalism holds true in the Indian context.

Notes

1 For example, while scholars like Shiva and Jalees (2005) observed that the Indian peasantry, the largest body of surviving small farmers in the world, faces a crisis of extinction, the recent report of Food and Agriculture Organization (2014: 10) notes that about a quarter of world's 570 million farms are from India and the vast majority of them are small by any definition.

2 Capitalist development is characterised mainly by three factors: production for the market, use of free wage labour and reinvestment of profit in technological change (see Patnaik 1972: 22, 1990: 41–44).

3 The term 'peasant' is understood as people involved in agriculture having direct access to the production of their means of subsistence (Araghi 1995).

Neoliberal reforms, agrarian capitalism and peasantry 189

4 According to Marx's conceptual category, peasants did not constitute a class as they own means of production as well as sell their labour power. For details, see Duggett (1975).

5 Marx used terms such as 'rural idiots' and 'potatoes in a sack' to refer to reactionary elements among the peasantry. See Mitrany (1951: 23–28).

6 For example, Djurfeldt (1981: 167) said, 'To date, history has falsified the classical conception of capitalism in agriculture. In Europe, the big estates have decreased in importance. The typical unit today is the family farm. The rural proletariat has decreased, not only in absolute size, but as part of the rural labour force'. He added, 'Wholesale application of the classical prediction to contemporary agriculture is both futile and dogmatic' (Djurfeldt 1981: 188).

7 For example, in states like Punjab the area under contract farming increased from 22,312 acres in 2002–3 to 216,183 acres in 2005–6. For details, see Singh (2009: 17).

8 In order to augment the reach of bank credit and increase the production of commercial crops, all contract farming arrangements are made eligible for availing special re-finance package from NABARD. Several initiatives have been undertaken by NABARD in this direction. For details, see https://www.nabard.org/english/contract_farm.aspx.

9 To go by the data furnished by the successive issues of *Agricultural Statistics at a Glance*, it is found that since 1990–91 there is a phenomenal growth of area under HYVs. In many states crops like wheat, cotton, sugarcane and paddy are largely covered by these varieties.

10 See *Eleventh Five-Year Plan (2007–2012): Agriculture, Rural Development, Industry, Services and Physical Infrastructure*, Volume III, Planning Commission, Government of India, New Delhi, 2008, p. 17.

11 The share of credit to agriculture by the scheduled commercial banks declined from 18 per cent in December 1987 to 11 per cent by March 2004. The number of agricultural loan accounts in scheduled commercial banks also declined from 27.7 million in March 1992 to 20.3 million by March 2004. For details, see Shetty (2006) and Shah (2007).

12 The following table provides information on compound annual growth rates of area, production, and yield indices of principal crops during 1990–91 to 1999–2000 (Base: TE 1981–82 = 100), and 2000–2001 to 2011–12 (Base: TE 1993–94 = 100) (percentage per annum):

Crops	1990–91 to 1999–2000			2000–2001 to 2011–12		
	Area	Production	Yield	Area	Production	Yield
Rice	0.68	2.02	1.34	0	1.78	1.78
Wheat	1.72	3.57	1.83	1.35	2.61	1.24
Coarse cereals	−2.12	−0.02	1.82	−0.81	3.01	3.85
Total pulses	−0.6	0.59	0.93	1.6	3.69	2.06
Sugarcane	−0.07	2.73	1.05	1.38	2.07	0.68
Total oilseeds	0.86	1.63	1.15	2.12	3.36	1.22
Cotton	2.71	2.29	−0.41	3.22	13.53	9.99

Source: *Economic Survey 2012–13*, GOI.

13 For details, see Government of India (2013a: pp. 174–75).
14 However, he holds the view that the present trend of agrarian change in India does not fit into classical pattern of agrarian transition and there is absence of link between industrialisation and agricultural development.
15 The Gini coefficient is estimated by Rawal (2013) based on pooled and normalised data from relevant rounds of NSSO surveys of employment and unemployment.
16 For details, see Vijay (2012).
17 The percentages of rural households self-employed in agriculture in 2011–12 are as follows:

AndhraPradesh	Bihar	Gujarat	Haryana	Himachal Pradesh	Karnataka	Kerala	Madhya Pradesh	Maharashtra	Odisha	Punjab	Rajasthan	Tamil Nadu	Uttar Pradesh	West Bengal	All India
28.2	37	40.4	37.2	36.2	37.4	14.3	45.2	37.6	35	25.2	45.7	15.8	39.15	18.9	34.3

Source: NSS, *Employment and Unemployment Situation in India* (68th round).

18 Distribution of internal migrants by rural–urban migration stream (percentage) for major states during the 64th round of NSSO is given below:

Andhra Pradesh	Bihar	Gujarat	Haryana	Himachal Pradesh	Karnataka	Kerala	Maharashtra	Madhya Pradesh	Odisha	Punjab	Rajasthan	Tamil Nadu	Uttar Pradesh	West Bengal	India
24.5	11.9	28	22.3	8.4	20.8	15.4	26.7	14.7	12.3	19.2	17.9	26.1	14	14.2	19.5

Source: NSSO Report No. 533: *Migration in India*: July 2007–June 2008 (64th round).

19 The Public Distribution System (PDS) is estimated to reduce the poverty-gap index of rural poverty by 18 to 22 per cent at the all-India level. For states with well-functioning PDS, the corresponding figures are much larger, for example 61 to 83 per cent in Tamil Nadu. For details, see Drèze and Khera (2013: 58). Similarly, Mahatma Gandhi National Rural Employment Guarantee Act (MGNREGA) since its inception has generated 13.48 billion person days of employment (Government of India 2013b).
20 According to Bernstein (2003: 4), '"peasants" become petty commodity producers when they are unable to reproduce themselves outside the relations and processes of capitalist commodity production, when those relations and processes become conditions of existence of peasant farming and are internalised in its organisation and activity'.

References

Araghi, F. 1995. 'Global Depeasantisation, 1945–1990'. *The Sociological Quarterly* 36 (2), 337–68.

Banaji, J. 1976. 'Summary of Selected Parts of Kautsky's The Agrarian Question'. *Economy and Society* 5 (1): 1–49.

Bernstein, H. 1992. 'Agrarian Structures and Changes: Latin America'. In Henry Bernstain, Ben Crow and Hazel Johnson (eds). *Rural Livelihoods Crisis and Responses.* New York: Oxford University Press, pp. 27–50.

Bernstein, H. 1994. 'Agrarian Classes in Capitalist Development'. In L. Sklair (ed.). *Capitalism and Development.* London: Routledge.

Bernstein, H. 1996. 'Agrarian Questions Then and Now'. *The Journal of Peasant Studies* 24 (1/2): 22–59.

Bernstein, H. 2003. 'Farewells to the Peasantry'. *Transformation: Critical Perspectives on Southern Africa* 52: 1–19.

Bernstein, H. 2006. 'Is There an Agrarian Question in the 21st Century?'. *Canadian Journal of Development Studies* 27 (4): 449–60.

Bhalla, G. S. and G. Singh. 2009. 'Economic Liberalisation and Indian Agriculture: A State Wise Analysis'. *Economic and Political Weekly* 44 (52): 34–44.

Bhalla, G. S. and G. Singh. 2010. *Growth of Indian Agriculture: A District Level Study.* New Delhi: Planning Commission.

Bhalla, G. S. and Gurmail Singh. 2012. *Economic Liberalisation and Indian Agriculture: A District-Level Study.* New Delhi: Sage.

Brass, T. 2008. 'Capitalism and Bonded Labour in India: Reinterpreting Recent (Re-) Interpretations'. *Journal of Peasant Studies* 35 (2): 177–248.

Brass, T. 2014. 'Debating Capitalist Dynamics and Unfree Labour: A Missing Link?'. *The Journal of Development Studies* 50 (4): 570–82.

Breman, J. 1996. *Footloose Labour: Working in the Indian Informal Economy.* London: Cambridge University Press.

Chand, Ramesh. 2009. 'Capital Formation in Indian Agriculture: National and State Level Analysis'. In D. N. Reddy and S. Mishra (eds). *Agrarian Crisis in India.* New Delhi: Oxford University Press.

Chatterjee, Partha. 2008. 'Democracy and Economic Transformation in India'. *Economic and Political Weekly* 43 (16): 53–62.

Chayanov, Alexander V. 1966. *The Theory of Peasant Economy* (translated by D. Thorner, B. Kerblay and R. E. F. Smith). Homewood, IL: Richard Irwin for the American Association.

Das, Raju. 2012. 'Reconceptualizing Capitalism Forms of Subsumption of Labor, Class Struggle and Uneven Development'. *Review of Radical Political Economics* 44 (2): 178–200.

Dev, Mahendra S. 2012. 'A Note on Trends in Public Investment in India'. Mumbai: IGIDR Proceedings/Projects series, PP-069-SMD2.

Dhanagare, D. N. 1983. *Peasant Movements in India 1920–1950.* Delhi: Oxford University Press.

Djurfeldt, G. 1981. 'What Happened to the Agrarian Bourgeoisie and the Rural Proletariat under Monopoly Capitalism?'. *Acta Sociologica* 24 (3): 167–91.

Drèze, J. and Reetika Khera 2013. 'Rural Poverty and the Public Distribution System'. *Economic Political Weekly* 48 (45/46): 55–60.

Duggett, Michael. 1975. 'Marx on Peasants'. *The Journal of Peasant Studies* 2 (2): 159–82.

Engels, Friedrich. 1894/1977. 'The Peasant Question in France and Germany'. In Karl Marx and Frederick Engels (eds). *Selected Works 3*. Moscow: Progress Publishers, pp. 457–75.

Food and Agriculture Organization. 2014. *The State of Food and Agriculture: Innovation in Family Farming*. Rome: Food and Agriculture Organization of the United Nations.

Friedmann, H. 2006. 'Focusing on Agriculture: A Comment on Henry Bernstein's "Is There an Agrarian Question in the 21st Century?"'. *Canadian Journal of Development Studies* 27 (4): 461–65.

Government of India. 2008. 'State wise Estimates of Value of Output from Agriculture and Allied Activities with New Base-Year 1999–2000 (1999–2000 to 2005–6)'. Ministry of Statistics and Programme Implementation, New Delhi.

Government of India. 2011. 'Reports of the Commission for Agricultural Costs and Prices (2011, 2010 and 2009)', accessed from http://eands.dacnet.nic.in/Cost_of_Cultivation.htm. Directorate of Economics and Statistics, Ministry of Agriculture.

Government of India. 2013a. '*Economic Survey, 2012–13*', Union Budget and Economic Survey. Ministry of Finance, New Delhi, p. 183.

Government of India. 2013b. 'Mahatma Gandhi National Rural Employment Guarantee Act, 2005: Report to the People', 2 February 2013, Ministry of Rural Development, New Delhi.

Government of India. 2014. 'Private Sector Companies Involved in Contract Farming in India', accessed from http://agmarknet.nic.in/ConFarm.htm on 14 November 2014. Directorate of Marketing and Inspection, Ministry of Agriculture, New Delhi.

Guérin, Isabelle. 2013. 'Bonded Labour, Agrarian Changes and Capitalism: Emerging Patterns in South India'. *Journal of Agrarian Change* 13 (3): 405–23.

Gulati, A., K. Ganguly and M. R. Landes. 2008. *Toward Contract Farming in a Changing Agri-Food-System*. New Delhi: ICAR, IFPRI, USDA.

Gulati, Ashok, Surbhi Jain and Nidhi Satija. 2013. '*Rising Farm Wages in India: The "Pull" and "Push" Factors*'. Discussion paper-5, Commission for Agricultural Costs and Prices, Department of Agriculture and Cooperation, Ministry of Agriculture, Government of India.

Gupta, Dipankar. 2005. 'Whither the Indian Village: Culture and Agriculture in Rural India'. *Economic and Political Weekly* 40 (8): 751–58.

Harriss, John. 2011. 'Agrarian Power and Agricultural Productivity in South Asia'. In Mary Kaldor and Polly Vizard (eds). *Arguing about the World: The Work and Legacy of Meghnad Desai*. UK: Bloomsbury Publishing Plc. Accessed from http://www.bloomsburyacademic.com/view/Arguing-About-The-World/chapter-ba9781849665469-chapter-007.xml on 25 January 2014.

Harvey, D. 2005. *A Brief History of Neoliberalism*. Oxford: Oxford University Press.

Hobsbawn, Eric. 1994. *Age of Extremes: The Short Twentieth Century 1914–1991*. London: Michael Joseph.

Jadhav, Vishal. 2006. 'Elite Politics and Maharashtra's Employment Guarantee Scheme'. *Economic and Political Weekly* 41 (50): 5157–62.

Jha B., N. Kumar and B. Mohanty. 2009. 'Pattern of Agricultural Diversification in India'. Working Paper Series No. E/302/2009, Delhi: Institute of Economic Growth.

Johnson, Heather. 2004. 'Subsistence and Control: The Persistence of the Peasantry in the Developing World'. *Undercurrent* 1 (1): 54.

Kannan, Elumalai and Sujata Sundaram. 2011. 'Analysis of Trends in India's Agricultural Growth'. Working Paper 276, Bangalore: ISEC.

Korovkin, T. 1992. 'Peasants, Grapes and Corporations: The Growth of Contract Farming in a Chilean Community'. *Journal of Peasant Studies* 19 (2): 228–54.

Lenin, V. I. 1964. *The Development of Capitalism in Russia*, vol. III. Moscow: Progress Publishers.

Lerche, J. 2007. 'A Global Alliance against Forced Labour? Unfree Labour, Neo-Liberal Globalization and the International Labour Organization'. *Journal of Agrarian Change* 7 (4): 425–52.

Lerche, J. 2013. 'The Agrarian Question in Neoliberal India: Agrarian Transition Bypassed?'. *Journal of Agrarian Change*, 13 (3):382–404.

Little, P. D. and M. Watts (eds). 1994. *Living under Contract: Contract Farming and Agrarian Transformation in Sub-Saharan Africa*. Madison: University of Wisconsin Press.

Marx, Karl. 1867/2007. *Capital: A Critique of Political Economy, Vol. III, Part II, The Process of Capitalist Production as a Whole*. New York: Cosimo, Inc.

Marx, Karl. 1906/n.d. *Capital: A Critique of Political Economy*, vol. I. New Work: Modern Library.

McMichael, P. 2006. 'Reframing Development: Global Peasant Movements and the New Agrarian Question'. *Canadian Journal of Development Studies* 27 (4): 471–83.

Mitrany, D. 1951. *Marx against the Peasant*. London: Weidenfeld and Nicolson.

Mohanty, B. B. 2009. 'Regional Disparity in Agricultural Development of Maharashtra'. *Economic and Political Weekly* 44 (6): 63–69.

Mohanty, B. B. 2012. 'Agrarian Studies in Indian Sociology'. In B. B. Mohanty (ed.). *Agrarian Change and Mobilisation*. New Delhi: Sage.

Moore, Barrington, Jr. 1967. *Social Origins of Dictatorship and Democracy, Lord and Peasant in the Making of Modern Word*. Middlesex: Penguin Books Ltd.

Narayanamoorthy, A. and R. S. Deshpande. 2001. 'Irrigation, Agrarian Relations and Agricultural Labourers: A State-Wise Analysis'. *Indian Journal of Labour Economics* 44 (4): 827–41.

National Sample Survey Organisation. 2005. 'Situation Assessment of Farmers: Indebtedness of Farmer Households, NSS 59th Round',

January–December 2003, Report No-498 (59/33/1), New Delhi: Ministry of Statistics and Programme Implementation.

Pal, S. 2009. 'Managing Vulnerability of Indian Agriculture: Implications for Research and Development'. *Agrarian Crisis in India*. New Delhi: Oxford University Press.

Papola, T. S., N. Maurya and N. Jena. 2011. *Inter-Regional Disparities in Industrial Growth and Structure*. New Delhi: Institute for Studies in Industrial Development, accessed from http://isidev.nic.in/pdf/ICSSR_TSP1.pdf on 6 November 2014.

Patnaik, Utsa. 1972. 'On the Mode of Production in Indian Agriculture: A Reply'. *Economic and Political Weekly* 7 (40): 145–51.

Patnaik, Utsa. 1990. 'Capitalist Development in Agriculture: A Note'. *Economic and Political Weekly* 6 (39): 123–30.

Ramachandran, V. K. 2011. 'The State of Agrarian Relations in India Today'. *The Marxist* 27 (1–2): 51–89.

Rawal, V. 2008. 'Ownership Holdings of Land in Rural India: Putting the Record Straight'. *Economic and Political Weekly* 43 (10): 43–47.

Rawal, V. 2013. 'Changes in the Distribution of Operational Landholdings in Rural India: A Study of National Sample Survey Data'. *Review of Agrarian Studies* 3 (2), accessed from http://www.ras.org.in/changes_in_the_distribution_of_operational_landholdings_in_rural_india on 17 January 2014.

Reddy D. N. and S. Mishra. 2009. 'Agriculture in the Reform Regime'. In D. N. Reddy and S. Mishra (eds). *Agrarian Crisis in India*. New Delhi: Oxford University Press.

Revathi, E. and A. V. Ramana Murthy. 2005. 'Challenging Seed Policy, Law and Regulation: An Appraisal of the Emerging Seed Markets in Andhra Pradesh'. GAPS Series Working Paper: 6, Centre for Economic and Social Studies, Hyderabad.

Scott, J. C. 1976. *The Moral Economy of the Peasant*. New Haven, CT: Yale University Press.

Shah, Mihir. 2007. 'The Crowning of the Moneylender'. *The Hindu*, 1 September.

Shah, Mihir, Rangu Rao and P. S. Vijay Shankar. 2007. 'Rural Credit in 20th Century India: Overview of History and Perspectives'. *Economic and Political Weekly* 42 (15): 1351–64.

Shetty, S. L. 2006. 'Monetary Policy and Financial Sector Liberalisation'. *Macroeconomics of Poverty Reduction: India Case Study*, Report submitted to United Nations Development Programme. Mumbai: Indira Gandhi Institute of Development Research.

Shiva, V. 1991. *The Violence of the Green Revolution: Third World Agriculture, Ecology and Politics*. London: Zed Books.

Shiva, V. and A. H. Jafri. 1998. *Seeds of Suicide: The Ecological and Human Costs of Globalisation of Agriculture*. New Delhi: Research Foundation for Science, Technology and Ecology.

Shiva, V. and K. Jalees. 2005. *Farmers Suicides in India*. New Delhi: Research Foundation for Science, Technology and Ecology.

Singh, Roopam. 2009. 'Effectiveness of Contract Farming Practices for Agricultural Development and Equity: A case of Hoshiarpur District in Punjab', Occasional paper-3, Consortium for trade and development, New Delhi.

Singh, S. 2002. 'Contracting Out Solutions: Political Economy of Contract Farming in the Indian Punjab'. *World Development* 30 (9): 1621–38.

Stokes, Eric. 1978. *The Peasant and the Raj: Studies in Agrarian Society and Peasant Rebellion in Colonial India.* London: Cambridge University Press.

Thorner, A. 1982. 'Semi-Feudalism or Capitalism? Contemporary Debate on Classes and Modes of Production in India'. *Economic and Political Weekly* 17 (49, 50, and 51): 1961–68, 1993–99, 2061–86.

Vaidyanathan A. 2006. 'Farmers' Suicides and the Agrarian Crisis'. *Economic and Political Weekly* 41 (38): 4009–13.

Van der Ploeg, J. D. 2010. 'The Peasantries of the Twenty-First Century: The Commoditization Debate Revisited'. *The Journal of Peasant Studies* 37 (1): 1–30.

Vanhaute, Eric. 2012. 'Peasants, Peasantries and (De)peasantisation in the Capitalist World-System'. In S. J. Babones and C. Chase-Dunn (eds). *Routledge Hand Book of World-Systems Analysis.* New York: Routledge.

Vijay, R. 2012. 'Structural Retrogression and Rise of "New Landlords" in Indian Agriculture: An Empirical Exercise'. *Economic and Political Weekly* 47 (5): 37–45.

Part III

Agrarian transition: regional responses

Chapter 7

Loosening ties of patriarchy in agrarian transition in Tamil Nadu

Judith Heyer[1]

This chapter traces the loosening of ties of patriarchy among Gounders in Coimbatore villages that underwent agrarian transition in the 1980s, 1990s and early 2000s. There are always other factors accompanying agrarian transition. Two of the more important factors in this case were increased participation in education and fertility decline.

This chapter focuses on Gounders in villages in western Tamil Nadu that were drawn into a process of industrialisation in the 1980s, 1990s and early 2000s. The villages concerned are in the hinterland of Tiruppur and Coimbatore, a region that has been involved in a process of industrialisation based primarily on textiles and engineering since the early decades of the twentieth century (Baker 1984). It was only in the 1980s that the villages in the study became at all seriously involved in this process however. This happened as industrialisation spread from larger to smaller towns and then into the villages themselves with the development of transport and communications. The move from a predominantly agricultural economy to an economy in which non-agricultural activities played a major part was accompanied by changes in gender relations. Increased levels of participation in education and fertility decline were important additional factors.

Many of the Gounder households in the study villages were capitalist households exploiting hired labour to generate surpluses on a relatively modest scale. They invested in agriculture, increased their spending on housing and consumer goods and invested increasingly in non-agricultural activities and in education. At the other end of the scale were Gounder labour households struggling to maintain themselves at increasing standards of living that became the norm. For them there was no question of investing in agriculture, self-employment, higher education, or spending on substantially better housing than before.

200 Judith Heyer

Their energies went into maintaining minimally adequate everyday standards of living instead.

Strong patriarchal relationships underpinned the organisation of Gounder households. The labour supplied by women and girls enabled male wages to be kept low and contributed to the survival of low-return male activities both in agriculture and outside agriculture(Ghosh 2009; Custers 2012). Patriarchal relations weakened as the non-agricultural economy evolved over the 1980s, 1990s and 2000s, and as levels of education increased. The recognition that female labour received improved. Nevertheless, female labour continued to be much less well rewarded than male.

Girls' upbringing was motivated primarily by marriage considerations and considerations relating to their role in the maintenance of their families' honour and reputation in this community. They received very little education until the early 1980s as more than a minimal level of education was considered to detract from their marriageability. There was a significant change in the later 1980s and 1990s however. By the 2000s education was considered an advantage as far as marriage was concerned. For boys and young men, the main driver behind increases in education was their link with better non-agricultural employment opportunities. Education both fuelled the exodus from agriculture and was driven by a desire to get out of agriculture.

Fertility decline was also an important factor in this case, reducing the pressure on resources and freeing up female labour. Its association with increasingly male sex ratios brought problems however. The CSR (child sex ratio) became significantly more male in the 1980s and 1990s contributing to the development of a shortage of brides among Gounders in the 2000s et seq. This left considerable numbers of poorer men unable to form households of their own (cf. Heyer forthcoming-b). The shortages of brides had other effects too. It put increasing pressure on education for boys and young men; it reduced the pressure on dowries; and it fuelled increased expenditure on houses in households that had sons to marry.

The chapter starts with a section providing background information on the villages. This is followed by sections on 1981–82, 1996 and 2008–9 to 2014. A final section concludes.

I. Background

The villages on which this chapter is based are villages with relatively good agricultural resources 20–30 km from Tiruppur, and 40–60 km

Loosening ties of patriarchy in Tamil Nadu 201

from Coimbatore. They were relatively remote in 1981–82 when the transport system was still poor. They were better connected subsequently. Coimbatore was already a major industrial centre in 1981–82. Tiruppur grew rapidly after 1981–82 as its knitwear industry took off. There were a number of smaller urban centres near the study villages that grew after 1981–82 as well.

The villages were multi-caste villages in a region in which caste played an important role. The major landowning groups were Naidus, Gounders and Chettiars, Gounders being the most numerous of the three (Table 7.1). Dalit agricultural labourers worked for the landowning groups. Gounders and Chettiars worked as agricultural labourers as well. There were small numbers of households belonging to a variety of other castes too.

Gounders from better-connected villages who migrated early to Tiruppur and settled there were prominent in the development of the Tiruppur knitwear industry (cf. Chari 2000, 2004; Vijayabaskar 2005; Damodaran 2008). The Gounders on whom this chapter focuses came into the Tiruppur knitwear industry late by which time it had become much more difficult to enter successfully.

The village Gounders were pursuing small-scale agriculture and business and achieving at most a low-level college education, leading to modest employment or self-employment in the early 2000s et seq (Heyer forthcoming-a). The majority were able to keep going on slow upward trajectories, reproducing themselves at progressively higher standards of living over time. Some of the less well endowed made progress through long periods of hard work in low-skilled jobs. It is noteworthy that none of them did better than this, given that they were operating in a region that had been the site of relatively successful agriculture and dynamic industrial development for so long. They are typical of the large majority of Gounders in the region nevertheless (cf. Carswell and De Neve 2011, 2013; De Neve and Carswell 2014; e.g. though the villages on

Table 7.1 Caste composition of village households in 1981–2

1981–82 households	Gounders	Naidus	Chettiars	Other non-Dalits	Dalits	All
Numbers	84	14	35	31	70	234
Percentages	36	6	15	13	30	100

Source: Village surveys.

202 Judith Heyer

which they focus were in the power loom belt where Gounders are more dominant still).

The data come from fieldwork starting with a brief stint in 1980. More extensive fieldwork was conducted in 1981–82, in 1996 and in 2008–9, with shorter periods in several years in the 2000s as well. The 1981–82 fieldwork involved a systematic survey of 20 per cent of the households in seven hamlets in two revenue villages, supplemented by in-depth interviews. In 1996, a second survey covered the descendants of the 1981–82 sample households still resident in the villages. Some information was also obtained on the 15 per cent or so that had left. A third systematic survey was conducted in 2008–9 as part of a larger project on the impact of the expansion of the knitwear industry in Tiruppur. That survey was based on a new 20 per cent sample. There were short bouts of fieldwork in 2003, 2004, 2010, 2011, 2012, 2013 and 2014 as well, updating some of the information and focusing on particular issues in more depth. More details on data collection can be found in Heyer (2014a, 2014b).

2. Gounders in the village economy in 1981–82

The village economy was predominantly agricultural in 1981–82 when the majority of Gounders were agriculturalists and agricultural labourers. Agriculture was based on land irrigated by large open wells and dry land on which rain-fed crops were grown.[2] Wells were powered by electricity. Bullocks were the major source of power for field operations and for transport. Bullocks, milch animals and sheep and goats were an integral part of the agricultural system.[3] The most important irrigated crops were cotton, turmeric and sugarcane. There were also a range of minor irrigated crops, including fruit and vegetables. Groundnuts and cholam (sorghum) were grown on dry land, interplanted with a variety of other pulses and oilseeds. High levels of purchased inputs were used. Gounder cultivators were known for working in the fields alongside hired labourers, thereby maintaining tight control.[4] Dalits, fellow Gounders and other Caste Hindus worked as hired labourers in 1981–82.

There were 358 Gounders in the sample in 1981–82, in 84 households averaging 4.3 members each. The average size of landholding was 5.4 acres (Table 7.2). The largest holding was 29 acres. There had been an increase in small and medium holdings in the 1960s and 1970s as earlier generations of large landowners moved out. The intensification of agriculture (wells and electrification, high-yielding varieties of crops, purchased inputs, etc.) meant that larger holdings were no longer as competitive as before.

Loosening ties of patriarchy in Tamil Nadu   203

Table 7.2 Landholding size distributions, Gounder households

Acres	0	>0<2.5	2.5<5	5<7.5	7.5<10	10+	All	Gounder area
1981–82								
Numbers	12	16	15	18	7	16	84	455 acres
Row percentage	13	19	18	21	8	19	100	acres/ household 5.4
1996								
Numbers	9	18	26	20	3	15	91	482 acres
Row percentage	10	20	29	22	3	16	100	acres/ household 5.3
2008–9								
Numbers	12	19	23	10	4	10	78	336 acres
Row percentage	15	24	29	13	5	13	100	acres/ household 4.3

Source: Village surveys.

A minority of Gounder households in the villages had sons involved in non-agricultural activities in 1981–82 when transport and communications were still weak and commuting was barely possible. These sons were not yet making significant contributions to household income. There were a few Gounder trade and service households as well.

Very few Gounders from the study villages had moved to urban areas in the period preceding 1981–82. This was very much a rural population. To the extent that whole households had moved, it was from one rural area to another.

The class composition of the Gounder population in the villages in 1981–82

Table 7.3 shows the class composition of Gounders in the villages in 1981–82, 1996 and 2008–9. In 1981–82 just over 50 per cent were agriculturalists, a small number combining agriculture and non-agricultural activities.[5] Most of the others were labour households with at least one member employed as an agricultural labourer or a low-skilled non-agricultural worker.[6] In the majority of these households, at least one member was employed as an agricultural labourer. There were relatively small numbers in low-skilled non-agricultural employment in 1981–82. A small minority of Gounder households were getting the bulk of their

204 Judith Heyer

Table 7.3 Class breakdown, Gounder households

Numbers of households	1981–82	1996	2008–9
Agriculturalists	43	39	36
Agriculturalists with some non-agricultural income	6	10	7
Agriculturalists with agricultural income only	37	29	29
Labour households	37	45	29
Labour households: no members agricultural labourers	10	16	14
Labour households: at least one member an agricultural labourer	27	29	15
Trade and service households	3	1	8
Dependents	1	6	5
All	84	91	78

Column percentages	1981–82	1996	2008–9
Agriculturalists	51	43	46
Agriculturalists with some non-agricultural income	7	11	9
Agriculturalists with agricultural income only	44	32	37
Labour households	44	49	37
Labour households: no members agricultural labourers	12	18	18
Labour households: at least one member an agricultural labourer	32	32	19
Trade and service households	4	1	10
Dependents	1	7	6
All	100	100	100

Source: Village surveys.

income from trade and services. There was one Gounder household consisting of dependents in 1981–82.

The majority of Gounder agriculturalists depended entirely on agriculture in 1981–82. About half of this group were relatively well-off 'thottam farmers', with enough irrigated land to justify the employment of permanent labour. Most of them were confident of their sons' futures in agriculture in 1981–82. The thottam farmers with the most substantial non-agricultural sources of income in this group were the VM (Village Munsiff)[7] and a teacher. None of them were farmer traders or farmer businessmen in 1981–82. The other half of the agriculturalist group relying entirely on agriculture was small and marginal farmers.

Gounder labour households were small and marginal farmers and landless agricultural labourers with one or more members employed as agricultural labourers and/or one or more members with a low-skilled non-agricultural occupation. The small numbers of small and marginal farmer households in this group had more to fall back on than those relying exclusively on agricultural labour, as they combined their own agricultural activities with low-status employment.

Most of the Gounder trade and service households were shopkeeper households in 1981–82. The one dependent household relied on sons living separately in the villages.

Very few of the Gounder households in the villages were doing more than reproducing themselves, albeit at a variety of levels in 1981–82.

Education

There were primary schools in several of the villages, a secondary school in one of the villages and another secondary school 4–5 km away. Only 14 per cent of the Gounder men and boys aged 15–25 years had completed secondary school in 1981–82 however, and only 7 per cent had gone any further than this (Table 7.4 and Figure 7.1). The position of women and girls was much worse. Not a single Gounder woman or girl aged 15–25 years had completed secondary school. Seventy-one per cent had never been to school at all. Most women's and girls' experience of other people and other places was limited to the family and kin group in the village in which they grew up, and in the village in which they were married, as well as their attendance at marriages and other life-cycle ceremonies both before and after marriage. It is worth noting that the majority of women did move to other villages on marriage though, unlike in the case of men.

The labour contribution of women and girls in Gounder households in 1981–82

Women and girls in Gounder households were under strict patriarchal control in 1981–82. This affected their care, their education, their marriages, the work they were expected to do and the way they were expected to behave.

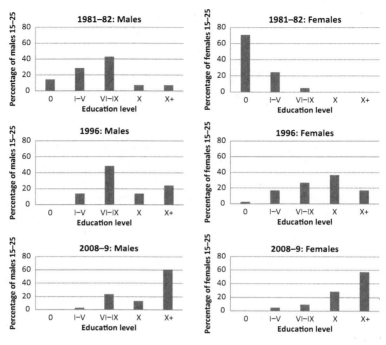

Figure 7.1 Education levels of males and females aged 15–25 years
Source: Village surveys.

In the households of agriculturalists, most of which were nuclear, women and girls did all the 'domestic' and 'reproductive' work. In most cases they also worked in the fields and with livestock. In households that employed agricultural labour, women supervised female agricultural labourers and cooked for male agricultural labourers as well. In many of the small and marginal farmer households, women worked hard in the fields and with livestock to keep the household afloat, with more or less support from men. Women also did a lot of the 'kin work', visiting relatives and attending marriages and life-cycle ceremonies. This could be burdensome. It was also an opportunity to engage in a wider world.

Girls were pulled out of education early both because it was useful to have them contribute to household tasks and because more than very little education was considered to be damaging to their marriage prospects. Only 50 per cent of 5- to 15-year-old Gounder girls were in school in 1981–82.

In Gounder labour households, many of them landless, women and girls worked as hired agricultural labourers and/or with livestock and/or on their own land. There were no women working in non-agricultural occupations in 1981–82. It was not unusual for it to be only the men who worked as hired labourers in these households.[8] Female agricultural labourers got less than half of the male wage.[9] There were also households in which women working as hired agricultural labourers were the sole income earners. Few women whose marriages had failed were accepted back into their natal households, and those who were had to pay their way.

In sum, in 1981–82 Gounder women made substantial contributions to household production and/or household income with low levels of remuneration when they worked as hired agricultural labourers, and low levels of recognition for the work they put in when they worked on their households' own account instead. Strong patriarchal structures underpinned all this.

Marriage

Marriages were used to build and cement alliances. It was expected that there would be continuing relations between families into which women married and families into which they had been born. It was considered important that they were not married too far away.[10] A number of marriages took place within the villages themselves. Cross-cousin marriages were still fairly widespread in this community in 1981–82.

Incoming brides were a valuable source of capital, of labour and of childbearing. They came with dowries, many of which were used to buy land, and/or for 'family expenses' in households that were doing less well. Dowry gold was also used as security for credit. Bride price had been the norm in this community in the 1930s and 1940s. It had gradually been replaced by dowry after that.

Women sometimes received land as part of their dowries, particularly if there were no sons in the family.[11] Fathers sometimes bought land for their married daughters after marriage too. Women's land ownership was nominal in most cases though. It may have strengthened their position within some marriages but it did not often appear to do so.

Women were treated fairly instrumentally in Gounder households in 1981–82, as bearers of family honour and reputations, and as conduits for alliances on which the success of their families relied. This changed over subsequent decades, but it was still very much the case in 1981–82.

208 Judith Heyer

Fertility decline and the child sex ratio (CSR)

Fertility had been declining among Gounders in the decades preceding 1981–82. The average number of children per couple in households starting families in the 1970s was approaching 2. This had repercussions on land accumulation and land concentration. It affected the channelling of resources for investment versus consumption. It also meant less childbearing and child rearing for women, and more time for other kinds of work.

As fertility declined, the CSR became more male (Heyer 1992, forthcoming-a). It was considered important to have sons – it was sons on whom parents relied as they got old – and this was less assured as the number of children per couple fell. Moreover, natal households did not feel that they got sufficient compensation for rearing daughters. Although there was no direct evidence of infanticide in the study villages,[12] foeticide was on the horizon,[13] leading to increasingly masculine adult sex ratios in the 2000s et seq. (see later).

Consumption versus investment

Gounders are often considered 'frugal', using their agricultural surpluses for investment rather than consumption. The most visible indicators of relative wealth among Gounders in the study villages in 1981–82 were houses, most of which were relatively modest. They had very few consumer durables. Their everyday clothing was modest too. A few had motorcycles, but these were very much the exception. They spent considerable sums on marriages and life-cycle ceremonies though. These expenditures bore more heavily on girls' families than on boys'.

3. Gounders in the village economy in 1996

Agriculture was under pressure in 1996 as growing industrialisation in surrounding areas made its impact on the village economy. Transport and communications had improved considerably, and significantly more men were now working outside agriculture, many of them commuting to nearby towns and other centres to do so. The demographic profile of Gounder households in the villages had changed. There were rural households with some of the younger generation missing – older couples managing in the absence of sons and daughters-in-law, brothers managing their brothers' land and so on. Remittances were beginning to feature in support of dependents too. There was some investment of agricultural surpluses in non-agricultural activities, but it was through changes in employment that increasing involvement in the industrial economy was really making itself felt.

Sixteen per cent of the Gounder households in the 1981–82 sample had left in their entirety by 1996, most for urban areas, not all selling their village land. Another 18 per cent of the households descended from 1981 to 1982 sample households some of whose descendants remained in the villages had also left, most of them retaining their land or an interest in family land that had not yet been divided. There were still 360 Gounders in the sample in 1996, in 91 households averaging 4.0 members each.

Agriculture was under pressure both because the water table had fallen and because wages had risen substantially. The deepest wells which had been 200 ft deep in 1981–82 were 600 ft deep in 1996. Bore wells had replaced open wells, and compressor and submersible pumps were now being used to lift the water to the surface. Less land was irrigated in 1996 and what was irrigated was irrigated less intensively.[14] Tractors and motor vehicles were replacing bullocks. The numbers of animals being kept for milk and meat had fallen too.[15] Less labour was being used in agriculture both because wages had risen and because more young men in cultivator households were continuing their education and/or were employed outside agriculture. There had also been a smaller increase in the numbers of young men as decreased fertility rates fed through. There was less female labour as well. Cropping patterns had changed. There were now substantial quantities of bananas alongside cotton, sugarcane and turmeric on irrigated land, and more cholam and fewer groundnuts on land that was rain fed. There were fewer minor crops as well.

The total area of land owned by Gounders had increased between 1981–82 and 1996 (Table 7.2)[16] despite the fall in numbers engaged in agriculture, and its distribution was less polarised. There had been an increase in holdings of 2.5–7.5 acres and a decrease in larger holdings. There had been a (small) decrease in the number of Gounders who were landless as well.

The class composition of the Gounder population in the villages in 1996

There were fewer Gounder agriculturalists in 1996, making up a smaller proportion of the Gounder population in the villages (Table 7.3). None of the thottam farmers had moved out. Several were now combining agriculture with agri-processing, trade and moneylending activities. The

210 Judith Heyer

majority now hoped for a non-agriculture future for their sons, but it was taking time to get their sons through the education that was necessary to achieve this. A number of small and marginal farmer households were educating their sons for higher-quality non-agricultural employment too. It was the small farmer group that had been depleted, some now falling into the labour group. There were still substantial numbers of small and marginal farmers concentrating exclusively on agriculture though.

The number of Gounder labour households had risen very substantially since 1981–82 (Table 7.3). This was partly because subdivisions had produced relatively large numbers of separate households in this group by 1996. An increase in small and marginal farmer households with members in low-status non-agricultural employment had also added to the number of labour households. There had been relatively little change in the number of households with one or more members working as agricultural labourers since 1981–82.

Dependent households now formed a significant minority (Table 7.3), most of them consisting of older parents supported by children living elsewhere. This was something that did not feature at all in 1981–82 when the only dependent household in the sample was being supported by sons living in the villages.

It was still the case that virtually none of the Gounder households in the villages were doing more than reproducing themselves. The VM had been replaced by a village administrative officer with better educational qualifications from elsewhere. No new households with substantial non-agricultural sources of income had emerged. The levels at which the majority of Gounder households were reproducing themselves had been rising though. This was reflected in better houses, better clothes, higher expenditures on education, more motorcycles and more consumer durables. There were also fewer Gounder households at the lower end of the distribution one or more of whose members were engaged in hired agricultural labour. Although the wages of hired agricultural labourers had increased very substantially in real terms by 1996,[17] working as a hired agricultural labourer was still an indicator of poverty where Gounders were concerned.

Education

There were higher levels of participation in education in 1996 than there had been in 1981–82 (Figure7.1), exposing more of the Gounder population to a wider world. (Television also contributed to greater

Loosening ties of patriarchy in Tamil Nadu 211

exposure, as did improved transport and geographical mobility.) Boys were being educated for roles outside agriculture. Girls were being educated for marriage in a context in which education was now considered an advantage, not a disadvantage as before. Twenty-four per cent of the men and boys aged 15–25 had gone further than secondary school, as opposed to only 7 per cent in 1981–82. The increase was even more marked for women and girls, 17 per cent of whom had gone further than secondary school in 1996 compared with none in 1981–82. This was a very significant change, given that going beyond secondary school meant travelling unescorted outside the village which would have been inconceivable in 1981–82. Equally striking in 1996 was the fact that virtually none of the women and girls aged 15–25 had not been to school at all.

The labour contribution of women and girls in Gounder households in 1996

Women in the better-off agriculturalist households did not work outside the domestic sphere when they were newly married and when they were bearing and/or looking after young children. Many in such households described themselves as 'housewives working on their own farms' after that.[18] Less labour-intensive agriculture meant less supervision of female agricultural labourers. There was also less cooking for male agricultural labourers who got fewer cooked meals both as their numbers fell and as employment relations changed. Fertility decline meant less childbearing and less work looking after children for Gounder women of all classes. Girls and young women spent more time in education, but the decline in the CSR also meant that there were fewer young girls. There had been some improvement in women's status in the better-off agriculturalist households both as they got more education and as they got more recognition for the roles that they played. The general rise in prosperity meant that there was also less of a struggle in small and marginal farmer households, and this affected women as much as men.

In agriculturalist households with non-agricultural sources of income, women were taking on more responsibility for managing the land and livestock of men who were involved in non-agricultural activities. There were only a few cases in which women were taking a leading role with respect to agriculture however. In many cases women were involved in more of the work in agriculture, as well as more domestic work supporting men involved in non-agricultural occupations, but their husbands and/or husbands' brothers were still taking the leading role.

212 Judith Heyer

Labour households were doing better than before. Agricultural wages had risen, as had wages for low-skilled non-agricultural work. The PDS (Public Distribution System), which provided subsidised food and other essential commodities, and the free mid-day meals being provided for children in school[19] were also helping women in labour households in 1996. The fact that more children in labour households were in school meant that there were less young girls working too. A few women in labour households were now describing themselves as 'housewives', or 'staying at home', but most were either agricultural labourers or working on their own land and/or with livestock. A few women in labour households were also working in garment units, and in power loom units, though there were still far more men than women doing this (Heyer 2013).

Marriage, fertility decline and the CSR

We come back to changes with respect to marriage, fertility decline and the CSR in the sections on the 2008–9 position later.

4. Gounders in the village economy in 2008–9

The impact of the industrial economy on the Gounder population in the villages had become stronger by 2008–9. The number of Gounders resident in the villages in the sample had fallen from 360 to 314. There were now only 78 Gounder households in the sample, averaging 4.0 members each. More erstwhile commuters were now living elsewhere, many of them still holding onto their village land. Gounders resident in the villages had become involved in more and better-quality non-agricultural occupations. There was a new element in the Gounder village population: people who had returned to live in the villages after spending the best part of their lives working elsewhere. They had held onto their land throughout. There were increasing numbers of couples who were still supporting themselves while their sons lived elsewhere. There were also old couples, widows and widowers being supported by children living elsewhere and in some cases by small pensions from the state. Mobile phones helped them all to keep in touch.

There was less land under cultivation in 2008–9 both as land was left fallow and as land had been sold for real estate. There had also been a decline in the intensity with which the land still under cultivation was being cultivated. The deepest bore wells were now 1200 ft deep. Drip irrigation which economised on labour as well as water first appeared in the villages in 2006–7 and it was spreading fast. Bullocks had been

Loosening ties of patriarchy in Tamil Nadu 213

almost completely replaced by tractors and motorised transport. There were also fewer dairy animals and fewer small stock being kept for meat.[20] There were fewer hired agricultural labourers. The main crops being grown on irrigated land were bananas, turmeric and sugarcane. Cotton had almost entirely disappeared. The main dryland crops were cholam and groundnuts still, but the balance had shifted further towards cholam. There were also fewer minor crops both on irrigated and on rainfed land.

The majority of Gounder holdings were now between 0 and 5 acres (Table 7.2). The mean was 4.4 acres. There had been land sales by Gounders resident in the villages as well as by some who had left. There were also Gounders not resident in the villages who were holding onto their land. A few Gounders resident in the villages were buying land in urban areas too. More village land was being used for non-agricultural business activities and for real estate, the latter almost entirely in the hands of outsiders. Land values were no longer related to agricultural productivity. Location was the determining factor in 2008–9.

Increasing numbers of small and marginal landholdings of residents and non-residents were linked to insecure and poorly paid employment in the non-agricultural economy. People were holding onto land both to supplement their non-agricultural earnings and as a backup in the event of failure of non-agricultural activities. They also held onto land with a view to returning to it after spending the better part of their working lives elsewhere. The proliferation of small and marginal holdings, many of which were only being operated half-heartedly, was one of many brakes on the development of capitalist agriculture.

Agricultural surpluses were being invested in agriculture and in education, housing and health care, the latter a new necessity that had emerged since 1996. There had been a substantial increase in non-agricultural investment since 1996 as well (see the next section).

The class composition of the Gounder population in the villages in 2008–9

There were still relatively large numbers of Gounder agriculturalists in 2008–9, relatively few combining agriculture with higher-status non-agricultural activities (Table 7.3). None of the better-off farmers had moved out. Some of their holdings had become smaller though, following the subdivision of their land. A few had invested in significant non-agricultural businesses: a spinning mill, one or two garment companies and so on, leaving behind the trade and agri-processing activities of 1996. The majority however were concentrating on educating their sons for professional (a lawyer, a dentist, an aspiring doctor), white-collar (IT, banking, accountancy, management) and skilled blue-collar (mechanical and mechanical engineering) occupations, based on diplomas and/or college degrees. A few former small farmers who had returned to the villages after working for many years elsewhere were also getting their sons through higher education as were a few hard-working small farmers. Most of the results of investment in higher education were still to come in 2008–9. In the five to six years following 2008–9, however, several of the sons concerned obtained employment at modest levels with prospects of promotion based on their college education. Thus, while most of the better-off Gounder households were continuing to obtain all of their income from agriculture, the next generation was getting set to move out of agriculture in significant numbers after 2008–9. There were still substantial numbers of small and marginal farmers pursuing agriculture alone. These included older couples whose children had left as well as people who had returned after working elsewhere.

The number of labour households had fallen significantly since 1996 (Table 7.3). The number with no members working as agricultural labourers was very similar to that in 1996. It was the number with at least one member working as an agricultural labourer that had fallen dramatically. Many of the households that would have been in this group either had taken up non-agricultural employment or had left.

There had been an increase in households involved in substantial trade and service occupations with little or no agricultural income (Table 7.3). These included a household with a transport business, a household with an electrical shop in a nearby centre, an LIC (Life Insurance Corporation) agent, a contractor, a banana trader, a shopkeeper and a milkman.

A small number of Gounders living in the villages were doing more or aspiring to do more than reproduce themselves in 2008–9. These included the spinning mill owner,[21] the owner of the transport business who was reputed to be making heavy losses in 2012, the LIC agent and the contractor.[22] Others doing more than reproducing themselves had left the villages to do so. Many of those reproducing themselves in the villages were doing so at better levels in 2008–9 than in 1996. This was reflected in better houses, better clothing, more motorcycles and a few cars, higher expenditure on education and substantial expenditure on health. Most households also had at least one mobile phone. At the other end of the scale, there were also considerably fewer Gounder labour households and these were also doing better than before.

Education

Gounders in the villages were now investing substantially in both boys' and girls' education (Figure 7.1). Significant numbers of young men were in college. Moreover, whereas in the 1980s and 1990s the young men who went into higher education did BA and BCom degrees, in the 2000s there was a heavy emphasis on engineering. These were routes into better-quality employment for boys and young men (see the previous section).

The proportion of women and girls aged 15–25 with post-X education had almost reached parity with that of men and boys in 2008–9 (Figure 7.1). Very few women and girls had been to private schools however, unlike men and boys, and the colleges to which they went, and the degrees for which they studied, were less costly and less prestigious than those of men and boys. The two exceptions in the sample were the older of two sisters in a family with no sons who had completed a bachelor's degree in international business followed by an MA, and a young woman who had completed a bachelor's degree in zoology followed by a BEd and an MSc. Both of these young women went on to do MPhils.

The labour contribution of women and girls in 2008–9

Women and girls in better-off Gounder households in the villages were now continuing in school or college until their early or mid-twenties. This involved them in new levels of independence from their families. It was a big change from 1996 when most ended their education aged 14–16. It was an even bigger change from 1981 to 1982 when few went further than primary school. The fact that more attention was being paid to education also increased the valuation of the contributions of married women in households attaching high priority to children's education. Women were getting more recognition in Gounder households generally in 2008–9.[23]

Women in the reduced number of Gounder labour households in the villages were doing somewhat better both as wages had continued to rise and as they were getting more state support in 2008–9. This included an expanded PDS, mid-day meals, and MGNREGA[24] in which Gounder women were beginning to participate alongside members of Dalit and other caste groups.

216 Judith Heyer

Marriage

Nearly all Gounder women and girls in the villages were being educated for marriage in 2008–9. Better-off Gounder households were now looking for educated brides, sometimes to compensate for relatively poorly educated bridegrooms, more often to complement bridegrooms who were well educated themselves. It was rare for women to be allowed to continue with their education or careers after marriage, which usually took place before they were 24 or 25 years old. Exceptions included the international business graduate who was married to someone who supported her aspirations for a career as a college lecturer, and the zoology graduate, married in 2012, who was hoping to become a teacher.

Women had more say with respect to marriage partners in 2008–9 than they had had earlier. They could now refuse a marriage proposal supported by their parents, something that had not been possible in 1996 still less in 1981–82. Parents still arranged the large majority of marriages though. Even highly educated young women usually accepted this. There were growing numbers of 'love marriages' however, marriages arranged by the couple concerned without the support of their parents. In labour households love marriages arose in the course of non-agricultural employment outside the villages. In agriculturalist households, they arose as young people in college together paired off. Nearly all love marriages were within caste. It was rare to find cross-caste marriages involving Gounders in these villages. There were reports of more such elsewhere.[25]

There were also increasing numbers of households with no sons in which the daughters had reached marriage age in 2008–9. There were generally two daughters in these households, one of whom was married in the usual way, the other to a bridegroom who agreed to reside with his bride's parents, or at least take responsibility for his bride's parents, inheriting their property and effectively taking the place of a son (Heyer forthcoming-b).

A striking new phenomenon in 2008–9 et seq. was the shortage of marriageable women that had emerged. This was a feature of the region as a whole, not just the study villages. What it meant was that a number of educated women from better-off households in the villages were married into urban families, as women from less well-off households were married into better-off households in the villages in turn. This left significant numbers of poorer men in the villages unmarried in their forties, something that would have been inconceivable in 1981–82 or 1996.

These men talked of continuing their search for brides, but given their inflexibility with respect to marrying out of region or out of caste, it seemed unlikely that many of them would ever get married at all (Heyer forthcoming-b).

One might have thought that the shortage of marriageable women would have led to an increase in the status of women.[26] One might also have thought that it would have reduced the pressure on dowries. Although the quantities of gold paid as dowry did not appear to have been increasing, the increasing price of gold meant that their value had continued to rise. (It was still uncommon for dowries to include anything other than gold, and sometimes land. It was very unusual for vehicles or consumer durables to be included here.)[27] The call on girls' natal households was increasing, taking education, increased spending on houses and dowries into account. The call on boys' households was increasing even more. Ostentatious spending on houses was very noticeable in 2008–9, particularly in households in which there were sons to marry, but also in households with only daughters.

Fertility decline and the CSR

There were more Gounder households with only one child, and fewer with more than two, in households starting families in the 1990s and early 2000s. Scans and foeticide which were reputed to have been common in the 1980s and 1990s were said to be much less common in the 2000s. The discourse concerning son preference had shifted too. In the 2000s, boys were said to be problematic, not studying well, not easy to manage, not easy to marry. Girls, in contrast, were said to study well, and there were no worries about marriage as they were much sought after as brides. In many cases daughters were said to be looking after ageing parents better than sons too. There had been a significant change in attitudes here (Heyer forthcoming-b).

5. Conclusion

Patriarchy tends to be strong in agrarian societies, with their tight-knit household and family relationships and communities playing strong roles in ensuring that patriarchal norms are followed. Patriarchy is weakened both by the break-up of households as members of younger generations move out of village communities and by the influx of new ideas and practices that come with increased exposure to a rapidly changing world. It is clear that patriarchy is directly weakened by education too. Education

218 Judith Heyer

involves rubbing shoulders with others, moving outside the confines of the village and being exposed to a wider range of influences and ideas. It was clear that patriarchy had weakened in the case under review. Patriarchy still remained remarkably strong, nevertheless. Women were still subordinated. Women were still not accessing anything like as many new and better opportunities as men.

The fertility decline that accompanied agrarian transition in this case has not been seriously addressed in this chapter. Suffice it to say that it decreased the pressure on agricultural resources and countered the tendency for the proliferation of small and marginal holdings to some extent, as did migration to urban areas, but the insecurities of the non-agricultural economy were also leading people to hold onto land. The net effect was an increase in the numbers of small and marginal holdings still.

Notes

1 The research on which this chapter is based was funded by the UK Department of International Development (DFID, formerly ODA), the Oxford University Webb Medley Fund, the Leverhulme Trust and the Queen Elizabeth House Oppenheimer Fund, at various stages. The 2008–9 research was funded as part of a project on the effects of the expansion of the knitwear industry in the Tiruppur region funded by a DFID-ESRC Research Award, a project in which Grace Carswell, Geert De Neve and M. Vijayabaskar were also involved. The research could not have been done without the support of Dr V. Mohanasundaram, my interpreter and co-researcher for most of the fieldwork since 1981–82, and without the contributions of M. V. Srinivasan, Paul Pandian, Selva Murugan, Arul Maran, Gowri Shankar, S. Saravanan and Jagan Subi who acted as research assistants at different stages in the field. The research has also benefitted from discussions particularly with K. Nagaraj, J. Jeyaranjan, Karin Kapadia and Barbara Harriss-White.
2 Forty-eight per cent of Gounder land was irrigated in 1981–82.
3 Average livestock holdings per household were 1.1 bullocks, 3.6 buffaloes and cows and 3.3 sheep and goats, in 1981–82. These were distributed over the majority of Gounder households. Very few livestock holdings were large.
4 Cf. Cederlof (1997).
5 These included a VM (Village Munsiff), a teacher, the milk society secretary, a fertiliser sales representative, someone with a general store and a household with a BSc clerk who later became a Coimbatore mill supervisor.
6 These included workers in garment units, ginning factories and textile mills, a watchman, a bus conductor, petty shopkeepers, a milkman and a village cooperative society employee.
7 The administrative officer responsible for tax collection, a position that has since been superseded by that of the village administrative officer.

Loosening ties of patriarchy in Tamil Nadu 219

8 In the 37 labour households, there were 31 male and 26 female agricultural labourers.
9 Gounder men got Rs 7 per day for casual labour in 1981–82. Women got Rs 2.50 or Rs 3.
10 See also De Neve (2011) on this.
11 In theory, the state ensured equal inheritance rights for women, including equal shares in land. In practice, this provision was not enforced.
12 There was evidence of female infanticide in similar communities in other parts of Tamil Nadu at the time (cf. George *et al.* 1992). See also Srinivasan and Bedi (2011) on this.
13 It became clear in later fieldwork that foeticide had been being practised by Gounders in the villages in the 1980s. See Heyer (forthcoming-b) for more details.
14 The distinction between irrigated and unirrigated land was more blurred in 1996 than in 1981–82. It was also clear that it varied from year to year. It was difficult to come up with a figure for the proportion irrigated in 1996.
15 It is not possible to be more specific about this because 1996 livestock numbers are incomplete.
16 Mean landholdings per household were very similar in 1996 to those in 1981–82 as smaller households meant that the number of Gounder households had increased.
17 In 1996 daily agricultural wages for men were Rs 40, Rs 45 and Rs 50. This represents an up to 100 per cent increase in real terms using the Coimbatore rural rice price, and up to 90 per cent using the Consumer Price Index for Agricultural Labourers (CPIAL). (The *India Labour Journal* is the source both for the rice price and for the CPIAL.) Women's daily wages were Rs 20 and Rs 25.
18 See Maria Mies (1982) on the use of the term 'housewives' reinforcing men's control over women's work. See Heyer (2014b) for a comparison between Dalits and Caste Hindus in this respect too.
19 Tamil Nadu's programme was launched in 1984, preceding the national programme which came into effect in the early 2000s.
20 Average livestock holdings per household were 2.4 buffaloes and cows, and 1.7 sheep and goats, in 2008–9. Milch animals were distributed over the majority of Gounder households. Only a minority of households had sheep and goats.
21 The spinning mill was closed in 2011 after heavy losses, but the son involved was developing other business ideas instead.
22 The contractor had educated and then set up his son with an automobile repair business in Tiruppur in 2013.
23 Rao (2014) elaborates on something similar in a study based on interviews with Gounder couples in a rural community in the vicinity.
24 MGNREGA (Mahatma Gandhi National Rural Employment Guarantee Act) under which each household applying for work was entitled to 100 days per annum at the minimum wage.
25 The Kongu Nadu Munnetra Kazhagam, the Gounder political party founded in February 2009, came out strongly against inter-caste marriages, that is marriages of Gounder women to Dalit men, in April 2013. This followed

220 Judith Heyer

reports from areas in which substantial numbers of such marriages were taking place. There were no virtually such marriages taking place in the study villages though.

26 Razavi (2009) and Jeffery (2014) caution us about making such simplistic assumptions though.

27 See Srinivasan (2005) for a contrary case.

References

Baker, C. J. 1984. *An Indian Rural Economy 1880–1995, The Tamilnad Countryside*. Oxford: Clarendon Press.

Carswell, G. and G. De Neve. 2011. 'Litigation against Political Organisation? Changing Gounder-Dalit Politics in Western Tamil Nadu', *Manchester Papers in Political Economy*, Manchester. Working Paper No. 1, February.

Carswell, G. and G. De Neve. 2013. 'From field to factory: Tracing Bonded Labour in the Coimbatore Powerloom Industry, Tamil Nadu'. *Economy and Society* 42 (3): 430–53.

Cederlof, G. 1997. *Bonds Lost: Subordination, Conflict and Mobilisation in Rural South India c. 1900–1970*. New Delhi: Manohar.

Chari, S. 2000. 'The Agrarian Origins of the Knitwear Industrial Cluster in Tiruppur, India'. *World Development* 28 (3): 579–99.

Chari, S. 2004. *Fraternal Capital, Peasant-Workers, Self-Made Men, and Globalization in Provincial India*. New Delhi: Permanent Black.

Custers, Peter. 2012. *Capital Accumulation and Women's Labour in Asian Economies*. New York: Monthly Review Press.

Damodaran, H. 2008. *India's New Capitalists, Caste, Business, and Industry in a Modern Nation*. New Delhi: Permanent Black.

De Neve, G. 2011. 'Keeping It in the Family: Work, Education and Gender Hierarchies among Tiruppur's Urban Industrialists'. In H. Donner and G. De Neve (eds). *Being Middle Class in India, A Way of Life*. Abingdon: Routledge, pp. 73–99.

De Neve, G. and G. Carswell. 2014. 'T-shirts and Tumblers: Caste, Politics and Industrial Work in Tiruppur's Textile Belt, Tamil Nadu'. *Contributions to Indian Sociology* 48 (1): 103–31.

George, S., A. Rajaratnam and B. Miller. 1992. 'Female Infanticide in Rural South India'. *Economic and Political Weekly* 27 (22): 2253–56.

Ghosh, Jayati. 2009. *Never Done and Poorly Paid, Women's Work in Globalising India*. New Delhi: Women Unlimited.

Heyer, J. 1992. 'The Role of Dowries and Daughters' Marriages in the Accumulation and Distribution of Capital in a South Indian Community'. *Journal of International Development* July–August: 419–36.

Heyer, J. 2013. 'Integration into a Global Production Network: Impacts on Labour in Tiruppur's Rural Hinterlands'. *Oxford Development Studies* 41 (3), September: 307–21.

Heyer, J. 2014a. 'Dalit Households in Industrialising Villages in Coimbatore and Tiruppur, Tamil Nadu: A Comparison across 3 Decades'. In V. K. Ramachandran and Madhura Swaminathan (eds). *Dalit Households in Village Economies*. New Delhi: Tulika, pp. 133–69.

Heyer, J. 2014b. 'Dalit Women Becoming "Housewives": Lessons from the Tiruppur Region, 1981/2 to 2008/9'. In Clarinda Still (ed.). *Mobility or Marginalisation: Dalits in Neo-Liberal India*. New Delhi: Routledge, pp. 208–35.

Heyer, J. forthcoming-a. 'Rural Gounders on the Move in Western Tamil Nadu: 1981/2 to 2008/9'. In Praveen Jha Himanshu and Gerry Rodgers (eds). *Longitudinal Research in Village India: Methods and Findings*. New Delhi: Oxford University Press.

Heyer, J. forthcoming-b. 'The impact of bride shortages in South India: Vellala Gounders in villages in western Tamil Nadu'. In Sharada Srinivasan and Shuzhuo Li (eds). *'Scarce' Women and 'Surplus' Men in Communities of Asia: Macro Demographics versus Local Dynamics*. New Delhi: Springer.

Jeffery, Patricia. 2014. 'Social Consequences of Demographic Change in India'. In Delia Davin and Barbara Harriss-White (eds). *China-India: Pathways of Economic and Social Development* (*Proceedings of the British Academy*). London: British Academy.

Mies, Maria. 1982. *The Lace Makers of Narsipur, Indian Housewives Produce for the World Market*. London: Zed Press.

Rao, Nitya. 2014. 'Caste, Kinship, and Life Course: Rethinking Women's Work and Agency in Rural South India'. *Feminist Economics*, published online in June, 20(3): 78–102.

Razavi, Shara. 2009. 'Engendering the Political Economy of Agrarian Change'. *Journal of Peasant Studies* 36 (1): 197–226.

Srinivasan, S. 2005. 'Daughters or Dowries? The Changing Nature of Dowry Practices in South India'. *World Development* 33 (4): 593–615.

Srinivasan, S. and A. S. Bedi 2011. 'Ensuring Daughter Survival in Tamil Nadu India'. *Oxford Development Studies* 39 (3): 253–84.

Vijayabaskar, M. 2005. 'Labour and Flexible Accumulation: The Case of Tiruppur Knitwear Cluster'. In K. Das (ed.). *Industrial Clusters, Cases and Perspectives*. Aldershot: Ashgate, pp. 37–54.

Chapter 8

Agro-ecological double movements?

Zero Budget Natural Farming and alternative agricultures after the neoliberal crisis in Kerala

Daniel Münster[1]

I. Introduction

This chapter introduces an ongoing ethnographic project on situated responses to agrarian crisis in the rural district of Wayanad, Kerala. In this project, I look at alternative agricultures that have emerged in response to a protracted crisis of commercial agriculture – a crisis that has repeatedly caused many smallholders to proclaim that agriculture has 'gone' (*poyi*) from the region. This chapter focuses on a particular response to the crisis: a natural farming movement, the so-called Zero Budget Natural Farming method (henceforth ZBNF), which came to Wayanad around 2006 at a time when the district made headlines for high incidences of farmers' suicides (Münster 2012). Within the larger picture of the political economy of agrarian transition in India, this chapter argues that agro-ecological movements and movements for food sovereignty, even if they operate within dubious ideological idioms, constitute important allies for the creation of a possible agrarian future in India – a future that I believe hinges on a necessary agro-ecological transition.

I conceive of contemporary alternative agricultures among smallholders in South Asia broadly as practical responses to the neoliberal crisis in agriculture. In Karl Polanyi's terms (2001 [1944]), they may be understood as protective double movements, aiming to regenerate rural society from the destructive consequences of the commodification of land (nonhuman nature) and labour (human nature). In Marxian terms, these alternative agricultures are the first steps towards repairing (Schneider and McMichael 2010) or reworking (Wittman 2009) the

Zero Budget Natural Farming and alternative agricultures   223

metabolic rift between humans and nonhuman nature brought about by capitalist agriculture(Foster 2000; Moore 2011). Such responses have become necessary as mainstream capitalist agriculture has reached an economic (Lerche 2011), social, ecological and scientific impasse, both at a planetary (Weis 2010) and at a regional (Reddy and Mishra 2009; Vasavi 2012) scale.

From a planetary perspective, all of humanity may be facing the same 'epochal crisis' that John Bellamy Foster has recently referred to as 'the convergence of economic and ecological contradictions in such a way that the material conditions of society as a whole are undermined, posing the question of a historical transition to a new mode of production' (Foster 2013: 1). While I largely follow the diagnosis of ecological Marxists such as Foster and Magdoff (Magdoff and Foster 2011), Jason Moore (2011), and James O'Connor (1998) in describing the contemporary agro-ecological crisis, which is often cast in Karl Marx's notion of the *metabolic rift* between human and nonhuman nature brought about by the logic of accumulation, I fear that the macro scale and abstract nature of their analysis might foreclose the possibility of practical alternatives to the epochal crisis, or of 'repairing the metabolic rift', as Schneider and McMichael (2010) put it. I agree with the latter's claim that the key to a post-capitalist political ecology of agriculture is to focus on farmers who 'know how to produce food in ways that are socially and ecologically sustainable' (Schneider and McMichael 2010).

The crisis in the dominant model of farming is most severely felt by smallholders,[2] or petty commodity producers who are faced with multiple 'vectors of rural dispossession' (Li 2009: 71) within the current global food regime. In the post-General Agreement on Tariffs and Trade dispensation, researchers across the world observe the 'piecemeal dispossession of small-scale farmers, unable to survive when exposed to the competition from agricultural systems backed by subsidies and preferential tariffs' (Li 2009: 72). Smallholders also face the environmental and health costs of the green revolution's techno-economic package, which has brought state agronomy, hybrid seed varieties and large quantities of chemical fertilisers and pesticides to Indian agriculture. Alternative agricultures such as ZBNF are responses to these challenges by reworking both production and exchange through innovative farming practices on one hand and by reworking relations to the market by limiting dependence on external inputs on the other. ZBNF also poses a cultural challenge to mainstream farming by rejecting mainstream agronomy and replacing the common focus on accumulation with a focus on autonomy, health and self-sufficiency.

224 Daniel Münster

Increasingly, scholars in the field of agrarian studies have been paying attention to alternative farming movements, as well as their in situ responses to the ecological and economic contradictions of capitalist agriculture and the contemporary food regime. Such movements are framed as agro-ecology (Altieri and Toledo 2011; Altieri, Funes-Monzote and Petersen 2012), agro(bio)diversity (Brookfield, Parsons and Brookfield 2003; Veteto and Skarbø 2009), food sovereignty (Patel 2009; Wittman 2009; Wittman, Desmarais and Wiebe 2010; for a sceptical view, see Bernstein 2014), re-peasantisation (Ploeg 2008, 2010) or ecotopia (Lockyer and Veteto 2013). Despite apparent contact with transnational agrarian movements such as Vía Campesina (Borras 2008), the movement under study here is part of that worldwide confrontation of globalisation and the practical reinvigoration of socially and environmentally sustainable peasant farming.

I suggest defining alternative agricultures thus broadly and including productive responses beyond 'green' agro-ecological movements. Alternative agricultures are all alternative responses to the large-scale exit from agrarian production (Li 2009) or what McMichael calls the 'displacement of peasant agriculture' (2006: 270). Anthropologist Mark Edelman, who studies the transcultural campaign towards a UN declaration on peasants' rights in analogy to the 2007 UN Declaration on the Rights of Indigenous Peoples (Edelman and James 2011), writes of smallholders' global situation: '[F]or peasant movements in recent decades and in diverse world regions […], [the right of subsistence] has broadened to the "right to continue being agriculturalists"'(Edelman 2005: 332).

In India, a large part of the scholarship on agro-ecology is concerned with resistance against genetically modified seeds and the 'science wars' regarding their risks and benefits (Assayag 2005; Shiva 2005; Herring 2006; Stone 2007; Glover 2010). Further scholarship deals with environmental justice movements (Martinez-Alier 2005; Zhang 2010) resisting globalisation and smallholders' displacement by large-scale development projects such as large dams (Baviskar 1995) or special economic zones (Cross 2014); with non-governmental organisations promoting sustainable development (Kumbamu 2012); with fair-trade and certified organic agriculture (Nicolaysen 2012; Thottathil 2012) and with innovations in farming science and technology, such as the system of rice intensification (Prasad et al. 2012; Harriss-White 2014).

Zero Budget Natural Farmers share many attributes of other agro-ecological movements across the world. According to their self-representation, however, they are entirely autonomous from the state

Zero Budget Natural Farming and alternative agricultures 225

and from non-governmental development actors: they do not collaborate with non-governmental organisations (NGOs), strongly oppose organic farming and other emerging alternative farming technologies and do not join other movements for environmental justice. Instead, their system of farming stands on two pillars: for one, they aim not to buy any farming inputs from the market (hence 'zero budget'), and furthermore, they produce a fermented cultivation of native cow products called *jivamrita* (literally 'nectar of life') that is the core component of their method for enhancing soil fertility. The ZBNF movement is focused on the teachings of its charismatic leader Subhash Palekar, who promotes the system in writing (Palekar 2010b, 2011, 2013), via the Internet,[3] and most important, in training camps, which he holds across South India.

The ethnographic research[4] presented here is largely located in Wayanad district in the Western Ghats of Kerala. In this district, which borders both Karnataka and Tamil Nadu, I originally investigated an epidemic of farmers' suicides (Münster 2012) and have detailed the debt and despair which have resulted from the increasing commercialisation and specularisation of agriculture at the forest frontier (Münster 2015b). In this chapter, I will abstain from a detailed content analysis of Palekar's writings and public performances, looking instead at the adaptation of his agronomical principles by smallholder farmers in Wayanad in the context of two competing responses to agrarian crisis: out-of-state ginger growing and certified organic agriculture. While there are some true devotees of Palekar among the ZBNF farmers of Wayanad, the majority of smallholders I spoke to take a pragmatic perspective on the 'spiritual' aspects of his instruction and creatively adapt the system into their lives by focusing on his system of soil management. However, all of them agree that ZBNF's more strictly agronomical principles regarding soil fertility, nutrient cycles, microbial activity, planting design and *jivamrita* have worked very well for them and saved many of their farmers from debt and unproductive or unhealthy agriculture in times of crisis. As a system of farming, many practitioners (and their neighbours) regard ZBNF as the best adaptive response to the multiple vectors of dispossession as South India becomes increasingly neoliberalised. I will first situate alternative agricultures in the regional context of agrarian crisis before I outline responses to the crisis with ZBNF at the centre.

2. Agrarian crisis in South India

Southwest Indian agriculture has been integrated into the modern world economy since 1498, when Vasco da Gama landed at Kappad

226   Daniel Münster

beach, some 50 km from the border of present-day Wayanad. Its agriculture was subsequently developed through exploration, warfare between the British and the Sultans of Mysore, timber extraction, elephant capture, the spice trade and plantations. The peripheral position of the Malabar coast in historical and contemporary food regimes marks it as a 'problem space' for alternative agricultures among 'petty commodity producers' (Harriss-White *et al.* 2009). The political-ecological history of Wayanad is well captured by the notion of the 'frontier': on the one hand, Wayanad is a hilly and forested landscape that has been constructed as relatively empty space since colonial times and has been up for grabs among colonial loggers and planters, entrepreneurial individuals and settler-migrants from the southwest Indian lowlands. On the other hand, Wayanad constitutes what has recently been called a 'resource frontier' (Tsing 2003, 2005). As Anna Tsing puts it, 'A frontier is an edge in space and time: a zone of not yet – not yet mapped, not yet regulated' (Tsing 2005: 28). The hills of Wayanad have been a frontier region for loggers, elephant catchers and gold diggers for centuries. After gaining independence, the region became a frontier of expanding agrarian capitalism. Its forested landscape turned into the site of a 'land rush' of internal colonisation by Syrian Christian settlers from central Kerala.[5] In the context of food shortages after the Second World War, agrarian expansion was an immediate developmental imperative for the young Indian state. Although the colonisation of Wayanad was not planned per se, the local state did little to stop the agrarian pioneers from encroaching on thousands of hectares of forested land.

On these fertile forest soils, settler farmers successfully established cash crop cultivation of a great variety of spices and export crops. A boom in these products brought considerable wealth to some parts of Wayanad in the 1980s and 1990s (on the notion of boom crops, see Hall 2011). To simplify a very complex story, the crisis hit the region at the end of the twentieth century as a dual crisis of production and prices. Fluctuations in the liberalised and globalised commodities market manifested themselves for farmers as a series of devastating price crashes of central commodities, most of all coffee and pepper (Jeromi 2007). Although these prices increased, the crisis of production turned out to be much more pervasive. Decades of overuse of chemicals and mono cropping and lack of management of soil fertility have depleted the formerly fertile forestland. New diseases have spread, wiping out entire plant species such as orange and vanilla. Pepper and ginger have also been widely decimated due to pathogens in Wayanad.

Zero Budget Natural Farming and alternative agricultures   227

In previous studies, I have described the 'rural angst' (Caouette and Turner 2009) of individual cultivators who navigate a precarious line between livelihood and ruin (Münster 2012). In documenting suicide cases and in many other conversations, I have recorded precarious life histories: choking struggles with pressing debts (mostly for chemical inputs), failing green revolution technologies, fluctuating markets, unpredictable prices and degraded, deteriorated soils full of pathogens, such as fungi and viruses, on fields that are hardly viable in terms of size. The ethnographic encounter with these precarious rural existences and their stories of depression, anxiety, 'tension', alcoholism, domestic abuse and suicide confirmed a widespread sense of the end of agriculture. *Ellam poyi* ('It is all gone') was a typical phrase I heard during fieldwork. Esha Shah has deemed such expressions, which are uttered in many parts of suicide-prone rural India, as 'dystopian declarations of future lessness' (2012: 1166).

On the other hand, I have studied the political and cultural effects of the Indian government's official declaration of the district of Wayanad as a suicide-prone district in 2006. From the first day of fieldwork, it has been brought home to me that farmers' suicides are highly political: not only in the sense of moral panic and the Left Democratic Front winning elections over the issues it engenders, but also in the sense that the production of knowledge about suicide and agriculture is enmeshed in the politics of development. Farmers' suicides, I argue, initiated a new push for governmental intervention in the countryside, both by NGOs and by the local state. Some of these interventions were in the form of financial support, chief among them the countrywide debt waiver in 2007 and the National Rural Employment Guarantee Scheme. But a large part of these interventions concerned farming practices themselves. The so-called Vidharba Scheme provided dairy cows for suicide widows; NGOs provided knowledge input for disease-afflicted fields; the Agricultural Department initiated several pepper rehabilitation schemes. In addition to that, the widespread institutional support both for certified organic agriculture and for green house horticulture was arguably initiated in response to farmers' suicides and agrarian crisis.

3. Productive responses to agrarian crisis

The developments described earlier have contributed both to the widespread sense that there is 'no future' for agriculture in Wayanad and to the recent proliferation of various experiments in alternative agriculture. I am interested in what Shrivastava and Kothari call 'stories

228 Daniel Münster

from tomorrow' (2012: 254–92): stories of farmers and farm workers who experiment with productive responses to crisis.

> Indeed, the country is brimming with stories of alternative experiments, many wildly successful, others struggling, but all pointing to the immense possibility of a world that is more ecologically sustainable and socially equitable than what globalised growth has given us.
>
> (Shrivastava and Kothari 2012: 255)

There are plenty of hopeful voices in Wayanad, and the self-representation of many settlers as historically more enterprising, daring and innovative than traditionally settled farmers may contribute to the experimental spirit among Wayanad's farmers. Settlers say that as they have adapted in the past to the forest soils of Wayanad, so they will also adapt to the challenged soils of the present.

Thinking of alternative agricultures in conjunction with agrarian crisis renders these agro-ecological innovations as similarly existential as has been argued for other so-called environmentalisms of the South (Guha 2000; Martinez-Alier 2005). Individual and collective quests for alternative relations between humans, soils, animals and markets are questions of survival for small-scale farm workers in India. In South India, I argue, the current agrarian crisis leaves smallholders with no other choice but to experiment with possible futures – or otherwise to exit agriculture entirely. These experiments in alternative agriculture, however, are located both outside and within what Peter Vandergeest (2009) has called 'the green box of sustainable agro-ecology'. My working definition of alternative agricultures for Wayanad district, and perhaps for other regions in South Asia as well, would thus include all experimental farming practices involving smallholders clinging to farming, situated in a regional context in which everyone seems to agree that agriculture has no future in the face of crisis.

In the case of Wayanad and many other regions of South Asia, sustainable agro-ecological knowledge, skills and practice have been lost in the 'epistemic rift' (Schneider and McMichael 2010) of decades of chemical farming. Farmers with a commitment to continue living as agriculturalists today cannot simply tap into traditional cultural reserves of pre-green revolution practices; instead, they are faced with a new plurality of competing and heterogeneous technologies and practices that they are expected to adapt. The emergence of alternative farming technologies, systems and philosophies contributes to a

Zero Budget Natural Farming and alternative agricultures 229

situation that might be called 'agronomical pluralism' (in analogy to the more established concepts of legal and medical pluralism) in which farmers are called upon to make conscious choices and to stand up for their productive relations to nonhuman nature (see also the notion 'contested agronomy' with Sumberg, Thompson and Woodhouse 2012). The sources of such agronomical knowledge vary from state agencies to farming gurus (such as Palekar) to other farmers (peers). In comparison to people seeking treatment from illness in South India, who have the option to choose from at least three medical systems (allopathy, homeopathy and Ayurveda) as well as the option to reject or combine them, smallholders, owners of a family plot and decision makers in agriculture also need to choose from a variety of agronomical techniques and systems. However, this agronomical pluralism and the decisions farmers take in adapting them are not entirely voluntary, but instead embedded in a situation of uncertainty and urgency in the context of a large-scale exit from farming. For heuristic purposes, I will distinguish between three distinct agronomical systems in Wayanad that are emerging as the most vibrant and innovative modalities of farming for small- and medium-sized landholders while keeping in mind that the reality of the situation is much more nuanced and indeterminate. These are:

- neoliberal agro-entrepreneurship, in particular ginger cropping on leased land;
- certified organic farming, mostly of export crops such as coffee and spices;
- Zero Budget Natural Farming.

From the outset, it should thus be clear that these varieties encompass a whole spectrum of responses to agrarian crisis, ranging in economic terms from a full embrace of the neoliberal market to a conscious repudiation of the market logic. To fully appreciate the unique position of Zero Budget Natural Farming, I will contrast it with ginger cropping, which is located at the other end of the spectrum in terms of social and ecological sustainability, and with organic farming, which occupies a socioecological middle ground but is seen by Palekar and his followers as even more exploitative and 'demonic' than chemical farming. My selection of these systems corresponds with ethnographic realities on the ground. In everyday usage, smallholders of Wayanad distinguish between three methods of farming that have come into existence after the crisis: chemical farming, called *rasa krishi* (*rasa* literally means 'medicine'), organic

230 Daniel Münster

farming, called *jaivakrishi*, and (Zero Budget) natural farming, called *prakritikrishi* (Zero Budget *krishi*) or simply 'Palekarkrishi'.[6]

Rasa krishi: entrepreneurial ginger croppers

When I confronted one Zero Budget farmer about the conspicuous display of wealth among some of the ginger croppers, he said, 'These people are not farmers, they are rapists of the soil!' The method of farming this farmer condemned in such strong moral terms is seen by many as the ultimate perversion of *rasa krishi*, or chemical farming. Entrepreneurial ginger cropping is a direct reaction, mostly by settler farmers, to the agrarian crisis of accumulation since the 1990s (Münster 2015a). Since the 1990s, agro-entrepreneurs from Wayanad have raised capital within groups of investors to experiment with the cultivation of ginger in the neighbouring state of Karnataka. What has begun as an exit strategy of settler farmers who lived close to the Wayanad Wildlife Sanctuary, where raids on farmland by wild animals made farming nearly impossible (Münster and Münster 2012), turned into a sizeable movement when the first ginger croppers returned from their enterprises as rich men and began building large houses, locally known as 'ginger mansions'. Ginger cropping is highly speculative and capital intensive. It requires a large initial investment of more than Rs 0.2 million per acre, but also promises returns of untaxed income of up to 1.8 million per acre. Such returns, and the individual success stories of some ginger croppers, continue to draw farmers to it.

However, there are several problems with ginger cropping. First of all, most cultivators can raise the required amount of capital by acquiring loans only from private sources, as banks do not give loans for enterprises on leased land. Capital is additionally organised through networks of kinship and friendship, in which silent partners invest in these enterprises. Ginger growing as an economic activity now blurs the line between farming and business, as it mobilises groups of investors who do not necessarily engage in the cultivation itself. But what makes ginger cropping into a real 'gamble', as many say in Wayanad, is the fact that it frequently fails. Floods and diseases often wipe out entire fields, leaving growers and investors with a total loss of harvest. The second risk factor is ginger prices, which have fluctuated between Rs 250 and Rs 3000 per bag throughout the period of study (2008–14). In reaction to the danger of diseases – a danger that rises exponentially with a second cultivation of ginger – these cultivators look out for new soils to lease every season. The frontier of ginger has thus

Zero Budget Natural Farming and alternative agricultures 231

expanded northwards from the district of Kodagu (Coorg) and has now reached as far as Goa in some cases. Soil fertility in these leased plots is enhanced short term by the massive application of chemical fertilisers and growth hormones. Ginger croppers also exercise little restraint in the use of pesticides and weedicides. When asked why this is, many of their critics in Wayanad cite the fact that these croppers do not bear the consequences of their actions anyway as they are going to move on to new soils.

As I have argued elsewhere (Münster 2015a), ginger is a boom crop that is both distress driven and profit driven. It is mostly cultivated by groups of men form Wayanad, who prefer to bring their own labourers with them as well. Knowledge about ginger cropping is reproduced within these networks of labourers and cultivators. It is driven by images of newly rich ginger kings and has remained the preferred exit strategy of the great majority of smallholders who found their agriculture in Wayanad unviable or had no access to land on which to cultivate cash crops. Ginger cropping has intensified the alienation of farmers – both from agriculture as a socio-natural process and from many of their social relationships. It is an alternative that fully embraces the neoliberal logic of speculative entrepreneurship (Münster and Strümpell 2014) and cares little about ecological and social sustainability. Ginger cropping is coproduced with new masculinities of independent, self-made men who largely see farming and their livelihood as a gamble. The high probability of failure in this speculative enterprise also makes ginger cropping the prime economic activity behind incidences of farmers' suicides in the region. It embodies almost every aspect of *rasa krishi* that Zero Budget farmers are critical of.

Jaivakrishi: *organic farming*

Many Zero Budget farmers of Wayanad are disappointed former organic farmers. Certified Organic Agriculture (COA) was introduced to Wayanad in the late 1990s and early 2000s in response to the income and fertility crisis in farming (the push factor) and increasing demand for 'quality-audited supply chains' (Friedmann 2005: 252) of agrarian commodities from Northern markets (the pull factor). COA used to have a strong institutional backing in church-based NGOs, who were the pioneers of the movement. In the case of the Catholic NGO Wayanad Social Service Society, which runs the largest consortium of organic farmers in the region, initial funding was acquired via the European Union's Export-Led Poverty Reduction programme. The 13 organic

NGOs currently running in Wayanad claim to include 17,000 farmers in their organisations; however, only a fraction of those have successful certification. COA has recently seen massive support by the development apparatus of Kerala state since the declaration of the Kerala State Organic Farming Policy, Strategy and Action Plan in 2010 (Thottathil 2012). COA is surely the most popular and best organised 'alternative' to chemical farming in Wayanad; pioneering NGOs have created clusters of COA farmers and turned entire villages into zones of organic production. These zones are scattered throughout Wayanad but have a stronger presence in northern Wayanad.

As the majority of the more radical Zero Budget farmers once started their alternative farming careers with a conversion to organic farming, they have a clear picture of why they found it unproductive, expensive and exploitative. Among the critical issues with COA is its export dependence and auditing process, which is called certification. For dissident farmers, export dependence manifests itself as rigidity in demand. 'They [organic certifiers] are very strict,' one Zero Budget farmer explained. He felt that he had lost control over what he could cultivate, as 'premium prices' were paid only for select export crops. There was no demand for vegetables or paddy, for example. According to these farmers, pressure from the international market in addition to the moral pressure from the NGO/church nexus also brought many farmers to organic farming who were not really committed to agroecology and were solely participating for economic benefit. They felt that the 'attitude' (*manobhavan*) within the movement was to change as little as possible and simply to replace chemical inputs with 'permitted' organic inputs. The process of certification became a matter of controlling adherence to a clear list of permitted practices and inputs, a process that was seen as removed from the actual concerns farmers had with the new methods. According to Zero Budget farmers, organic farming is green revolution farming with alternative inputs, but it does not possess the kind of agronomical paradigm shift that natural farming entails: fundamental changes have been overlooked in the way soil fertility and health are approached. Certification is also seen as excessively costly, especially for smallholders.

The state government's organic policy, which aims to phase out chemical farming entirely, seems to accelerate the convergence of technologies and markets of COA with those of chemical farming. Both chemical and organic farming surrender farm autonomy to the forces of the market, and both understand soil fertility as a matter of adding the right quantity and quality of external input.

Zero Budget farmers also criticised the practices of organic farming itself. Many of these methods, such as the preparation and application of composts, were perceived as too labour intensive and costly. Organic inputs and bio-control agents that require larger quantities to be effective are often more expensive than chemical fertilisers and biocides; in addition, the recommendations given were viewed by farmers as confusing and arbitrary. At the time Wayanad's alternative developers plunged into organic farming, it was already a well-developed transcultural field of globally travelling methods and models. Many Zero Budget farmers can look back today at a decade of trial and error in which they trialled such diverse techniques as effective microorganisms, vermicompost, Varanasicompost, Panchagabiyam, liquid potash, 'BD' biodynamic farming, Fukuoka farming and Agnihotra rituals, to list only some of the technologies mentioned in conversations. Each of these was fraught with uncertainty and difficulties; this-top down, unsophisticated and market-driven approach to organic farming has kept many smallholders struggling. Disappointed, many of them have exited intensive agriculture, while the environmentalists among them have embraced Zero Budget farming.

According to Mr Chacocan, a senior leader and pioneer in the organic movement of Wayanad, the strong opposition of Palekar and his followers to organic farming, and their classification of farming methods into chemical, organic and natural farming, is wrong: 'There are only two types of farming . . . one is conventional farming and one is organic farming.'[7] Among the many strands of organic farming, Palekar's method is one; hence, his organisation has no problem in recommending aspects of ZBNF to its certified farmers. As a matter of fact, Palekar's very first teaching camp in Wayanad was organised by the NGO Organic Wayanad and held at its compound near Pulpalli. Other organisations, including the M. S. Saminathan Research Foundation, have embraced ZBNF and added recipes for *jivamrita* preparation to their extension teaching material. This embrace is rhetorically rejected by Subhash Palekar, who never tires in debunking organic agriculture as an 'exploiter system' and 'preplanned foreign conspiracy not to create humus in the soil' (2010b: 130). Palekar's arguments against COA also focus on the cost of production, export dependency, dependency on external commercial inputs and the foreign origin of the methods. Most vehemently of all, Zero Budget farmers oppose the practice of vermicomposting and the application of compost manure because it removes biomass from the field and because vermicompost worms are foreign (*videshi*) surface feeders that do not allow the humus creation near the roots of plants, which is at the centre of the Zero Budget method.

Prakritikrishi: *Zero Budget Natural Farming*

Zero Budget Natural Farmers are perhaps the most radical farmers, in terms of both their disregard for state agronomy and their work towards personal independence of agrarian markets. The majority of Wayanad's ZBNF farmers are disappointed former organic farmers who quit organic farming for one of two reasons: they found it unaffordable and the policies 'strict' and coercive, or organic farming lacked self-determination and had been co-opted by mainstream farmers – who didn't truly care about human–nonhuman relations – and by the Kerala state bureaucracy and its irrational subsidy policies. Prior to becoming organic farmers, the majority of ZBNFs had practised chemical farming and were concerned about spiralling debt, increasing plant diseases, declining yields and the growing amounts of pesticides necessary. ZBNFs are arguably the most radically environmentalist and non-capitalist of farmers, who embrace the method as part of a discourse of coping, resilience and resistance.

The movement was introduced to Wayanad in 2008 when Palekar held his first meeting – locally known as 'Pulpally Camp' – on the invitation of Organic Wayanad in Pulpally, the centre of a Christian settler region. Another camp was held in 2012 in Sultan Bathery, and there are currently between 80 and 100 farmers organised in the Wayanad Natural Farmers Forum; according to members, these numbers are growing. Wayanad came late to the movement, which is much larger in South India: according to Mr. Palekar, there are some 30 million practitioners in South India, mostly in the four Dravidian states and in Maharashtra. In Kerala, the movement was first introduced in Palakad district, which remains its largest base of followers.

ZBNF is centred on the charismatic personality of Palekar; since the inception of his movement in 1997, he conducts most of his outreach through books (translated to Malayalam, among other Indian languages), the Internet and his outreach events, called 'camps', which he holds personally across the country. These events usually span several days and rely on the attendance of several hundred farmers, NGO workers, agricultural officers and *kudumbashree* (women's self-help group) workers. In these meetings, after lecturing extensively on the dangers of chemical and organic farming, Palekar makes his audience take vows on several occasions to never again use chemicals in their farming and to commit to a natural lifestyle. Farmers' suicides, exploitative globalisation and the current agrarian crisis are key elements in illustrating the impasse in conventional farming and mainstream agricultural sciences. But the larger segment of these conventions is dedicated to teaching principles of agro-ecology, in

Zero Budget Natural Farming and alternative agricultures   235

particular the importance of humus creation in the soil, microbial activity and the transformation of nutrients into absorbable forms.

Palekar's style of writing and speaking makes alliances with other progressive social movements difficult, for it is confrontational, exclusivist, nationalist – even verging on chauvinist – and involves the glorification of all things Indian (Hindu) and the demonisation of all technologies and ideas of foreign origin (see Vogel 2013). Some of the spiritual aspects of this renegade agronomy are outright obscurantist and pseudoscientific.[8] The strong emphasis on vegetarianism and the glorification of the native (desi) cow and its 'protection' brings the movement uncomfortably close to right-wing Sangh Parivar forces.[9] Palekar's critique of mainstream agronomy, chemical farming and organic farming does not feature any theory of capitalism, agrarian class relations, the commodification of land and labour or a sophisticated analysis of structural forces within historical food regimes. Instead, according to him, Indian farmers have fallen victim to the great 'preplanned foreign conspiracy' (Palekar 2010b: 130) of an agricultural exploiter system which manifests itself in both chemical and organic farming.

Reservations aside, Palekar's methods and teachings resonate unlike any other method of farming with the situated experiences of farmers in suicide-prone regions, who are permanently in danger of overburdening themselves with debts, face health issues from the overuse of biocides and have been confronted with the reality of declining soil fertility. In other words, as an agro-ecological double movement, ZBNF is wildly successful in restoring financial autonomy to farmers and in producing high yields of chemical-free food and commodities. The ideological proximity to the Hindu Right has also been partially lost in the system's adaptation by the Zero Budget farmers of Wayanad, many of whom, as former organic farmers, are Syrian Christians.

ZBNF is a system of farming that has two principal aims. The first is to maximise farmers' self-reliance and autonomy from market forces; the second is to build and manage soil fertility through the conscious design of cropping patterns and, most important, the application of the fermented preparation *jivamrita*. Farmers' autonomy from the market is seen as achievable by making farmers independent from loans and external inputs. 'We do not take a single Paisa to the market,' Palekar repeated over and over again at the camp I attended. The primary targets of his criticism are what he calls 'parallel input industries' (2010b: 119), which he identifies as the prime cause of indebtedness, and ultimately, suicide. According to natural farmers, these external inputs hinge on an incorrect (chemical) theory of soil fertility that sees soil as deficient matter. In ZBNF, soil is instead conceived of as *Annapurna*

236 Daniel Münster

(mother earth), a living part of 'nature' and an abundant 'ocean of nutrients'. As a consequence, everything a farmer needs for building soil fertility can be found on the farm if farmers keep a native cow. Cutting ties with the market also involves a shift to the cultivation of mixed crops and more food crops (*bakshakrishi*). Furthermore, and importantly, the healthier food produced by natural farming is supposed to reduce medical expenses. Currently, the movement has not yet dealt with the problem of selling to the market. Thus far, most of the farmers have pooled their produce with conventionally grown (or organically grown, if they retain their certification) commodities when selling to dealers. Aside from neighbours occasionally buying vegetables directly from farms, there are no initiatives to create alternative forms of exchange or to demand fairer prices.[10] The importance of native cows for ZBNF creates a further contradiction for Zero Budget farming. In Kerala, native cows have been almost completely eradicated with the introduction of high-yielding hybrid cows and are consequently very difficult to obtain. Since 2008, the price of native cows has risen from Rs 5000 to Rs 20,000, an initial expense that has emerged as an entry barrier for farmers ready to trial 'Zero Budget' farming. Yet according to its practitioners, all these problems are meaningless when viewed in relation to the abundant yield this system of soil management promises.

The second pillar of ZBNF holds the management of soil fertility, mulching practices, symbiotic intercropping and the fermented *jivamrita* at the core of the method. *Jivamrita* is prepared on each farm by mixing the urine and dung of a native (desi) cow, pulse powder and a sweet component such as jaggery or fruit with water and letting it ferment for several days. The importance of the native (desi) cow is explained by the alleged superabundance of micronutrients in its dung and urine as compared to high-yielding hybrid cows. Tending to native cows has become something of a telling distinction between 'real farmers' and entrepreneurial cash croppers in Wayanad. The native cows, which produce no milk and therefore have no other economic value besides contributing to soil fertility, distinguish a naturalist avant-garde of farmers. When applied to the soil, *jivamrita* does not act as a fertiliser – which means it is not absorbed by the plants. Instead, it enhances microbial activity in the soil, which in turn attracts earthworms that bring nutrients from lower levels of the earth to the topsoil. Microbes also decompose the organic matter that is placed as mulch onto the soil.

According to Palekar, Indian soils are naturally fertile and abundant in nutrients that need to be activated with the help of *jivamrita*. From the perspective of comparative agro-ecology, ZBNF may be understood as a combination of permaculture principles (Mollison and Holmgren

Zero Budget Natural Farming and alternative agricultures   237

1990) with the kind of dissident science that alternative models such as biodynamic farming (Steiner 1924) or do-nothing farming (Fukuoka 2009) represent. Central is the paradigm shift in conceptualising fields as 'self-sufficient forests', as one farmer put it, that require no input from outside the farm. In Palekar's rhetoric, his method is a superior form of science with a strong focus on microbial soil activity, which claims to represent a genealogy with Vedic science and spiritual principles. Soil properties are thus of fundamental importance to Zero Budget farmers, and a great deal of their conversations, as well as of Palekar's teachings, circle around themes such as microbes, biota, nutrients, humus, earthworms, nitrogen fixing, mulch and other earthly matters. According to all the farmers I spoke to, the results of *jivamrita* application and mulching are amazing: farmers report of highly increased yields, healthier plants, less need for irrigation and highly reduced labour input. The success of the principles of natural farming also attracts farmers who are not ready to fully follow Palekar's teachings or are not ready to commit to keeping a native cow. As a result, farmers circulate *jivamrita* far beyond the actual practitioners of ZBNF.

For actual devotees of Palekar, ZBNF entails a change of personality as well as a change in the culture of farming. Palekar camps double as revival meetings in which farmers solemnly vow to shift from being a 'demon destroyer of nature' to a 'saint protector of nature'. In his book, Palekar defines natural farming thus:

> Natural farming is a self-developing, self-nourishing and self-sufficient farming. So, in this system, there is no any human made exploitation. There is no any chance for it. It is a pain free, care free, loan free, passion free farming.
>
> (Palekar 2010b: 194)[11]

Wayanad natural farmers express their different 'mindset' (*manobhavam*) most explicitly in relation to ginger growers, whose entire enterprise is geared towards moneymaking. 'These people are looking for an easy way out. We have the willingness to do the [farm] work,' one natural farmer explained. The most important values ZBN farmers mentioned include a healthy life, care for the soil and for future generations and pride in being a farmer. Palekar calls his ideal the 'easy natural life style' (2010b: 131) – a lifestyle that is focused on the joy of working with nature and one in which human dignity does not depend on participation in consumerism. When I discussed the incomplete and partial adoption of his system in Wayanad with Mr. Palekar, he replied with a popular stereotype about Malayalees: 'They have a different mentality,

238 Daniel Münster

they want money; and Kerala mentality is more, they want money.' In addition to that, vegetarianism is part of Palekar's 'easy natural life style', a demand that poses a great challenge to his Christian followers who are great lovers of meat.

The ZBN farmers of Wayanad are mostly smaller owner-cultivators, with landholdings ranging from a few cents (1/100 of an acre) to 14 acres (7 ha). While there are some committed followers who embrace the entire philosophy of ZBNF, many consider Zero Budget farming to be an aspect of the period of great experimentation that began in Wayanad with the onset of the agrarian crisis and the consequent and necessary quest for alternatives. A full 'conversion' to natural farming is rare, as it is considered odd (*vatta*) among many mainstream farmers, but many farmers experiment with *jivamrita*. All farmers who have adopted it, whether partially or fully, claim without exception that it has increased yield, reduced their costs of production to almost zero, reduced both their own and external labour input, increased their pleasure working the field without having to handle toxic substances and significantly reduced the water requirements for their fields. In short, *jivamrita* has given these farmers a sense of an agrarian future in a situation of crisis and structural futurelessness.

4. Conclusion

This chapter has discussed Zero Budget Natural Farming in the context of ongoing experiments and projects in response to the ecological and social crisis of agriculture in India. Not all alternative agricultures are anti-capitalist; most cultivating smallholders seek practical alternatives to declining incomes and are oriented towards survival and livelihood. I have thus presented three agrarian responses to crises that operate both within and against neoliberalism. Emerging agrarian possibilities range from farmers embracing neoliberal capitalism and accelerating destructive chemical farming, on one side, to an outright rejection of the state/capital/science nexus in Zero Budget farming that points towards a revival of India's agronomic heritage and alternative economies, on the other. Not all of these alternatives are available to all cultivators' precarious economic circumstances: there are entrance barriers to most of them in terms of capital needed and networks that are more or less closed, in addition to caste barriers. However, these systems are even more fluid and disaggregate than presented here. Smaller technological innovations, such as the so-called system of rice intensification, may be picked up by farmers interested in paddy cultivation. What is important is that the knowledge of these alternatives is available to cultivators in

Zero Budget Natural Farming and alternative agricultures   239

Wayanad. Taken together, these agrarian possibilities constitute a situation of agronomical pluralism in which no farmer can claim to simply cultivate. Every farmer cultivating within this situation of economic and environmental uncertainty is called upon to explain his farming system or combination of technologies. There is neither existing tradition nor hegemony of agronomic science to be taken for granted. Instead, agronomical pluralism points towards complex ethical and practical choices when confronted with the power-laden entanglements of situated knowledges, official science and alternative science.

My chapter shows that in India, many radical land-based productive alternatives emerge as responses to situated experiences of health problems, ruin, degradation and despair. I have thus presented these radical engagements with land, food and capitalism in conjunction with regional ethnography of agro-ecological crises in the context of contemporary capitalism. In his discussion of protective double movements against the ravages of the free market ideology and the violence of commodified land and labour, Karl Polanyi has included a politically broad range of counter-movements, including fascism. Zero Budget Natural Farming is not an easy partner for transformative politics in India given its incessant nationalist populism, exclusivity, anti-science and anti-state rhetoric. Cultivators in this land-based project rarely share an explicit anti-capitalist sentiment (beyond the danger of 'the market') and an understanding of a global agro-ecological crisis (beyond a demonisation of green revolution technologies), but they may practically contribute to the 'cultivation' of post-capitalist futures and, by doing so, constitute a pragmatic first step towards inevitable agro-ecological transition not only in India, but worldwide.

Notes

1 Acknowledgements: Earlier versions of this chapter were presented at the panel on *New Ground for Revolutionary Engagements with Land, Food, and Capitalism* at the American Anthropological Association's 2013 annual meeting in Chicago (20–24 November 2013); at the conference on *Cultivating Futures: Ethnographies of Alternative Agricultures in (South) Asian Landscapes of Crisis* at Heidelberg University (12–14 December 2013); and at the international seminar on *Agrarian Transition in India* at Pondicherry University (28–30 January 2014). I gratefully acknowledge the feedback of all participants in these events, and in particular the helpful comments by Haroon Akram-Lodhi, Ursula Münster, Cristóbal Valencia and Peter Vandergeest. Research was affiliated with the Centre for Development Studies (2011–12), Trivandrum, and with the Ashoka Trust for Research in Ecology

240 Daniel Münster

and the Environment, Bangalore (2012–13). I owe deep gratitude to my research collaborators Joby T. Clement and C. K. Vishnudas.

2 I prefer the term 'smallholder' over 'peasant' in order to avoid the latter's association with debates about pre-capitalist and subsistence modes of agrarian production.

3 Subhash Palekar runs his own website, which also features video lectures he has given, http://palekarzerobudgetspiritualfarming.org, accessed on 15 November 2013.

4 This chapter is based on ethnographic fieldwork among a great number of farmers in Wayanad since 2008. Recent field trips in 2013 and 2014 have focused exclusively on ZBNF and included participation in a ZBNF training camp (Nilambur, February 2014), which also gave me the possibility to interview Mr. Subhash Palekar.

5 Kerala state was formed in 1956. When the internal colonisation of Wayanad began in the 1940s, the settlers came from the semi-independent state of Travancore.

6 The alternative name Zero Budget *Spiritual* Farming is hardly in use in Wayanad. This may have to do with the fact that most of its practitioners are Syrian Christians and that most of Palekar's 'spirituality' is a confusing medley of Hindu traditions incompatible with their worldview. Another explanation could be that Kerala's farmers are very eager to present their alternative model as located within the confines of reason and science.

7 Interview with author on 22 February 2014, Vanamoolika, Pulpally.

8 Most of Palekar's teachings, however, are very much in line with recent advances in agro-ecology; see Magdoff and van Es (2009).

9 The relationship between agro-ecological and other environmental movements in India and forces of the Hindu Right deserves separate investigation. While Palekar stresses that his agro-nationalism follows the spirit of Mahatma Gandhi and the ideal of *gram swaraj* (village self-rule) (see 2011: 6–13), he does not really control appropriations of his movement from the right. In Kerala's Palakad district, the pioneers of ZBNF are said to have been RSS activists. Both Palekar and his followers aim at foregrounding their innovative farming techniques, but the centrality of the desi cow in their system repeatedly brings them close to the RSS-run Goshala (cow shelter) movement and other right-wing cow protectors (see Alter 1994). In 2007, Palekar received the so-called Gopal Gaurav Award on the occasion of the Vishwa Gou Sammelan, or World Conference on Indian Cattle Breed, a convention held in Shimoga district (Karnataka) featuring participation across the entire spectrum of Hindutva activists and organisations (*The Hindu*, 21 April 2007).

10 In his writings there are some first ideas about exchange in terms of a parallel certified market: 'There should be our own non-governmental internal certification system. Our cost will be zero. The income will be bonus. The rates for our poisonless products will be doubled' (Palekar 2010a: 8).

11 I refrain from marking language errors in Palekar's writings with [sic], as they are ubiquitous in his writings and, as he proclaims in the preface, part of his attempt to write 'simple no literal English' (2010b: 11) for his farmer-readers 'so they will accept this rustic or boorish English language, no doubt'.

References

Alter, J. S. 1994. 'Somatic Nationalism: Indian Wrestling and Militant Hinduism'. *Modern Asian Studies* 28 (3): 557–88.

Altieri, M. A., F. R. Funes-Monzote and P. Petersen. 2012. 'Agroecologically Efficient Agricultural Systems for Smallholder Farmers: Contributions to Food Sovereignty'. *Agronomy for Sustainable Development* 32 (1): 1–13.

Altieri, M. A. and V. M. Toledo. 2011. 'The Agroecological Revolution in Latin America: Rescuing Nature, Ensuring Food Sovereignty and Empowering Peasants'. *Journal of Peasant Studies* 38 (3): 587–612.

Assayag, J. 2005. 'Seeds of Wrath: Agriculture, Biotechnology and Globalization'. In Jackie Assayag and Chris J. Fuller (eds). *Globalizing India: Perspectives from Below*. London: Anthem Press, pp. 65–88.

Baviskar, A. 1995. *In the Belly of the River: Tribal Conflicts over Development in the Narmada Valley*. Delhi and New York: Oxford University Press.

Bernstein, H. 2014. 'Food Sovereignty via the "Peasant Way": A Sceptical View'. *Journal of Peasant Studies* 41 (6): 1031–63.

Borras, S. M. J. 2008. 'La Vía Campesina and Its Global Campaign for Agrarian Reform'. *Journal of Agrarian Change* 8 (2–3): 258–89.

Brookfield, H. C., H. Parsons, and M. Brookfield. 2003. *Agrodiversity: Learning from Farmers across the World*. Tokyo and New York: United Nations University Press; UNEP; GEF.

Caouette, D. and S. Turner. 2009. *Agrarian Angst and Rural Resistance in Contemporary Southeast Asia*. London and New York: Routledge.

Cross, J. 2014. *Dream Zones: Anticipating Capitalism and Development in India*. London: Pluto Press.

Edelman, M. 2005. 'Bringing the Moral Economy Back in . . . to the Study of 21st-Century Transnational Peasant Movements'. *American Anthropologist* 107 (3): 331–45.

Edelman, M. and C. James. 2011. 'Peasants' Rights and the UN System: Quixotic Struggle? Or Emancipatory Idea Whose Time Has Come?' *Journal of Peasant Studies* 38 (1): 81–108.

Foster, J. B. 2000. *Marx's Ecology: Materialism and Nature*. New York: Monthly Review Press.

Foster, J. B. 2013. 'The Epochal Crisis'. *Monthly Review* 65 (5): 1–12.

Friedmann, H. 2005. 'From Colonialism to Green Capitalism: Social Movements and Emergence of Food Regimes'. In Frederick H. Buttel and Philip McMichael (eds). *New Directions in the Sociology of Global Development*. Amsterdam: Elsevier, pp. 227–65.

Fukuoka, M. 2009. *The One-Straw Revolution: An Introduction to Natural Farming*. New York: New York Review Books.

Glover, D. 2010. 'The Corporate Shaping of GM Crops as a Technology for the Poor'. *Journal of Peasant Studies* 37 (1): 67–90.

Guha, R. 2000. *Environmentalism: A Global History*. New York: Longman.

242 Daniel Münster

Hall, D. 2011. 'Land Grabs, Land Control, and Southeast Asian Crop Booms'. *Journal of Peasant Studies* 38 (4): 837–57.

Harriss-White, B. 2014. 'Towards a Lower Carbon Agriculture: An Experiment with Expert and Situated Knowledge'. Paper presented at International Seminar on Agrarian Transition in India, 28–30 January in Pondicherry University.

Harriss-White, B., D. K. Mishra and V. Upadhyay. 2009. 'Institutional Diversity and Capitalist Transition: The Political Economy of Agrarian Change in Arunachal Pradesh, India'. *Journal of Agrarian Change* 9 (4): 512–47.

Herring, R. J. 2006. 'Why Did "Operation Cremate Monsanto" Fail? Science and Class in India's Great Terminator-Technology Hoax'. *Critical Asian Studies* 38 (4): 467–93.

Jeromi, P. D. 2007. 'Farmers' Indebtedness and Suicides. Impact of Agricultural Trade Liberalisation in Kerala'. *Economic and Political Weekly* 42 (31): 3241–47.

Kumbamu, A. 2012. 'The Agri-Food Sector's Response to the Triple Crisis: Sustaining Local Social Initiatives in Andhra Pradesh, India'. *Development* 55 (1): 104–11.

Lerche, J. 2011. 'Agrarian Crisis and Agrarian Questions in India'. *Journal of Agrarian Change* 11 (1): 104–18.

Li, T. M. 2009. 'Exit from Agriculture: A Step Forward or a Step Backward for the Rural Poor?' *Journal of Peasant Studies* 36 (3): 629–36.

Lockyer, J. and J. R. Veteto. 2013. *Environmental Anthropology Engaging Ecotopia: Bioregionalism, Permaculture, and Ecovillages*. New York: Berghahn Books.

Magdoff, F. and J. B. Foster. 2011. *What Every Environmentalist Needs to Know about Capitalism: A Citizen's Guide to Capitalism and the Environment*. New York: Monthly Review Press.

Magdoff, F. and H. van Es. 2009. *Building Soils for Better Crops: Sustainable Soil Management*. Beltsville, MD: SARE.

Martinez-Alier, J. 2005. *The Environmentalism of the Poor: A Study of Ecological Conflicts and Valuation*. New Delhi: Oxford University Press.

McMichael, P. 2006. 'Global Development and the Corporate Food Regime'. In Frederick H. Buttel and Philip McMichael (eds). *New Directions in the Sociology of Global Development*, vol. 11. Bingley: Emerald (MCB UP), pp. 265–99.

Mollison, B. C. and D. Holmgren. 1990. *Permaculture One: A Perennial Agriculture for Human Settlements*. Tyalgum, Australia: Tagari.

Moore, J. W. 2011. 'Transcending the Metabolic Rift: A Theory of Crises in the Capitalist World-Ecology'. *Journal of Peasant Studies* 38 (1): 1–46.

Münster, D. 2012. 'Farmers' Suicides and the State in India: Conceptual and Ethnographic Notes from Wayanad, Kerala'. *Contributions to Indian Sociology* 46 (1–2): 181–208.

Münster, D. 2015a. '"Ginger Is a Gamble": Crop Booms, Rural Uncertainty, and the Neoliberalization of Agriculture in South India'. *Focaal: Journal of Global and Historical Anthropology* 71: 100–113.

Zero Budget Natural Farming and alternative agricultures   243

Münster, D. 2015b. 'Farmers' Suicides and the Moral Economy of Agriculture: Victimhood, Voice, and Agro-Environmental Responsibility in South India'. In Ludek Broz and Daniel Münster (eds), *Suicide and Agency: Anthropological Perspectives on Self-Destruction, Personhood and Power*. Farnham: Ashgate, pp. 105–25.

Münster, D. and U. Münster. 2012. 'Human-Animal Conflicts in Kerala: Elephants and Ecological Modernity on the Agrarian Frontier in South India'. *Rachel Carson Center Perspectives* 2012 (5): 41–49.

Münster, D. and C. Strümpell. 2014. 'The Anthropology of Neoliberal India: An Introduction'. *Contributions to Indian Sociology* 48 (1: special issue on The Making of Neoliberal India): 1–16.

Nicolaysen, A. M. 2012. 'Empowering Small Farmers in India through Organic Agriculture and Biodiversity Conservation'. PhD thesis, University of Connecticut.

O'Connor, J. 1998. *Natural Causes: Essays in Ecological Marxism*. New York: The Guilford Press.

Palekar, S. 2010a. *Five Layer Palekar Model's: Mixed Lashyadhisha Pattern*. Amravati: Zero Budget Natural Farming Research, Development and Extension Movement.

Palekar, S. 2010b. *The Philosophy of Spiritual Farming: Zero Budget Natural Farming* (5th revised). Amravati: Zero Budget Natural Farming Research, Development and Extension Movement.

Palekar, S. 2011. *The Symbiosis of Spiritual Farming*. Amravati: Zero Budget Natural Farming Research, Development and Extension Movement.

Palekar, S. 2013. *The Principles of Spiritual Farming* (8th edition). Amravati: Zero Budget Natural Farming Research, Development and Extension Movement.

Patel, R. 2009. 'Food Sovereignty'. *Journal of Peasant Studies* 36 (3): 663–706.

Ploeg, J. D. v. d. 2008. *The New Peasantries: Struggles for Autonomy and Sustainability in an Era of Empire and Globalization*. London: Earthscan.

Ploeg, J. D. v. d. 2010. 'The Peasantries of the Twenty-First Century: The Commoditisation Debate Revisited'. *Journal of Peasant Studies* 37 (1): 1–30.

Polanyi, K. 2001 (1944). *The Great Transformation: The Political and Economic Origins of Our Time*. Boston, MA: Beacon Press.

Prasad, C. S., T. M. Thiyagarjan, O. P. Rupela, T. Amod and G. V. Ramanjaneyulu. 2012. 'Contesting Agronomy through Dissent: Experiences from India'. In J. E. Sumberg and John Thompson (eds). *Contested Agronomy: Agricultural Research in a Changing World*. New York: Routledge, pp. 175–85.

Reddy, D. N. and S. Mishra (eds). 2009. *Agrarian Crisis in India*. New Delhi: Oxford University Press.

Schneider, M. and P. McMichael. 2010. 'Deepening, and Repairing, the Metabolic Rift'. *Journal of Peasant Studies* 37 (3): 461–84.

Shah, E. 2012. '"A Life Wasted Making Dust": Affective Histories of Dearth, Death, Debt and Farmers' Suicides in India'. *Journal of Peasant Studies* 39 (5): 1159–79.

244 Daniel Münster

Shiva, V. 2005. *Biodiversity Wars and the Global Giants: India Divided*. New York: Seven Stories Press.

Shrivastava, A. and A. Kothari. 2012. *Churning the Earth: The Making of Global India*. New Delhi: Viking.

Steiner, R. 1924. *Geisteswissenschaftliche Grundlagen zum Gedeihen der Landwirtschaft: Landwirtschaflicher Kurs* [The Agriculture Course: Birth of the Biodynamic Method]. Koberwitzbei Breslau.

Stone, G. D. 2007. 'Agricultural Deskilling and the Spread of Genetically Modified Cotton in Warangal'. *Current Anthropology* 48 (1): 67–103.

Sumberg, J. E., J. Thompson and P. Woodhouse. 2012. 'Contested Agronomy: Agricultural Research in a Changing World'. In J. E. Sumberg and John Thompson (eds). *Contested Agronomy: Agricultural Research in a Changing World*. New York: Routledge, pp. 1–21.

Thottathil, S. E. 2012. 'Incredible Kerala? A Political Ecological Analysis of Organic Agriculture in the "Model of Development"'. PhD thesis, University of California, Berkeley.

Tsing, A. 2003. 'Natural Resources and Capitalist Frontiers'. *Economic and Political Weekly* 38 (48): 5100–106.

Tsing, A. 2005. 'How to Make Resources in Order to Destroy Them (and Then Save Them?) on the Salvage Frontier'. In Daniel Rosenberg and Susan Harding (eds). *Histories of the Future*. Durham: Duke University Press, pp. 51–75.

Vandergeest, P. 2009. 'Opening the Green Box: How Organic Became the Standard for Alternative Agriculture in Thailand'. Paper Presented at Berkeley Workshop on Environmental Politics, UC Berkeley.

Vasavi, A. R. 2012. *Shadow Space: Suicides and the Predicament of Rural India*. Gurgaon: Three Essays Collective.

Veteto, J. R. and K. Skarbø. 2009. 'Sowing the Seeds: Anthropological Contributions to Agrobiodiversity Studies'. *Culture and Agriculture* 31 (2): 73–87.

Vogel, L. C. 2013. Koalitionen: Zur Inszenierung von Fakten im 'Zero Budget Natural Farming' Subhash Palekars [Coalitions: On the Performance of Facts in Subash Palekar's 'Zero Budget Natural Farming']. MA thesis, Martin-Luther-Universität, Halle (Saale).

Weis, T. 2010. 'The Accelerating Biophysical Contradictions of Industrial Capitalist Agriculture'. *Journal of Agrarian Change* 10 (3): 315–41.

Wittman, H., A. A. Desmarais and N. Wiebe, (eds.) 2010. *Food Sovereignty: Reconnecting Food, Nature and Community*. Halifax: Fernwood Publishing.

Wittman, H. 2009. 'Reworking the Metabolic Rift: La VíaCampesina, Agrarian Citizenship, and Food Sovereignty'. *Journal of Peasant Studies* 36 (4): 805–26.

Zhang, S. 2010. 'Conceptualising the Environmentalism in India: Between Social Justice and Deep Ecology'. In Qingzhi Huan (ed.). *Eco-Socialism as Politics: Rebuilding the Basis of Our Modern Civilisation*. Dordrecht: Springer, pp. 181–91.

Chapter 9

Stressed commerce and accumulation process
A farm-level study of agrarian transition in West Bengal

Santanu Rakshit

1. Introduction

Studies on agrarian transition in India of recent times show that it is not following the classical form of transition as envisaged. The distortion or deviation in terms of classical notion of agrarian transition, sometimes termed as 'arrested capitalist development', needs to be explicated in a different environment. The process need not be wholly Marxist or wholly non-Marxist. It is also important to discern the different politico-economic environment through which post-Independent India has traversed. Studies on agrarian transition in the 1970s and 1980s to the early 1990s explicate the dynamics of the indigenous development of capitalism in a government-supported environment. With the advent of neoliberalism in the 1990s we perceived a different economic environment controlled by capital, global in nature and state slowly withdrawing from the productive support to agriculture. These induced changes were mostly irreversible in nature. Therefore, the closed circuit with limited external intervention in agriculture transformed it into an open circuit with limited or zero government intervention. Indian agriculture started to be included in the capital's global sphere. The global linkages and intervention of neoliberal capital started transforming the agrarian structure, initially through forced exchange. The latter became the medium through which transfer and accumulation of surplus in the form of money from the agrarian sphere to global circuit took place. This started inducing permanent changes in the agrarian relations and structure. Most important is the change in the accumulation process – erstwhile government-supported indigenous capitalist accumulation, that is state-led capitalism transformed into primitive accumulation (observable as mercantile accumulation in agrarian sector) of capital and/or both. Nevertheless, primitive accumulation is the dominant

246 Santanu Rakshit

source of surplus appropriation. The process of primitive accumulation started expanding the non-capitalist sector in agriculture, which was apparently in a diminishing condition under closed circuit with government support. Primitive accumulation of capital in this non-capitalist sector also entailed another burgeoning sector, that of the 'excluded'. Wherein the direct producers after getting dissociated from their means of production are transformed into free labourers. However, they remain excluded because of the lack of productive sectors to get absorbed. This is an expanding sector excluded from productive activities – termed 'Limbo-space' or 'MOM'.[1] Therefore, we find three sectors in agriculture:

Capital (becoming/arising)

This group includes those who survived the neoliberal capital's hegemony and were able to get included in the global circuit. They are undergoing capitalist accumulation. This group also includes those who got appropriated or incorporated in ambit of global capital, for example Lumpen bourgeoisie (as defined by Andre Gunder Frank) or Comprador bourgeoisie (as defined by Mao Tse Tung).

Non-Capital

This group is subjected to primitive accumulation of global capital (observable as mercantile accumulation in agrarian sector). It also includes those who are structurally transformed from *capital arising*[2] (in pre-neoliberal era) to *non-capital* in the neoliberal regime.

Excluded

This group actually represents the emerging non-farm space inhabited mostly by labourers and those people forced to get involved in non-farm occupation. The people of this group have been dissociated from its state as direct producers in non-capital space to get excluded from the productive sphere. This group needs to be sustained by Capital's Development Management or reverse primitive accumulation (Sanyal 2007).

Recent publications mostly theoretical and some even non-essentialist in nature have become popular in propagating ideas conceptually close to the structure explicated earlier (Chowdhury et al. 2000; Chakrabarti and Cullenberg 2003; Sanyal 2007; Patnaik 2008a, 2008c). These studies are very much acclaimed and depict the agrarian transition from a different standpoint of Marxist, Neo-Gramscian or Neo-Althusserian

Stressed commerce and accumulation process   247

Marxist viewpoint. Sanyal's study (2007) is an all-round view of the Indian economy rather developing world economy and its theorisation.

2. Capitalist development: a brief exposition of the agrarian transition in West Bengal

This study is an attempt to find an outlet for the debate of agrarian transition or development of capitalism in Indian agriculture in the neoliberal regime of Capital. Neoliberalism seems to be a higher moment in the broad journey of capital in global economy. Keynesianism at least for least developed countries (LDCs) should be a forgone chapter as far as Keynesian developmental-ism specifically practiced in LDCs is concerned. Neoliberal capital had been able to maintain a multipronged approach towards maintaining its complete hegemony on the LDCs that were seriously practising Keynesianism till may be the late 1980s. Keynesianism, as Araghi (2009, 2010) defines 'unruly developmental-ism', is a form of active government intervention actually helped in the process of capital accumulation in agriculture in India. As Keynesianism or government support in agriculture faded away from the productive agricultural sector, signs of distortion in agrarian transition started to manifest.

Academicians involved in the wonderful mode of production debate were finally unanimous on the point that substantial development of capitalism has been experiential in Indian agriculture. The mode of production debate and the importance of the study of class formation and class differentiation were summarised by Utsa Patnaik (1990) by the following words, 'Concept of mode of production, theoretically an analytical concept, could not be cavalierly treated as one might an elastic glove, stretching it here and there to fit varying empirical reality. Such a procedure would logically imply as many "modes of production" as there were historically existent social formations and therefore represent a subversion of the analytical concept of mode of production itself.' Subsequently, the discussion veered back to the original questions of class formation and class differentiation in agriculture. That is the Leninist position on the correspondence of 'class differentiation' and 'capitalist development'. During the debate we have come across many strains of thought, arguments of Ashok Rudra, Amit Bhaduri, Jairus Banaji,[3] Ranjit Sau, Nirmal Chandra, Sharat Lin and Nirmal Mukhopadhyay, Gunder Frank[4] and others.[5] In their subsequent works they became unanimous at least on one point that substantial capitalist development has taken place in Indian agriculture along with some pre-capitalist relics, mostly semi-feudal.[6] They had to agree to this because with the spread of new technology (green revolution) along with the government support (subsidies), Indian agriculture was fast moving towards capitalist development. We can consider this outcome as capital (arising or becoming) looking forward for its completion to 'being'. Class differentiation study of many later researchers[7] all over India affirmed that in terms of all economic factors – input, assets, output and surpluses – there was a definite tendency of increasing differentiation in peasantry leading towards the culmination of capitalist development.

Let us now follow the diagrammatic exposition of the first part of the schema (given in Figure 9.1) that we perceive to be working or have worked in the process of agrarian transition in West Bengal. The schema can be generalised to Indian agriculture in some cases, and it even appears to be applicable to developing countries as well. In West Bengal, after independence we can safely assume the structure that is given in Figure 9.1. It shows the consequences in closed circuit of productive agricultural sphere with active government support.

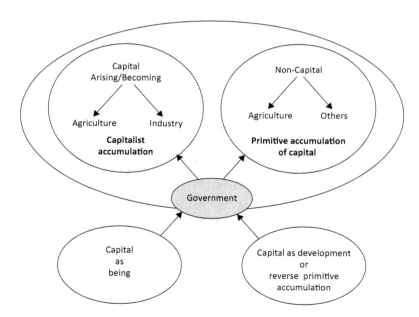

Figure 9.1 Closed circuit with government support
Source: Author's conceptual construct.

We assume that *capital-non-capital* complex (Sanyal 2007) existed in the following way under closed economic circuit with government support. The capital sphere represented by *capital-arising* or *capital-becoming* was found to follow classical capitalist accumulation, leading to the development of the indigenous *capital-arising* or *becoming*. On the other hand, a subset of agricultural sector was also undergoing capital's primitive accumulation represented by non-capital. That is the part where *capital as being* was capable to intervene and carry on its primitive accumulation against the barrier posed by government – centre or federal state of West Bengal. Figure 9.1 also depicts the presence of *capital as being* ready or trying to intrude with its development management or governmentality, a process termed as 'reverse primitive accumulation' by Sanyal (2007).

The overwhelming presence of state supporting production sphere, that is agriculture helped development of the *capital-arising*, however short of getting transformed to *capital as being*. This was due to the step-by-step withdrawal of state from production sphere in post-liberalisation era (after 1991). This is the reason why debate on the mode of production enthusiastically concluded that agrarian transition by nature is directed towards capitalist development. In the neoliberal era, the process got stunted. This indicates that development of capitalism in agriculture as envisioned by the stalwarts in mode of production debate was not *capital as being* rather *capital-arising*. If it would have been *capital as being*, then it would have been able to replicate, reproduce and grow amidst unfavourable conditions posed in the neoliberal regime. Authors have amply exemplified the scenario in Rakshit (2011, 2014), showing that peasant class differentiation though exists in production sphere in terms of assets, inputs, product and product marketed is conspicuously absent in exchange arena. Exchange sphere is important because that determines the amount of surplus and the question of reinvestment thereof. If the peasants and producers fail to retain the surplus, it would hamper accumulation and reinvestment of the surplus for growth and productivity. The study of the author in 2003 and 2013 empirically shows that agrarian producers are failing to retain the surplus during the process of exchange. This is due to the phenomenon of 'stressed commerce'. It has been exemplified in detail in Rakshit (2011, 2014).

3. Agrarian transition in the new millennium

I feel the conclusion of the mode of production debate as summarised by Utsa Patnaik (1990) seemed partially correct till the first decade of

250 Santanu Rakshit

the current millennium. During my study undertaken in 2003–4, (the year of agrarian crisis worldwide, those years when Condoleezza Rice, an American diplomat, had the audacity to say that Asians consume too much of food grains), I definitely found intense differentiation of the peasantry with respect to factors like input, assets, output and output marketed except in the 'retention of the surplus'. However, preliminary results of my recent study – a repeat survey of the same region with the same sample in 2013–14 – cast doubt even on the existence of differentiation or concentration in terms of the factors (mentioned earlier), which were found to be skewed in favour of richer economic class both by my predecessors and by my study in 2003. This brings us to Figure. 9.2. In my view this must be the depiction of the current scenario. After nearly 20–22 years of vigorous implementation of neoliberal tenets, we can now safely term it as 'open economic circuit' (agriculture) under neoliberalism.

This was even the feeling among many noted academicians. Even Utsa Patnaik (2007) defined the agrarian transition in India as arrested development of capitalism. Prabhat Patnaik (2012) clearly stated that Indian agriculture is undergoing primitive accumulation of capital. Sanyal (2007) was of the view that Indian economy as a whole like other developing economies is undergoing primitive accumulation. It was fascinating to understand from him the concept of development management or reverse primitive accumulation. It is so true in the case of Indian agriculture as well as that of West Bengal.

Let us try to digress upon the other opinions of academicians who have greatly influenced the debate on agrarian transition in India and other developing countries. Byres (2003) made some predictions about Indian agriculture: first, predictions of the growth of strong capitalist producers and, second, strong home market for industrial goods and siphoning of surplus for the development of non-agricultural sector. However, in the case of West Bengal we do not find the first prediction to be true after ten years of his publication. On the contrary, it seems to be moving in the opposite direction, that is from *capital-arising* to *non-capital*. However, his other prediction of strong home market for industrial goods and siphoning of surplus for the development of non-agricultural sector seems to be phenotypically true. Mercantile supremacy in commerce (rather stressed commerce) siphoning of surplus from the agricultural sector is the reality. We would highlight this point by empirical evidence from the study of 2003 and 2013–14. Primitive accumulation in Indian agriculture would eventually dissociate direct producers from its means of production. The siphoning of surplus to large non-agricultural capital can be re-channelised in the agricultural sector in numerous ways, which surely is an important arena of future study in this line. Currently, nothing very assertive can be said about the nature of ploughing back of the surplus to the agrarian sector. However, governments' intervention in the form of development management (e.g. Mahatma Gandhi National Rural Employment Guarantee Act) is creating a market for non-agricultural sector in agrarian India.

Bernstein (1996) interestingly opined that the agrarian question of capital has been bypassed in India. However, his recent argument (2014) though refuting primitive accumulation of capital seems on the contrary to be rationalising it more by questioning the importance of acknowledging the very existence of peasants. According to Bernstein, this particular group is no more important as it seems to be on the verge of extinction. In my view the dissociation of producers or peasants from their means of production due to primitive accumulation and loss of occupational identity had been justified putting a question mark on the rationality of acknowledging the existence of peasantry by Bernstein. He tried to put the peasantry out of the purview of transition debate because primitive accumulation in reality is dissociating it from productive sphere to sphere of *non-capital* or *excluded*.

On the discussion on structural transformation of agriculture, I agree with Lerche (2011). To him, in Indian context, capitalist development is progressing without a proper agrarian transition and the group of farmers still accumulating must be numerically small, as there is no evidence that successful capitalist farming is becoming more broad based under the present neoliberal conditions. While non-institutional credit is spreading anew to a regionally diverse degree of intensity, it may well be that increasing share of the agrarian profits is being appropriated elsewhere (Lerche 2011). This observation is rational and corroborates my findings in the survey done in the current millennium. Lerche's observation is to a very large extent a correct depiction of agrarian transition in India, particularly in West Bengal.

From the above discussion, our starting point of the analysis of the agrarian transition can be the findings of Sanyal (2007), Patnaik (2007), Lerche (2011) and Patnaik (2012).

We would first give some empirical evidence about the current nature of accumulation process and agrarian transition, and then move over to substantiate our schema undergoing in this neoliberal regime in West Bengal.

As we have said earlier, empirical evidence would be basically a comparative study of the data of the most developed agricultural region in West Bengal taken in 2003–4 and 2013–14.

252 Santanu Rakshit

4. Methodology of the studies in 2003–4 and 2013–14

Any inference to be drawn on the aforementioned issues from a micro-level study necessarily requires a sample survey which is comprehensive enough in capturing the diversity in the agrarian structure in West Bengal. The investigator made a thorough survey in 2003–4 during his PhD research in the advanced district of Bardhaman (Memari-I block), a region with higher capitalistic development along with high fertility (advanced region), West Bengal. The repeat survey in 2013–14 was carried on exactly the same sample of households. So the methodology for selecting districts, villages and households exercised in 2003–4 is discussed here.

Selection of districts

The indices of economic development and other parameters on the basis of which the selection of the district Bardhaman was done are given in Tables 9A.1 and 9A.2. The rationale which evolved from the development indices eventually influencing the selection of the districts are thoroughly discussed in the following two broad categories: (1) strictly economic criteria and (2) other criteria which include topography, demography and geographical location of the two regions. Regarding the economic criterion, the following characteristics of the district of Bardhaman in comparison with other districts were observed:

First, in terms of per capita district domestic product, Bardhaman ranks third behind Kolkata and Darjeeling, respectively. Among the rural-based districts, it ranks first by this criterion. Second, regarding rural monthly per capita consumption, again Bardhaman ranks third with Rs 520, behind Haora and North 24 Parganas. Third, by the criterion of rural poverty ratio, in Bardhaman the ratio is 19 per cent. Fourth, considering district per capita income, the rank of Bardhaman is third with Rs 17,537.98, which is higher than the average district per capita income of West Bengal behind only to Kolkata (Rs 33,299.5) and Darjeeling (Rs 18,529.18). Finally, when per capita real income (1993–94 prices) is considered, Bardhaman ranks second (Rs 11,445), only after Kolkata (Rs 19,896).

Thus, selection of the Bardhaman district seems to be appropriate and congruous to the objective of the study. In view of some criteria Haora, North 24-Parganas and Darjeeling are marginally ahead of Bardhaman.

However, these districts were not selected considering the following criteria: first of all, their proximity to state capital, second, their urban and industrial bias, and finally, their dependence on non-conventional or special economic sectors (e.g. tourism in Darjeeling). Moreover, in terms of agro-based economy, Bardhaman among the rural districts projects a consistent pattern of high development in all the indices considered. This is evident from Table 9A.1.

The other criteria related to overall development which had an influence on selection of the district follows.

First, topographically Bardhaman, except the northern industrial belt, is covered by vast tracts of alluvial plain, with major perennial rivers like Bhagirathi and Damodar flowing through it: as a result, the district is covered by a wide network of these rivers in the forms of rivulets and canals. Moreover, the annual rainfall is 140 cm, high compared with the country and the state itself. All these favourable topographical conditions have contributed to high fertility and extremely good irrigational facility. In consequence, it enjoys high productivity, leading to consecutive bumper crops.

Second, the distribution of population shows that density of population is 985 per sq. km, highest among the predominantly rural districts of West Bengal.

Third, literacy rate is high in Bardhaman (71 per cent in 2001 and 62 per cent in 1991), whereas it is low in Purulia (56.1 per cent in 2001 and 45 per cent in 1991). Fourth, in the districts a majority of the inhabitants are dependent on agriculture around, 65 per cent.

Selection of the sample villages

The process adopted in the selection of the sample villages in this study was little different. It chose to select directly the sample villages from the village-level disaggregated data of the census. It chose two sets of data that were obtained from the Census Department, Government of India: (1) Rural Primary Census Abstract and (2) Village Directory – Bardhaman. There are numerous criteria, nearly 120 in the two sets of data. Broadly, these two combined data sets can be classified into two types – (1) quantitative, that is absolute numbers such as data on population, land, irrigation, category of workers, literacy and others; and (2) indicative, based on the availability of different amenities such as schools, health centres, electricity, pucca road, daily hat and so on, and their distances from the villages.

254 Santanu Rakshit

Table 9.1 Quantitative criterion for village selection

No.	Quantitative criterion fixed	First level	Second level	Third level
1	Percentage of literacy	>30	>40	>50
2	Percentage of irrigated land to total cultivable area	>40	>50	>60
3	Percentage of cultivable land to total land	>70	>80	>90
4	Percentage of canal irrigation to cultivable land	>30	>40	>50
5	Percentage of canal irrigation to total irrigation	>50	>60	>75

Source: Author's criterion set on Census Data, 1991.

This study took extensive help of MS Access. Next, the villages where survey would be undertaken were selected. This was done on the basis of the relative measures. The first round of query was run in MS Access by assigning three different levels of percentages successively to the aforementioned criteria shown in Table 9.1.

The criteria in the third level were finally set. In the first two levels, percentages were set much in the lower end, as shown in Table 9.1. Subsequently, percentages were increased to the third level. In consequence, nearly 142 villages out of nearly 26,000 villages came under the purview of selection. The maximum of these 142 villages, nearly 50 per cent, were from Memari-I and Memari-II blocks.

After pursuing the first round of query, a second round of query was run in MS Access where the qualitative or indicative measures were taken into consideration. The broad criteria important and relevant for the study were at first selected, which are shown in Table 9.1. All the selected criteria were adjusted to their optimum qualification level. The indicators for the different amenities available in the Village Directory Census are set numerically 0, 1, 2, 3.[8] As 1 represents the optimum quality level, all the criteria important for our purpose were adjusted to 1, given as quality indicator in Table 9.2, which summarises the process followed in detail.

In the completion of the aforementioned round of query, the 142 villages after round one got reduced to 25 only. Interestingly, the maximum numbers of the villages were found to be under Memari-I and II blocks, nearly 60 per cent.

Stressed commerce and accumulation process 255

Table 9.2 Indicative criterion for village selection

No.	Indicative criteria	Quality indicator
1	Educational facilities	ONE
2	Health facilities	ONE
3	Availability of electricity for all purposes	ONE
4	Availability of Hat (market) day	ONE
5	Approach pucca road	ONE
6	Access to railways	ONE
7	Availability of post office, bank, telephone connection, etc.	ONE

Source: Author's criterion set on Census Data, 1991.

Table 9.3 Final villages selected in Memari, Bardhaman

No.	Name of villages	Village code	Tehsil code	District code
1	Genraghata	47	260	16
2	Dalui-bazar	55	260	16
3	Chaknara	134	260	16
4	Rasulpur	136	260	16

Source: Author's selection of villages from Census, 1991.

From the reduced set of 25 villages, 4 villages were selected, which are given in Table 9.3 with their village, tehsil and district codes.

The villages were purposively selected from Memari-I, since they are geographically adjoining. This was done in expectation of less deviation and fair amount of homogeneity among them, as depicted in Table 9.3. To reiterate, our only objective was to select the villages with maximum economic development from the advanced district of Bardhaman.

Selection of sample households

Households were selected on the basis of simple random sampling without replacement. A complete list of households was obtained from local panchayat office in voter list or list compiled from different economic surveys undertaken by it.

256 Santanu Rakshit

Classifying the households

Households have been classified by two different criteria, namely farm size and labour exploitation. In 2013–14 preliminary trends of primary survey show that operational holdings have decreased over all classes except landlord class. Table 9.4 shows the comparative situation of the operational holding. Average landholding of the 57 households which were studied in 2003–4 (out of 116) in Memari-I indicates decreasing trend over all the classes. In absolute terms also, the decrease is significant. Land concentration is in favour of the richer classes. In 2003–4, increasing returns to scale (IRS) were found in the case of output produced in the advanced region (Memari-I) with respect to class status and acreage (NSSO stratification)[9] published in Rakshit (2011).

The problem in 2003–4, however, was with both net and gross surpluses. The expected monotonic relation between surplus and class status was totally absent and showed a completely different picture. Besides, farm labour surplus or farm disposable surplus[10] per acre or per household showed u-shaped relation (Figure 9.3) along with gross value added per acre and household (Rakshit 2010, 2011, 2014). This breakdown of monotonicity actually signifies the basic problem of reinvestment of surplus or accumulation for further capitalisation. It also indicates the collapse of class status or class structure according to adopted E-criterion or Acreage. This is surely and doubtlessly a distortion in the process of agrarian transition within the standard parameters of capitalist development (Rakshit 2010). Figures 9.2 and 9.3 justify the argument of deviated transition and also represent the state of affairs in 2003–4.

Table 9.4 Average operational holding according to economic class in acres

E-criterion	Number of HH	2003–4 average	2013–14 average	2003–4 total	2013–14 total
LLD	10	5.80	4.42	58.00	44.2
RP	14	4.16	2.33	58.19	32.6
MP	7	1.25	1.06	8.73	7.4
SP	11	1.31	0.03	14.45	0.33
PP	3	0.89	0.22	2.68	0.66
LLS	12	0.003	0.000	0.04	0
	57	2.24	1.34	142.09	85.19

Source: Primary Survey by author.

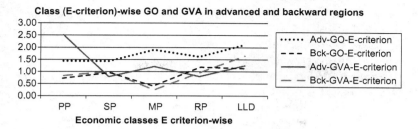

Figure 9.2 Trends of gross output, gross value added in advanced and backward regions in 2003–4

Source: Rakshit (2014).

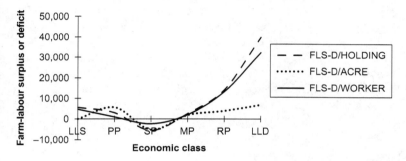

Figure 9.3 Trend of farm-labour surplus or deficit per holding, acre and worker

Advanced Region

Source: Rakshit (2010, 2014).

Even Utsa Patnaik, the ardent advocate of capitalist development in agriculture, came out with her new position of arrested capitalist development in Indian agriculture (Patnaik 2007). In later studies conducted in 2009–10 also, it is established that in advanced regions the gross value added (GVA), farm labour surplus (FLS) and farm disposable surplus (FDS) are negative! (Dey 2012). That is monotonicity in fourth quadrant of standard graphical representation implying increasing negativity with increasing class status. This conclusively proves that there is a serious question mark on the viability of farm irrespective of its class status.

Transition-distorted or arrested-the phenomenon is abnormal and points to things outside the production periphery. For the time being, I thought of naming the state as capitalistic rather being capitalist in nature. However, the question needs to be resolved and I pursued further to find out the anomaly in the process of differentiation in the peasantry separately for production and exchange sites. The main question, however, was, why does the surplus retention become non-monotonic in relation to the economic class? Formulation of my study pointed out to many variables: rent extraction (like Akram-Lodhi 1993), high minimum wages or withdrawal of subsidies by government and of course lower prices fetched. In general, there would have been a temptation to blame everything on the increasing cost elements in agricultural production.

If these are the reasons, then the question that arises would have affected all the classes equally, but that was not the case. Why are the farmers more integrated with market (broadly richer class) of advanced region failing to retain higher surplus even under the condition of IRS? If cost would have been the reason, then IRS would not have prevailed in increasing cost conditions. Everything pointed to the other side of the state, that is low price. The reason was actually the failure to procure comfortable price level. This phenomenon I termed as 'stressed commerce' (Rakshit 2011). It depicts the condition of forced variation in local farm-level price and the retail price of agricultural product, the condition that is now perceived as evidential in current economic activities in India (different from the forced commerce popularised by Amit Bhaduri).

In fact, the *Journal of Agrarian Change* advised me to replace the word 'forced' with 'stressed commerce'. This peculiar and exploitative exchange process is perpetrated by 'outside traders'[11] through their local agents by recurrent price shocks in terms of high price fluctuations[12] in the local agrarian economy. Stressed commerce entails a psychological terror on all the classes of farmers rich and poor – to sell away their products at throwaway prices, which is still continuing in agrarian West Bengal. Perhaps these are the preliminary steps towards moving to contract farming. The rich farmers through different locally practicable economic processes such as leasing out land in crop-to-crop basis try to transfer the operational loss to poor farmers, and in turn making them more dependent on land and agriculture. The monetary loss of the rich farmers manifests in impoverishment of the poor farmers. A recent experience in Bardhaman and Hoogly district on the surge of contract farming of potato vindicates the point. This actually implies submission of the peasantry to the large capital (global) and get included in *capital-non-capital* complex as Lumpen Bourgeoisie-Frank or compradorisation

Stressed commerce and accumulation process 259

of the bourgeoisie-Mao Tse Tung on the one hand and the others being forced to the spaces of *non-capital* or *excluded*.

Then I looked upon the share of the surplus retained[13] by the different classes of producers vis-à-vis traders. This showed a very dismal picture expressed in Table 9.5. One will find the ratio to be decreasing as we move from lower to higher economic classes. This completes our brooding behind the surplus retention and the question of distorted transition. It is perverse market intervention in agrarian sector that is leading to such a distortion and thus putting a serious question on indigenous capitalist development.

During the recent spate of survey of the same advanced region after ten years, we calculated the surpluses as depicted earlier. It is found that the surplus retention capability has further decreased. In many cases there will not be any surplus if the imputed wage of the family labour is incorporated. Inclusion of the family labour cost would lead to deficit. Even the situation assessment survey in 2004–5 by NSSO shows that in West Bengal and India the farmers are experiencing deficit. Tables 9.6a and 9.6b depict the surplus distribution between the producers and traders. There were some grim signals indicating the perpetual decrement of the economic status of the farmers. From our study in 2003–4, we came to know that the farm viability was already in question. Still the farmers were optimistic and were not averse to experiment with different options, though they were not able to take them out of this sorry state of affairs. The irreversible declensions of the viability of the farmers are now totally clear in 2013–14. The richest and the most progressive farmer of the region, Shri Nanda Lal Ghatak owning 16 acres of land having three tractors, truly capitalistic, boasting of his superior and modern methods of farming practices and ever optimistic in those initial years of crisis, was found totally dejected. He had stopped producing Boro Rice. In 2003–4 I did not come across any rich farmer not producing HYV rice, though they started showing their scepticism about its future. Current survey shows that some 5 per cent farmers produce HYV rice. Nitai Ghatak, erstwhile capitalist farmer, had sold out all of his land and had become landless. Initial data of 2013–14 show decrease in land ownership, increased landlessness and leasing in of land by small farmers from rich farmers (the predominant trend in 2003–4, – the initial period of agrarian crisis) had stopped. Small and poor farmers are getting increasingly engaged in non-farm activities. The stark phenomenon is that the producers are increasingly getting dissociated from their means of production and are getting excluded from productive sphere.

Table 9.5 Surplus retention ratio 2003–4

		Total cost incurred by producers for marketed product	Total value received by producers for marketed product	Retail value of the marketed product by producers	Surplus accruing to producers, A = col (2 – 1)	Surplus accruing to traders, B = col (3 – 2)	Sum of total surplus, A + B = X	Ratio of producers surplus to total, A/X	Ratio of traders surplus to total, B/X	Ratio of producers to traders surplus A/B
		1	2	3	4	5	6	7	8	9
ADV-Region	PP	23,981	38,695	60,287	14,714	21,593	36,307	0.41	0.59	0.68
	SP	167,595	197,799	296,502	30,204	98,703	128,906	0.23	0.77	0.31
	MP	410,069	583,481	898,264	173,412	314,783	488,195	0.36	0.64	0.55
	RP	2,705,667	3,510,833	5,686,756	805,166	2,175,923	2,981,090	0.27	0.73	0.37
	LLD	1,784,151	2,856,098	4,890,868	1,071,947	2,034,770	3,106,717	0.35	0.65	0.53
	Total	5,091,463	7,186,906	11,832,678	2,095,443	4,645,772	6,741,215	0.31	0.69	0.45

Source: Rakshit (2014).

Table 9.6a Details of cost, production and surplus – producers/traders in 2013–14

E-criterion	Total cost incurred by producers for marketed product	Total value received by producers for marketed product	Retail value of the marketed product by producers	Retail value of the marketed product by producers	Surplus accruing to producer, A = col(4 – 3)	Surplus accruing to traders (WB), Bwb = col(5 – 4)	Surplus accruing to traders (India), BIndia = col (6 – 4)
1	2	3	WB-4	India-5	6	7	8
LLD	1,984,376	2,846,400	6,073,359.4	7,441,624.3	862,024	3,226,959.4	4,595,224.3
RP	1,231,975.5	1,669,910	3,350,898.5	4,163,152	437,934.5	1,680,988.5	2,493,242
MP	232,393.5	325,510	623,513.25	775,721.5	93,116.5	298,003.25	450,211.5
SP	2,547,871.5	3,508,550	7,385,862.9	9,065,176.3	960,678.5	3,877,312.9	5,556,626.3
PP	668,480	1,007,760	2,038,395	2,539,600	339,280	1,030,635	1,531,840
Total	6,665,096.5	9,358,130	19,472,029.05	23,985,274.1	2,693,033.5	10,113,899.05	14,627,144.1

Source: Primary survey by author.

Table 9.6b Details of surplus distribution and retention between traders and producers

E-criterion	Sum of total surplus-WB	Sum of total surplus-Ind	Ratio of producers surplus to total-WB	Ratio of traders surplus to total-WB	Ratio of producers to traders surplus-WB	Ratio of producers surplus to total-Ind	Ratio of traders surplus to total-Ind	Ratio of producers to traders surplus-Ind
	A + Bwb = Xwb	A + Bind = Xind	A/Xwb	Bwb/Xxb	A/Bwb	A/Xind	Bind/Xind	A/Bind
1	9	10	11	12	13	14	15	16
LLD	4,088,983.4	5,457,248.3	0.21	0.79	0.27	0.16	0.84	0.19
RP	2,118,923	2,931,176.5	0.21	0.79	0.26	0.15	0.85	0.18
MP	391,119.75	543,328	0.24	0.76	0.31	0.17	0.83	0.21
SP	4,837,991.4	6,517,304.8	0.20	0.80	0.25	0.15	0.85	0.17
PP	1,369,915	1,871,120	0.25	0.75	0.33	0.18	0.82	0.22
TOTAL	12,806,932.55	17,320,177.6	0.22	0.78	0.28	0.16	0.84	0.19

Source: Primary survey by author.

Thus, we find clear and vivid symptoms of primitive accumulation of capital.

From the earlier discussion I propose the schema (Figure 9.4a and 9.4b) which seems to be undergoing in agrarian West Bengal. Perhaps it can also be generalised to Indian and developing agricultural system as well. Figure 9.4a describes the synoptic view of the process of accumulation of surplus and retention described earlier. It describes the process of inclusion of the agricultural sector into the ambit of the global capital

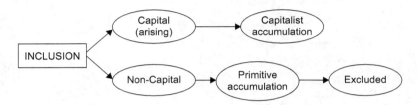

Figure 9.4a Synoptic view of the process described for agriculture only (Capital and Non-capital)

Source: Author's conceptual construct.

INCLUSION → CAPITAL → Market/govt. incentives

→ NON-CAPITAL- (primitive accumulation)

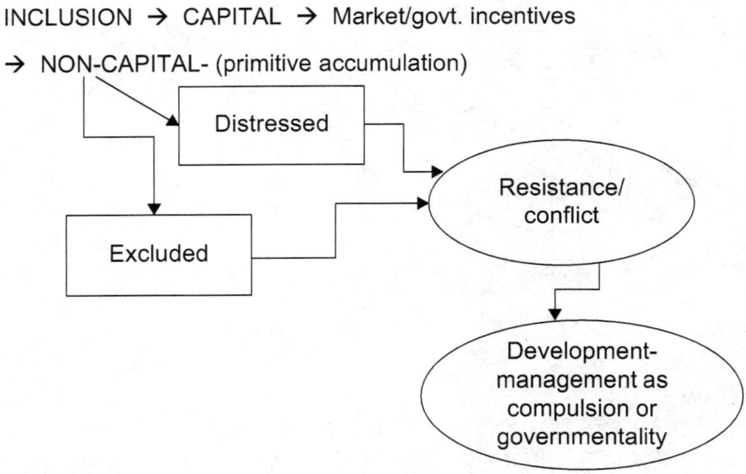

Figure 9.4b Synoptic view of the process described for agriculture only (Non-capital)

Source: Author's conceptual construct.

264 Santanu Rakshit

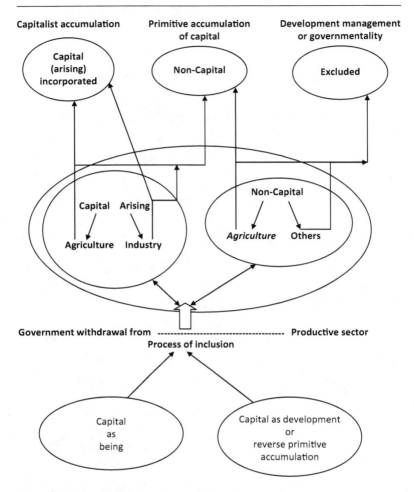

Figure 9.5 Open circuit under neoliberalism
Source: Author's conceptual construct.

in the neoliberal era. Taking cue from Figure 9.1, the government-sheltered *captial-arising* and *non-capital* are now open to global market environment. In the inclusion process *captial-arising* group is supposed to be subjected to capitalist accumulation. These are the appropriated classes more nearer to the lumpen Bourgeosie or comprador Bourgeosie (Frank and Mao).

On the other hand, the *non-capital* initially included in the ambit of capital's primitive accumulation is finally dissociated from its means of production to be *excluded* finally from the productive sphere. Figure 9.4a depicts how the appropriated *captial-arising* group continues to get the market and government sops to accumulate faster and larger.

Finally, the complete picture of the schema is depicted in Figure 9.5. It is basically the combined picture of Figures 9.4a and 9.4b. Rather, a whole depiction of the process of accumulation along with the nature of transition in agrarian Bengal has been attempted.

Caption given for Figure 9.5 defines the scenario that is agriculture in open circuit under neoliberalism. Open implies both liberalised and globalised. As described in Figure 9.4b the dissociation of the *non-capital* from its means of production would lead to increasing distress culminating into resistance and conflict. This requires pacification wherein the role of reverse primitive accumulation comes into play. Sanyal (2007), taking cue from the concept of governmentality from Foucault, had opined that this burgeoning *excluded* sector needs to be managed. He termed this pacification role of state of sustenance of the *excluded* as 'Development Management', which is basically re-channelising of the accumulation of surplus done through primitive accumulation, and hence termed as 'reverse primitive accumulation' (Development Management or governmentality). Figure 9.5 vividly describes the state of affairs regarding agrarian transition.

5. Conclusion

Neoliberalism is a higher moment in the journey of capital in this global economy. Neoliberalism applies multipronged approach towards maintaining its complete hegemony over the political, economic and social spaces. Specifically in the agrarian sector we observe the process of capitalist accumulation in the case of *capital (arising)*, the process of primitive accumulation of capital in case of *non-capital* and developmental management (governmentality) for the *excluded*. The aforementioned process got expedited with the withdrawal of government from productive sphere in the post-liberalisation period. The study mainly highlighted the process of inclusion of the agrarian sector in the capital-non-capital complex propagated by global capital. It also depicted the different instruments of exchange and commerce in practice, particularly the stressed commerce, that are instrumental in maintaining a systematic surplus appropriation process through mercantile and subsequently primitive accumulation. The stressed commerce on the farmer along with the richer farmers is found to have serious economic consequences, such as impact on the rate of surplus appropriation, profitability finally culminating into the dissociation of the producer class from its means of production which enforces displacement. Finally, it also attempted to highlight how these simultaneous interventions induce the process of agrarian transition. Pattern of surplus distribution and production structure signify distorted agrarian transition quite different from capitalist development envisaged in the classical sense (Lenin 1977). The study undertaken in two phases (2003–4 and 2013–14) after the time gap of nearly 12–13 years of the implementation of reform programme, 1991, made it possible to comprehend the post-reform impact in its entirety. The time gap was sufficient to understand the significant impact, if any, in the liberalised Indian economy and made possible to find the distortion that has crept in the development of capitalism in agrarian sector, particularly productive activity and realisation of surplus thereof. Repeat survey of the advanced region in 2013–14 reaffirms the contentions made on the basis of 2003–4 (Rakshit 2010, 2011, 2014). In fact, the picture has become clear, and now we can safely conclude that the agrarian sector in West Bengal is undergoing primitive accumulation of capital and thus is the main rationale behind the economic consequences such as impact on the rate of surplus appropriation, profitability and displacement. The typical manifestation of the consequences described was visible in the agrarian conflicts in Nandigram and Singur where the rich peasant and landlord classes eagerly gave consent to sell their land, but majority of the poor peasantry resisted it, leading to such massacre and bloodbath. Agrarian crisis consequent to land acquisition spree for industrialisation gives such indications (Patnaik 2007). At the end, we again stress that existence of socioeconomic differentiation in peasantry does not imply that capitalist development is taking place in the classical sense; rather in the case of West Bengal it appears to have stalled in the classical sense and has given rise to a distorted or deviated path resembling primitive accumulation of capital in agriculture. The growth of free capitalism in agriculture is no more possible in the globalised agrarian economy. It is only capital's primitive accumulation in agriculture.

Appendix

Table 9A.1 Development indices of the districts of West Bengal

Districts	Development indicators							
	Per capita district domestic product rank	District per capita income	Rural poverty ratio percent	Per capita real income at 1993–94 prices (Rs 1)	Per capita real income at 1993–94 rank	Rural monthly per capita consumption (Rs.)	Population density (/sq. km)	Literacy rate (%) 2001
Darjeeling	2	18,529	19.66	10,415	3	465.42	510	73
Jalpaiguri	4	16,749	35.73	8831	11	416.43	547	64
Koch Behar	13	13,855	25.62	7780	16	466.43	732	67
Uttar Dinajpur	12\18	11,183	27.61	6779	18	484.56	778	49
Dakshin Dinajpur	12\18	14,579	27.61	8866	10	484.56	677	64.5
Malda	10	14,777	35.4	8339	13	428.67	881	51
Murshidabad	15	13,392	46.12	8009	14	385.69	1101	55
Birbhum	17	12,792	49.37	7738	17	382.81	663	62
Bardhaman	3	17,538	18.99	11,445	2	501.58	985	71
Nadia	6	16,211	28.35	9606	6	458.29	1172	66.5
North 24 Parganas	11	14,768	14.41	9440	7	550.84	2181	78.5
Hugli	5	16,280	20.43	10344	5	486.9	1601	75.5
Bankura	7	15,742	59.62	9361	8	353.28	464	64

Purulia	16	13,045	78.72	7905	15	280.15	405	56
Medinipur	9	15,526	19.83	9263.5	9	490.2	685	75
Haora	8	15,591	7.63	10,365.5	4	590.19	2913	78
Kolkata	1	33,299.5	n.a.	19,896	1	n.a.	24,760	81
South 24 Parganas	14	13,630	26.86	8395	12	453.2	694	70
West Bengal	n.a.	16,072	n.a.	n.a.	n.a.	n.a.	n.a.	n.a.

Source: (1) Bureau of Applied Economics and Statistics, Government of West Bengal; (2) Census of India, Preliminary District Report-2001.
n.a. – not available.

Table 9A.2 Village-wise distribution of population and sample

Name of districts and blocks	Name of villages	Village-wise total household	Village-wise sample household	Household sample %-age	Village-wise population		Population sample percentage
					Total	Sample	
Burdwan (MEMARI)	Genra-ghata	146	30	20.5	662	129	19.5
	Dalui-bazar	587	10	1.7	2850	54	1.9
	Chak-nara	535	66	12.3	2710	341	12.6
	Rasul-pur	718	10	1.4	3654	46	1.3
	Total	1986	116	5.8	9876	570	5.8

Source: Census of India, Village Directory-1991.

Notes

1 MOM – Margins of Margins as explicated by Ajit Chaudhuri (Choudhury *et al*. 2000).

2 Capital (arising) here is a category taken from the Marx's (1993) idea of 'capital in arising' as explained in Grundrisse and appropriately illustrated in Sanyal (2007). Capital arising here means capital not self-sustaining and needs to depend on outside support, in the Indian context the government support before the neoliberal advents in 1991 of the capital (global). That is the indigenous capitals development under the support of nation-state.

3 According to Banaji, the most important aspect of colonial India was the absence of a process of capitalist expansion for six decades in manufacturing and for about a century in agriculture. He proposed to accept the reality of colonial modes of production with its own coherence and laws of development. Existence of such a mode of production warrants the existence of capitalist production whose function is to finance primary accumulation outside the colonial world, acting as a circuit through which capital can be drained out in different forms and transmit to the colonies pressure of accumulation process in the metropolis without unleashing any corresponding expansion in the forces of production (Patnaik 1990).

4 Andre Gunder Frank criticised Patnaik's definition on capitalism in agriculture as 'far out'. He also criticised her for looking for the criterion of the mode of production on the individual farm and her assertion for the reproduction and accumulation of surplus value on the very spot where it has been produced, that is in agriculture itself or in agriculture in the same geographical area. Supporting the colonial mode of production, he asserted that surplus can well be re-invested in the centre in place of periphery.

5 A wonderful summarisation of the different strains of mode of production debate can be found in Utsa Patnaik's *Agrarian Relations and Accumulation – 'Mode of Production Debate'*.

6 Amit Bhaduri (1973) on the basis of a survey conducted in 26 villages in West Bengal concluded that the dominant character of existing production relations can be best described as semi-feudal because the existing production relations have more in common with classic feudalism than with industrial capitalism. Prasad (1974) lent his support to Bhaduri on the basis of his survey conducted in 2000 households in the three districts of Bihar. Chandra (1974) on the basis of laws of motion of agriculture formulated by Kautsky and Lenin regarding agrarian transformation suspects that India has not been going through a capitalist transformation at all and there are important socioeconomic forces that are impeding it. Sau (1975) expresses his concurrence to the views of Chandra. He adds another rationale for the resolute persistence of semi-feudalism and that is the determination of the small peasants to continue cultivation with low return because of the lack of alternative employment opportunities. In an uncanny reversal of his earlier position, Rudra (1974) asserted that there are increasing manifestations of capitalism in the agriculture of eastern India. He completely denounced the position of semi-feudalism taken by Bhaduri, Prasad, Chandra and Sau by citing from his first-hand experience in an enquiry of the agrarian relations in the different districts of

272   Santanu Rakshit

the state of West Bengal. Semi-feudal mode of production was also suggested by Sengupta (1977), who was of the view that India being a part of world capitalist system should have the continuation in the capitalist trend which manifests itself in semi-colonial society. This along with the existence of feudal mode of production runs in an assimilative form with a variety of proportionality between the feudal and capitalist modes. Sengupta labelled this semi-colonial and semi-feudal. Lin (1980) puts forward a new term 'dual mode of production', where two primary modes of production, capitalist and pre-capitalist, interpenetrate each other to give rise to a single mode of production with dual character having at once both accommodating and conflicting internal dynamics. Regarding state power he opines that since two historically opposed ruling classes would share it, it cannot remain stable forever (Patnaik 1990).

7 Bhattacharyya (2001) along with Utsa Patnaik (1987) has shown that there exists monotonic relation between class status and surplus, which decisively proves the contention of capitalist development in agriculture.

8 Zero implies non-availability of the amenities; and from 1 to 3, increasing order of the numerical implies decreasing order in quality of amenities available. Quality otherwise generally refers to distance at which the amenities are available. One=>(0–5) km, Two=>(5–10) km, Three=>(>10).

9 Patnaik's Labour Exploitation Criterion:

$$E = X/Y = \{(Hi - Ho) + (Lo - Li)\}/F$$

where X = (net labour days hired in) + (net labour days appropriated through rent); Y = family labour spent in cultivation on the operation holding; and where E = exploitation criterion

Hi = labour-days hired on the operational holding of the household

Ho = family labour days hired out to others

Li = labour days worked on leased-in land (whether by family or hired labour)

Lo = labour days similarly worked on land leased out by the household

F = labour days worked by household workers on the operational holding. According to Utsa Patnaik, the following ranges of the value of E determine the corresponding classes in the agrarian sector:

$E = +\infty$	$\Rightarrow$	*landlord* – LLD
$\infty > E \geq +1$	$\Rightarrow$	*Rich peasant* – RP
$+1 > E > 0$	$\Rightarrow$	*Middle peasant* – MP
$0 \geq E > -1$	$\Rightarrow$	*Small peasant* – SP
$-\infty > E \leq (-1)$	$\Rightarrow$	*Poor peasant* – PP
$E = -\infty$	$\Rightarrow$	*landless worker* – LLS

Stressed commerce and accumulation process 273

NSSO

1. Landless households have been categorised as (0 acre) household group;
2. Households whose operated land is positive but less than 2.5 acres (i.e. $0 < OL \leq 2.5$ acres) as (0–2.5) acre household group;
3. Operated land is higher than 2.5 acres but less than or equal to 5 acres ($2.5 < OL \leq 5$ acres) as (2.5–5) acres group;
4. Operated land higher than 5 acres but less than or equal to 10 acres ($5 < OL \leq 10$ acres) as (5–10) acres group; and
5. Households which have operated land higher than 10 acres – above-10 or >10.

10 Definitions and derivation of net output and surpluses:

1. Value of agricultural production = gross output of all crops + value of by-product and livestock production
2. Gross value added (GVA) of all crops = value of agricultural production – total material input cost
3. Farm labour income (FLI) = gross value added (GVA) of all crops – wages (kind and cash)
4. Farm labour surplus or deficit (FLS) = farm labour income (FLI) – imputed value of family labour income
5. Total income = agricultural income (A) + non-agricultural income (B) where agricultural income is the sum of (1) farm labour income (A_1); (2) income from agricultural wages (A_2); (3) income from hiring out equipment and so on (A_3); and (4) non-cultivation income from rent (A_4). Therefore, $A = A_1 + A_2 + A_3 + A_4$
   And non-agricultural income is the sum of (1) income from salaries, pension and remittances (B_1) and (2) non-cultivation income from other sources (B_2). Therefore, non-agricultural income = $B = B_1 + B_2$
6. Farm-disposable income (FDI) = farm-labour income (FLI) – rents paid
7. Total disposable income = farm disposable income (FDI) + non-agriculture income + agricultural wage + rents + income from hiring out
8. Farm-disposable surplus or deficit = farm disposable income – imputed value of family labour

11 The local peasantry has named these non-local traders as 'outside traders'. The latter are persons working mostly for the (1) the newly developed multinational food processing units located near the fertile agricultural land of rural West Bengal, in our case the place of field survey and (2) traders of the metropolitan cities like Kolkata, engaged as exporters or as suppliers to different transnational food processing units located in different parts of India.

12 (In our survey period of two months, on an average 10–12 fluctuations per month was observed. Out of this only once or twice for one or two days in a month the price remained at the highest level and mostly remained at the miserably lowest level and sometimes at breakeven level. Fluctuation was terrible and not a single farmer in our survey was able to get the highest price level. Some farmers of rich peasant and landlord class stored their product for future price rise for hedging the risk, and selling more than 70 per cent of their product at the existing price level from the field itself with minimum loss or profit.) Election of 2006 was astonishing.

274 Santanu Rakshit

13 Ratio of surplus taken away by the traders in terms of price-differential from the local producers to that of the surplus accrued by the local producers deducting the cost of production from the gross value added was greater than one. Price for outside traders was taken to be the product-specific state-level retail price available from West Bengal Economic survey for the same period (2003–4). Calculation:

Traders' surplus = (retail price – field-level price) × (total product marketed in the survey area)
Producers' surplus = (GO of total product marketed) – (total cost of production of marketed product only)
Total surplus generated = traders' surplus + producers' surplus
GO – Total material input cost = GVA (Rakshit 2010).

References

Akram-Lodhi, H. 1993. 'Agrarian Classes in Pakistan: An Empirical Test of Patnaik's Labour Exploitation Criterion'. *The Journal of Peasant Studies* 20 (4): 557–89.

Araghi Farshad. 2009. 'The Invisible Hand and the Visible Foot: Peasants, Dispossession and Globalisation'. In A Haroon Akram-Lodhi and Cristóbal Kay (eds). *Peasants and Globalisation: Political Economy, Rural Transformation and the Agrarian Question*. New York: Routledge, pp. 111–47.

Araghi, Farshad. 2010. 'The End of "Cheap Ecology" and the Crisis of "Long Keynesianism"'. *Economic and Political Weekly* 45 (4): 39–41.

Bernstein, H. 1996. 'Agrarian Questions Then and Now'. *The Journal of Peasant Studies* 24 (1): 22–59.

Bernstein, H. 2014. 'Revisiting Agrarian Transition: Reflections on Long Histories and Current Realities'. Paper presented in International Seminar organised by the Department of Sociology, Pondicherry University.

Bhaduri, A. 1973. 'A Study in Agricultural Backwardness under Semi-Feudalism'. *Economic Journal* March 83 (329): 120–137.

Bhattacharyya, Sudipta. 2001. 'Capitalist Development, Peasant Differentiation and the State: Survey Findings from West Bengal'. *Journal of Peasant Studies* 28 (4): 95–126.

Byres, T. J. 2003. 'Structural Change, the Agrarian Question and the Possible Impact of Globalisation'. In J. Ghosh and C. P. Chandrasekhar (eds). *Work and Well-being in the Age of Finance*. New Delhi: Tulika Books, pp. 171–211.

Chakrabarti, Anjan and Cullenberg Stephen. 2003. *Transition and Development in India*. London and New York: Routledge.

Chandra, Nirmal K. 1974. 'Farm Efficiency under Semi-Feudalism: A Critique of Marginalist Theories and Some Marxist Formulations'. *Economic and Political Weekly*, 09 (32–34): 1309–1332.

Choudhury, A., D. Das and A. Chakraborty. 2000. *Margin of Margins: Profile of an Unrepentant Postcolonial Collaborator*. Kolkata: Anustup.

Stressed commerce and accumulation process 275

Dey, Rajiv. 2012. 'Problem of Farm Viability, Poverty and Agrarian Crisis-The case of West-Bengal'. In K. Suman Chandra, V. Suresh Babu and Pradip Kumar Nath (eds). *Agrarian Crisis in India – The Way Out*. Academic Foundation in Association with National Institute of Rural Development (NIRD).

Lerche, J. 2011. 'Agrarian Crisis and Agrarian Questions in India'. *Journal of Agrarian Change* 11 (1): 104–18.

Lin, Sharat G. 1980. 'Theory of a Dual Mode of Production in Post Colonial India'. *Economic and Political Weekly* XV (10 and 11): 516–529; 565–573.

Marx, Karl. 1954. *Capital*. Vol. 1, Part VIII. Moscow: Progress Publisher.

Marx, Karl. 1993. *Grundrisse*. London: Penguin Classics.

Patnaik, Prabhat. 2008a. 'The Accumulation Process in the Period of Globalisation'. *Economic and Political Weekly* 43 (26): 108–13.

Patnaik, Prabhat. 2008b. 'Return of the State'. *Frontline*, 7 November 2008.

Patnaik, Prabhat. 2008c. *The Value of Money*. New Delhi: Tulika Books.

Patnaik, Prabhat. 2012. 'The Nature of the Current Capitalist Crisis'. Keynote address given in a seminar on 'The Current Crisis of Capitalism and the Third World'; 20 January 2012, Centre for Marxian Studies, Jadavpur University.

Patnaik Utsa. 1987. *Peasant Class Differentiation: A Study in Method with Reference to Haryana*. Delhi: Oxford University Press.

Patnaik, Utsa (ed.). 1990. *Agrarian Relations and Accumulation: Mode of Production Debate in India*. Bombay: Oxford University Press (published for Sameeksha Trust).

Patnaik Utsa. 2007. 'New Data on the Arrested Development of Capitalism in Indian Agriculture'. *Social Scientist* 35 (7/8): 4–23.

Rakshit, Santanu. 2010. '"Agrarian Transition"-Diversity in Nature, Notion and Observations – A Survey of Theoretical Expositions and Empirical Studies with Reference to India and West Bengal'. *Research in Social Stratification and Mobility* 28 (4): 465–81.

Rakshit, Santanu. 2011. 'Capital Intensification, Productivity and Exchange – A Class-Based Analysis of Agriculture in West Bengal in the Current Millennium'. *Journal of Agrarian Change* 11 (4): 505–35.

Rakshit, Santanu. 2014. 'Output, Surpluses and "Stressed Commerce": A Study on Farm Viability and Agrarian Transition in West Bengal, India, in the New Millennium'. *Journal of Peasant Studies* 41 (3): 343–63.

Rudra, A. 1974. 'Semi Feudalism, Usury Capital Etcetera'. *Economic and Political Weekly* IX (48): 1996–1997.

Sanyal, Kalyan. 2007. *Rethinking Capitalist Development*. New Delhi: Routledge.

Sengupta, Nirmal. 1977. 'Further on the Mode of Production in Agriculture'. *Economic and Political Weekly* XII (26): 55–63.

Chapter 10

Punjab's small peasantry
Thriving or deteriorating?

Sukhpal Singh and Shruti Bhogal[1]

I. Introduction

Following the technological breakthroughs in the mid-1960s, subsistence agriculture in Punjab was transformed into a market-oriented operation. The growth of the rapidly progressing agricultural economy levelled out over time in terms of profits because of the rising cost of cultivation and stagnant productivity. The liberalisation of the economy in the 1990s provided ideological support to free trade and minimised state intervention in economic activities. As a result, downsizing of the public sector and reducing subsidies became key issues. Public-sector investment in agriculture and allied activities has declined continuously in India. The percentage of the budget that was spent on agriculture was 14.9 per cent during the First Five-Year Plan (1951–56). It declined to 12.3 per cent during the Fifth Plan (1974–79), and further to 3.7 per cent during the Eleventh Plan (2007–12).

The upshot has been that farmers' own investment in agriculture has increased over the decades, and the capital intensity of Punjab's farms has increased manifold. There are now 477,000 tractors, 1.384 million tube wells, 0.624 million threshers and about 13,000 harvesting combines in the state (GoP 2013: 17). The demand for human labour in the farm sector has decreased significantly since the late 1980s – from 479 million man-days in 1983–84 to 422 million man-days in 2000–2001 (Sidhu and Singh 2004: 4132–33), and further to 401 million man-days in 2009–10. It is not only large farmers who have mechanised their farms, but also small ones – 13 per cent of the marginal farmers and 31 per cent of the small farmers in the state own tractor-operated farms (Singh *et al.* 2007b: 14–15). As a result, farmers have surplus family labour, which was 85 per cent in the case of marginal farmers and 82 per cent in the case of small farmers in

2009–10 (Singh *et al.* 2012: 40). But the unfavourable nature and structure of the non-farm sector in the state prevents these farmers from being fully absorbed outside agriculture – 24 per cent of the depeasantised people want to shift to new professions (Singh 2009: 225–26). Hence, there exists a large 'reserve army of labour' in the state's economy. About 3.5 million people were unemployed in the state during 2006, of which about 2.4 million were from rural areas (Singh *et al.* 2007a: 3).

Though the government of Punjab offers various benefits to the farm sector such as subsidies for power and fertilisers, and credit to augment productivity and profitability, they do not cater to the needs of small farmers. The power subsidy to the farm sector was Rs 47.78 billion in 2012–13, of which just 6 per cent went to small farmers, who comprise 34 per cent of the total farmers in the state. The other subsidies had a similar reach (Singh 2014: 84). This shows that small farmers are deprived of even the support/facilities provided by the government. The most vulnerable groups at the bottom of the pyramid of the farming population are the peasantry. It is being suggested that farming on small landholdings is not viable unless it is supported with supplementary income (Chandra 2001: 1–4). Keeping this scenario in view, this study analyses the status of marginal and small farmers in the agriculturally developed state of Punjab.

2. Sampling design

The primary data were collected from sample households through personal interviews during 2012–13. Punjab is divided into three well-defined agro-climatic zones – the sub-mountainous zone (zone I), central zone (zone II) and south-western zone (zone III), which occupy 9, 65 and 26 per cent area of the state, respectively. Zone I comprises 3 districts, zone II 13 and zone III 6. For this study, one district was selected from zone I, three from zone II and two from zone III. All the farmers of the selected villages who had left farming after 1991 were chosen for the study. The number of depeasantised families in all the sampled villages was 150. One-third of each category of marginal, small and other farmers (including semi-medium, medium and large farmers) were taken from the selected villages. In this way, the total sample of farmers was 450, which comprised 150 depeasantised respondents, 28 marginal farmers, 66 small farmers and 206 farmers of other categories (Table 10.1). The data relate to the agricultural year 2012–13.

278 Sukhpal Singh and Shruti Bhogal

Table 10.1 Sampling design of the study

Zone	Total districts	Selected districts	Selected villages	Sample (number)			
				Farmers who left farming	Marginal farmers (<1 ha)	Small farmers (1–2 ha)	Other farmers (>2 ha)
Sub-mountainous (zone I)	3	Roop Nagar	1	12	7	7	32
Central (zone II)	13	Patiala	1	25	4	13	33
		Jalandhar	1	30	5	16	36
		Ludhiana	1	25	4	13	34
South-western (zone III)	6	Bathinda	1	28	4	9	35
		Ferozepur	1	30	4	8	36
Total	22	6	6	150	28	66	206

Source: Made by the author.

3. Changing structure of landholdings

Punjab is an agriculturally developed economy, but it faces the problem of absorbing labour on small farm landholdings, which has seen the number of smallholders decline over time. The number of total operational holdings has been almost constant during the past four decades, but the trend in the number of marginal and smallholdings has been different in the 1980s and 1990s. During this period, the number of landholdings increased from 396,000 in 1980–81 to 500,000 in 1990–91 (Table 10.2). This may have happened due to the high rate of farm profitability, lower land rent and pure tenancy relations. But after the 1990s, falling profitability, declining land rent and reverse tenancy saw the number of small landholdings decline to 296,000 in 2000–2001. However, the number of small landholdings increased slightly to 318,000 in 2005–6, which may have been due to increasing profitability after the introduction of Bt-cotton and larger families dividing their property.

In any case, the overall number of small farmers has been declining since the 1990s. This decline in the number of smallholdings indicates that they are unviable under modern capital-intensive technologies. Even households with holdings up to 4 ha find it increasingly difficult to meet their living expenses from farming alone in Punjab. Given an opportunity, most of them would leave farming (Singh *et al.* 2007a: 10).

Punjab's small peasantry: thriving or deteriorating? 279

Table 10.2 Distribution of number of operational holdings in Punjab and India

Year	Punjab			India		
	Marginal (<1 ha)	Small (1–2 ha)	Total	Marginal (<1 ha)	Small (1–2 ha)	Total
1980–81	197,000 (19.20)	199,000 (19.40)	396,000 (38.6)	505,960 (56.60)	160,910 (18.00)	666,870 (74.60)
1990–91	296,000 (26.50)	204,000 (18.26)	500,000 (44.76)	633,420 (59.4)	200,470 (18.8)	833,890 (78.2)
1995–96	204,000 (18.66)	183,000 (16.74)	387,000 (35.40)	711,970 (61.6)	216,130 (18.7)	928,100 (80.3)
2000–2001	123,000 (12.35)	173,000 (17.37)	296,000 (29.72)	753,900 (62.90)	226,870 (18.90)	980,770 (81.8)
2005–6	135,000 (13.43)	183,000 (18.21)	318,000 (31.64)	837,350 (64.8)	239,710 (18.5)	1077,060 (83.3)

Source: *Statistical Abstract of Punjab*, various issues.

Note: Figures in brackets are percentages.

On the other hand, the number of marginal and small farmers at the all-India level has been increasing. The total number of operational holdings rose from 666,870 in 1980–81 to 833,890 in 1990–91. This further increased from 928,100 in 1995–96 to 980,770 in 2000–2001 and 1,077,060 in 2005–6. This shows that the trend in Punjab is the reverse of that in the country as a whole.

4. Changing structure of rural workforce

Policymakers in developing countries increasingly recognise that diversification in the structure of rural employment holds the key to reducing unemployment and poverty. This is associated with a shift of the workforce from the farm sector to non-farm sectors of the economy. Many economists have focused on structural shifts in employment patterns. Bhalla and Hazell (2003: 3473–84) show that economies experience shifts in their structure of employment. A major reason for this is that the agricultural sector in many countries is in trouble from declining employment elasticity, falling productivity and shrinking returns (Singh *et al.* 2007a: 6).

In Punjab, the total rural workforce was 3.556 million in 1981, which increased to 4.303 million in 1991 and 6.360 million in 2001. However,

280 Sukhpal Singh and Shruti Bhogal

Table 10.3a Changing structure of rural workforce in Punjab

Year	Cultivators (million)	Agricultural labour (million)	Other rural workers* (million)	Total rural workers (million)	Total rural population (million)	Rural work participation rate (percentage)
1981	1.640 (46.11)	1.132 (31.82)	0.784 (22.07)	3.556 (100.00)	12.141	29.28
1991	1.897 (44.08)	1.356 (31.52)	1.050 (24.40)	4.303 (100.00)	14.289	30.11
2001	2.014 (31.66)	1.408 (22.14)	2.938 (46.20)	6.360 (100.00)	16.096	39.51
2011	1.840 (29.78)	1.474 (23.85)	2.865 (46.37)	6.179 (100.00)	17.344	35.62

Source: Census of India, various issues.

*Other rural workers include workers in allied activities, mining and quarrying, manufacturing, servicing, processing and repairing, trade and commerce, transport and communication and other services.

it declined to 6.179 million in 2011 (Table 10.3a). Similarly, the number of cultivators increased from 1.640 million in 1981 to 1.897 million in 1991, and 2.014 million in 2001. But it declined to 1.840 million in 2011. On the other hand, the number of agricultural labourers increased from 1.132 million in 1981 to 1.356 million in 1991, 1.408 million in 2001 and 1.474 million in 2011. The number of other rural workers – those engaged in allied activities, mining and quarrying, manufacturing, servicing, processing and repairing, trade and commerce, transport and communication and other services – also followed a similar pattern. It was 0.784 million in 1981 and increased to 1.050 million in 1991, and 2.938 million in 2001. But it declined to 2.865 million in 2011. The total rural agricultural workforce, both cultivators and agricultural labourers, numbered 3.422 million in 2001. It declined to 3.314 million in 2011. On the whole, the total rural workforce had declined from 6.360 million in 2001 to 6.179 million in 2011. Similarly, the rural work participation rate increased from 29.28 per cent in 1981 to 30.11 per cent in 1991, and 39.51 per cent in 2001. But it declined to 35.62 per cent in 2011. This shows that labour absorption in agriculture and allied activities in the rural economy of the state was positive until 2001. After that, a squeeze on work opportunities made employment elasticity negative.

Punjab's small peasantry: thriving or deteriorating? 281

Table 10.3b Percentage point change in the structure of rural workforce in Punjab

Year	Cultivators	Agricultural labour	Other rural workers*
1981–91	–2.03	–0.3	2.33
1991–2001	–12.42	–9.38	21.8
1981–2001	–14.45	–9.68	24.13
1981–2011	–16.33	–7.97	24.3
1991–2011	–14.30	–7.67	21.97
2001–11	–1.88	1.71	0.17

*Other rural workers include workers in allied activities, mining and quarrying, manufacturing, servicing, processing and repairing, trade and commerce, transport and communication and other services.

The change in the proportion of the workforce engaged in different activities of the rural economy reveals different trends (Table 10.3b). The percentage point change in the workforce engaged in agriculture as cultivators and agricultural labourers was negative from 1981 to 2001, which shows that farming could not absorb the increasing workforce, either as cultivators or as agricultural labourers. On the other hand, the share of other rural workers in the total rural workforce shows a positive trend, but at a declining rate. It grew rapidly from 1981–91 to 1991–2001 (from 2.33 to 21.80 per cent), but was sluggish from 2001 to 2011 (0.17 per cent). This corroborates the theory that not only the farm sector but also the rural non-farm sector has been unable to absorb the growing rural workforce in the state.

5. Dimensions of agrarian crisis

Agricultural surplus

Despite the productivity of major crops increasing over time, net returns have followed a declining trend in the state. In the age of globalisation, profitability has declined at a faster rate because of a mismatch between input and output prices. Between 2000 and 2005, the minimum support price of wheat and paddy increased by around 2 per cent, but the cost of cultivation increased by 8 to 9 per cent (Singh *et al.* 2012: 1). As wheat and paddy cover 85 per cent of the state's arable area, the decline in profitability has seriously affected the economic health of Punjab's farmers.

282   Sukhpal Singh and Shruti Bhogal

As a result, the surplus with farmers has declined. The surplus from agriculture is the amount remaining after meeting farm and domestic expenditure. Table 10.4 shows that an average farm family in the state recorded an annual surplus of Rs 240,443, of which Rs 217,678 was from agriculture and Rs 22,765 from non-farm income. Many farmers earn their livelihood from dairying and non-farm activities. Those whose income from dairying was more than 25 per cent of their total income were less prone to indebtedness (Singh et al. 2007b: 43). In addition, small farmers who used hired machinery were getting better returns than those who owned machinery (Singh 2013: 5–6).

The highest amount of surplus was in zone II (Rs 285,895), of which Rs 245,784 was from agriculture and Rs 40,111 was from non-farm income. However, the total surplus of farmers in zone III was Rs 268,930, of which Rs 261,284 and Rs 7645 were from agriculture and non-farm

Table 10.4 Surplus from agriculture and non-farm income on various farm categories in different zones of Punjab (Rs/household)

Zone	Particulars	Marginal (<1 ha)	Small (1–2 ha)	Other farmers (>2 ha)	Average
I	Surplus from agriculture	−13,720	−5318	15,961	2543
	Non-farm income	18,259	45,717	0	16,085
	Total	4539	40,398	15,961	18,628
II	Surplus from agriculture	33,433	133,594	318,218	245,784
	Non-farm income	79,846	35,886	33,480	40,111
	Total	113,279	169,480	351,698	285,895
III	Surplus from agriculture	49,223	78,965	309,550	261,284
	Non-farm income	31,217	263	6675	7645
	Total	80,439	79,227	316,225	268,930
Overall	Surplus from agriculture	23,201	87,602	286,328	217,678
	Non-farm income	48,416	25,978	17,139	22,765
	Total	71,617	113,579	303,467	240,443

Source: PAU (2010–11).

Punjab's small peasantry: thriving or deteriorating? 283

income, respectively. The sub-mountainous zone of the state (zone I) lagged behind with Rs 18,628, which was about 15 times less than that of zones II and III. The surplus in zone II was an outcome of the availability of non-farm employment and earning.

A size-wise analysis shows that the surplus from agriculture varied, by and large, in accordance with the size of a farm. In zone I, the surplus from agriculture with marginal and small farmers was negative. The cropping pattern is maize–wheat in zone I, paddy–wheat in zone II and cotton–wheat in zone III. Zone I is a low-productivity zone as the yield of maize is 40.80 quintals/ha, and that of wheat is 45.07 quintals/ha, which is lower than the yields of wheat in zone II (53.75 quintals/ha) and zone III (50.00 quintals/ha). This is a major reason for reduced farm returns in zone I, which is responsible for the negative farm surplus. The zone-wise and size-wise scenarios on agricultural surplus are quite consistent with state-level observations. It is worth mentioning that marginal farmers earned a major share of their total surplus from non-farm sources, whereas large farmers earned their surplus from agriculture by virtue of their larger land size.

Severity of debt

Punjab's farmers are reeling under debt. Of the sampled farmers, 88 per cent had an average debt of Rs 218,092 per household (Table 10.5). The amount of debt per hectare was inversely related to farm size. It was the highest among marginal farmers (Rs 170,184), followed by small farmers (Rs 104,155) and other farmers (Rs 44,069). In the era of globalisation, the rate of increase in the costs of cultivation has been much faster than that of farm produce prices (Singh et al. 2012: 1). Therefore, the increase in income from farming was not sufficient to meet domestic and farm expenditure, which led a large proportion of farmers in Punjab into a debt trap. It was found that 89 per cent of marginal farmers and 91 per cent of small farmers were in debt. Marginal and small farmers were indebted for about Rs 170,000 per hectare and Rs 104,000 per hectare, respectively. Compared to this, other farm categories had an outstanding debt of Rs 44,069 per hectare. It is important to underline that the relative indebtedness of marginal and small farm households was many times higher than that of large farm households. The debt income ratio was also the highest (1.39) in the case of marginal farmers, followed by small (0.94) and other farmers (0.33). This showed that marginal farmers were the major sufferers as their debt was much more than their annual income, followed by small farmers.

284 Sukhpal Singh and Shruti Bhogal

Table 10.5 Magnitude of debt in Punjab

Farm category	Sampled farmers			Debt (Rs)		Debt income ratio
	Total	Number of indebted farmers	Percentage	Per hectare	Per household	
Marginal (<1 ha)	28	25	89.28	170,184	107,216	1.39
Small (1–2 ha)	66	60	90.91	104,155	146,859	0.94
Other farmers (>2 ha)	206	179	86.89	44,069	255,985	0.33
Total	300	264	88	50,021	218,092	0.37

Source: Field survey.

Stress level of debt

The stress level of indebtedness can be gauged from the magnitude of indebtedness in relation to total family income. Farm households that could return their loans in one season were considered stress-free households. Table 10.6 shows that about 25 per cent of marginal farmers and 39.4 per cent of small farmers were in this group as their indebtedness was less than 50 per cent of their income. The percentages of farmers

Table 10.6 Degree of indebtedness in relation to income, Punjab

Stress level	Total loan in relation to total income (%)	Percentage of holdings			
		Marginal (<1 ha)	Small (1–2 ha)	Other farmers (>2 ha)	All holdings
No stress	Less than 50	25	39.39	44.66	41.67
Manageable	51–100	25	26.75	27.18	27
Under stress	More than 100	39.28	25.75	14.56	19.33
Bankruptcy	More than 200	25	12.12	3.39	7.33
	More than 300	14.29	9.09	2.43	5
Total number of holdings		28	66	206	300
Loan as a percentage of income		139.2	97.01	40.5	45.96

Source: Field survey.

whose indebtedness was considered to be manageable (from 51 to 100 per cent of their annual income) were 25 and 26.75 per cent of marginal and small farmers, respectively.

The remaining 39 per cent of marginal and about 26 per cent of small farmers, whose indebtedness was more than their annual income, were taken to be under stress.

Indebtedness approaches bankruptcy when a loan is more than two times a family's annual income, which is close to acute/extreme stress. It was found that this was inversely associated with farm size. About one-fourth of marginal and 12.12 per cent of small farmers were under acute stress, compared to 3.39 per cent of other farmers. Households also face a severe debt crisis when the loan is more than what the family earns in three years. About 14 per cent marginal and about 9 per cent small farmers were in this category, against 2.43 per cent of other farmers.

Farmers' suicides

Small farmers in Punjab are in a state of crisis, both economic and social. Their traditional source of livelihood is unviable because of rapidly increasing input costs, stagnant productivity, falling profitability and increasing living costs. This leads to farmers opting to end all their miseries by committing suicide. In a census-based study (Singh *et al.* 2012: 1–45) on farmers' suicides in six districts of Punjab during 2011, it was found that the largest number who took their own lives belonged to the category of small farmers (Table 10.7).

Of the 3507 farmers who committed suicide between 2000 and 2011 in the state, about 80 per cent were marginal and small farmers (up to

Table 10.7 Farmers' suicides in Punjab, 2000–2011

Total number of suicides	3507	
Suicides, category-wise	Small farmers (up to 2 ha)	Other farmers (>2 ha)
Number of suicides	2788 (79.51)	719 (20.5)
Suicides due to debt	2186 (78.4)	409 (56.9)
Average debt (Rs)	234,541	361,229
Average income (Rs)	30,420	135,800
Debt–income ratio	7.71	2.66

Source: (Singh *et al.* 2012).

Note: Percentages from the respective categories in brackets.

286 Sukhpal Singh and Shruti Bhogal

2 ha). Though the relationship between landholding size and average amount of debt was direct, the relationship between landholding size and average household income was indirect. These small farmers had an average debt of Rs 235,000 per household and they earned only Rs 30,420 per annum. The debt–income ratio of marginal and small farmers was about three times higher (7.71) than that for other farm categories (2.66). This clearly indicates the poor and miserable conditions that plague marginal and small farmers in Punjab.

Process of depeasantisation

The shift of the workforce from the farming to the non-farming sector can be categorised under two heads – growth-led transformation and distress-induced transformation. The first is related to developmental factors such as the mechanisation of agriculture, increasing employment and income, high levels of education, urbanisation, the development of the secondary and tertiary sectors and even state intervention in generating employment opportunities. These are 'pull factors', which attract the workforce from farming to more lucrative non-farm activities. On the other hand, distress-induced transformation is based on crisis-driven factors such as falling productivity, increasing costs and decreasing returns, unemployment and underemployment and indebtedness. These 'push factors' force the agriculture workforce towards non-farm activities, leading to depeasantisation.

It was found that 14.40 per cent of the farmers in the state had left farming since 1991 (Table 10.8). Of this, the proportion of marginal farmers was 26.50 per cent and small farmers 18.26 per cent.

Only a relatively small proportion (5.78 per cent) of farmers from other farm categories had left farming in the state. Of the total sample that had left farming, 39 per cent were marginal, 43 per cent were small and 18 per cent were other farmers, which included semi-medium, medium and large farmers who had more than 2 ha of operational land.

The field survey identified various reasons that had induced farmers to leave farming (Table 10.9). One of the most common reasons was the non-profitable nature of farming (30.67 per cent). About 53 per cent of marginal farmers, 18 per cent of small farmers and 11 per cent of other farmers had left farming as it was non-remunerative.

Joining another profession was the second most common reason (19 per cent) for leaving farming. Of the total sample, 17 per cent of marginal farmers, 23 per cent of small farmers and 11 per cent of other farmers gave up farming because they joined other professions. Farmers were

Punjab's small peasantry: thriving or deteriorating? 287

Table 10.8 Number of families who had left farming in Punjab

Category	Total number of farm families in sampled villages	Sample farmers who had left farming		Percentage of farmers who had left farming
		Number	Percentage	
Marginal (<1 ha)	219	58	38.67	26.5
Small (1–2 ha)	356	65	43.33	18.26
Other farmers (>2 ha)	467	27	18	5.78
Total	1042	150	100	14.4

Source: Field survey.

Table 10.9 Reasons for leaving farming in Punjab

Reasons for leaving farming/ farm category	Marginal (<1 ha)	Small (1–2 ha)	Other farmers (>2 ha)	Total
Non-profitable farming	31 (53.45)	12 (18.46)	3 (11.11)	46 (30.67)
Land leased out due to high rent	4 (6.90)	15 (23.08)	7 (25.93)	26 (17.33)
Joined another profession	10 (17.24)	15 (23.08)	3 (11.11)	28 (18.67)
Land sold due to high debt	4 (6.90)	6 (9.23)	3 (11.11)	13 (8.67)
Emigration	3 (5.17)	5 (7.69)	7 (25.93)	15 (10.00)
Less family labour due to old age/death/disease/ drug addiction	6 (10.34)	11 (16.92)	2 (7.41)	19 (12.67)
To buy more land elsewhere	–	1 (1.54)	2 (7.41)	3 (2.00)
Total	58 (100)	65 (100)	27 (100)	150 (100)

Source: Field survey.

leasing out their land because they could get a rent that was higher than the return from farming, and this was the third most common reason (17 per cent). Marginal farmers 7 per cent, small farmers 23 per cent and other farmers 26 per cent reported high land rent as their reason for leaving farming. About 13 per cent of farm households faced the problem of less family labour, which was due to various factors such as old age, disease, drug addiction and death of main earners in families. The proportions of marginal, small and other farmers that reported this were 10.3, 16.9 and 7.4 per cent, respectively.

Emigration was the next most common factor, with 10 per cent of the sampled farmers citing it. About 5 per cent of marginal farmers, 8 per cent of small farmers and 26 per cent of other farmers were reported to have migrated abroad. High debt burdens forced 9 per cent of the sampled farmers to sell their land. About 7 per cent of marginal farmers, 9 per cent of small farmers and 11 per cent of other farmers left farming for this reason. Due to price differentiation, a few farmers (2 per cent) gave up farming in their villages to buy land elsewhere and thus increase the size of their holdings.

Leaving farming has a two-way impact. It is a healthy trend if a person joins a more lucrative profession, but it becomes disastrous if a person joins a low-paid profession or enters the labour market. The secondary and tertiary sectors have witnessed growth in the recent past, compared to the primary sector. The overall increase in rural non-farm employment is explained by the increase in the proportion of casual non-agricultural workers and self-employment (Basant and Joshi 1994: 222–57). Our survey showed that small farmers in distress had been leaving farming. Table 10.10 reveals that of the sampled farmers who had left farming (150), the majority (28 per cent) were working as labourers. This proportion was very high among marginal (47 per cent) and small (22 per cent) farmers. Among them, 4 per cent joined the farm sector and the remaining 24 per cent the non-farm sector, mainly as construction and factory workers. This transformation of the peasantry into wage labour is psychologically painful given the state's sociocultural traditions.

About 12 per cent of the sampled farmers, which included 12 per cent marginal farmers, 11 per cent small farmers and 15 per cent other farmers, set up small businesses. The percentages of marginal, small and other farmers that did so were 12, 11 and 15 per cent, respectively. Of the total who left farming, about 3 per cent became shopkeepers, milkmen and animal traders. About a similar percentage began other businesses such as becoming *atta-chakki* owners or mechanics. As much as 23 per cent of the sampled farmers joined the public or private sector. About 21 per cent of marginal, 31 per cent of small and 11 per cent of other farmers did so. Those engaged in government jobs were around 12 per cent of the sample, and those engaged in private jobs were 4.67 per cent. Further, 5.17 per cent of marginal farmers, 7.69 per cent of small farmers and 25.93 per cent of other farmers went abroad. However,

Punjab's small peasantry: thriving or deteriorating? 289

Table 10.10 New occupations of farmers who left farming

New occupation	Marginal (<1 ha)	Small (1–2 ha)	Other farmers (>2 ha)	Total
Labour	27 (46.55)	14 (21.54)	1 (3.70)	42 (28.00)
(1) Agricultural labour	4 (6.90)	2 (3.08)	–	6 (4.00)
(2) Non-agricultural labour	23 (39.65)	12 (18.46)	1 (3.70)	36 (24.00)
Self-enterprise	7 (12.07)	7 (10.77)	4 (14.81)	18 (12.00)
(1) Shopkeeper	2 (3.45)	1 (1.54)	1 (3.70)	4 (2.67)
(2) Milkman	2 (3.45)	2 (3.08)	1 (3.70)	5 (3.33)
(3) Animal trader	1 (1.72)	2 (3.08)	1 (3.70)	4 (2.67)
(4) Others*	2 (3.45)	2 (3.08)	1 (3.70)	5 (3.33)
Job	12 (20.69)	20 (30.77)	3 (11.11)	35 (23.33)
(1) Government job	7 (12.07)	8 (12.30)	3 (11.11)	18 (12.00)
(2) Private job	5 (8.62)	12 (18.46)	–	17 (4.67)
Working abroad	3 (5.17)	5 (7.69)	7 (25.93)	15 (10.00)
Idle/nothing	9 (15.52)	11 (16.92)	10 (37.04)	30 (20.00)
Others**	–	8 (12.31)	2 (7.41)	10 (6.67)
Total	58 (100.00)	65 (100.00)	27 (100.00)	150 (100.00)

Source: Field survey.

* Includes self-enterprises of becoming atta-chakki owners, mechanics and so on.
** Includes occupations such as dealers and commission agents.

about 16 per cent of marginal farmers, 17 per cent of small farmers and 37 per cent of medium and large farmers were idle, or were not engaged in any kind of profession after leaving farming. About 7 per cent of the sampled farmers were working as dealers, commission agents, brickkiln owners and so on.

Farming carries social status in an agrarian society. Farmers find it very difficult to leave their occupation and take up jobs that pay less and have less social status. Some who had found jobs in the public sector or taken up other better-paid activities were satisfied with their new professions.

290 Sukhpal Singh and Shruti Bhogal

Table 10.11 Level of satisfaction from present profession of sample families, Punjab (percentage)

Farm categories	Level of satisfaction					Wanted to expand	Want to go to new profession
	Fully	Medium	Less	Dissatisfied	No response		
Marginal (<1 ha)	18.20	21.34	17.78	35.56	7.11	25.00	32.14
Small (1–2 ha)	19.53	21.26	22.77	33.40	3.04	30.30	19.70
Other farmers (>2 ha)	37.22	28.70	17.94	12.56	3.59	48.21	16.07
Overall	25.87	24.04	20.04	26.05	4.01	36.00	20.67

Source: Field survey.

However, some were less than satisfied with these occupations, even if they were earning better than what they did while farming. Table 10.11 measures the level of satisfaction of the new professions of farm families.

A large majority of small and marginal farmers were not satisfied with their new occupations. About 36 per cent of marginal, 33.4 per cent of small and 12.6 per cent of other farmers were dissatisfied with their new professions. It was found that about 26 per cent of the persons who left farming were fully satisfied with their new occupation, whereas 24.04 per cent reported a medium level of satisfaction. On the other hand, 20.04 per cent of the respondents were somewhat satisfied, and 26.05 per cent were dissatisfied. About 18 per cent of marginal farmers, 19.53 per cent of small farmers and 37.22 per cent of other farmers were fully satisfied with their new occupations. The better the resource base, the better seemed to be the level of satisfaction with the new occupation. However, the willingness to expand their business was more or less similar among both categories of farmers – 25 per cent of marginal farmers and 30.30 per cent of small farmers were willing to do so.

6. The way out

The farming sector of agriculturally advanced Punjab is showing signs of sickness. It is suffering from declining employment elasticity, falling productivity and shrinking returns. As a result, the percentage of the workforce engaged in cultivation has been falling. Despite the rising productivity of major crops over time, farm profitability has declined due to a mismatch between input and output prices. As a result, the surplus from the farming sector is decreasing – it was even negative for marginal and small farmers in the sub-mountainous region of the state. Farmers are reeling under debt. The intensity of the agrarian crisis can be judged from the fact that about 14 per cent of marginal farmers and about 9 per cent of small farmers have become bankrupt, with their loans exceeding more than two years of their family income. Due to the low profitability of farming, small farmers are leaving farming and around 28 per cent of them have entered the labour market. The majority of small and marginal farmers were dissatisfied with their new occupations. Obviously, small is no longer beautiful. Small farmers operate under severe economic constraints – their earnings are very low, they are indebted and many are compelled to leave farming. Tragically, some reach a stage where they take their own lives.

It is of utmost significance that the problems of marginal and small farmers in Punjab are addressed. First, small farming has to be made viable through a massive public investment in agriculture, which reduces the cost of cultivation and contributes to marketing produce more efficiently. Second, off-farm employment opportunities must be increased by developing the non-farm sector of the economy. Cooperative farming can give a fillip to small farmers by supplying them with machinery and farm inputs at subsidised rates. The problems of indebtedness, depeasantisation and suicides must be solved through a multipronged strategy, which assures small farmers of a nominal rate of interest on credit, custom hiring of farm machinery, inputs at subsidised rates, better marketing, free health care and education facilities and a minimum level of income. Such policy measures may help in mitigating some of the major problems that small farmers in Punjab face today.

Note

This chapter first appeared as an article 'Punjab's Small Peasantry: Thriving or Deteriorating?' Economic and Political Weekly 49 (26–27): 95–100, 2014.

References

Basant, R. and H. Joshi. 1994. 'Employment Diversification in an Agriculturally Developed Region: Some Evidence from Rural Kheda, Gujrat'. In P. Visaria and R. Basant (eds). *Non-Agricultural Employment in India: Trends and Prospects*. New Delhi: Sage, pp. 222–57.

Bhalla, G. S. and Peter Hazell. 2003. 'Rural Employment and Poverty – Strategies to Eliminate Rural Poverty within a Generation'. *Economic and Political Weekly* 38 (33): 3473–84.

Chandra, D. 2001. 'Crucial Agriculture Problems Facing Small Farmers'. *Political Economy Journal of India* 10: 1–4.

GoP. 2013. *Agriculture at a Glance*, Information Service, Department of Agriculture, Chandigarh.

PAU 2010–11. 'Economics of Farming and Pattern of Income and Expenditure in Punjab Agriculture'. Research Scheme, Department of Economics and Sociology, Punjab Agricultural University (PAU), Ludhiana.

Sidhu, R. S. and Sukhpal Singh. 2004. 'Agricultural Wages and Employment in Punjab'. *Economic and Political Weekly* 39 (7): 4132–35.

Singh, Karam. 2009. 'Agrarian Crisis in Punjab: High Indebtedness, Low Return, and Farmers' Suicides'. In D. Narasimha Reddy and S. Mishra (eds). *Agrarian Crisis in India*. New Delhi: Oxford University Press, pp. 261–84.

Singh, Sukhpal. 2013. 'Custom Hiring of Farm Machinery: A Boon for Small Farmers'. *Progressive Farming*, April, pp. 5–6.

Singh, Sukhpal. 2014. 'Problems of *Arhtiyas* (Commission Agents) vis-à-vis Farmers in Punjab', NABARD funded research report, Department of Economics and Sociology, Punjab Agricultural University, Ludhiana, pp. 1–124.

Singh, Karam, Sukhpal Singh and H. S. Kingra. 2007a. 'Status of Farmers Who Left Farming in Punjab'. Research report, Punjab State Farmers' Commission and Punjab Agricultural University, Ludhiana, pp. 1–51.

Singh, Sukhpal, H. S. Kingra and Manjeet Kaur. 2007b. 'Flow of Funds to Farmers and Indebtedness in Punjab'. Research report, Punjab State Farmers' Commission and Punjab Agricultural University, Ludhiana, pp. 1–77.

Singh, Sukhpal, R. S. Sidhu, S. K. Sidhu, H. S. Kingra and M. S. Sidhu. 2012. 'Farmers' and Agricultural Labourers' Suicides Due to Indebtedness in the Punjab State'. Research report, Department of Economics and Sociology, Punjab Agricultural University, Ludhiana, pp. 1–49.

Index

accumulation: accumulation by dispossession 44, 167; agrarian crisis 230; agrarian question 12, 13, 69, 74, 94, 95, 97–9, 102; capitalist accumulation 3, 17, 22, 23, 32, 33, 49, 50, 52, 53, 68, 85, 96, 118, 127;class differentiation 28; industrial accumulation process 76, 77, 80, 81, 86; Preobrazhensky'sproblematics 31; primitive accumulation 4, 17, 21, 22, 29, 54–7, 59, 72, 79, 93, 109, 116, 117, 123, 128, 168, 180, 188, 246, 249–51, 263–6; procrustean orthodox materialist approach 30; surplus accumulation 27; world historical change 14

Africa 3, 15,45, 59,71, 75, 79, 87,100, 101, 103,123, 124, 128, 134, 142

Agnihotra 233

agrarian question: AQ1 (problematic of politics) 69, 86, 87, 94, 95, 97, 99, 100, 102; AQ2 (production) 69–71, 74, 75, 77, 82, 93–5, 99, 110; AQ3 (accumulation) 69–71, 74–8, 82, 94, 95, 97, 99, 100, 110; agrarian question of capital 13; agrarian transition 8, 12; classical agrarian question13, 14, 29; global value relations 24;Kautsky 6, 43; peasant question 25; resolution of agrarian question 61, 70, 71, 74, 77, 94, 109

agribusiness 21, 78, 79, 87, 167

agro-ecological 27, 222, 223, 224, 228,232, 234, 235, 236, 239, 240

agro-entrepreneurs 230

agro-entrepreneurship 229

agro-nationalism 240

agronomy 223, 229, 234, 235

Akram-Lodhi, H. 2, 5, 8, 9, 11, 12, 13, 14, 15, 24, 28, 29, 31, 43, 45, 52, 59, 62,86, 92, 104, 109, 239, 258

Alavi, H. 18

alcoholism 227

alienation 231

Allen, R. C. 119

Alter, J. S. 240

Althusser, L. 47, 49

Altieri, M. A. 224

Amerindians 123

Amjad, R. 20, 32

anachronism 100

Anderson, P. 47

Andhra Pradesh: capitalist development18; disappearance of peasantry 187;land distribution 107; farmer suicide 148; rural to urban migration 185

aquaculture 154

Araghi, F. 5, 14, 59, 167, 188, 247

Aristotle 122

Arora, S. 3

Arunachal Pradesh 22

Arvind, P. 161

Asia 15, 16, 25, 45, 59, 75, 78, 79, 92, 97, 98, 100, 101, 103, 109,126, 141, 142, 156,222, 228

294 Index

Aston, T. H. 30, 51, 52
Australia 70, 123, 124
Ayurveda 229

Bagchi, A. 17
Baker, C. J. 199
Bakshakrishi 236
Baliber, E. 47, 85
Banaji, J. 6, 18, 49, 58, 59, 86, 96, 166, 176, 247, 271
Banerjee, A. 109
Bangalore 159, 240
Bangladesh 32, 101, 156
Bankura 268
Bardhaman 252, 253, 255, 258, 268
Bardhan, P. 18
Basant, R. 288
basmati 151, 152
Basole, A. 82, 86, 105
Basu, D. 22, 82, 86, 105, 108
Bath, S. V. 117
Bernstein, Henry: agrarian question13, 31, 45, 55, 69, 79, 99, 100, 102, 103, 109, 116, 251; agrarian transition11, 12, 24, 80, 82, 85;class differentiation 84; food sovereignty 14
Bhaduri, A. 18, 32,77, 247, 258, 271
Bhagirathi 253
Bhalla, G.S., 170, 171, 173, 175, 279, 292
Bhardwaj, K. 20
Bhattacharya, S. 96, 118
Bhogal, S. 27, 28, 276
Bhoodan 107
Bihar 18, 155, 170, 171, 173, 174, 176, 178, 181–7, 190, 271
Borras, S. M. J. 108, 224
Brass, T. 23, 57, 174
Brazil 87, 142
Breman, J. 19, 23, 84, 155, 174
Brenner, R. 9, 10, 11, 12, 30, 51–3,72–4
Brewer, A. 53
bureaucracy 140, 160, 234
Byres, T. J. 6, 11–13, 31,43–5, 53, 69–82, 85, 92–4, 97–9, 109, 250

Canada 70, 123
Caouette, D. 227

Carswell, G. 201, 218
Chacocan 233
Chaknara 255, 270
Chakrabarti, A. 3, 19
Chakraborty 246
Chandra, N. 18, 19, 247, 271, 277, 292
Chatterjee, P. 21, 22,92, 168, 188
Chattopadhyay, P. 18,49
Chaudhuri, A. 271
Chayanov, A. V. 7, 10,84,166
Chhattisgarh 148, 155, 157, 182
Chicago 159, 239
China 78, 87, 100, 101, 120, 121, 123, 124, 125, 131, 133, 134, 142
class: capitalist class 16, 55, 56; class configuration 105, 106; class differentiation 7, 19, 27, 28, 44, 59, 62, 83, 84, 90, 105, 109, 166, 180, 247, 248, 249, 275; class dynamics 14, 80, 84; class relations 10, 11, 67, 85, 94, 97, 104, 108, 235; class structure 19, 20, 22, 31, 52, 53, 74, 87; class struggle 12, 23, 51, 53, 85
classrelations 10
Claude Meillassoux 47
Clement, J.T. 240
Coimbatore 199, 201, 219
colonialism 20, 68, 73, 98, 121,169
commercialisation 10, 19, 22, 172, 225
commodification 44, 51, 69, 84, 177, 222
communism 139
The Condition of Working Class in England 4
Condoleezza, R. 250
Connor, J. O. 87, 223
Cullenberg, S. 19, 246

Damodaran, H. 201
Darjeeling 252, 253, 268
Das, D. 22, 82, 105, 108
Das, R. 173, 180
depeasantisation 7, 14, 19, 151, 166, 167, 169, 183, 185, 285, 286
Deshmukh, V., 149, 150
Deshpande, R. S. 3, 181
Desmarais, A. A. 224
Dev, M. S. 175

Index 295

Development of Capitalism in Russia
(Lenin) 5, 17, 94
Dey, R. 257
Dhanagare, D. N. 25, 28, 138, 139,
140, 169
Die Agrarfrage (Kautsky) 5
Dinajpur 268
Dipankar, G.87, 168
Djurfeldt, G. 189
Dobb, M. 8, 9, 10, 50, 51
Doshi, L. 161
Dreze, J. 32, 190
Duggett, M. 4, 30, 189
Dunkel Draft 142, 143

Edelman, M. 224
Engels, F. 4, 5, 31, 43, 44, 45, 62, 69,
70, 93, 165
England 4, 30, 50–3, 55, 56, 68, 69, 72,
74, 93, 117, 119, 123, 132, 165, 188
epistemic rift 228
estates 86, 189
*Essay on the Influence of a Low Price of
Corn on the Profits of Stock* (David
Ricardo) 119
Europe: agrarian transition 1, 5, 6,
9; capitalist transition 8, 10, 50,
51, 53, 68, 70, 72, 93, 189; class
struggle 52
exclusionist 123
exploitation: capitalism 5, 108;
colonial 123; family labour 7;
exploitation of labour 19, 256, 272;
exploitation of peasants 58, 77;
oppression 81
expropriation 4, 55, 56, 188
extinction; extinction of peasantry
188, 251; small agricultural
producer 5
extraction: extraction of rent 258;
extraction of surplus 22, 51, 52, 76,
87, 95; extraction of timber 226;
extraction of tax 120

fair-trade 224
fallacious theory 121, 127
FAO (Food and Agricultural
Organisations) 134
farmer suicide 148, 149, 195, 227,
235, 285

fascism 139, 239
FDI (Foreign Direct Investment)143,
150, 159, 273
Federici, S. 72
Ferozepur 278
feudalism 2, 6, 8, 9, 10, 12, 18, 20, 30,
50, 51, 52, 68, 72, 73, 87, 271
foeticide 208, 217, 219
Foreign Trade Agreement (FTA)
142, 152
Foster, J. B. 15, 59, 223
Foucault, M. 265
France 4, 5, 11, 30, 52, 69, 75, 93
Frank,A.G. 96, 246, 247, 259,
264, 271
Frankfurt 159
Friedmann 14, 167, 231
Fukuoka 233, 237
Funes-monzote 224

GATT (General Agreements on
Tariffs and Trades) 164
GDP (Gross Domestic Product) 21,
25, 32, 123, 125, 140, 145, 146,
159, 160
Geert De Neve 218
Genraghata 255, 270
George, S. 219
Germany 5, 69, 93, 121
Ghosh, J. 200
giant economies 78
Gibbon, P. 58
Gini coefficient 106, 177, 190
globalisation: agrarian crisis 25;
agrarian economy 266; agrarian
question 29; commodities market
226; farmer suicides 234; forms of
labour subsumption 62; neoliberal
capitalism 15, 77–9, 94, 101–3,
115; peasant farming 224;
Glover, D. 224
Goa 231
Goldman, M. 139
Goodman, D. 80
GopalGaurav Award 240
Goshala 240
Gough, K. 19
Gounder 26, 199, 201, 202–5,
208–17, 219
Grabowski, R. 120, 122

296 Index

gram swaraj (village self-rule) 240
gross capital formation(GCF) 175
Guha, R. 228
Gujarat 18, 155, 159, 170–4, 176–8,
 180–2, 184–7, 190
Gulati, A. K. 172, 181, 182
Gupta, D. 21, 22, 87, 168, 188
Gupta, S. C. 16, 31
Guérin, I. 23, 174

Hague 30
Haldea, G. 158, 159
Hall, D. 226
Hammen, O. 5
Haora 252, 269
Harriss, J. 19, 22, 82, 105, 107, 183
Harriss-White, B. 86, 87, 95, 97, 105,
 106, 108, 109, 219, 224, 226
Harvey, D. 44, 79, 139, 140–2, 167
Haryana 151, 153, 154, 155, 170–4,
 176–8, 180–7, 190
Hazelkorn, E. 5
Hazell, P. 279, 292
Heidelberg 239
Heller, H. 72
Herring, R. 224
Heyer, J. 3, 26, 28, 29, 109, 199,
 200–202, 208, 212, 217–19
Hilton, R. H.51, 52
Himachal Pradesh 170, 173, 174,
 176, 177, 178, 181, 182, 184,
 186–8, 190
historical materialism29, 30, 43
Hobsbawm, E. J. 100,166
Holmgren, D. 236
Hoshiarpur 150, 195
Huang, P. C. C. 87
Hugli 268
HYV (high yielding varieties) 172,
 189, 259

IFAD (International Fund for
 Agricultural Development) 71
ILO (International Labour
 Organisation) 157, 181
IMF (International Monetary Fund)
 139, 140, 142, 159
imperialism 18, 48, 49,71, 80,
 87,124,167

impoverishment 186, 258
India 2, 3, 15–32, 45, 49, 54, 68,
 69, 77, 78, 81, 82, 86, 87, 92,
 94, 95, 96, 98, 99, 101, 103–7,
 109,119–31, 133, 134,138, 140–6,
 148, 150, 152, 153, 155–61, 164,
 168, 170–4, 176, 177, 181–95,
 219, 222, 224, 225, 227–9, 234,
 238–40, 245, 247, 248, 250, 251,
 253, 258, 259, 261, 269, 270–6,
 279, 280, 292
Indonesia 32, 101
Ireland 117, 123

Jadhav, V. 171
Jafri, A. H. 172, 195
Jaivakrishi 230, 231
Jalandhar 278
Jalees, K. 188, 195
Jalpaiguri 268
James C. 87, 223, 224
Jammu and Kashmir 107
Jansen, K. 14
Japan 68, 69, 70, 75, 86, 120
Jawandia, V. 145, 147
Jeromi, P. D. 226
Jeyaranjan, J. 219
Jha, B. N. 171
Jha, P. S. 20
Jharkhand 182
Jivamrita 225, 233, 235, 236–8
Jodhka, S. S. 19, 23, 155
Johnson, H. 167, 185
Joshi, H. 288
Joshi, S. 161

Kalecki, M. 32
Kannan, E. 171
Kappad 225
Karnataka 148, 154, 170–4, 176, 177,
 179, 181, 182, 184, 185, 187, 190,
 225, 230, 240
Kautsky, K. 5, 6, 7, 11, 12, 31, 43, 44,
 45, 58, 62, 69, 70, 94, 99, 165, 166,
 176, 271
Kelly, P. F. 2
Kenwood, A. G. 118, 122, 124
Kerala 26, 28, 29, 147, 155, 170, 171,
 173, 174, 176, 177, 179, 181–7,

Index 297

190, 222, 225, 226, 232, 234, 236, 238, 240
Keynesianism 247
Khera, R. 32,190
KisanMandis 146
Kodagu 231
Kolkata 252, 269, 273
Korea 69, 70, 71, 75, 76, 77, 120
Korovkin, T. 172
Kothari, A. 227, 228
Kotovsky, G. 16, 31
Kritsman, L. 50
kudumbashree 234
Kumbamu, A. 224
Kuznets, S. 116, 132

labour: farmlabour 257, 273; labourdays 272; labourintensive 125, 211; labourmarket 55; labourproductivity 53; labourretrenchment 127; unfreelabour 23, 57, 95, 122, 173, 174; wagelabour 56, 58–60, 165
laissez-faire 138
Landless: hired agricultural labourers 207; households 106, 107, 177–80, 210; land dispossession and debt accumulation 172; landless waged labour 44, 103, 158, 205; landless worker 83, 102, 272; proletarianised landless rural workers 84, 167; scheduled castes 157, 158
Latin America 15, 59, 68, 78
Laughlin, B. O. 15
La ViaCampesina 79, 224
Lenin, V. I. 5, 6, 7, 11, 12, 17, 31, 43, 44, 45, 62, 82, 94, 99, 165, 166, 168, 266, 271
Lerche, J. 15, 19, 22, 23, 78, 81, 82, 96, 99, 104, 105, 106–9,174, 177, 223, 251
Lewis, A. 32,120–2
Leys, C. 83
Li, T. M. 87
liberalisation125, 249, 276
Limbo-space 246
Lin, S. 247

Littlejohn, G. 50
Lockyer, J. 224
Lucchesi, V. 101
Lucknow 146
Ludhiana 278, 292
lumpenBourgeosie 246, 259, 264
Luxemburg, R. 47, 128

Macao 152, 161
Maddison, A., 120
Madhya Pradesh 148, 154, 170, 171, 173, 174, 176, 178, 181, 182, 184, 185, 187, 190
Madras 18
Magdoff, F. 223, 240
Maharashtra 145, 147, 148, 149, 153, 155, 159, 161,170–4, 176, 177, 179, 180, 181, 182, 184–7, 190, 234
Mahatma Gandhi 32,150, 190, 240, 251
Malabar 226
Malayalam 234
Malaysia 3
Malda 268
Malthusian 10
Manchester 159
Manobhavan 232, 237
Maran, Arul 218
Marathwada 155
Maria, M. 219
market fundamentalism 139, 160
Markfed 151
Marx, K. 3–7, 9, 11, 12, 17, 24, 28, 30, 31,43, 45–47, 50, 53–62, 72, 74, 82, 84, 93, 96, 100, 117, 118, 124, 131, 165, 168, 188, 189, 223, 271
McMichael, P. 13, 14, 79,167, 222, 223, 224, 228
Medinipur 269
Meillassoux, C. 47
Memari 255, 270
Mencher, J. P. 19
MGNREGA (Mahatma Gandhi National Rural EmploymentGuarantee Act) 145, 150, 158, 190, 216
Mies, M. 219

298 Index

migration 2, 21, 26, 32, 81, 105, 124, 160, 164, 168, 185, 188, 190, 218
Mishra, S. 3, 172, 223
Mitra, A. 77
Mitrany, D. 189
Mohan, V. 143
Mohanasundaram, V. 218
Mohanty, B. B. 1, 19, 26, 28, 29,109, 150, 161, 164, 169, 171
Mollison, B.C. 236
money lending 101
Moore, B. Jr. 169
Moore, J., 87, 223
Moyo, S. 3, 15, 80,104, 108
MPCE (monthly per capita expenditure) 130, 133
MSP (Minimum Support Price) 146, 160
Mukherjee, R.K. 31
Mukhopadhyay, N. 247
Mumbai 149, 161, 195
Munsiff 205, 219
Murshidabad 268
Murthy, A. V. R. 172
Münster, D. 26, 27, 28, 29, 138, 222, 225, 227, 230, 231, 239

NABARD (National Bank for Agriculture and RuralDevelopment) 154, 189, 292
Nadia 268
Nagaraj, K. 127,219
Namboodiri 155
Nanda LalGhatak 259
Nandigram 266
Napoleonic Wars 118
Narasimham Committee 175
Naratarajan, J.142
Narayanamoorthy, A. 181
Narodniks 5
Neocosmos, M. 58
neoliberalism: accumulation by dispossession 44;agrarian crisis 28, 238; agrarian question 29;governance of neoliberal state 140; national sovereignty 139; open economic circuit 250, 264, 265
New Zealand 70

Nicolaysen, A.M. 224
NSSO (National Sample Survey Organisation) 144, 157, 174, 177, 185, 190, 256, 259, 273

OBC (other backward caste)26
Odisha 17, 18, 155, 170, 171, 173, 174, 176, 179, 181, 182, 184–8, 190
Omvedt, G. 19
Oya, C. 80, 85

Pakistan 32, 101, 156
Palakad 234, 240
Palekar, S. 225, 229, 233–7, 240
Panagaria, A. 161
Panitch, L. 83
Papola, T. S. 186
Parashar, B. K. 146
Patiala 278
Patnaik, Utsa: agrarian question 29, 80, 83, 92, 96, 99, 120; agrarian transition 49, 50; capitalist accumulation 68; debate over mode of production 17–19, 247, 249, 250, 257; development of capitalism in agriculture 22, 188; Industrial Revolution 86; labour exploitation 272; neoliberal global capitalist accumulation 3
Pawar, S. 145, 148, 149, 152
PDS (public distribution system) 32, 190, 212, 216
The Peasant Question in France and Germany 5
Penrose, E. F. 120
Philippines 3
Pogge, T. W. 131
Polanyi, K. 222, 239
populism 82, 139, 166, 239
Prakritikrishi 230, 234
Prasad, C. S. 224
Prasad, P. 18, 271
Preobrazhensky, E. 31, 76, 77, 94, 100
proletarianisation5, 6, 19, 104, 150, 166, 168, 177, 182, 185, 186
Prussia 5, 6, 12,69, 75, 97

Index 299

Punjab 17, 27, 28, 140, 150, 151, 153,
154, 155, 157, 158, 159, 170–174,
176, 177, 179–87, 189, 190, 195,
276–87, 290, 292
Purulia 253, 269

Raj, K. N. 20
Rajasekhar, B. 107
Rajasthan 155, 157, 170, 173, 174,
176, 179, 181, 182, 184, 185,
187, 190
Rakshit, S. 27, 29, 245, 249, 256,
257, 258, 260, 266
Ramachandran, V. K. 69, 82,105,
109,175
Rao, P. V. N. 143
Rao, V. K. R. V. 16
Rasa Krishi 229, 230, 231
RBI (Reserve Bank of India) 150, 161
Reddy, B. 107
Reddy, D. N. 25, 29
Revathi, E. 172
Rey, P. P. 47, 48
Ricardo, D. 119, 121, 122
Rudra, A. 17, 18, 19, 31,247, 271
rural dispossession 223, 225
Russia: class politics7;social relations
of production 50
Ruttan, V. W. 120

Sainath, P. 161
Samajwadi Party 146
Sanyal, K. 22, 30, 96, 246, 249–51,
265, 271
Sau, R. 18,247, 271
Saul, S. B. 119
Schneider, M. 222, 223, 228
Scott, J. C. 169
semi-feudalism 18, 32, 68,
95,195, 271
semi-proletarianisation 104
Sen, A. 4
Sengupta, N., 272
Sengupta, R. 152
Sethi, N. 144
Shah, A.82, 95, 97, 105, 108
Shah, E. 227
Shah, M. 189
Shanghai 159

Shanin, T.60
Shaw, A. 82
Shetty, S. L. 189
Shiva, V. 172, 188, 195, 224
Shrivastava, A. 227, 228
Sidhu, R. S. 276, 292
Singh, G.170, 171, 173, 175
Singh, K. 277
Singh, N. K. 142
Singh, R. 151, 152, 189, 195
Singh, S. 27, 28, 152, 172, 276,
277,282, 292
Skarbø, K. 224
Smith, A. 138
Srinivasan, M. V. 218
Srinivasan, S. 219
Srivastava, R. 108
Stiglitz, J. E. 142
Strümpell, C. 138, 231
Subaltern 3
Sundaram, S. 171
surplus: surplus accumulation 27;
surplus appropriation 50, 51, 52,
74, 104, 246, 265, 266; surplus
distribution 259, 262, 266; surplus
retention 258–60; surplus value 18,
23, 56,128, 271
Sweezy, P. 8, 9, 10,50, 51, 52

Tamil Nadu 26, 28, 29,155, 170–4,
176, 177, 180–7, 190, 199, 219,225
targeted priority lending 175
Tata 159
Taylor, J. 49
Thailand 3
Therborn, G. 85
Thorner, A.19, 49, 92, 95, 96, 169
Thorner, D. 7, 16, 31
Tiruppur 200–202, 218
Toledo, V. M. 224
trade liberalisation 152
Tripathi, S. N. 155
Tung, M.T. 125, 246, 264
Turner, M. E. 119, 132, 227
Turner, S. 227

United Nations 104, 133, 134, 157, 195
United States 68, 69, 70, 75, 77, 86,
119, 120, 133, 134, 141

300 Index

UPA (United Progressive Alliance) 143
Uttar Pradesh 31, 146, 147, 154, 157, 170–4, 176, 180–5, 187, 188, 190, 268

Vaidyanathan, A. 175, 195
Van der Lindon 57
Van der Ploeg, J. D. 82, 167, 195, 224
Vanhaute, E. 167, 195
Vasavi, A. R. 223
Vasco Da Gama 225
vegetarianism 235, 238
Vidarbha 148, 149
Vijay, R. 190, 195
Vijayabaskar, M. 201, 218
Vikram, K. 154
Vishwa Gou Sammelan 240
viticulture 171
Vogel, L. C. 235

Watts, M. 15
Wayanad 26, 27, 222, 225–40
Weis, T. 15, 87
West Bengal 18, 27, 29,107, 148, 154, 170–7, 180–5, 187, 190, 245, 247, 248–53, 258, 259, 263, 265, 266, 268, 269, 271–3
Western Ghats 225
Wilkinson, J. 108
Wittman, H. 222, 224
Wood, E. M. 10, 30,53, 59
WTO (World Trade Organization) 139, 142, 143, 152, 159, 164, 172

Yawatmal 148

zamindari 104
ZBNF (Zero Budget Natural Farming) 222, 223, 225, 233–8, 240
Zemstvo Statistics 5
Zhang, S. 224